Where
Did
We Go
Wrong?
Industrial Performance, Education and
the Economy in Victorian Britain

Where
Did
We Go
Wrong?
Industrial Performance, Education and
the Economy in Victorian Britain

Edited and Introduced by
Gordon Roderick
and
Michael Stephens

 The Falmer Press
(A member of the Taylor & Francis Group)

First published 1981

ISBN 0 905273 11 7

Illustration and jacket designed by Leonard Williams

Printed and bound in Great Britain by
Taylor & Francis (Printers) Ltd., Basingstoke, Hampshire for

The Falmer Press
Falmer House
Barcombe, Lewes
Sussex BN8 5DL
England

Contents

1 **BACKGROUND**

Introduction: Britain 1851–1914
Gordon Roderick and Michael Stephens   3
The Economy, Management and Foreign Competition
Derek H. Aldcroft   13
Progress in Artisan Literacy
E.G. West   33
The Labour Force: Some Relevant Attitudes
P.W. Musgrave   49
Population and the Bio-social Background
W.H.G. Armytage   67

2 **CASE STUDIES**

The Coal Industry
Neil Buxton   85
Iron and Steel
J.K. Almond   107
The Textile Industries
Stanley Chapman   125
Engineering
Geoffrey Sims   139
The Chemical Industry
Keith Trace   155

3 **EDUCATION AND GOVERNMENT**

Technical Education 1850–1914
Michael Le Guillou   173
The Universities
Gordon Roderick and Michael Stephens   185
Technical Education and the University College of Nottingham
Brian Tolley   203
The Role of Government
Gordon Roderick and Michael Stephens   219
Conclusions
Gordon Roderick and Michael Stephens   231

Contributors   251

Index   253

I
Background

Introduction: Britain 1851–1914

Gordon Roderick and Michael Stephens

In 1851, the year of the Great Exhibition, Britain was almost exactly at mid-point of the period at which, it is claimed, she was 'the workshop of the world'.[1] The period, which began in the 1820s and ended with the depression of the 1870s, was the high noon of economic advance. Britain's natural resources (especially of coal and iron), her skilled, adaptable manpower and the industrial developments of the eighteenth century enabled her by 1851 to rise to a position of global influence and power[2] and to lead the world in the supply of machinery, manufactured and textile goods. At this time, Britain was experiencing a level of industrial production and foreign trade which set her far ahead of all other countries.[3]

Although natural resources and inventiveness were central to Britain's rise to economic power, other factors also played a part: her naval strength guarded her overseas trade routes and had removed all danger of destructive wars; the growth of population gave manufacturing industries an increasing home market as well as a supply of workers; free trade encouraged overseas commerce; and the railways accelerated industrial and commercial development. The Great Exhibition, whilst confirming Britain's position as the leading industrial nation, also marked the beginning of an age of rapidly accelerating industrial production of coal, iron and steel and many other commodities. The mood of euphoria and complacency lasted for the next twenty years, at the end of which period the foreign trade of the United Kingdom was still more than that of France, Germany and Italy together, and four times that of the United States.

By the end of the century, however, a dramatic transformation had come about as a decline set in in the rate of increase of industrial production relative to her competitors. There appeared to be a failure of British industry to maintain the momentum it displayed in the first half of the nineteenth century. During the final quarter of the century prices fell, factories closed down, unemployment went up and there was widespread distress. The age of British economic supremacy was over.

In steel, American production passed Britain's in 1890, followed six years later by that of Germany; by 1900 the United States and Germany between them were producing three times as much steel as Britain. Steel was only one element in the challenge, although the most significant one. The British chemical industry in 1913 accounted for only 11 per cent of world output as against 34 per cent by the United States and 24 per cent by Germany, while the latter exported twice as much as Britain.[4] The initiative had passed to Germany, particularly in the production of synthetic dyes from coal tar (which replaced the traditional dyes from natural sources) and in the production of a whole new range of products – fertilisers, explosives, cyanides and pharmaceuticals. The British had pioneered electrotechnics yet by 1913 the output of the British electrical industry was only a third of Germany's and its exports barely half. By 1913 Britain ranked a poor second to the United States in car production whilst in the machine tool industry, which had been British in origin, 'nowhere did foreign countries and yet again chiefly the United States leap ahead more decisively'.[5] By the outbreak of World War I in 1914, Britain was short of khaki dye, acetone for explosives and magnetos for transport because Germany had become the chief source of supply.

Yet it would be wrong to assume from the foregoing that Britain stagnated industrially. Rather, industrial activities developed on a great scale: basic industries increased their output – between 1893 and 1913 coal, shipping and steel increased 75 per cent, 100 per cent and 136 per cent respectively; others such as boots and shoes, brewing, soap and tobacco also grew fast and new technical inventions led to electrical engineering, motor cars, bicycles, aluminium, ferro-concrete and artificial silk. What cannot be denied, however, is that the bare facts of industrial production reveal lower increases in Britain than was the case for her competitors, Germany and the United States.

With regard to exports, the position was even worse. There was little ground for complacency as competition caused Britain to lose export markets in America, industrialised Europe and underdeveloped countries. By 1913 Britain's share of world trade in manufactures was 25.4 per cent as compared with 37 per cent in 1883 (in the same period Germany increased her share from 17 per cent to 20 per cent and the United States from 3.4 per cent to 11 per cent). In a group of fifteen manufactures, British exports to protected foreign markets between 1895 and 1907 increased by 44 per cent while those of Germany and America increased by 125 per cent and 500 per cent respectively. The same exports to identical markets in the British Empire registered an increase of 91 per cent for Britain as against 129 per cent and 559 per cent for Germany and the United States. By 1913, textiles still accounted for one third of total exports, while the share of total exports of the new categories (machinery, chemicals and electrical goods) stood at only 15.9 per cent in 1910. The fastest growing export category before 1914 was the staple product coal; in general Britain tended to retain her specialisation in the older lines rather than in the more recently developed products – inorganic rather than organic chemicals, locomotives rather than motor vehicles, textiles and farm machinery rather than machine tools and electrical goods.

The entry of the United States into world markets occurred in the mid-1890s and appeared to have fewer harmful effects on British exports. This was partly because her export structure was complementary to Britain's rather than competitive, and partly because American export growth was concentrated on areas like Canada and Latin America. Industrialization in the United States, behind tariff barriers, affected British exports to the American markets. Germany, on the other hand, posed a far greater threat. Together with Belgium she made great strides in capturing European markets which were former British preserves: by 1913 Germany was selling more than Britain to nearly every European country. She was also expanding her trade more rapidly with the economically underdeveloped countries such as Russia, Latin America and Turkey. By 1913 Germany monopolised the Russian market, her exports to that country being four times greater than those of Britain.[6]

Clearly there seemed to be something 'radically wrong' both with regard to industrial productivity and to Britain's ability to sell goods abroad. Few students, of the period after 1870, deny that there was a slowing down in the rate of economic growth during the final quarter of the century. Some argue that a break occurred in the 1870s, whereas others point to the 1890s. If figures for real income per head are examined, it is evident that the real check to growth, apart from a temporary break in the 1870s, did not occur until towards the end of the nineteenth century. On the other hand, in the case of exports and industrial production, the break in growth trends occurs somewhat earlier, probably around the 1870s. Thus whilst it is generally accepted that there was a slowing down of the rate of economic growth sometime after 1870 there is no measure of its exact timing, its extent or its causes.

The Great Debate about Britain's decline was begun by the Victorians themselves. There was little doubt in the minds of contemporary observers in the late nineteenth century that a decline had set in in Britain's industrial progress. A flood of documentary evidence was produced which, although prejudiced, was not entirely inaccurate for the more scholarly and analytical accounts contained similar conclusions. There must have been an element of truth since informed opinion was almost unanimous on the question. Up to recent years, there was a consensus also among twentieth century historians that a decline had set in between 1870 and 1914, a decline which was attributable to a failure of British industry and to management in particular. Serious reservations however are now being expressed.

Contemporary observers and earlier historians based their assessments on statistics relating to industrial output and trade figures which clearly indicated a 'relative decline' vis-a-vis Britain's competitors. Economic historians of more recent times, on the other hand (in particular mathematical economists and ecomoneticians), have attempted to provide an assessment based on quantitive tests using a variety of more sophisticated economic measures. Their results, whilst invalidating many earlier arguments, have at the same time triggered off a spate of arguments and counter-arguments over the applicability of these methods.

Was there a 'failure' of the British economy as a whole to maintain the momentum of the earlier years? There may well have been individual industries which were deficient, but it appears that such a charge may no longer be justified for British industry as a whole. Indeed, an extreme view is that there is little left of the dismal picture of British failure painted by historians and the conclusions of a conference of economic historians in 1970 was that 'during the critical period 1870 to 1900 when the balance tilted from dominance to dependence the British economy . . . performed as one would expect a competitive and prosperous economy to perform'.[7] Nevertheless, the argument about Britain's 'assured failure' is by no means over.

Of the many factors advanced as being contributory to the failure of British industry to innovate and increase production as rapidly as its competitors, two have stood out as being of overriding importance; these were the quality of entrepreneurs and the role of education and training.

The theory of entrepreneurial failure reached its culminating point with David Landes' (1969) *Unbounded Prometheus* in which he points to the leads lost, the opportunities missed and the markets relinquished that need not have been. The theory embraces familiar accusations of amateurism, indifference and complacency; incompetent and indifferent salesmanship involving the unwillingness to try new products; a stubborn refusal to suit goods to the needs of potential clients or to engage technical salesmen with a facility in foreign languages; lack of dynamism and adventurousness by managers; technical and organizational lag within individual firms; conservatism in the face of new techniques and a reluctance to abandon individuality and tradition. Because England industrialized early English entrepreneurs were second or third generation entrepreneurs in the critical period 1879 to 1900 and were more likely to be distracted from business life by social life. Furthermore, their lack of formal training told against them – they lacked technical expertise and were less able to judge the commercial prospects of particular innovations.

The early entrepreneurs, pioneers of the Industrial Revolution, had been untutored, lacking formal education, products of the ancient traditions of British craftsmanship – men such as Crompton, Smeaton, Bramah and Maudslay. The Industrial Revolution, it seemed, owed little to education systems or to direct action from the state. At mid-century the prevailing philosophy was that Britain owed her success to the natural character and qualities of her entrepreneurs, to her craftsmen and engineers endowed with native ability. These, allied to daring entrepreneurship and individualism, had brought Britain to the top. What indeed was owed to education?

In 1851 Lyon Playfair, in his lecture to the School of Mines, drew attention to the fact that the ready availability of cheap natural resources had been in Britain's favour but in the future, with the widespread development of transport and communications systems, the race would go to the nation which commanded the greatest scientific skill. But belief in individualism and the superior qualities of British workmanship, together with a dislike of state interference, held back state intervention to create systems of scientific education and training. Arnold (1892) summed up the British attitude to the state in the words 'as an alien, intrusive power in the community, not summing up and representing the action of individuals, but thwarting it'. This attitude, together with 'our high opinion of our own energy and prosperity'[8] were stumbling blocks to progress. In Germany – the main continental rival – there was extensive state and municipal support for education, whereas the attitude to education in England is well represented by a statement of Robert Lowe when Chancellor of the Exchequer: 'I hold it as our duty not to spend public money to do that which people can do for themselves'.[9] These attitudes led to grave deficiencies in secondary and higher technical education and to a lack of central direction by Government. The absence of an overall plan or blueprint led to a situation which contrasted the haphazard British system with the organized German system.

Despite the impressive performances of British industries in winning medals at the Great Exhibition, England was one of the few major competing countries without an organized system of technical education. The aim in the early part of the century was to produce an industrious workforce. The conviction grew during the first quarter of the century that, with increasing industrialization, there was a need for the industrial worker, variously described as a mechanic or artisan, to have a knowledge of science related to his industrial practice. Consequently, technical education, from its origins, became associated in the public mind with the education of the artisan. At elementary level, prior to mid-century, education was in the hands of the voluntaryists. The church bodies were anxious to preserve their dominant position and the progress of a state system of education was hindered by the secular-religious power struggle over the control of education. Manufacturers and landowners, too, had their own economic interests to defend whenever the state attempted to introduce new legislation requiring school attendance. The first central government support came in the form of a grant of £20,000 in 1833, but not until 1870 were the proper foundations of a system laid down. Widespread poverty and apathy and indifference to educational needs were common among the populace. A comprehensive survey by the Newcastle Commission, which reported in 1861, discovered that the average attendance at elementary schools was only 76 per cent; one third of pupils attended for less than a hundred days, and less than one fifth stayed on after the age of ten. Following Robert Lowe's Revised Code of 1861 the passing of examinations in the three Rs became the necessary condition for the award of grants to schools. Government policy and action in the next two decades were more often activated by the concern for cheapness rather than efficiency. Prior to this many teachers had taken a delight in teaching elementary science, but as it now no longer counted for grant purposes innovation and experimentation of this kind disappeared from the schools.

Deficiences in day school education were compensated for by the evening schools. The principle of supplementary early schooling and of remedying defects had been adopted by the Sunday Schools and adult schools at the end of the eighteenth century. By the mid-nineteenth century, evening schools and night schools had become an established part of the educational scene. They were very much a second best, and their grave deficiencies were revealed by Michael Sadler, Professor of the History and Administration of Education at Manchester University, in 1907. They were

> in some respects little but a makeshift for what should have been done in elementary day schools. Much that was attempted in the evening schools would have been better done by a well organized system of day schools . . . There was no legal compulsion to attend them and they left untouched large sections of the community.[10]

In Sadler's (1907) view:

> the question to be decided is whether we in England gain more through

stimulating and rewarding the energy of the few by our voluntary system of continuation schools than is lost through our failure to raise the general average of trained and disciplined efficiency by means of compulsory attendance for all. The same question comes up in some form or other in every attempt to balance the advantages of what may broadly be distinguished as the English and German forms of educational organization. The Germans make thriftier use of their average material than we succeed in doing ... Can we afford the waste which our lack of organization entails?[11]

In the field of secondary education there was a greater reluctance on the part of the state to interfere or to allocate adequate resources. Government action was largely confined to the setting up of numerous Commissions, few of whose recommendations were implemented, and of a Charity Commission whose function it was to oversee the considerable number of endowments, many of which were grossly abused. In the 1860s and 1870s, three Royal Commissions under the Chairmanship of the Earl of Clarendon, Baron Taunton and the Duke of Devonshire all revealed that Britain had remarkably little education, much of it inadequate in quality, and drew attention to the deplorable state of scientific education. Thirty years later the Board of Education in its Report of 1905–6 concluded: 'The most conspicuous fact that emerges is of how much there is yet to be done in secondary education ... the short-comings are too often less than disastrous'. A few years later it highlighted a fundamental weakness when it pointed to the lack of positive state action:

That the state has any concern with secondary education is a comparatively modern idea in England ... This isolation and consequent neglect of secondary education over so long a period is at the root of the difficulties which have had to be faced in the last few years in all grades of education in England ... The formidable inertia of the nation reinforced by intense jealousy of state interference and dislike of public control held up much needed reforms.[12]

A cohesive pattern of secondary education was not laid down until the turn of the century. By the time the Bryce Commission was appointed in 1894 there were numerous bodies participating in the provision and funding of secondary education. Fragmentation and lack of cohesion were the hallmarks. There was an uneven distribution of endowments; an overall inadequacy of finance; an absence of inspection; a too narrow curriculum and a paucity of free places. The Bryce Commission was the first body to attempt a visionary definition of secondary education. It was the springboard for the formation of the Board of Education in 1899 and the Education Act of 1902. To overcome 'the usual results of dispersed and unconnected forces, needless competition between the different agencies and a frequent overlapping of effort' the Bryce Commission proposed a single statutory body presided over by a Minister, which would supervise action by local authorities in whom responsibility for secondary education was to be invested.

Throughout the greater part of the century the main middle-class schools – the public and grammar schools – were almost exclusively classical. The Devonshire Commission (1872) carried out an extensive survey of the place of science in the schools:

> We regret to observe in many of the larger schools the number of science masters is totally inadequate. We fear that the fewness of the science masters in the great schools and the slowness with which their number is allowed to increase must, to a certain extent, be due to an inadequate appreciation on the part of the authorities of those institutions of the importance of the place which science ought to occupy in school education.[13]

In defending themselves against criticisms the schools sought a scapegoat in Oxford and Cambridge which offered few scholarships and fellowships in the sciences; the vast majority being awarded for classics. Sir John Lubbock, a member of the Devonshire Commission, observed:

> They do not prepare them (in science) at schools because there is not the same number of awards for it in the universities and the universities do not award them because science is not taught in the schools and the schools do not teach them because they are not rewarded in the universities.[14]

Few products of the leading schools went on to study science and engineering, with the notable exception of some schools. A Committee set up under Sir J.J. Thomson in 1916 found a deplorable state of affairs fifty years after the Clarendon Commission had first drawn attention to the poor state of science education:

> Not for the first time educational conscience has been stung by the thought that as a nation we are neglecting science . . . We cannot regard it as anything but unsatisfactory that it should be impossible to form even a rough estimate of the number of children receiving secondary education in this country nor of the value of that education.[15]

The fortunes of the leading schools were bound up with the ancient universities and a great deal of blame attached to the latter. Oxford and Cambridge, with their continued adherence to traditional studies and their neglect of science, were a stumbling block to progress. They were a perpetual thorn in the flesh of those who viewed with concern the rise of the German universities and technical high schools. Royal Commissions to Inquire into the State, Discipline, Studies and Revenues of the Universities and Colleges were set up in the 1850s. They discovered that the wealth of the Universities resided in the colleges which resisted reforms and were reluctant to devote funds to science. The Devonshire Commission discovered that the funds devoted to science were 'lamentably deficient'. Of a total of 449 fellowships, 212, (46 per cent) were in classics and 125, (27 per cent) were in mathematics, whereas seven only were in natural science. Teaching was predominant over research, of which little was done.

Early in the nineteenth century the two London colleges – University and King's – had been established to provide for the sons of the middle classes studies which were not available at Oxford and Cambridge. Later (beginning with Owens College,

Manchester, in 1851) a spate of 'civic' colleges were set up in the major cities with the teaching of science and technology as a principal aim. These colleges were handicapped in their development by government indifference; financial support not forthcoming until the first Treasury Grant in aid of £15,000 was awarded in 1889 – the colleges having to rely on donations and subscriptions from individuals, civic leaders, manufacturers and traders. Chronic lack of funds led to a paucity of research scholarships. Professor Moore, the first holder of the chair of biochemistry at Liverpool University, wrote in 1911:

> It is much to be regretted that in the financial system of our universities no separate provision is made for the endowment of research apart from undergraduate teaching ... The result is a perpetual struggle between teaching and research for the partition of a sum of money inadequate to supply completely the needs of both and in such a struggle, research, though equally or even more important, comes off worst because it is usually regarded by administrators as a luxury whereas teaching is deemed an essential function in the work of a university.[16]

The underlying philosophy of English education was 'class based'. The grammar and public schools were exclusively middle class, whereas the cornerstone of technical education was the artisan; the perceived needs of the artisan underpinned thinking about technical education throughout the greater part of the century. The widespread concern felt about the general education of the artisan, and in particular the lack of basic instruction in science, gave rise in the second quarter of the nineteenth century to the Mechanics' Institutes which were to provide instruction in the various branches of science related to the industrial arts which the members practised. Government action in the early 1850s led to the creation of a Division of Science being added to the Department of Practical Art to form a new Department of Science and Art for the encouragement of the teaching of the applied sciences. But the working man, due to the absence of efficient primary and secondary systems of education, lacked the basic educational skills necessary to enable him to benefit from such provision created for him. An even greater weakness in technical education was middle and higher technical education. There was little provision at higher levels until the formation of technical schools and civic university colleges during the final quarter of the century, and these were badly handicapped by lack of adequate funds and suitable pupils. In contrast, higher technical education in Germany was catered for by a system of well endowed state-sponsored technical high schools which produced cadres of well trained and qualified scientists and technicians for the rapidly expanding German industrial machine. The neglect of 'higher' technical education can be seen as a fundamental weakness of the English scene. In Germany money was allocated according to pre-determined needs and the whole of education was characterised by zeal and systematic thoroughness.

Professor Margaret Gowing in her Wilkins Lecture,[17] delivered to the Royal Society in 1976, lists five factors as affecting Britain's industrial progress. These were finance, administrative structure, social class, the Church and imperial purpose. She points to the absence of any wide and sustained interest in scientific and technical education among the upper and middle classes, and quotes Professor Rolleston, Professor of Physiology at Oxford who, in evidence to the Devonshire Commissioners, referred feelingly to a French report of higher education in Britain which talked of '*snobbisme* as a *vanité très Anglaise*'.[18] According to Professor Gowing (1977), obsession with social class, which appeared on almost every page of the great educational reports, was a cause of British backwardness. She observes that it is

> strange that a country which had experienced such swift social mobility in the eighteenth and nineteenth centuries, and which had much admired its self-made industrial and engineering heroes, was so dominated by class and so reluctant to accord social prestige to science and technology. In some other European nations class divisions were as rigid, and in France much more bitter. In no other Western country did the class differences prevent scientific and technical education from permeating national life.

The administrative structure of education was a weakness. The Education Department at Whitehall which looked after elementary education and the Department of Science and Art both came under the Privy Council Committee on Education, but they were geographically and administratively separate. Secondary education fell in the gaps between the Departments while yet another body administered the endowed schools. Administrative practice was too complex. The Department of Science and Art's voluminous and ever-changing rules were unintelligible to local committees and students; it was a 'nest of nepotism' with strangely mixed functions and it remained the arbiter of scientific and technical education. Professor Gowing concludes 'the late Victorians, sometimes portrayed as creative administrative reformers, emerge in this story as patchers, improvisers and procrastinators'.

Notes and References

1 CHAMBERS, J.D. (1968) *The Workshop of the World: British Economic History 1820–1880*, Oxford, Oxford Press p. 1, defines this as the period between the financial crisis of 1821 and the Great Depression of 1873.

2 HOBSBAWM, E.J. (1968) *Industry and Empire*, Pelican Economic History of Britain, Vol. 3, Harmondsworth, Penguin Books, p. 13.

3 THOMPSON, D. (1950) *England in the Nineteenth Century*, Pelican History of England, Vol. 8, Harmondsworth, Penguin Books, p. 101.

4 HOBSBAWM, E.J. (1968) *op. cit.*, p. 180.

5 *Ibid.*, p. 181.

6 GAY, J.E. (1917) 'Anglo Russian Economic Relations', *Economic Journal*, XXVII, pp. 316–7.

7 McCLOSKEY, D.N. (Ed.) (1971) *Essays on a Mature Economy: Britain after 1840*, Papers and Proceedings of the Mathematical Social Science Board Conference of the The New Economic History of Britain, 1840–1930, London, Methuen, p. 7.

8 ARNOLD, M. (1892) *Higher Schools and Universities in Germany*, Second Edition, London, Macmillan, p. 20.

9 CARDWELL, D.S.L. (1972) *The Organization of Science in England*, London, Heinemann, p. 98.

10 SADLER, M.E. (1907) *Continuation Schools in England and Elsewhere*, Manchester, Manchester University Press, p. 3.

11 *Ibid.*, pp. 70–1.

12 *Board of Education Reports* 1905–6, pp. 31–2.

13 *Royal Commission on Scientific Instruction and the Advancement of Science* (Devonshire Commission) (1872), Vol. III, Sixth Report, p. 5.

14 *Ibid.*, Vol. I, p. 32.

15 'Natural Sciences in Education' in the *Report of the Committee on The Position of Natural Science in the Educational System of Great Britain*, (Thomson Committee) (1918), p. 11.

16 *Researches in Biochemistry*, 1908–11, Harold Cohen Library, University of Liverpool.

17 GOWING, M. (1976) *Science, Technology and Education*, The Wilkins Lecture, reprinted from notes and records of the Royal Society of London, Vol. 32, No. 1, July, 1977.

18 *Royal Commission of Scientific Instruction and the Advancement of Science* Papers, Vol. 25, p. 3731.

The Economy, Management and Foreign Competition

Derek H. Aldcroft

The retardation debate

It seems to be a favourite pastime of the British public to criticize the performance of their country's economy. For a century or more now Britain's economic performance and her industrialists have been under close scrutiny by economists, historians, journalists. and others and, generally, the tenor of their observations has been unfavourable. British businessmen, in particular, have frequently been the target for critical comment, if not outright abuse, and it is curious that a country which pioneered the breakthrough into modern industrial growth should have so little admiration for its industrial leaders.[1] Indeed, the present author, while having a high regard for thrusting and dynamic enterprise, has contributed his share to tarnishing the image of industrialists and, ironically, it has been foreign observers, notably American scholars, who have come to the rescue of the maligned British businessman.

The origins of the businessmen's 'bad press' date from the latter part of the nineteenth century.[2] This was the period when Britain's industrial supremacy began to be challenged by the newer industrializing nations and when, by all accounts, Britain's economic performance began to falter. Much has been written about the nature and extent of this decline and it is not the purpose of this paper to rehearse all the arguments and data yet again. While acknowledging the fact that the subject is still somewhat controversial, there are several points on which a broad measure of agreement has been reached. First, no one would dispute the fact that in the half century or so up to 1914 Britain steadily lost her former supremacy as industrialization proceeded abroad (notably in Germany and America) and foreign competition consequently increased. In terms of both world production in manufactures, and world trade in those products, Britain's importance declined considerably through to 1914; a not unexpected happening given her domination in the middle of the nineteenth century. Second, rates of growth of total output and industrial production decelerated in this period, though the timing and the extent of that deceleration are still being debated.[3] Not only was growth less rapid than it had been previously but it also compared unfavourably with the growth performance of some of the later industrializing countries, notably Germany and the United States. Third, and more serious, there was a marked slowing down in the rate of growth of industrial productivity. Though the statistical data leave room for improvement, evidence so far seems to indicate a significant check to productivity growth at quite an early date and by the beginning of the twentieth century industrial productivity was scarcely rising at all.

It is true that the tentative nature of some of the statistical data makes it difficult to determine precisely the timing of the break in the trend and the extent of the retardation. Nor do all series show the same pattern of deceleration. Most observers are prepared to accept, albeit with varying emphases on its timing and severity, that there was some element of lagging in Britain's economic performance. However, a few writers have not been prepared to accept fully this conventional wisdom. McCloskey (1970), for example, maintains that the growth performance of the economy was reasonably satisfactory and that the slowing down in productivity growth amounted to no more than a check in the 1900s which was 'too short, too late, and too uncertain to justify the dramatic description "climacteric"'.[4] He also argues that there was very limited potential for faster growth through either home demand or exports due to inelastic supplies of labour and capital, and, at the same time, dismisses the suggestion that a diversion of resources from foreign to domestic investment would have made much difference.[5] Similarly, in a recent study on British industry, Musson (1978), while acknowledging the debate about retardation, paints a fairly glowing picture of the period 'as that in which the Industrial Revolution really occurred, on a massive scale, transforming the whole economy and society much more widely and deeply than the earlier changes had done'.[6]

Despite such reservations, the general interest shown in Britain's retardation, and the variety of causes adduced to explain it, seem to indicate that it was more than just a myth. Indeed, as with Britain's current problems, some of which are not unlike those of a century ago, the reasons for the poor performance have been one of the most hotly debated subjects in economic history; a debate which looks like continuing for some years to come. The list of causes includes the handicap of an early start; over–commitment to basic industries; a slowing down in export growth due partly to industrialization abroad and partly to excessive commitment to certain products and markets; the lack of technical education and trained workers; obsolete machinery and a low rate of capital accumulation; imperfections in the capital market and excessive foreign investment; a low rate of technical progress and, of course, entrepreneurial deficiences of one sort or another. Such a long 'laundry list' of faults has not, however, done much to clarify the issue since it has usually proved difficult in practice to quantify the importance of each factor and thereby rank the order of priority.

It is not the purpose of this essay to traverse familiar ground yet again by discussing in detail the retardation debate and all its possible causes. There are, indeed, many loose ends still to be tied up but in this paper we shall concentrate attention on two important issues around which the debate has crystallized in recent years: first, the potential for faster growth via structural change and shifts in the use of resources; and second, the vexed question of the rate of technical progress in British industry and the associated issue of the calibre of British management and enterprise. In fact, a good part of the recent controversy has centred around the entrepreneur and his alleged failings or otherwise. Indeed, part of the original impetus for the current debate developed from earlier comments by contemporaries and later writers, which implied that much of the blame for Britain's deteriorating performance in late-Victorian Britain could be attributed to the 'malpractices' of businessmen of the period. Not surprisingly, an attack along such lines eventually brought forth a response, especially from American scholars, who have been more anxious to rescue the name of the British businessman than his compatriots have been. McCloskey, Sandberg, Harley and others have argued that it is misleading to generalize on an economy-wide basis given the wide diversity of performance between industries and between different branches of the same industry. Furthermore, where there was a recognizable lag in the adoption of new techniques (as for example in iron and steel, cotton, coal, chemicals and parts of the engineering industry) this, it has been claimed, did not necessarily signify a failure of enterprise. Indeed, it could be argued that in many instances British industrialists were behaving in a rational manner in response to a given set of economic conditions, which included relative factor prices, market structure and profit opportunities. Only when the particular conditions no longer held, that is after World War 1, did it become apparent that the pre-1914 entrepreneurial response was misplaced, but then the businessman's time horizon and powers of perception do not encompass the long-run.

The structural potential for faster growth

At any particular point in time most economies have some potential for faster growth through structural change, but this potential may remain unexploited for one reason or another. For example, many European countries had enormous growth reserves locked away in an inefficient and low productivity primary sector and these were eventually unleashed, with dramatic consequences, after World War 2.[7] Alternatively, many mature industrial countries of the present day devote a large share of their resources to services of one kind or another, many of which have low productivity levels. In Britain, in the late nineteenth and early twentieth centuries, the scope for boosting growth by shifting resources from agriculture to industry was obviously fairly limited given the already small size of the farm sector. However, one can deduce at least two possible sources of faster growth: first, a large share of resources were tied up in the basic staple industries with low rates of productivity growth, whilst at the same time there was a lag in the development of newer lines of activity or faster growing sectors; and second, a large proportion of British savings was channelled abroad. What potential was there then for improved growth through a reallocation of resources?

McCloskey's (1970) doubts about the potential for improved growth through resource reallocation have been noted earlier. He believes that the economy was growing as rapidly as its resources permitted; supplies of labour and capital were, in his opinion, relatively inelastic, and a diversion of capital invested abroad to domestic use would not have made all that much difference to the perceived growth rate. His assumptions can be challenged on several grounds. First, it is doubtful whether factor supplies were as inelastic as he suggests; second, the implications of significant structural change within the economy are not properly explored; and third, he tends to ignore the scope for productivity improvements through the adoption of best practice techniques and 'better industrial housekeeping'. The last of these points will be taken up in the section on innovational response. Here we shall deal with the 'inelastic factor supply' argument and the important question of structural change.

It is difficult to believe that factor supplies were inelastic in Victorian Britain or, alternatively, that they could have not been augmented had the need arisen. Indeed, in a recent paper, Harley (1974) has argued that it was the very abundance of skilled labour which slowed down the rate at which new techniques were adopted in Britain.[8] More generally, there may have been supply constraints with respect to labour in the short-term but, given the right conditions on the demand side, the long-term manpower potential could be improved in several ways: by lower emigration, reduction in unemployment, increased use of female labour or by improving labour utilization within the labour-intensive staple industries. With regard to capital inputs, again one can argue that better utilization would have improved the situation but, more importantly, domestic capital supplies could easily have been raised by diverting savings from foreign investment.

The structural potential for faster growth might at first glance appear to have been fairly limited, at least if one confines attention to the traditional 'old' versus 'new' industries. That too many resources were being committed to the basic trades – coal, cotton, shipbuilding – is not in question, at least from the long-term point of view. Britain also lagged in developing the newer industries – automobiles, new chemicals and electrical products. The latter were, however, at an early stage of commercial development in most countries up to 1900 and it is difficult to envisage any remarkable improvement in the growth performance of the British economy emanating from more rigorous development of these industries given that their quantitative importance was so small at that time. In fact, some doubts have recently been expressed as to their importance in inter–war growth, especially in the recovery of the 1930s, when they accounted for quite a significant share of industrial production. However, a wider interpretation of structural change would involve a more fundamental shift of resources within the economy as a whole and a shift from foreign to domestic investment.

Work by William Kennedy (1976) on growth and structural change in this period has made one aware of some of the possibilities in this direction. Preliminary calculations suggest that, had Britain made a commitment of resources to tele-communications, electricity, engineering (including electrical), car manufacturing, construction and related industries similar to that made in the United States, then the implied increase in growth would have been sufficient to raise British per capita incomes to 55 per cent above the level actually recorded in 1913.[9] In subsequent detailed work on structural change and resource reallocation, Kennedy (1978) sets out possible growth profiles contingent upon a greater commitment of resources to those sectors capable of sustaining rapid expansion and technological progress. The upper bound growth potential is substantial, producing up to a doubling of the realised per capita income of 1913. The structural change envisaged is also considerable, involving a commitment of resources to dynamic sectors greater, in relative terms, than that in the United States during the same period. But this reallocation was by no means outside the realms of feasibility, given earlier historical experience during the industrial revolution, or compared with contemplated shifts in the light of current needs.[10] It would, of course, have involved a substantial switch of resources from foreign to home investment,[11] a shift which would be economically rational on the assumption that most foreign investments yielded less than the average domestic return.[12]

The fact that structural adaptation did not take place along the lines posited can, according to Kennedy (1978), be largely attributed to the imperfections of the capital markets which concentrated their activities on fixed interest issues (foreign bonds and government securities) and well-established industrial undertakings in order to satisfy the risk-averting predilections of the British investor. What this meant in practice was that, far from encouraging the shift of resources and new technological developments, more rewarding albeit more risky, the institutional financial mechanism acted as a constraint and thereby led to an ossification of the existing structure.

> By affecting both the structure of capital supplies available domestically to British firms and the level and structure of demand for the output of British firms, foreign investment, perhaps more than any other single factor, acted to freeze the structure of the British economy in the position seen to be so precarious in the inter-war period.[13]

Furthermore, the fact that the large proportion of British savings flowing into foreign investment restricted the growth of the economy in turn conditioned the behaviour of entrepreneurs.

There are many implications of this structural counter-factual which need to be explored more fully before we can be completely satisfied with it. For example, the gains on the domestic front from 'collapsing' foreign investment would in part be offset by losses on the latter and, therefore, the net gains must be stated more explicitly. In addition, there is the question of the relative rates of return on home and foreign investments which remains to be settled. Further, it is by no means certain that the institutional rigidity of the capital markets was as strong and perverse as Kennedy (1978) implies since there is evidence that growth-orientated firms (even in the newer more risky fields of endeavour) could raise the capital required. Edelstein (1971), in particular, is doubtful about the alleged irrational bias of the British capital market towards foreign investment.[14] Finally, the analysis posits an ideal world, or an upper bound to growth through structural change, a condition not likely to be achieved in practice though a second-best order might be attainable. However, these reservations apart, the main point to emerge is that we should be wary of adopting a complacent view about the Victorian economy. As with the British economy today, everything was not alright with the Victorian economy; it could, and should, have grown faster and there was certainly room for some structural change which would have helped to achieve a better result.

Innovational response and business enterprise

Victorian industrialists have long been berated for their lack of enterprise. They have been criticised on three main counts: first, reluctance to adopt new technologies and labour-saving methods; second, the weakness of their commercial methods, especially in export markets; and third, the failure to appreciate the importance of applied science and the value of technical education. The traditional view has been set forth in a long list of writings.[15] More recently, it has been countered by a vigorous attack seeking to show that some sectors of industry were dynamic and that entrepreneurial response was rationally based.[16]

There is no doubt that British industrialists appear to have been slow to adopt new techniques and processes and improved methods of production when compared with their counterparts in the United States and Germany. One can run through a long list of industries and find something wrong with them on this score – iron and steel, coal, cotton textiles, engineering, boots and shoes, chemicals, shipbuilding, watchmaking and the railways, not to mention the newer sectors such as electrical engineering and automobiles.[17] The details are now familiar enough and they need not therefore be recounted again. However, the position was not one of unrelieved gloom. First, some industries, or branches of industry, performed creditably enough. For example, parts of the engineering industry – notably textile, steam and sewing machinery – were technically very advanced[18] while, after the 1870s, British arms manufacturers could fully match the Americans in a mass-producing export industry.[19] Nor does there seem to have been very much wrong with machine tools or the letter-press printing industry.[20] Second, one can point to a number of enterprising and innovating firms in retailing, rubber, soap and fats, pottery, glass, engineering, cotton thread, food manufacturing, clothing, furniture, tobacco and pharmaceuticals.[21] Third, from the 1890s onwards there are signs in some trades of a definite improvement in competitive position and a greater willingness to adopt new techniques. This was in part a reponse to the stimulus imparted by foreign competition, as in the case of boots and shoes, bicycles and some branches of engineering.[22] The railways too seem to have put up a better performance, at least on the freight side, in the early twentieth century.[23]

Notwithstanding these bright spots, there still remained large sectors of industry which were technically backward compared with American and German practice. In some cases, notably the electrical industry, chemicals and the Scottish cotton industry, deficiencies of enterprise can be found.[24] Lindert and Trace (1971) in their careful analysis of the chemical industry uncovered certain failures, particularly the reluctance of the Leblanc producers to switch over to the Solvay process of soda making, from which they inferred that 'the Leblanc management exhibited early-start mentality, with its profit-losing attachment to continuity and its reluctance to admit a major mistake'.[25] The virtual demise of the Scottish cotton industry has also been attributed to entrepreneurial shortcomings. The vulnerability of Scottish production to changes in fashion, coupled with a difficult labour force, played a part but, according to Robertson (1970), the crucial factor was a lack of enterprise and initiative since the experience of the Glasgow cotton spinning company, J. and P. Coats, and one or two other firms, demonstrated that given the will to succeed Scottish cotton mills could compete successfully with Lancashire or anyone else up to 1914. Scottish cotton manufacturers gave up too easily; they retired or drifted into other pursuits.[26]

Whether these are representative examples is another matter. Indeed, the general concensus of much recent work is that the British industrialist was not so bad after all.[27] There may well have been technical lags but it does not necessarily follow that entrepreneurs were inefficient or that they behaved irrationally. It is possible to explain their behaviour as a rational response to costs, market and other conditions peculiar to Britain. Thus, in the case of cotton textiles, Sandberg (1969) argues that past criticisms of the industry's technical and productive performance have been exaggerated. By not investing in ring spindles and automatic looms, as American firms did, British millowners were not sacrificing a great deal in terms of profitable investment opportunities. Given Britain's market and cost conditions with increasing emphasis on quality and ready supplies of skilled labour, it was rational for manufacturers to retain the old technology in contrast to the position in countries where skilled labour was less abundant and concentration on coarser counts was greater.[28] More generally, Harley (1974) attributes the neglect of new processes and machine techniques in several industries – iron and steel, textiles and engineering – to the abundance of skilled labour in Britain. 'So long as factor prices left "handicraft" methods the low cost technique in Britain there was little incentive to specialize' and thereby adopt modern production techniques in engineering.[29] Market conditions may also have been partly responsible for slowing down the rate of technical progress, especially in iron and steel and engineering.[30]

The most spirited defence on behalf of the entrepreneur has come from McCloskey (1971), especially with respect to the coal and iron and steel industries, which have been heavily criticized in the past for their failings. The difference in labour productivity between the American and British coal industries he explains largely in terms of the more favourable resource base which the Americans worked, thicker seams, shallower pits and fewer faults.[31] But while geological factors were important in terms of relative productivities they do not fully explain the continuing decline in British productivity or the failure to mechanize as resources diminish or become more difficult to work. Postwar experience certainly showed the gains to be derived from mechanization as seams became thinner and less accessible. A possible explanation is that relative factor prices did not justify the use of mechanical cutters up to 1914, but that after the war, when labour became more costly and disruptive, it paid to mechanize.[32] As for iron and steel, McCloskey (1973) can find very little wrong with it. That productivity growth continued in America after the 1880s when it stagnated in Britain should occasion no alarm since it simply reflected the American industry's process of catching up from an initial position of inferiority. 'The eventual cessation of productivity growth in the early 1880s in Bessemer steel, in the late 1880s in pig iron, and in the early 1900s in open hearth steel was a reflex of the exhaustion of available technology, not of slower growing demand. The rate of productivity growth in America did finally come to exceed the rate in Britain, but only because Britain had earlier achieved high levels of productivity'.[33] Britain had a good record in the open hearth process, showed no failure in the use of basic ores and, in general, the industry responded in a rational manner to the given market conditions and economic incentives then prevailing.

While the notion of entrepreneurial failure has clearly undergone some revision in recent years one must be careful not to take too complacent a view of British industry and enterprise in this period. Certainly, there were examples of technical lags, productivity stagnation and deficient enterprise. Some of these failings can be explained in terms of relative costs, factor supply conditions and market conditions, in which case one could argue that entrepreneurial behaviour was in some way rational.[34] On the other hand, much of the revisionist work is only partial in scope, since it concentrates on one or two selected issues and then attempts to make broad generalizations about the aggregate performance of the industries concerned. For example, McCloskey's (1973) analysis of the iron and steel industry takes as the basis of comparison the productivity gap between Britain and the United States. Since Britain was superior initially, America would inevitably catch up and therefore there was little need for worry even though British productivity was stagnating. It is difficult to believe, however, that there was no scope for further productivity growth unless, as McCloskey infers, technology was exhausted in Britain, a point which is neither credible nor proven since he does not analyse all the possible ways of raising productivity. The analysis of the coal industry is even more restricted. Again, the comparison with America is useful in that it demonstrates the greater yields possible in a country endowed with richer resources. However, this is only part of the story. We must also know why productivity stagnated in Britain, whether there was scope for improving it by mechanization, and if so why this was not accomplished. The thinner seams and more difficult geological conditions only explain part of the problem since the record of the twentieth century shows that productivity could be improved when mechanization was adopted. Finally, one more example might be taken, that of cotton. Sandberg (1969)[35] reckons that at the very worst British cotton firms ignored a marginally good investment in not adopting ring spindles. Continued investment in mule spinning in Britain as opposed to ring spinning in the United States could be attributed to relative labour costs; mule spinning required skilled labour and the costs were nearly one third higher in America than in Britain. Yet the labour cost of ring spinning was similar in both countries and decidedly cheaper than mule spinning in both cases, which raises the question why it was not profitable for Britain to adopt the cheaper process.

On a more general level, one should emphasise again that the revisionist school of thought would have us believe that there was very little wrong with the British economy. However, while there may well have been a variety of conditioning factors which partly explain the retardation in productivity and the behaviour of industrialists in terms of innovational response, it would be mischievous to assume that there was little that could have been done to improve efficiency and the performance of the economy in general. At the macro level, Kennedy (1976)[36] has illustrated the possibilities in terms of a substantial structural shift in the allocation of resources, while in the case of individual industries and firms there were opportunities for improved efficiency which were missed. Whether these were excusable on economic or non-economic grounds is another matter, but the fact remains that the British economy did not realise its full potential in late-Victorian and Edwardian Britain.

Foreign competition and commercial response

There is no doubt that Britain found herself in a much more competitive world in the later nineteenth century as other countries industrialized. Clearly therefore, she could not hope to retain her semi-monopolistic trading position in manufactures of the mid-Victorian period and, hence, it is not surprising to find that her share of world trade in manufactured products fell steadily in the period 1870–1914. However, though some loss of trade share was only to be expected, it has frequently been suggested that her export growth could have been stronger had a better commercial response been made to countering foreign competition in both home and overseas markets. Thus, apart from unfavourable trends in prices[37] and industrial structure,[38] there was the additional problem that British industrialists lost orders to foreign competitors simply because they would not adopt more aggressive selling methods to counter the challenge. The string of complaints listed by consular officials stationed abroad is all too familiar: too few and badly trained salesmen; lack of direct selling agencies and a consequent heavy reliance on the merchanting system; poorly produced catalogues; badly packaged goods; late delivery of goods and so on.[39] While the consular reports no doubt somewhat exaggerated the situation – and it should be noted that British consuls were strong on criticism but weak on constructive assistance – it is evident from other sources that there was more than a grain of truth in their allegations.

The weakness of British selling methods was especially noticeable in the late 1880s and 1890s, the time when American and German competition became really acute in the British domestic market and in overseas markets.[40] In a wide range of products – iron and steel, bicycles, boots and shoes, chemicals, electrical products, engineering manufactures, farm machinery, clocks, gloves and gas mantles – American and German firms appeared to be invading world markets. The strength of the invasion was exaggerated at the time but nevertheless it was significant. Moreover, the success achieved by Britain's competitors was not simply due to their superior products. Indeed, in many cases British wares were as good as, if not better than, the equivalent foreign products, though quite often the British product was not suited to the particular market in question. This was the case in the cycle industry, for example, where British firms concentrated on producing high-price, quality bicycles which could not compete with cheaper American cycles in the lower end of the market. But at the same time, British firms could not in the 1890s match the superior salesmanship of the Americans who employed technically competent salesmen and advertised widely.[41] A similar experience occurred in the boot and shoe industry,[42] and again, the loss of British dominance in the market for farm machinery in the state of Victoria, Australia between 1870 and 1900 can be explained largely in terms of non-price competition. The Americans replaced the British as the major suppliers not because the latter concentrated on traditional lines but largely because American firms were prepared to market their goods more vigorously through product adaptation, market testing and sales promotion campaigns.[43]

One of the main problems with regard to overseas sales was that British firms still relied heavily on the traditional merchant system which had served its purpose well in the early days of iron and cotton, but, as Lewis (1957) has pointed out, was less suited to selling sophisticated capital equipment to industrial countries in a more competitive environment.[44] There were obvious drawbacks in a system in which selling and production organizations were separated. Many merchant houses acted as agents to a number of firms and this inevitably produced a certain conflict of interests between competing firms. All too frequently the system of indirect selling provided an inadequate reflection of the needs and requirements of customers, both at home and abroad, partly because of the poor system of communication between firm and agency. Moreover, many merchants were accustomed to selling relatively simple consumer goods and were not equipped to promote sales of technically complex products of the later nineteenth century and, even for fairly simple consumer goods, the merchanting system was becoming increasingly unsatisfactory. By the 1890s the footwear specialists, C. and J. Clark, admitted that they had lost a good deal of business by their reliance on agents and were slowly coming to the conclusion that direct selling was the only alternative.[45]

The obvious answer to the defects of the merchanting sytem was to switch to direct selling. Both the Americans and Germans found that, with widening markets, increasing competition and more complex products, the agency or merchant system was becoming something of an anachronism and that the only real solution was to invest capital in establishing sales networks. Originally, up to the 1870s, the majority of American industrial concerns had concentrated their activities on manufacturing and they purchased their supplies, and sold their finished products, through wholesale and commercial agents. This practice changed during the later nineteenth century with the growth of large integrated concerns and, by 1900, many enterprises did much more than simply manufacture. They handled their own purchasing and controlled their own raw materials; they established their own nation-wide distribution networks, through which they carried on wholesaling and retailing, and they set up selling agencies abroad. The building up of extensive sales organizations sometimes required more in terms of capital, employment and entrepreneurial skills than did the expansion of production facilities.[46] Advertising was also extensively employed; in the marketing of breakfast cereals, for example, W.K. Kellog at times spent nearly one third of the company's working capital on advertising.[47]

German firms also went in for marketing in a big way with considerable emphasis on the promotion of exports. The country's whole commercial policy was said to be directed towards the enlargement and extension of foreign trade. To achieve their objectives all manner of expedients were tried. As Lewis (1978) reflects:

> The world was flooded with German salesmen. All kinds of sales organiza-
> tion were tried: wholesale export houses, manufacturers' representatives
> selling directly to the foreign buyer, manufacturers' export co-operatives,
> sales through foreign commission agents, and so on. Numerous consulates
> were opened at strategic points, and consuls were expected to promote
> sales of German goods, a decision which shocked British conceptions of
> diplomatic behaviour.[48]

The investigation of selling methods has been somewhat neglected by historians
and so our knowledge of the subject is far from complete. However, the record to
date still seems to indicate that British firms were weak in this field, especially on
the export side. There were important exceptions of course – firms such as Lever,
Beecham and J. and P. Coats were as advanced as any American firm in sales
techniques. Furthermore, there is some evidence to suggest that a number of
British firms made a spirited response to the American and German commercial
challenge of the late nineteenth and early twentieth century[49] but, generally speaking,
there was no revolution in sales techniques in industry taken as a whole and one hears
very little among British firms about the recruitment and training of manpower in
sales and distribution. One suspects that technical expertise in this field was thinner
on the ground than in the laboratory and that the occupation remained very much
the province of the amateur.

One can suggest reasons for the reluctance to alter or adapt selling methods. The
small scale of the typical firm, together with a marked lack of cooperation among
firms for marketing purposes, made it difficult to establish viable, direct selling
organizations or to maintain large staffs of qualified salesmen. It is possible, too,
that the innate satisfaction with existing arrangements and an apparent ignorance
regarding the deficiences of the merchant system go some way towards explaining
the situation. But perhaps more important were the consequences of the failure to
improve selling techniques. There is certainly plenty of evidence to suggest that
British firms lost export business through lack of sales drive, and, in turn, the
consequent slower growth in exports may have reduced the incentive to make
technical improvements. Moreover, reliance on the merchanting system may, as
Kindleberger (1964) suggests, have inhibited technical progress.[50] The division of
functions between producing and selling agents interposed barriers of communication between producer and consumer and thereby rendered external to the firm the
benefits of technical change. He cites the case of cotton textiles where the merchant
was partly responsible for the large number of separate qualities of product because
he lacked the incentive or ability to induce customers to standardize their requirements. Similarly, in the case of machine tools, the lack of close liaison between
producer and customer, because of the interposition of the merchant, restricted
both the standardization of tool design and the development of new tools.

More generally, we know that the merchant system was geared to selling traditional goods in traditional markets and less suited to selling new and sophisticated
products in the rich and expanding markets of Europe and America. By 1914 nearly

70 per cent of Britain's exports went to primary or semi-primary producing countries and the types of exports which were sold to these countries did not provide the same kind of incentive to adopt modern production methods and advanced technology as those to America and Europe. In effect therefore, the merchant system may well have tended to intensify the relative over-commitment to traditional products and traditional markets. Indirectly, this could have contributed to slowing down the rate of technical progress and, in turn, productivity growth, though by how much is anybody's guess.

Science, education and trained manpower

Another area of weakness in British industry in the later nineteenth century was in the application of science to industry and in the recruitment of a trained labour force. It is true that there were plenty of traditional craftsmen trained in particular skills through long plodding apprenticeships. But scientists, technicians and creative workers were thin on the ground. British firms had a poor record in scientific research; they employed relatively few scientists and technologists, and there was a big gulf between academic science and industry. The implications for the more science-based industries – iron and steel, chemicals and electrical engineering for example – were serious and have been outlined in some detail elsewhere.[51] Moreover, as Lewis (1978) has pointed out, the gap existed not only at the top but also at the intermediate level of foremen, supervisors and technicians.[52] Though considerable investigation still remains to be done in this area it seems very likely that Britain's workforce was less well-educated than those of Germany and America.

The failure of industry to recruit more trained personnel, both at the higher and lower levels of educational attainment, can be attributed largely to two factors: lack of interest on the part of employers and the defects of Britain's educational sytem. Most industrialists had little faith in applied science and adhered to the cult of the practical man. Scientists were accorded a lowly status in the firm's hierarchy and many employers regarded training on the job as preferable to formal technical education. Technical schools were regarded more as places of correction than as centres of skilled instruction. As Robertson (1974) has noted in his study of ship-building ' ... technical education for skilled workmen was deemed beneficial because it discouraged vandalism, promoted moral strength, and broadened a man's outlook as well as giving him a better grasp of the job. It was important not so much because it imparted a better knowledge of the principles of shipbuilding and engineering, but because it helped to inculcate habits of good conduct'.[53]

Such attitudes were by no means uncommon among employers though, of course, there were enlightened firms who did take advantage of the educational facilities available. These facilities were, however, somewhat limited since Britain's educational system was not very well adapted to a modern industrial society. Britain had little to compare with the scale and provision of university, technical and elementary education in Germany, which ultimately provided that country with an army of trained scientists and technicians for its science-based industries such as chemicals, iron and steel and engineering. Until the middle of the nineteenth century there was little in the way of formal science teaching other than that provided by the new University of London, the Mechanics' Institutes, occasional evening classes and a few courses in elementary science in the more progressive grammar schools. During the latter part of the century improvements were made at all levels, the most notable advances being the establishment of the more science-based universities in the provinces and the beginnings of technical education by local authorities.

These developments, as Michael Sanderson (1972) has shown, coincided with the greater readiness of some of the larger firms to develop their own research activities and employ qualified graduates.[54] As a consequence the demand for science graduates rose and the links between universities and business were strengthened. Even so, progress on the higher educational front was limited, especially in technical education, and by the early twentieth century the British system of scientific and technical instruction was still far behind that of Germany, especially from the point of view of providing trained recruits for industry.[55] In 1910 Germany had some 25,000 university students in science and technology compared with a mere 3,000 ·in Britain and many of the latter drifted into teaching or emigrated because of the lack of suitable openings in the business world.[56] No doubt in qualitative terms some of our science and engineering graduates ranked on a par with those of Germany but 'by any criteria as a major industrial power our quantitative lag in producing scientists for industry was plain compared with the capability of our chief competitors'.[57]

Even worse was 'the general backwardness of British mass education compared with the American. The big deficiency was in secondary education, which the British reserved for the handful, with the result that the intermediate industrial class was better educated in Germany or the United States than in Britain. This class, being on the shop floor, plays an important role in improving production techniques'.[58] Despite the advances in state education from the early 1870s onwards it is clear that Britain was losing ground to Germany and the United States. Even by the 1880s the share of educational expenditure in GNP in these two countries had surpassed the British level and continued to advance more rapidly in subsequent decades.[59]

This advance was reflected at both the higher and lower levels of education. Even as early as the 1860s, the German craftsman received a better general and technical education than his British counterpart; by the turn of the century the disparity in standards was even greater. According to Lee (1978), the average German worker, *circa* 1900, would have spent about 32 hours a week for nine years in a primary school as against 20 hours for seven years in the case of the English worker, while the former would more than likely have had the benefit of an average of five hours a week for two to four years in a continuation school. Educational investment was one of Germany's major assets in the economic rivalry of the period and Lee reckons that by 1914 Germany had established 'not merely the finest university system but also the finest technical and commercial educational system the world had yet seen'.[60]

The lag in educational facilities and the indifference of employers to scientific research and technical training of work forces meant that down to 1914 British industry invested less in human capital than her main competitors. The full implications of this neglect still remain to be analysed. However, it certainly limited the range of opportunities open to businessmen in both a productive and technical sense and probably explains in part the weak innovational response in some industries. As Sir William Armstrong, one of the more enlightened employers, remarked:

> The ignorance of the great masses of persons engaged in industry as regards natural science and technical knowledge is a bar to the progress of the individual, as well as a loss to the nation. Almost every branch of skilled labour could be developed if the persons engaged in it were trained in the elements of natural science, which come into account in the labour.[61]

Labour management

Finally, one area which has not received the attention it deserves is that of labour management and utilization of the workforce. It has frequently been alleged that British industry, both then and now, did not use its labour force efficiently; that by comparison American and German firms exploited their labour resources more effectively either by providing labour with more capital per head and/or by adopting methods of work organization which maximised output. American workers in particular were 'driven' at a faster rate than the British.

In Britain, in the latter half of the nineteenth century, there was considerable slack to be taken up in terms of resource utilization. The bursts of innovation of the first half of the nineteenth century had led manufacturers to neglect the possibilities of economizing on the use of labour. According to Hobsbawm (1964):

> The increase in output due to technical innovation was so vast that it was easy to forget how much greater it might have been with efficient exploitation ... It seemed not to matter that they might have turned out more, because few entrepreneurs realised the potential economies of really efficient labour exploitation.[62]

In fact, industrialists devoted very little effort to exploring the possibilities of boosting productivity by more efficient work methods, while handbooks for industrialists and managers neglected the subject almost entirely. Employers tended to assume that the lowest wage bill for the longest hours meant the lowest labour costs per unit of time. Productivity was conceived largely in terms of mechanization and disciplining the workforce, and little regard was paid to the way in which it might be increased by using more efficient work methods and incentive payments.

It would be wrong to assume that no improvements at all were made in this period. Indeed, with pressure on profit margins, increasing competition and the limited possibilities of cutting costs by extending hours of work or forcing down wages, employers were obliged to find alternative ways of reducing costs. But the advances made with modern management methods were limited and were never commensurate with the degree of slack which prevailed in the system. Even in America, where much greater emphasis was placed on the efficient use of manpower, evidence of under-utilization was still common in the early twentieth century. The author of *The Economics of Efficiency* was told by a number of prominent American manufacturers that they were getting only between 50 and 60 per cent of the possible output from their workers.[63] The position was clearly very much worse in Britain since American methods of labour management, work and time studies were still in their infancy. New methods of industrial remuneration (for example, payment-by-results) despite their obvious implications for improved productivity,[64] were adopted only slowly in this country. In fact, by 1914, rationalized methods of production and scientific management of the labour force had made only very limited progress in British industry.

One reason given for the slow progress on this front was the attitude of workers. Generally speaking they were anything but receptive to new work methods and, at times, they were openly hostile towards attempts to boost output by rationalizing production methods and the introduction of incentive payments. Such attitudes might be regarded as natural enough given the consequences in terms of employment and the past history of redundancy in certain trades as a result of technological progress earlier in the century. However, the situation was no doubt exacerbated by the fact that management did little to assuage workers' fears on this count or to improve the system of industrial relations. There was a wide gulf between management and workers, the latter being regarded merely as units of labour, and little effort was made to bridge this gap. Hence,

> the workers' natural reaction to this was alienation from the system, and unwillingness to co-operate in any measures which might reduce the demand for labour, coupled with the conviction that the nation's leaders were an enemy, in whom no confidence should be reposed.[65]

Had British employers shown the capacity of their American counterparts for mutual cooperation and a greater willingness to encourage their workers to share in the benefits and profits from improved methods and new machinery, the unions might well have been more receptive to new ideas and new practices. Even Edwin Pratt (1904), who was by no means sympathetic to the restrictive practices of the unions, conceded that British employers had much to learn from American methods of labour management.[66] And indeed they had, since few manufacturers in Britain were sufficiently familiar with American methods and the teachings of Taylor to be able to apply them effectively and, at the same time, to reconcile the interests of labour. 'Taylorism' was as much misunderstood and misinterpreted by the managerial hierarchy in Britain as by the rank and file workers. With some notable exceptions, scientific management got a 'vague, cool and distant' reception from British businessmen whose notions about business were still very much redolent of the industrial revolution period. Not surprisingly 'the industrial *milieu* presented an infertile soil because of scepticism and apathy – an incapacity to understand that anything other than technology was of consequence – rather than because of any active opposition or obstructive ignorance'.[67]

Conclusion

The debate on Britain's economic performance in the late nineteenth century will no doubt continue for many years to come, with optimist and pessimist interpretations vying for pride of place. It should not, however, be regarded as a sterile one even if at times the frontiers of knowledge seem to shift forward imperceptibly. The controversy concerning Victorian growth is not without its counterpart today; the big difference being that there are fewer optimists about the current situation and a great deal more apathy. However, the study of past economic performance almost certainly acts as a useful 'learning' device.

This short essay has only been able to touch upon some of the major issues in dispute; it does not claim to be original, rather its function is to provide an up-to-date survey of the main areas of debate. From the author's point of view the main conclusions to emerge are as follows. First, the performance of the Victorian and Edwardian economy cannot be regarded as completely satisfactory. The optimists appear to have been too complacent in their interpretation of Britain's track record in this period. Second, it is clear that there was considerable scope for improvement in performance through structural change and resource reallocation, faster technical progress and better management of resources. The most important and difficult problem is explaining why that potential remained unexploited. There are a number of possible causes which have been explored in some depth in recent years, though in practice it has proved difficult to weight their relative importance. They include institutional constraints, market conditions, relative factor supplies, managerial deficiences and a hostile economic environment. The current trend is towards lifting some of the burden of guilt from the much maligned entrepreneur by interpreting his behaviour as rational in terms of the economic environment and constraints under which he operated. Perhaps the role of future research might be towards a more explicit specification of the relative importance of the various conditioning factors.

It is worthwhile here to add a contemporary postscript. Britain's relative decline, which began in the later nineteenth century, has continued almost without check to the present day. And it looks like continuing into the future with the prospect even of *absolute* decline if something drastic is not done soon. Yet an attitude of complacency still prevails among the British people and, no doubt, later writers will feel constrained to argue that Britain's current performance was not really that bad, just as academics are trying to whitewash the record of the later nineteenth century. But if, as Peter Jenkins (1978) suggested in his series of articles in *The Guardian*,[68] social, political and cultural deficiencies are at the root of our relative decline, such complacent views about our past and present performance will serve no useful purpose in terms of achieving the radical transformation of the British economy which is so desperately required in the near future.

Notes and References

1 Fortunately Neil McKendrick is doing an admirable job in promoting the image of the British business-man. See his excellent introductions to the Europa Business Biography Series, three of which have so far been published: OVERY, R.J. (1976) *William Morris, Viscount Nuffield*, Europa Publications; TREBILCOCK, R.C. (1977) *The Vickers Brothers*, Europa Publications; DAVIES, P.N. (1978) *Sir Alfred Jones: Shipping Entrepreneur par Excellence*, Europa Publications.

2 Though even in the heyday of the industrial revolution the businessman was rarely praised, at least not by the novelists of the period.

3 The literature is enormous. For two recent surveys see LEWIS, W.A. (1978) *Growth and Fluctuations 1870–1913*, Allen and Unwin and MUSSON, A.E. (1978) *The Growth of British Industry*, (Chapter 8) Batsford.

4 McCLOSKEY, D.N. (1970) 'Did Victorian Britain Fail?', *Economic History Review*, 23.

5 For alternative interpretations see ALDCROFT, D.H. (1974) 'McCloskey on Victorian growth: a comment', *Economic History Review*, 27 and KENNEDY, W.P. (1974) 'Foreign investment, trade and growth in the United Kingdom 1870–1913', *Explorations in Economic History*, 11. See also below.

6 MUSSON, A.E. (1978) *op. cit.*, pp. 150–1.

7 See ALDCROFT, D.H. (1977) *The European Economy, 1914–1970*, Croom Helm. A very stimulating analysis of the process and implications of structural change in mature western economies is given by CORNWALL, J. (1977) in his *Modern Capitalism*, Martin Robertson.

8 HARLEY, C.K. (1974) 'Skilled labour and the choice of technique in Edwardian industry', *Explorations in Economic History*, 11.

9 KENNEDY, W.P. (1976) 'Institutional response to economic growth: capital markets in Britain to 1914', in HANNAH, L. (Ed.) *Management Strategy and Business Development*, London, Macmillan, p. 183, note 97.

10 I should like to thank Dr. Kennedy for allowing me to consult and to quote from his paper *Economic Growth and Structural Change in the UK, 1870–1914*, Discussion Paper No. 112 (May 1978), Department of Economics, University of Essex.

11 KENNEDY, W.P. (1974) in *Explorations in Economic History*, 11. In fact Kennedy calculates the upper bounds to growth on the assumption that the only limits to growth were imposed by the constraint that *all* capital formation occurred at home.

12 There is by no means full agreement on this matter; see EDELSTEIN, M. (1976) 'Realised rates of return on UK home and overseas portfolio investment in the age of high imperialism', *Explorations in Economic History*, 13.

13 KENNEDY, W. P. (1974) *op. cit.*, p. 439.

14 EDELSTEIN, M. (1971) 'Rigidity and bias in the British capital market, 1870–1913' in McCLOSKEY, D.N. (Ed.) *Essays on a Mature Economy: Britain after 1840*, London, Methuen.

15 For a selection of pessimist views see LANDES, D.S. (1969) *The Unbound Prometheus*, Cambridge University Press; LEVINE, A.L. (1967) *Industrial Retardation in Britain 1880–1914*, Weidenfeld; ALDCROFT, D.H. (1964) 'The Entrepreneur and the British Economy 1870–1914', *Economic History Review*, 17 and 'Investment in and utilisation of manpower: Great Britain and her rivals, 1870–1914' in RATCLIFFE, B.M. (Ed.) (1975) *Great Britain and Her World, 1750–1914*, Manchester University Press.

16 See for example, McCLOSKEY, D.N. (1971) *op. cit.*; 'Did Victorian Britain fail?', *Economic History Review*, 23, (1970); and with SANDBERG, L.G. (1971) 'From damnation to redemption: judgements on the late Victorian entrepreneur', *Explorations in Economic History*, 9; SAUL, S.B. (1967) 'The market and the development of the mechanical engineering industries in Britain, 1860–1914', *Economic History Review*, 20.

17 In the last mentioned one could say there was too much enterprise, that is too many small producers.

18 SAUL, S.B. (1967) *op. cit.*

19 TREBILCOCK, C. (1969) 'Spin-off in British economic history: armament and industry 1760–1914', *Economic History Review*, 22.

20 FLOUD, R.C. (1976) *The British Machine Tool Industry 1850–1914*; ALFORD, B.W.E. (1965) 'Business enterprise and the growth of the commercial letter-press printing industry, 1850–1914', *Business History*, 7.

21 MUSSON, A.E. (1978) *op. cit.*, pp. 163–4; WILSON, C. (1965) 'Economy and society in late Victorian Britain', *Economic History Review*, 18.

22 SAUL, S.B. (1966) 'The American impact on British industry, 1895–1914', *Business History*, 3; CHURCH, R.A. (1968) 'The effect of the American export invasion on the British boot and shoe industry, 1885–1914, *Journal of Economic History*, 28; HARRISON, A.E. (1969) 'The competitiveness of the British cycle industry, 1890–1914', *Economic History Review*, 22.

23 IRVING, R.J. (1978) 'The profitability and performance of British railways 1870–1914', *Economic History Review*, 31; see also GOURVISH, T.R. (1978) 'The performance of British railway management after 1860: the railways of Watkin and Forbes', *Business History*, 20.

24 See KENNEDY, W.P. (1976) *op. cit.*, p. 172; LINDERT, P.H. and TRACE, K. (1971) 'Yardsticks for Victorian entrepreneurs' in McCLOSKEY, D.N. (Ed.) (1971) *op. cit.*; ROBERTSON, A.J. (1970) 'The decline of the Scottish cotton industry, 1800–1914', *Business History*, 12.

25 LINDERT, P.H. and TRACE, K. (1971) *op. cit.*, pp. 263–4.

26 ROBERTSON, A.J. (1970) *op. cit.*, p. 128; Byres lists a whole string of other failures in Scottish industry and lays much of the blame on the entrepreneur: BYRES, T.J. (1967) Entrepreneurship in the Scottish heavy industries, 1870–1900', in PAYNE, P.L. (Ed.) *Studies in Scottish Business History*, London, F. Cass.

27 For a recent review see PAYNE, P.L. (1978) 'Industrial entrepreneurship and management in Great Britain' in MATHIAS, P. and POSTAN, M.M. (Eds.) *The Cambridge Economic History of Europe, Vol. VII, The Industrial Economies: Capital, Labour and Enterprise, Part 1, Britain, France, Germany and Scandinavia*, Cambridge University Press, pp. 201–11. Payne argues that there have always been entrepreneurial deficiencies even in the period of the industrial revolution, and while he has certain misgivings about entrepreneurial performance in what he calls the 'critical period' (1870–1914) on balance he comes down on the side of the optimists. He does not explain however the productivity lag.

28 SANDBERG, L.G. (1969) 'American rings and English mules: the role of economic rationality', *Quarterly Journal of Economics*, 83, and *Lancashire in Decline* (1974), Columbus, Ohio State University Press.

29 HARLEY, C.K. (1974) *op. cit.*, p. 410.

30 TEMIN, P. (1966) 'The relative decline of the British steel industry, 1880–1913' in ROSOVSKY, H. (Ed.) *Industrialisation in Two Systems*; SAUL, S.B. (1967) *op. cit.*

31 McCLOSKEY, D.N. (1971) 'International differences in productivity? Coal and steel in America and Britain before World War I' in McCLOSKEY, D.N. (1971) *op. cit.*

32 See WALTERS, R. (1975) 'Labour productivity in the South Wales steam-coal industry, 1870–1914', *Economic History Review*, 28 (1975); for the influence of the growth of unionism on productivity before 1914 see PENCAVEL, J.H. (1977) 'The distributional and efficiency effects of trade unions in Britain', *British Journal of Industrial Relations*, 15.

33 McCLOSKEY, D.N. (1973) *Economic Maturity and Entrepreneurial Decline: British Iron and Steel, 1870–1913*, Boston, Harvard University Press, p. 125.

34 In fact the present author attempted to define some of the conditioning factors affecting entrepreneurial behaviour in 'Technical Progress and British Enterprise, 1875–1914', *Business History*, 8, (1966).

35 SANDBERG, L.G. (1969) *op. cit.*

36 KENNEDY, W.P. (1976) *op. cit.*

37 British export prices rose relative to those of Germany and the United States between 1883 and 1913. LEWIS, W.A. (1978) *op. cit.*, p. 122.

38 Britain's industrial structure was weighted towards those products whose export growth potential was limited. See TYSZYNSKI, H. (1951) 'World trade in manufactured commodities, 1899–1950', *The Manchester School*, 19.

39 A full account can be found in HOFFMANN, R.S.J. (1933) *Great Britain and the German Trade Rivalry, 1875–1914*; PLATT, D. (1971) *The Cinderella Service: British Consuls since 1825*, Longman, p. 103, *et seq.*

40 NOVAKS, D.E. and SIMON, M. (1965–66) 'Commercial responses to the American export invasion, 1871–1914' *Explorations in Entrepreneurial History*, 3.

41 HARRISON, A.E. (1969) *op. cit.*

42 CHURCH, R.A. (1968) *op. cit.*

43 McLEAN, I.W. (1976) 'Anglo-American engineering competition, 1870–1914: some third-market evidence', *Economic History Review*, 29.

44 LEWIS, W.A. (1957) 'International competition in manufactures', *American Economic Review*, 47, p. 578.

45 SUTTON, G.B. (1964) 'The marketing of ready made footwear in the nineteenth century: a study of the firm of C. and J. Clark', *Business History*, 6.

46 CHANDLER, A.D. (1963–64) 'Entrepreneurial opportunity in nineteenth century America', *Explorations in Entrepreneurial History*, 1, p. 118.

47 SILK, A.J. and STERN, L.W. (1963) 'The changing nature of innovation in marketing: a study of selected business leaders, 1852–1958', *Business History Review*, 37, p. 190.

48 LEWIS, W.A. (1978) *op. cit.*, p. 122.

49 For examples in boots and shoes and bicycles: see CHURCH, R.A. (1968) *op. cit.*; and HARRISON, A.E. (1969) *op. cit.*

50 KINDLEBERGER, C.P. (1964) *Economic Growth in France and Britain 1851–1950*, pp. 148–9.

51 ALDCROFT, D.H. (1975) 'Investment in and utilisation of manpower: Great Britain and her rivals, 1870–1914' in RATCLIFFE, B.M. (Ed.) (1975), *op. cit.*, pp. 289–92.

52 LEWIS, W.A. (1978) *op. cit.*, p. 129.
53 ROBERTSON, P.L. (1974) 'Technical education in the British shipbuilding and marine engineering industries, 1863–1914' *Economic History Review*, 27, p. 227.
54 SANDERSON, M. (1972) 'Research and the firm in British industry, 1919–39', *Science Studies*, 2, pp. 108–12; and *The Universities and British Industry 1850–1970*, London, Routledge and Kegan Paul.
55 LANDES, D.S. (1969) *op. cit.*, pp. 339–45.
56 RODERICK, G. and STEPHENS, M. (1974) 'Scientific studies and scientific manpower in the English civic universities 1870–1914', *Science Studies*, 4, p. 62. The authors blame the government more than industry for the tardy development of higher education.
57 SANDERSON, M. (1972) *op. cit.*, p. 24.
58 LEWIS, W.A. (1978) *op. cit.*, p. 130.
59 WEST, E.G. (1975) 'Educational slowdown and public intervention in nineteenth century England: a study in the economics of bureaucracy', *Explorations in Economic History*, 12, p. 80.
60 LEE, T.J. (1978) 'Labour in German industrialisation', in *The Cambridge Economic History of Europe*, Vol. VII, Part I, p. 459.
61 Quoted in VON SCHULZE-GAEVERNITZ, G. (1895) *The Cotton Trade in England and on the Continent*, p. 140.
62 HOBSBAWM, E.J. (1964) *Labouring Men: Studies in the History of Labour*, Weidenfeld, p. 354.
63 BRISCO, N.A. (1914) *The Economics of Efficiency*, New York, pp. 5–6.
64 For examples of the benefits to be derived from payment by results see SCHLOSS, D.F. (1898) *Methods of Industrial Remuneration*, p. 120.
65 LEWIS, W.A. (1978) *op. cit.*, p. 127.
66 PRATT, E.A. (1904) *Trade Unions and British Industry*, p. 186.
67 URWICK, L. (1949) *The Making of Scientific Management, Vol. 2, Management in British Industry*, London, Pitman, pp. 88–92.
68 JENKINS, P. (1978) 'Castles in the Air', *The Guardian*, 28, 29 and 30 September.

Progress in Artisan Literacy from 1790*

E.G. West

Sharp differences of judgment appear to persist on the precise extent and timing of literacy changes in the eighteenth and nineteenth century Britain and their relationship to economic growth. This chapter will explore the exact nature of the differences and will attempt to resolve some of the main issues.

Recent research among British historians seems to have been sensitive to the seminal work of the American economists Bowman and Anderson in 1963.[1] From statistics of cross-sectional comparisons of literacy rates in the 1950s they generalized that a literacy rate of 30 to 40 per cent was a necessary condition for a country to make a significant per capita income breakthrough. Several British historians seem to have been uneasy about Bowman and Anderson's inclusion of eighteenth and nineteenth century Britain as one of the many 'industrial and literacy success' examples. Their critical response to the American authors has included the following three arguments; first, that literacy deteriorated in the Industrial Revolution; second, that growth produced literacy, not *vice versa*; third, that private educational activities were inadequate.

This response has no doubt been conditioned by the long established tradition in British history that the Industrial Revolution, especially in its early stages, was generally inimicable to reasonable *material* comforts, let alone educational improvements, among the working class. Typical of the originators of this tradition, for instance, were the Hammonds (1937). Their conclusion was that in the new manufacturing towns of the Industrial Revolution:

> ... all diversions were regarded as wrong, because it was believed that successful production demanded long hours, a bare life, a mind without temptation to think or remember, to look before or behind.[2]

> The ruling class argued ... that with the new method of specialization, industry could not spare a single hour for the needs of the man who served it. In such a system education had no place.[3]

* This chapter is taken from the article 'Literacy and the Industrial Revolution' which appeared in *Economic History Review*, Summer 1978.

... politicians were prepared to leave the nation to a hopelessly inadequate provision made by voluntary societies, and it was not until 1833 that education received any help from the public funds.[4]

Richard Altick (1957), a more recent upholder of this tradition, summed it up in one sentence:

The occupational and geographical relocation of the people – the total disruption of their old way of life, their conversion into machine-slaves, living a hand to mouth existence at the mercy of their employers and of uncertain economic circumstances; their concentration in cities totally unprepared to accomodate them, not least in respect to education; the resultant moral and physical degradation – these, as we shall see, had significant consequences in the history of the reading public.[5]

The supporters of this traditional view, nevertheless, have had to face the challenge not only of Anderson and Bowman, but also of the new empirical work of writers (including the present author) who claim that education did not decline.[6] The response to this challenge has been interesting. Some historians, whether traditionalists or not, have reacted by concentrating on intensive surveys of particular localities that suggest apparent exceptions to the rule of progress. Sometimes, too, the 'new sceptics' have challenged the reliability of the statistical sources used in recent work, but then they have proceeded, regardless of the inconsistency, to rely themselves on the same sources, but with their own particular interpretation.[7] More important, the sceptics have concluded that the verdict, that the industrial revolution period (which most participants in the debate seem to take to be 1760–1840) was favourable to educational growth, is, at best, appropriate only for the last few years of the period.[8] They base their main argument on large scale sample data on eighteenth century marriage register signatures first published in 1973. Previously, scholars had been limited to national figures from 1839 in the Registrar's annual reports and to one or two small local samples.

In this chapter I shall take the opportunity to examine the new data, especially since I did not get access to it until 1974 when I had finished writing my last book *Education and the Industrial Revolution*, (published in 1975). I shall argue that, on correct interpretation, it does not support the sceptics.[9] The chapter will also consider the claim of the sceptics that wide regional variations in nineteenth century literacy throw doubt on any generalized conclusion on the relationship between industrialization and educational growth. The main focus will be on the regional example that is so often cited, the case of Lancashire. It will be argued that here some important variables have been missing from the discussion. Finally, it will be shown that, in reaching their conclusion, the sceptics have gone from figures of literacy to figures of schooling, and that, in this latter field, their argument is equally unconvincing.

The discussion will begin with a re-examination of the Lancashire case, will go on to analyse the new data on eighteenth century literacy and will discuss critically the current interpretation of it. It will then link the evidence of changing literacy with that of changing educational institutions, and especially the innovations of 'free', 'compulsory', and publicly-provided schools, in a way that tests hypotheses about such linkage that is commonly employed by the sceptics but not efficiently tested by them.

It is generally agreed by all participants, that people were more literate at the end of the Industrial Revolution period, 1760–1840, than they were at the beginning. Social historian Michael Sanderson's (1972) survey of Lancashire, however, has suggested to him initial decline or stagnation that only reversed itself after over one half of the period was over.[10] Sanderson based his survey on a selection of what he believed to be fairly representative instances of the industrializing centers in the country.

After adding further data, Thomas Laqueur (1974), using the same measure as Sanderson – marriage register signatures – also pointed to an early decline in literacy in Lancashire. The low point was 48 per cent of men and 17 per cent of women able to sign their names in 1814–16.[11] Laqueur, however, rejected Sanderson's suggestion that the low point might have been *caused* by the introduction of large scale factories using steam-power in the 1790's which, according to Sanderson, was the beginning of real social dislocation. This is unproven, Laqueur insisted, because the downward literacy trend had by then already been in progress for forty years. Sanderson's argument, moreover, could not explain the beginning of a long-term rise in the literacy rate which Laqueur placed at around 1800, when the full influence of the factory system was beginning to be felt.

> In fact, it appears that the Industrial Revolution reversed a downward
> spiral of working-class literacy which began in the mid-eighteenth century
> . . . By the time the full effects of the factory system came to be felt, literacy
> was once again on the rise.[12]

Laqueur emphasized that the marriage literacy test reflected an education that ended about twelve to fifteen years before, as was likely, for instance, with a marriage age of 25 and a school leaving age of 10. It was for this reason that the correct date for the improvement in literacy was around 1800. Laqueur's article also stressed that the adult literacy rates in the same Lancashire towns were below the national averages just *before* the Industrial Revolution. In his reply in 1974, Sanderson did not satisfactorily meet Laqueur's point that the downward trend in literacy had been in progress for forty years before the introduction, in the 1790s, of steam-powered factories and that the latter were not, therefore, the obvious cause of the low point in literacy in 1800. Instead, Sanderson shifted the debate to the later end of the period. He argued that his own figures of literacy in Lancashire at the time of marriage did not show a 'consistent' upturn before 1820. The graph of his data[13], however, shows that there *was* a distinct upturn before 1820, as Laqueur argued. First, Sanderson's nine point moving average curve rises steadily from its first point in the year 1817. Second, and much more importantly, his graph needs an adjustment lag to account for the interval between school and marriage. Sanderson (1974) accepted Laqueur's argument that literacy records in marriage registers reflected a schooling of twelve to fifteen years earlier. On the assumption that schooling creates literacy (which all participants accept) his nine point average curve of literacy should, on his own concession, start twelve to fifteen years *before* 1817, that is in 1802–5. Third, neither Laqueur or Sanderson give the source for their belief that the lag was twelve to fifteen years. My own research (1965, p. 133) suggests that on the average it was about seventeen years. On this estimate, Sanderson's graph reveals the rise in literacy starting in 1800, as Laqueur argued on the basis of his own data. Notice that the argument, that the full effects of the large scale factories in 1800 caused a social dislocation that was inimical to education, requires evidence that literacy *declined* at this time. Sanderson's evidence shows instead that the period around 1800 was the beginning of an *increase*.

The question whether industrial change in the past hindered or helped literacy is much more complex when other substantial changes were occurring. The most dramatic change in the late eighteenth and early nineteenth centuries, apart from the Napoleonic War, was the unprecedented expansion of population. The true test of the question is whether literacy rates would have fared better if the same late eighteenth population explosion *had occurred in the pre-factory environment*. Even if we ignored the previous criticisms, this consideration would make Sanderson's argument much more hypothetical. Laqueur mentions a 60 per cent increase in the Lancashire population between 1781 and 1800. Not only was the natural increase well above the national average, but so was the rate of immigration. The total increase in the Lancashire population was four times the national average. According to rough estimates, just under half of the increase between 1781 and 1800 was by immigration (126,319 increase by immigration and 146,852 by natural increase).[14] This means that if the typical immigrant family consisted of two adults and two children, then for every two 'local born' children, there was about one immigrant child needing education over this period. The more that immigrants consisted of young single adults, the more the early marriage signatures would be represented by them. Also relevant is that between 1801–31 population increase reached its peak in absolute numbers (637,543) as did the natural increase (474,009) and immigration (183,543).[15] The *ratio* of immigrants to natural increase, however, was evidently falling by this time.

Because a considerable proportion of the immigrants were low-income Irish, and since by all accounts they had the poorest of education,[16] the growth of Irish arrivals relative to the local born Lancashire population must have had a significant depressing effect on the local literacy records, especially between 1781 and 1800. According to Arthur Redford (1968), Lancashire contained a greater number of Irish settlers during the period than any other county, and the majority of them settled in the Industrial Revolution towns.[17] In 1835, Dr. J.P. Kay estimated that the Irish and their immediate descendents in Manchester had grown to about sixty thousand. This was between one quarter and one third of the town's total population.[18]

It is surprising that, in the works cited above, neither Sanderson or Laqueur connect the Irish immigration with the relatively low literacy rates in the Lancashire of the Industrial Revolution. Indeed, Laqueur argues the possibility that the immigrants were typically the more accomplished and literate. Clearly, the data produced by Sanderson and Laqueur would benefit by a re-examination and search for a correlation between Irish settlement and literacy rates in the various parishes so far studied. Their investigations are surely significantly incomplete without it.

If the explanation of a depressant effect of immigrants holds up, the view that literacy had no major connection with economic growth in the period would be even weaker.[19] The quickening of economic activity in the Industrial Revolution stimulated the demand for new construction of houses, port facilities, canals, and roads. This in turn increased the demand for general labourers, among whom, it is generally agreed, literacy is not of the strongest relevance to their particular productivity. As Redford (1968) observes:

> Much of the work done by the Irish in Great Britain was of the same general manual nature as their harvesting and agricultural labour ... An immense number of Irish were employed as hodmen in Lancashire ... By 1833 there were at least seven hundred Irish hod-carriers working in Liverpool, and two years later it was said that four-fifths of the bricklayers' labourers in Stockport were Irish.[20]

Such a picture is quite consistent with a situation of significant 'threshold' literacy among the indigenous population enabling them better to concentrate in 'key' growth areas, like manufacturing, where literacy *was* of more consequence. But even if this were not the case, insofar as the literacy of the immigrant Irish improved compared with its normal attainment at their place of origin, we can still speak of this as a growth in education; and one that was associated with industrialization. The positive association could still prevail *despite* the stagnation or even decline shown in Lancashire marriage signatures in particular localities. This kind of explanation, too, could give its own kind of support to a 'threshold'-type argument similar to Bowman and Anderson's. And it is noteworthy that at the end of his recent debate, even Sanderson comes to reconcile his position with theirs:

> Yet I find credible the notion that pre-industrial Britain had already crossed a threshold of literacy sufficient for industrialization and that, however much it fell during early industrialization, it did not regress beyond that threshold.[21]

One other modern specialist, R.S. Schofield (1973), still rejects the 'threshold' theory. After referring to Bowman and Anderson's association of literacy with growth he observes:

> Inferences sometimes drawn from this association are that an illiteracy rate of about 60 per cent is a threshold above which economic growth is unlikely ...

Schofield then objects:

> Although it is true that the national male illiteracy rate had crossed the
> 60 per cent threshold before 1750, the female rate only crossed it definitely
> around 1795, and female illiteracy was very high in areas of high female
> industrial employment; for example, it was still 84 per cent in Oldham in
> 1846.[22]

These objections do not stand up. First, the threshold described by Bowman and
Anderson is not 60 per cent, but between 60 and 70 per cent;[23] and it is relevant
that these authors also suggested from their data that within the range from 30 to 40
per cent literacy there was 'remarkably little' increase in income with rising literacy
rates.[24] Schofield's figures show that the national rate for women was about 37
per cent in 1755, rising steadily to 40 per cent around 1795, and still rising thereafter.
Clearly, this was well within Bowman and Anderson's relevant threshold.

Second, Bowman and Anderson's figures refer in any case to *adult* literacy rate
(men and women combined). In England, according to Schofield's figures, this rate
started well above the limit at about 50 per cent (in 1755), and rose to about 60
per cent in 1840. Finally, Schofield is misleading when he supports his argument
that female industrial employment by taking 'for example' the case of Oldham with a
16 per cent female literacy rate in 1846. This was an extreme instance. The figure for
industrial Lancashire as a whole, which is the more relevant one, was about 31.1
per cent.[25]

Schofield's article has the distinction of offering the strongest defence hitherto
of the marriage signature measure of literacy. His main point is that it is the most
standard, direct, and inclusive. One can agree with this up to a point;[26] and one can
accept, as reasonably representative, the national estimates from his random sample
of 274 parishes (out of a total of 10,000) relating to the pre-1839 years, the period
before the Register General recorded aggregate literacy. What is debatable is his
interpretation of these figures.

Schofield argues that the 'long period of stability' in literacy in the eighteenth
century suggests that 'for England, at least, the usual causal relationship between
literacy and economic growth might profitably be reversed.' But taking the conventional dates of the first 'industrial revolution' to be between 1760 and 1840,
and assuming, as Schofield does, that entry into the labour force may be taken to be
15 years prior to marriage (i.e., at school leaving), then 1790 is the date when the
long term stability in male literacy changed to one of definite improvement.[27]
It follows that, despite the unprecedented population growth after 1760, England
was not only able to *maintain* the male literacy rate that had been constant for twenty
years *preceding* the industrial revolution, but well before half the 'revolution' period
was over, and at a time when the population explosion was in full force, it managed
to begin an upward trend. It is interesting again to notice that the date of upturn,
1790, coincided with the beginning of the large-scale factory system and the widespread commercial use of steam-power.

The influence of the British tradition on educational history (as exemplified by
the quotation from the Hammonds at the beginning of this chapter) might be one

factor inhibiting Schofield from drawing the central attention to the 1790 'take-off' point, and from making reference to the enormous handicap of the sudden growth of population. For such an early year suggests a growth in the *means* of literacy improvement such as private schools for all classes, while the tradition argues the impossibility of any progress (or avoidance of decline) until *public* action was taken.[28] Interestingly enough, Schofield eventually moves from his major data, on literacy, and into the evidence on schooling. Since the evidence he uses refers to the post-1830 years we must, for the moment, shift our focus from the early (eighteenth century) industrial revolution period, and from literacy to schooling.

Schofield starts by rejecting the 'rash of educational surveys' in the 1830s as being too restricted in date span to be useful for a study of trends over a long period. Yet, inconsistently, he himself eventually leans heavily on one of them; and he does this to demonstrate that schooling (over a long period) was seriously deficient. More significantly still, he here makes serious errors in interpretation and reporting. Referring to 1750–1850, he argues, '*All* schools had great difficulty in securing attendance'.[29] He supports the statement about this 'long period' from one example of the numerous surveys of the 1830s, the survey of education in Westminister in 1837–38. According to Schofield, this reported 'that school attendance in winter was down to between a quarter and a half of the number enrolled'.[30] But, to be precise, the Committee of the Westminister Statistical Society was reporting, in 1838, on a total of eight different types of school. Its comments on decreased attendance in the winter months related to only two of them; and these contained 29 per cent of the total scholars in the area.

With respect to this subset the Committee reported: '*In some instances* the decrease thus caused was stated to amount to one-fourth, to one third and even to one half'.[31] If we take a quarter to be the proportion of scholars absent in the *whole* of this sub group of schools this would amount to an absence rate of about seven per cent of the *total* school population of the area – although to be realistic we should add some *small* rate of absence in the other schools outside the sub group. Even this absence rate referred to part of the year (the winter) only. The *annual* rate of absence would have been smaller.

Next, the winter of 1837–38 was not typical. There were three causes of absence reported by the Committee. One was 'the sickness of the children', the second, 'the unwillingness of the parents to expose their children to the inclemency of the weather'. The Committee added: 'This was particularly the case during last winter, which was remarkable for its great and long-continued severity'. The third cause of school absence in the sub group was unemployment. This factor, which could have been related to the severity of the winter, obviously prevented some parents paying the fees. Schofield mentions neither the sickness nor the severe winter. He simply deduces the general statement that the fees in most schools were an important barrier; and he does this in a way that gives the impression that they prevented the *average* family from buying education in the typical school. But whatever the balance of causes, the real absence rate reported by the Westminister Committee for 1837–38 would not look unusual in the English state schools of the 1970s, especially in the winter months, and more especially when sickness epidemics (like influenza) occur.

Schofield switches from his literacy figures into *schooling* statistics in order to support his hypothesis that education was more the effect than the cause of economic growth. His argument is that if schooling was of economic value the parents would have invested in it widely and voluntarily. Because the education that really promoted productivity was related to more practical skills, the schools, which provided literary skills only, were not well patronized. This argument is difficult to accept for three reasons. First, parents *did* invest in education widely and voluntarily. Second, Schofield's argument does not explain satisfactorily how the literacy rates did manage to improve so strikingly. Third, he makes errors in his numerical estimates of schooling. The latter he gathers from the same single example from the independent surveys of the 1830s (apparently having forgotten that he warned readers that this route is 'fraught with danger'). Referring once more, and exclusively, to the survey of education in Westminster to show that the parents wanted a practical not a literary education, Schofield concludes: 'Consequently, few children were regular in attendance, and few remained at school for more than one and a half years'.[32]

The incorrectness of his estimates of *attendance* has already been explained. The next issue is school duration. Nowhere in the Committee's Report is there any statement about the typical child receiving in his lifetime a schooling of not more than one and a half years. What *is* included is an investigation of each of the eight prevailing types of school and a reference to the fact that, in three types of school, the entrances within the course of the year exceeded the number of children upon the books. This suggested, at most, a high turnover in these particular schools. But in those days of high mobility and competition between schools, the children typically accumulated several years of schooling from several schools, having relatively short stays at each.[33] Schofield's estimate of one and a half years neglects this fact and is therefore far too low.

The Newcastle Report for 1859 found that on the average for the whole country the children of the working class alone were receiving an education of 5.7 years. Horace Mann, the compiler of the special educational extension to the national census of 1851, stated that for that year working class children over the whole country were receiving a schooling that was 'certainly above four years'.[34] For these reasons, it is difficult to accept Schofield's judgment that 'the prospect of upward mobility for their children did not lead many working class parents to invest heavily in education'.[35] The four and above years of schooling on average for working class children in 1851, reported by Horace Mann, was paid for substantially by the parents.

Both Schofield and Sanderson venture the arguments that fee paying was a significant barrier to the working class and that accordingly they had to wait for public action to provide nearly free schooling. Neither of these arguments can be accepted. According to the Manchester Statistical Society, 80 per cent of the schoolchildren's education in Manchester in 1834 was paid for entirely by parental fees. The remaining 20 per cent was paid for *party* by fees.[36] The same study suggests that at least four out of five Manchester children were being schooled. Neighbouring Pendleton (Salford) schooled 97 per cent of its children in 1838 and, according to the particularly intensive survey of this township by the Manchester Statistical Society, one third of the schoolgoers remained for three to five years, one third above five years, and one third less than three years (figures that are fairly consistent with the national estimate of Horace Mann).[37]

E. J. Hobsbawm (1975) has recently given the opinion that the quantitative study of education that has made so much progress since 1963 is largely due to the study of parochial records of marriage signatures. The study of *school* statistics (attendance and availability) Hobsbawm adds, have also been scrutinized for 'optimistic' purposes, 'but their value remains in serious doubt'.[38] If their value is in such doubt then this would reduce confidence in much of the reasoning of Schofield and Sanderson who themselves ultimately rely on them. In the context of the precise facts reported in the Westminster Statistical Report, Hobsbawm presumably might describe Schofield as selectively scrutinizing the school statistics for 'pessimistic' purposes. The truth is that there are dangers in using all sources, including the parochial returns, as the earlier discussion has shown. Consider Hobsbawm's own conclusions. He argues that the marriage signature studies suggest a halt or even a reversal in the long-term progress of literacy during the early industrial period, at least in industrial Lancashire up to the late 1820s. Schofield's figures, however, show that average literacy rates (males plus females) measured at the school leaving stage were slowly rising throughout. Second, the same figures point to 1790 as a significant improvement point for men (1800 Lancashire). Third, in all cases the trend of the *early* industrial period was about the same as the two decades that preceded it. The new industrialism therefore *cannot* be argued to have had a depressing effect.

It is too hasty, however, to dismiss immediately any data, whether of literacy or of schooling, the moment a difficulty or complexity arises. Usually, after some sensible, expressed qualification, the information from most sources can be employed, tentatively at least; and confidence will be increased if a consistent pattern from the *various* sources seems to emerge.

Now a general pattern *does* emerge from the various sources on schooling. Such is the case, for instance, concerning national statistics of school population, attendance, and years' duration. It is not persuasive to argue against them that, in contrast, the literacy figures are preferable because they derive from an official government source and one, therefore, that provides the *most* standard and disinterested test of education. The 1851 figures of Horace Mann on schooling also came from a central government official source and indeed from the same office – the Registrar General's. Moreover, this was an all-inclusive universal *census*. The marriage signature test of literacy, in contrast, was not all inclusive, but related only to the 90 per cent or so of the population who were even married. And for the years before 1839 we have to rely on *samples* of parishes.

The 1851 Census figures reported 2.14 million scholars with an average of over four years schooling. Further confidence in these figures is encouraged when we look at their consistency with those of the Newcastle Commission for the year 1859 (with its larger population) which reported 2.54 million scholars. Horace Mann, who completed the 1851 figures for the Registrar General, encourages the same view with his statement that 'the estimate of 1859 (Newcastle Commission) is supported by the results of the previous and more extensive (1851 Census) inquiry'.[39] And the Newcastle Commission reported that 'almost every one receives some amount of school education', and this long before schooling was 'free' and compulsory.

When we consider the 1760–1840 period we certainly have to 'reach back' from the 1851 census and rely on a great variety of education surveys and circumstantial evidence. But if the marriage signature specialists do the same, they cannot simultaneously object that these sources are completely 'unreliable'. All sources should be carefully sifted for what threads they have to offer, despite initial difficulties. Even the marriage signature evidence is often ambiguous, at least in the first instance. This is clear, for example, when we remember the questions or assumptions one has to make about migration before one can use the parochial returns.

Obviously the evidence on literacy and schooling is inter-dependent. Those who set out to be 'pure' specialists in the one invariable succumb to the temptation to merge their findings with information they obtain about the others. Literacy specialists usually describe figures of schooling as 'indirect evidence' of literacy. Schooling specialists, meanwhile, regard literacy as 'indirect evidence' of schooling. Surely the two specialisms or approaches can converge. And this should be welcomed, for total knowledge will progress better with competition and cross checking from both sides.

The remaining part of this chapter will attempt to illustrate by showing how Schofield and Sanderson can use the data on *literacy* to check their speculations or hypotheses about *schooling*. Schofield offered the hypothesis that a substantial number of parents did not school their children when 'very few genuinely free places were available'.[40] Similarly, Sanderson argued that fees were a strong barrier to the 'lower orders'.[41] Schofield's second hypothesis stated that compulsion of the law was even more important in obtaining universal investment in education and, therefore, literacy. A third hypothesis, which is more explicit in Sanderson, but is at least hinted at in Schofield, is that the supply of education was largely an 'exogeneous' event to industrialism and to individual (family) self-help; that is, it came largely from the initiative of 'public agencies' whose task it was eventually 'to combat . . . those adverse effects of industialization . . . '[42]

Consider now the latest data on nineteenth century literacy. Schofield plotted national annual illiteracy rates (percentages unable to sign) on a semi-logarithmic scale showing percentage of illiteracy on the vertical ordinate and on two horizontal ordinates – marriage dates and schooling leaving. His diagram is reproduced here as *figure 1*.

Schofield argues that 'The fastest rate of improvement was amongst those . . . leaving school after about 1870'.[43] In *figure 1* he is referring to the graph that relates to the bottom horizontal axis that refers to school leaving. Schofield assumes that marriage signatures reflect on the average school leaving fifteen years before mar-

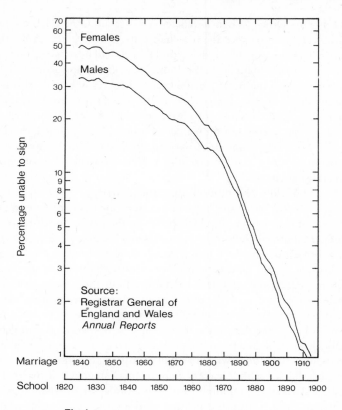

Fig. 1
Annual percentages of males and females
unable to sign at marriage,
England and Wales, 1839–1912.

riage. Whether he intended it or not, 1870 will trigger off in most minds the famous Forster Education Act of the same year, the most vigorous, ambitious, and celebrated piece of Victorian education that eventually made 'public agencies' supersede private in school provision. When we refer exclusively to the bottom (school) axis, both curves in *figure 1* do indeed show a distinct point of inflexion (or kink) in the later part of the century. But Schofield is wrong in locating it at 1870. Rather it is in 1867, three years *before* the Forster Act.

The first time Forster's legislation could have had any significant influence on schooling, must, in any case, have been some few years after 1870. The legislation did not pass through Parliament until after the middle of the year in 1870. It then took some time to establish school boards. When they were elected their time was initially taken up electing chairmen, vice-chairmen, finance committees, school sites and building committees, school staffing committees, and education committees. The boards then had to make extensive inquiries about educational deficiencies in their areas, and this often resulted in protracted correspondence with the Registrar's Office. Where a deficiency was found, the private schools were given a period of grace to give them a chance to 'fill the gaps'. After this period and, where 'deficiencies' remained, the school boards had next to draw up and debate various plans, negotiate loans from the Public Works Commission, and eventually appoint architects and builders. To illustrate, the first effective school board in Northampton was elected in January 1871. But the various procedures took two years to carry out, while the first (newly-built) board school was not opened until October 1874.[44] On the assumption that an efficient schooling lasts six years at minimum, the Act's effects on education and literacy in Northampton would not, therefore, begin to show until the school leavers of 1880 who, of course, were married several years later.

Return to Schofield's assumption that the marriage registers reflect school leaving 15 years before marriage. (I shall not press my own preference, explained above, for a lag of seventeen years). The point on the graph, for instance, for 1870, reading from the bottom (school) axis, represents the marriage signature rates in 1885. This must next be qualified. If individuals were married on the *average* 15 years after school, there would be a certain number on either side of the average. We must therefore make some qualification. Throughout these years individuals who married under 20 years of age were under a half of one per cent of the total population.[45] For practical purposes therefore I shall take the twenty year-old brides and bridegrooms as being 'the first of the few' to appear in the nineteenth century who could possibly have benefited from Forster's Act. To give the Act the fullest chance, I shall also assume that those who married youngest needed education most. But even supposing that *all* school leavers were in this category (all married ten years after school), and assuming building time 'lags' similar to Northampton's, the first school leavers to benefit from the Forster schooling (as in Northampton) would not appear until well to the right of the kink in the curve, say 1876 at the earliest. This point is indicated in *figure 2*. This figure is identical with *figure 1* except for the addition of my vertical arrows with associated explanations.

If we now extrapolate the curve onwards to the late 1890s from that part of the curve between the turning point of 1867 to 1876, the latter year, to repeat, being the first possible influence of the 1870 Act, we obtain an almost linear trend result. This pre-Forster trend *shows approximately the same 'success rate' as that in figure 1.* The data in the diagram therefore does not, at least at first sight, support the third hypothesis that major literacy improvement had to wait for *public* (government) initiative. We should remember, however, that *some* intervention was operative before 1870. This was a system of subsidies to all kinds of private schools. More precisely, the diagram suggests that this mixed private and public system (dating from 1833) was just as efficient as the new apparatus of 'nationalized' school intervention introduced by Forster.[46]

With respect to making education 'free', the extrapolation of the trend established between 1867 and 1876 suggests that it made no difference. And even if it did, its maximum effect shown in the diagram is merely an improvement in the national literacy rate of one per cent – from 98 per cent to 99 per cent. Similarly, the extrapolated trend suggests that compulsion had negligible effect. And even if it

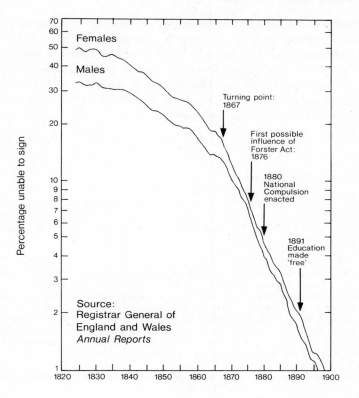

Fig.2
Annual percentages of illiterate male and female
school leavers as determined by their
inability to sign the marriage register
15 years later.

did, it could have affected literacy at most by making only 3.5 per cent of the total population literate.

I conclude first, that the recent attempts to reject Bowman and Anderson's 'threshold theory' of literacy, as it applies to England and Wales, have not been successful; second, that available national estimates do *not* demonstrate that the Industrial Revolution depressed literacy – even if we consider the rate for males or females exclusively; third, that the date of distinct improvement in the national literacy trend coincided with the beginnings of the large-scale factory system; and fourth, that the apparent local exception of Lancashire is closer to the national trend than has been believed, and that in any case when we take Irish immigration into account, the association between education and economic growth is considerably strengthened. Finally, I have shown that, despite the attempts by historians of *literacy*, and historians of *schooling*, to keep their studies separate, this is not easily achieved in practice. The convergence of the two disciplines nevertheless is necessary, although it is still important for the one specialist to cross check carefully the use of his sources by the other. Evidence on literacy has its difficulties and problems, just as does evidence on schooling. But, if properly handled, both can still yield the *truest*, rather than the most 'pessimistic' or 'optimistic', view of the eighteenth or nineteenth educational progress.

Notes and References

1   BOWMAN, M.J. and ANDERSON, C.A. (1963) 'Concerning the role of education in development' in GEERTZ, C. (Ed.) *Old Societies and New States*, New York, Free Press of Glencoe, pp. 247–79.
2   HAMMOND, J.L. and B. (1937) *The Rise of Modern Industry*, 5th Edition, London, Longmans, p. 229.
3   *Ibid.*, p. 231.
4   *Ibid.*
5   ALTICK, R.D. (1957) *The English Common Reader*, Chicago, University of Chicago Press, p. 207.
6   WEBB, R.K. (1955) *The British Working Class Reader, 1790–1848*, London, Allen and Unwin; NEUBERG, B.E. (1971) *Popular Education in Eighteenth Century England*, London, The Woburn Press; who argues (p. 139) that there was a 'mass reading public' by 1800; ROBSON, D. (1966) *Some Aspects of Education in Cheshire in the Eighteenth Century*, Manchester, The Chetham Society; LAQUER, T.W. *The English Sunday School and Formation of a Respectable Working Class 1780–1850* (unpublished thesis, Princeton University); STONE, L. (1969) 'Literacy and education in England 1640–1900', *Past and Present* No. 42, February; WEST, E.G. (1965) *Education and the State*, London, Institute of Economic Affairs; also *Education and the Industrial Revolution*, London, Batsford, 1975; HARTWELL, M. (1971) *The Industrial Revolution*, London, Methuen.
7   This was a central point in my reply to J.S. Hunt's article 'Professor West on early nineteenth century education', *Economic History Review*, XXIV, 1971.
8   See, for example, Michael Sanderson's review of my 1975 book in *Economic History Review*, Summer, 1976.
9   On the same reasoning the opinion of Sanderson (1976) that 'the recent debates on literacy' render some of the conclusions of my book 'seriously outdated', will be rebutted.
10 SANDERSON, M. (1974) 'Literacy and social mobility in the industrial revolution in England', *Past and Present*, No. 56, August, pp. 75–104.
11 LAQUER, T.W. (1979) 'Literacy and social mobility in the industrial revolution in England', *Past and Present*, 64, August, pp. 96–107.
12 *Ibid.*, p. 100.
13 SANDERSON, M. (1974) *op. cit.*, p. 87.
14 DEANE, P. and COLE, W.A. (1962) *British Economic Growth 1688–1959*, Cambridge, Cambridge University Press, p. 109.
15 *Ibid.*
16 WEST, E.G. (1965) *op. cit.*, pp. 113–4.
17 REDFORD, A. (1968) *Labour Migration in England*, New York, Kelly, p. 154.
18 MITCHELL, B.R. (1962) *Abstract of British Historical Statistics*, Cambridge, Cambridge University Press, p. 24.
19 See the view of SCHOFIELD, R.S. (1973) 'Dimensions of illiteracy, 1750–1850', *Explorations in Economic History*, Vol. 10.
20 REDFORD, A. (1968) *op. cit.*, p. 154.
21 SANDERSON, M. (1974) *op. cit.*, p. 111.
22 SCHOFIELD, R.S. (1973) *op. cit.*, pp. 437–51.
23 BOWMAN, M.J. and ANDERSON, C.A. (1963) *op. cit.*, p. 252.
24 More precisely, this was the case in 27 out of 32 countries studied.
25 LAQUER, T.W. (1979) *op. cit.*, p. 99.
26 I gave almost as strong support for the marriage signature test of literacy, but from different arguments, in my *Education and the State* (1965), p. 134.

27 Schofield agrees with this timing, p. 446.

28 The government did not intervene until 1833, and even then only with very modest subsidies to private schools WEST, E.G. (1965) *op. cit.*, p. 75.

29 SCHOFIELD, R.S. (1973) *op. cit.*, p. 439 (my emphasis).

30 *Ibid.*, p. 439.

31 Second Report of a Committee of the Statistical Society of London, appointed to enquire into the State of Education in Westminster, *Journal of the Statistical Society of London* (1838), pp. 193–215 (my emphasis).

32 SCHOFIELD, R.S. (1973) *op. cit.*, p. 452.

33 WEST, E.G. (1965) *op. cit.*, p. 83.

34 Minutes of evidence to the Newcastle Commission taken on 6 December, 1859.

35 SCHOFIELD, R.S. (1973) *op. cit.*, p. 415.

36 WEST, E.G. (1965) *op. cit.*, p. 86.

37 *Ibid.*, p. 18.

38 HOBSBAWM, E.J. (1975) 'The standard of living debate', in TAYLOR, A.J. *The Standard of Living in the Industrial Revolution*, London, Methuen, p. 83.

39 MANN, H. (1869) 'National education', *Transactions of the British Association for the Promotion of Social Science*, British meeting.

40 SCHOFIELD, R.S. (1973) *op. cit.*, p. 439.

41 SANDERSON, M. (1974) *op. cit.*, p. 80.

42 *Ibid.*, p. 111.

43 SCHOFIELD, R.S. (1973) *op. cit.*, p. 443.

44 *Northampton Mercury*, 25 November, 1876. I am grateful to Victor A Hartley of Northampton for supplying me with this source. I am aware that some boards opened schools earlier but these were usually existing private schools that were soon taken over by them. I am only concerned here with net improvements in school supply which would show up in entirely new buildings.

45 MITCHELL, B.R. (1962) *op. cit.*, table 5, p. 151. The average marriage age was nearly 28 years in 1881 according to the Registrar's General Report (Vol. IV) for that year.

46 This finding supports a central argument in my *Education and the Industrial Revolution* (1975); an argument that Sanderson (1976) in his review seems strangely to have overlooked; for he presents me as arguing simply that 'state intervention was of doubtful necessity'.

The Labour Force: Some Relevant Attitudes

P.W. Musgrave

The way in which any social structure reacts to change can be usefully analysed in terms of the attitudes, held by those within it, to the various innovatory experiences of their times. In the Victorian era great economic changes were occurring that were seen to put an increasing emphasis upon the scientific and rational elements in industrial and commercial processes and, as a consequence, upon the education which could provide the knowledge now needed by those within the labour force so that they might operate efficiently. If we wish to examine some of the reasons why an economy performed as it did, we may well start by studying the relevant attitudes at each level of the labour force.

Here, the attitudes held towards industry, change, science and education during the second half of the nineteenth century will be outlined. Four levels of the labour force will be considered: managers and technicians, foremen, skilled workers and unskilled workers. This chapter will not therefore, analyse the position of entrepreneurs, to whose failure the stagnation of the British economy during the period has sometimes been attributed; that argument has been dealt with elsewhere in this book. Not only did the four attitudes chosen for study affect economic performance, but they also influenced the development of the educational system. Hence, the inter-relationships between these four attitudes and education will be given consideration.

At the time there was much comparison with the apparently successful German economy, so that in the attempt to weigh the effects upon economic performance of these attitudes held within the labour force brief reference will be made to the German experience. Finally, some conclusions will be drawn.

The labour force

Managers

One excellent measure of the low standing of industry amongst the upper and upper middle class is the infrequency of its mention by such successful contemporary novelists as Trollope. Commerce was somewhat more acceptable, though to be avoided if possible. The destination of those leaving the public schools that served these classes provides further evidence. Less than one fifth of those leaving Uppingham entered business between 1854 and 1887, whilst at Marlborough, a school of higher status, the proportion over much the same period was about a tenth.[1] Indeed, the qualities of personality encouraged in the post-Arnoldian public schools were probably not appropriate to success in industry. Thus, in 1909, in his address on the fiftieth anniversary of Wellington College, the Dean of Lincoln saw it as a school where boys 'learn to put honour before gain, duty before pleasure, the public good before private advance'.[2] Hence, whatever the qualities of those who bore the white man's burden it was not surprising that British engineers were said in 1899 not only to lack 'professional efficiency, but culture, diplomatic skills and linguistic attainment'.[3]

Amongst the middle classes the position was very different. 'The existence of a considerable literature of success',[4] and especially the best-sellers of Samuel Smiles, is evidence of the importance of industry as an acceptable arena within which to work out one's life. In 1864, *The Economist* described the lower-middle class as 'probably . . . the worst educated of any class that is educated at all in this country'.[5] This was said on the appointment of the Taunton Commission which during 1864–68 examined what *The Economist* called 'the middle class schools'. Yet thirty years later it was still necessary to appoint a Royal Commission (Bryce, 1894–95) to examine the state of secondary education. Certainly at the beginning of the period, many in the middle class questioned the relevance of education for industry, a field in which illiterates could succeed. For example, in the late 1850s it was reported of Dudley, an iron-making area:

> Many prosperous employers are found conducting very large operations who have themselves risen from the lowest occupations in the pit or at the furnace, or the forge, and have never acquired the rudiments of writing or reading, or any language but collier's English.[6]

One result was that many managers, technicians and clerks were recruited from the continent where the educated young learnt more appropriate attitudes to industry. Even after the Education Act of 1870, which enabled the establishment of mass elementary education and, therefore, made available a more literate populace, advertisements such as the following were common throughout the 1880s and 1890s:

> Wanted by a Young German Gentleman . . . a situation in the office of a Metal Merchant or Broker. Correspondence in French and German. Salary no object.[7]

Evidence for the employment of such foreign labour covers many industries including the chemical, engineering, iron and steel, silk and woollen industries as well as commerce.[8]

Contemporary attitudes to change were complex. In *Locksley Hall*, written during the year Victoria came to the throne, Tennyson had these lines, 'Let the great world spin for ever down the ringing grooves of change.' A little later J.S. Mill spoke of 'the consciousness of living in a world of change.' Yet paradoxically many examples can be cited in mid-Victorian Britain of the slow acceptance at the managerial level of economic change. The Admiralty and Lloyds underwriters held back the use of Bessemer steel in shipbuilding. Similarly, resistance by railway officials delayed the adoption of steel tyres on railway wheels. At the end of the era in 1896 a cartoon drawn by Tenniel was published in *Punch* showing an old lady asleep by a road having her skirt, labelled 'British Trade', cut away by a German pedler with scissors, labelled 'Competition'. Though the direct point related to commercial inefficiency, clearly it was a slowness to adapt to change that was at the root of the criticism.

For many the main relevant change seemed to be the growing importance of science in industrial processes. In his Presidential Address to the British Association at Aberdeen in 1885 Lyon Playfair, a constant publicist for science, attempted

> to point out how it is that science lags in its progress in the United Kingdom owing to the deficient interest taken in it by the middle and upper classes

An important cause in his view was sheer ignorance due to the curriculum of the public schools. In 1890, Lankaster, the founding editor of *Nature*, described the British view of science as 'dreamy, vague, untrustworthy and useless to practical men'.[9] This theoretical subject was associated with the universities, especially the two ancient English ones, where those with high social status were educated, whilst the simple and practical branches of science were mainly taught in the lower status institutions connected with technical education.

During the latter part of the century, as a result of legislation following the Report of the Taunton Commission (1868), there was some expansion of facilities for secondary education but the new schools, whether for boys or girls, largely imitated the higher status public schools then gaining popularity in large part because of the demand of the upwardly socially mobile to establish their children in their new class. Thus, science, particularly in its practical aspects, continued to be given a low priority. The result was a feeling that the pure scientist was a gentleman, whilst the applied scientist had lost his amateur status and become a tradesman. A good example of an engineer of this type was Menelaus, manager of the Dowlais works in the 1880s who

> made the best guess he could as to the strength there should be, multiplied by four and the thing never broke. But he was pained by the weight of his creations.[10]

By the 1890s there were signs of change. Chemists were employed in the iron and steel industry, but their laboratories were 'mere sheds, placed, say, behind the boiler house'. The chemist was poorly paid and regarded as 'a mere analytical machine'.[11] What J.S. Mill once called 'the dogmatism of common sense' was a powerful feeling. Research was not necessary in industry and in any case its results could be purchased. The Patent Laws provided an institutional framework within which scientific ideas that were worthwhile could be bought and scientists themselves could be protected and rewarded.

The scientific rationality that was now admitted to be applicable to industry was only slowly seen to be applicable to management itself. In the 1860s the name of Alfred Krupp of Essen recurred in discussions of German industry. He employed 8,000 in his works in the mid-1860s. He did not use rule of thumb methods, but showed a great belief in science and its use in industry. Furthermore, he applied the same methods to management. He had brought the making of large steel castings 'to such a pitch that he (had) a thousand pots or more of steel all ready melted at the right moment, to be poured into a common reservoir and then cast ... '.[12]

The use of sub-contracting, still common in large works in Britain at the end of the century, did not encourage the growth of scientific management. However, once again there were signs of change, probably due to the ending of the Great Depression and to the growth of size in manufacturing concerns. Such factors seem to have encouraged some graduates to enter industry, particularly after 1900, and some of these came from the newly established schools of 'professional' economics at the London School of Economics and the Universities of Birmingham and Cambridge.[13] Yet the numbers of trained managers flowing into the iron and steel industry by 1900 was apparently still inadequate.[14]

Like so much else in Britain in 1850 education was on the whole seen as a service to be provided by laissez-faire. After the 1870 Act a minimal education might be provided for the working class by the state when no one else stepped in to do so, but the middle and upper classes were expected, and themselves expected, to provide the education of their children. By 1900 clerks and salesmen, however, were largely recruited from the lower classes who had undergone state education. Such employees in the main learnt on the job. There was some distrust of technical education.[15] In 1868 *The Economist* wrote that 'every workshop or factory in the kingdom' was a technical school in which trades could be 'learned with far more efficiency than under the most learned professors'.[16] Similar feelings gainst education were still common at the turn of the century. In 1904, a leading Sheffield steelmaker felt that 'degrees stood in the way of (young men) obtaining positions in the industry'.[17] Thus, when the government included educational measures as a part of their policy to alleviate the effect of the slump there were some, at least in the steel industry, 'who smiled superciliously when one proposed to associate depression in trade with anything in the nature of incompetence on the part of themselves'.[18]

Foremen

British foremen gained their industrial knowledge by working on the job. They were working class successes in the tradition of Samuel Smiles. Industry for them was the avenue to the equivalent of a middle class career. Many of them had served apprenticeships as craftsmen, a training held by many to lead to conservative attitudes. According to Siemens, speaking in 1881, this system produced 'a man of notions with a supreme contempt of theory or science'.[19] In 1889, the ironmaster, Sir John Kitson, asked one of his foremen whether his men would work any better with a little scientific knowledge. 'No', said the foreman, 'in my opinion they would do it a great deal worse ... '.[20] Long service was the usual pre-requisite for promotion to the position of foreman. Employers did not want innovators at this level or highly educated persons who might question their decisions and the process whereby foremen reached their position did not encourage positive attitudes towards innovation, science or education. Many, indeed, as already indicated, were illiterate and were unable to take advantage of such new opportunities as the foundation in 1880 of the City and Guilds of London Institute which took over the industrial examination of the Royal Society of Arts, started the year before. Furthermore, because promotion to this position took time, it is unlikely that even by 1900 much effect was felt at this level of the increase in literacy begun by the 1870 Education Act. Contemporary industrialists might have seen their foremen as stabilising influences, deeply committed to their firms but, from the standpoint of the economy as a whole, they were probably overly conservative and incapable of appreciating the changing needs of the times.

Skilled Workers

Like the foremen, the craftsman was amongst the successful who had made their way by dint of what employers saw as attitudes appropriate to industry; he has been described as 'Rochdale Man, the respectable, self-helping, self-educating working man with his cooperative society, savings bank and chapel'.[21] In the Final Report of the Royal Commission on Labour (1894) phrases can be found that give some impression of how 'skilled workers' were viewed by those with power and how their own representatives, the officials of their unions, saw their members. The Majority Report speaks of the improvement of conditions of life 'among the more settled and stable population of skilled work people; . . . this part of the population possesses in a highly remarkable degree the power of organization, self-government, and self-help.' Furthermore, the existence of 'powerful trade unions, on the one side, and powerful associations of employers on the other led to "mutual education" so that industrial peace is promoted by the knowledge acquired by workmen and capitalists meeting in conference together.'

Yet the Minority Report denied this picture of a committed labour force, speaking of 'unsatisfactory relations between employers and employed as but one inevitable incident of the present industrial anarchy' and pleaded for 'the substitution, as fast as possible, of public ownership of a capitalist enterprise'.[22] Undoubtedly, 'the demoralising conditions', to which the Minority Report referred, more commonly affected unskilled than skilled workers. Yet unemployment ran at a high level even amongst the skilled. Thus, for all the unions reporting during the period from 1879 to 1895 the percentage of unemployed varied from 11.4 (1879) to 5.8 (1895), and for those in engineering, metals and shipbuilding from 15.3 (1879) to 7.7 (1892);[23] most of the workers covered in both sets of figures were skilled.

Under such conditions attitudes to change were almost irrelevant and had little connection with education. Where skilled men had strong unions, as in Sheffield, they used their power to oppose the changes that German and American competition seemed to demand.[24] Where unions were weak or did not exist workers did what their employers told them if they wanted jobs at all. For skilled men this situation was complicated by the presence of apprentices, needed to ensure the future supply of skilled men but seen by many employers as a reserve supply of cheap labour in depressed times when apprentices could not be put off in the same way as skilled men out of their indentures. Yet there is evidence to show that some were coming to see formal education in general, and technical education in particular, to be of importance at this level of the labour force, especially where the apprenticeship system had broken down in new industries or in new industrial areas. A Leeds woollen manufacturer told the Royal Commission on Depression of Trade and Industry (1886) that he thought the better educated people now growing up made better weavers, and a trade union official from the cotton industry said that technical education 'improve(d) the general intelligence and capacity of the operatives for understanding and getting through their work'.[25] There were, however, those who saw technical education as a subtle way of putting more profits into the pockets of capitalists. Magnus (1910), an active publicist for technical education and the founding Secretary and Director of the City and Guilds Institute of London, said of the 1890s that 'trade unions . . . , at that time, were by no means active supporters of technical education, its necessity and adventages'.[26]

Yet the views of the trade unions on education were by no means monolithic. Studies in Birmingham and Manchester show that the representatives of the working class decided their views according to their religious denomination or political affiliation.[27] Craft unions tended to oppose technical education because the teaching of trades was seen by them to be done outside the control of the unions. A little earlier, in the 1870s, however, technical education by evening class was seen by these unions as part of self-help and they had worked themselves to organise the transmission of craft skills though with little success. The growth of such socialist groups as Hyndman's Socialist Democratic Federation and of the new unions of unskilled workers began to change some of these attitudes although we must not think that even by the Edwardian era any large sections of the working class were characterised by political feelings against their 'betters' in the higher social classes.[28] But in relation to education, the change was reflected in the resolutions of 1894 and 1897, at the Trade Union Congress, demanding secondary education for all and in the interest shown by the working class in the struggle over the 1902 Education Act during which meetings of eighty to a hundred thousand at Leeds and of fifteen thousand in Manchester were reported. A general working class view of education, at the time related more to structure than to content, was beginning to develop.

Unskilled Workers

It was the view of the Royal Commission on the Depression of Trade and Industry (1886) that apart from 'a deplorably large residuum of the population . . . who lead wretchedly poor lives'; 'unskilled labour . . . (had) probably benefited no less than the skilled worker from the increased efficiency of production conferred by the various legal and economic advances of industrialisation'.[29] Whatever one's feelings about the debate over the contemporary standard of life of the working class, this conclusion probably truly represents the view of the time. A large proportion of the contemporary population had no alternative but to become 'unskilled labourers', especially at a time when competitive conditions were driving them off the land.

Opposition to change amongst workmen was generally felt to have diminished, though in discussing this two representatives of the Birmingham Chamber of Commerce told the Royal Commission on Depression, 'There is a very strong feeling against making changes, and it is very intelligible in some respects'; workers knew what was done before and objected to disruption of their feeling of security.[30] The Report noted that:

> the displacement of labour . . . owing to the increased use of machinery and other changes in the methods of production cannot fail to create a certain amount of distress of a more or less temporary character among the working classes, who are nationally less able to adapt themselves to sudden changes than those whose capital is of a more moveable form . . . [31]

Workers did not need to be literate to understand the major implications of such unemployment and, indeed, illiteracy was common, though diminishing throughout the period. The 1851 Census showed that 45 per cent of boys and 43 per cent of girls aged three to fifteen were 'scholars'. At the time of the debates on the 1870 Elementary Education Act, W.E. Forster, the minister responsible, supplied the House with figures relating to recruitment to thirteen English and eighteen Scottish militia regiments that give a fair idea of the contemporary levels of literacy:[32]

	Read				**Write**			
			Imper-				Imper-	
	Total	Well	fectly	Not at all	Total	Well	fectly	Not at all
English	7506	2360	2503	2360 (30%)	8563	1657	3302	3604 (47%)
Scottish	4970	1839	2170	961 (19%)	4970	1128	2395	1447 (29%)

This situation is not surprising, since prior to 1870 education was not compulsory, and in the eyes of a working man for his children to go to school brought no advantage and had the major disadvantage that he was deprived of their earnings during years when, certainly in some trades, children earned comparatively high wages. Furthermore, until the end of the period, the trade unions representing such men, only recently established, had no educational policy since their energies were largely absorbed in gaining adequate legal security and ensuring their own viability as organisations.

There is some evidence to show that, prior to the 1870 Education Act, some of the ruling class saw education as a form of idleness that prevented children from learning the virtues of work.[33] However, and particularly after this Act, the education of the unskilled came to be seen as an agent of social policy. If their schooling was not to be supplied through the workings of laissez-faire, as the passing of the 1870 Act recognised, then it could be justified on political, economic and broad moral principles. All these strands can be seen in the description given in 1866 by Ruskin to a group of Bradford businessmen of the characteristics of their ideal worker; they wanted 'workers who never drink, never strike, always go to church on Sundays, and always express themselves in respectful language'.[34]

More specifically, Robert Lowe pointed out the political need in discussing the 1867 Reform Act. Now that working men had the vote we must 'compel our future masters to learn their letters'. Forster used arguments connecting education with greater economic efficiency in the debates on the 1870 Elementary Education Act. Throughout the period moral functions were often attributed to education. In his commentary on the educational statistics gathered for the 1851 Census Horace Mann noted that 'the habits of the people have been so conspicuously improved'; his standard of comparison were 'the groups of gambling, swearing children' who attended the first Sunday Schools in the 1780s.[35]

These better 'habits' were felt to have various economic effects. In 1866 *The Economist* claimed that in relation to strikes

> there had been an absence of the extreme violence and lawlessness not uncommon in these strikes ten or fifteen years ago. Education, reading rooms, and the cheap Press (had) done something to establish a community of modes of proceeding, if not a community of views or aims between the workmen and masters.[36]

Commitment to the industrial labour force, particularly of those who moved out of agriculture, was seen as a possible outcome of the education of the working class. In a minority report of the Royal Commission on Depression this striking passage occurs:

> There is one department in the work of elementary schools which, though of vital importance to the success of our industries, has not yet, we think, received sufficient attention. We allude to the disciplinary training of children. But the children who now come to them from elementary schools are not, to say the least, more receptive of that industrial training which is required to make them skilful and active workers, than those who came in former years endowed with a smaller amount of schooling. We think that the careful and thorough training in habits of punctuality and order, of alacrity and diligence, and of close attention and prompt and implicit obedience to instructions, ought to occupy more of the time and thought of teachers in elementary schools . . .[37]

However, as already noted, labour discipline was enforced at that time in other than normative ways. When the rate of unemployment was high workmen, at the very least, had to be obedient to retain their jobs. Employers could also use the law. Menelaus, when discussing the Masters and Servants Act (1867), went as far as saying in his usual direct way, 'I do not think that without the gaol in the background we could properly conduct the works'. He claimed to use the law only against individuals who broke their contract – 'just to show them again that there is a law to protect us' – or who misbehaved grossly by, for example, walking off in the middle of a melt or coming to work drunk.[38]

This last case relates to what was seen as one of the major problems of contemporary labour discipline. Le Play said that the basic recreation of English workers was 'the use and abuse of spirits'.[39] Education was felt to be one possible way of ensuring a more temperate labour force, and this in its turn was related to economic benefits in that much bad work would be stopped, timekeeping would be improved and many accidents, most common on Mondays and Tuesdays, would be eliminated.[40] 'St. Monday' was worshipped, particularly amongst skilled men up to the 1870s. There is evidence that after this date, for instance, Sheffield mechanics who were 'not so temperate as (they) should be' in times of good trade 'improved (their) social and moral condition very much' in times of 'lesser wages'.[41] The peak of consumption of beer and spirits was in the 1870s. Up till then, the real level of wages of skilled men had risen enabling them to maintain a high rate of consumption; after then, the real wages of the unskilled were to permit their consumption to rise.[42]

This problem was very definitely seen as one of educational significance and, by the turn of the century, temperance syllabuses were in circulation in the schools. What is very clear is that what is now called 'the hidden curriculum' was then quite openly seen as part of the manifest goal of the schooling of the working class, and that the social implications of elementary education were clearly appreciated by the owners and managers of industrial and commercial enterprises.

The educational system

These attitudes both had their effects upon, and were sustained by, the contemporary educational system. Frequently, comparisons were made with Germany. In the next section, the comparable situation in that country will be examined briefly, but here, before outlining the relevant qualitative characteristics of the British system, two quantitative comparisons will be presented to establish the magnitude of the educational differences between the two countries. In 1899, the numbers of boys in public elementary schools per 1,000 population in Birmingham and Berlin was 52 and 57 respectively, and in public secondary schools 3.4 and 10.0. Even allowing for the omission of British boarding schools and post-elementary schools of the secondary type the contrast at that level is striking. Furthermore, in 1903, there were 5.0 students per 10,000 of this population in British universities and university colleges as against 7.87 per 1,000 in Germany.[43]

Though by the turn of the century children had to attend elementary school up to the age of fourteen, questions must be asked about the quality of the education received. The Code upon which grants were given was a somewhat liberalised version, but a direct spiritual descendant, of the Revised Code of 1862 which was in turn a consequence of the recommendations of the Report of the Newcastle Commission on the State of Popular Education (1859). This Commission had defined elementary education in terms of the ability to read 'a common narrative', write 'a letter that shall be both legible and intelligible' and knowing 'enough of ciphering to make out, or test, the correctness of a common shop bill', together with a little geography, and the ability 'to follow the allusions and arguments of a plain Saxon sermon'[44] – in other words, a minimal and Christian version of the 3Rs. Certainly such competences were needed by future members of the labour force, but two criticisms are possible and were made. First, the elementary schools were seen as 'clerkly' and many of the attitudes that were encouraged were unfavourable to work in industry, as they were associated with the lower middle class, into which many of the teachers involved had successfully climbed,[45] and for which many parents had ambitions for their children. Second, science, when it finally entered the curriculum, was taught in an academic manner that had little direct relevance to the working class.[46]

The nature of the schools then seen as secondary was said in 1899 to be 'almost as doubtful a matter as the topography of Central Africa'.[47] Facilities that to-day would be called secondary were supplied by the famous public and other private schools and, in addition, – under the diverse auspices of the Education Department – the Department of Science and Art, the Board of Agriculture and the Charity Commissioners. There was no real coordination between these bodies. The Bryce Commission was appointed in 1894 to examine the situation and reported in 1895. Largely in consequence, the 1899 and 1902 Education Acts allowed state-financed and coordinated growth in this field where previously, by and large, laissez-faire had ruled. Prior to 1899, expansion, defined in 1899 as illegal, had occurred within the elementary system in what would now be called secondary education. This version of secondary schooling was seen by some as excessively vocational, as indeed sometimes was the case. It was, then, not difficult for Morant, the senior civil servant at the new Board of Education, to direct the development of the new grammar schools, provided by the local authorities, along the lines traced out in the second half of the nineteenth century by the public schools. These new secondary schools, therefore, became Arnoldian in spirit and in curriculum and not connected in any vital way with the world of industry and commerce as might have been the case. The Bryce Commission, probably under the influence of Sadler, took a very different view of the possible way in which secondary education might develop, believing that 'no definition of technical instruction is possible that does not bring it under the head of Secondary Education, nor can Secondary Education be so defined as absolutely to exclude from it the idea of technical instruction'.[48]

The technical instruction movement had been strong in Britain in the 1870s and 1880s, though it is noteworthy that despite the work during 1870–75 by the Royal Commission on Scientific Instruction and the Advancement of Science (Devonshire) there were no related debates in either House on technical education. The movement eventually succeeded, in 1889, in forcing legislation; the Technical Instruction Act. Yet, ironically, it was the availability, after Goschen's Budget of 1890, of 'the whiskey money' that probably had the greatest influence on growth. Funds originally intended to compensate licensees of redundant public houses, an arrangement presumably necessary because elementary education still had not fully 'gentled' the working classes, could not be used for the intended purpose due to the opposition of both the liquor trade and the temperance movement and so became available for technical education. Courses were financed, often within secondary schools, under the auspices of the Department of Science and Art, though their nature was sometimes severely criticized. Huxley, for example, was afraid that the students would 'merely learn the ordinary technique of their business, varnished over with scientific phraseology'.[49] At a somewhat lower level, there were the examinations of the City and Guilds of London Institute. These had a basis of literacy, provided by the 1870 Act, that was firmer than had been available to the Mechanics Institute earlier in the century. Whereas these institutes had by 1860 become largely recreational in function and served the lower middle class, the numbers sitting the two systems of examinations, mainly taken through evening study, rose yearly throughout the depressed last quarter of the century.[50]

As to the universities, J.S. Mill in his Rectoral Address at St. Andrews in 1867 described their spirit well,

> There is a tolerable general agreement about what a university is not. It is not a place of professional education. Universities are not intended to teach the knowledge required to fit men for some special mode of gaining a livelihood. Their object is not to make skilful lawyers and physicians and engineers, but capable and cultivated human beings.

This broad approach to university education closely fitted the English amateur tradition, and governed the development of the curricula of the new universities founded in the second half of the nineteenth century, even though they were situated in industrial cities and were often associated with local industries. Their addiction to pure rather than to applied science was much criticized. As the Board of Education noted in 1909, 'There still exists amongst the generality of employers a strong preference for the men trained from an early age in the works, and a prejudice against the so-called "college-trained man"'.[51]

Yet this feeling was becoming less strong as three pressures were working to weaken the anti-vocational view of university education. First, pure subjects like mathematics, and even classics, were coming to be seen as vocational if only because they could be justified according to the tenets of the then fashionable doctrines of faculty psychology in that they trained some aspects of the mind that could be valuable in management. Second, science itself was seen to be of increasing relevance in industry, particularly as enough was now known to form the basis for such worthwhile and internationally popular text-books as Percy's *Metallurgy of Iron and Steel* (1864). Third, scientific thought was now seen as applicable in the field of commerce; the day of the useful social sciences could now be foreseen.

The situation in Germany

Although comparisons with the USA were, by 1900, becoming common it was to the economic progress of Germany, after 1870 a political entity, that self-conscious British industrialists usually pointed with fear. In 1902, in his Presidential Address, Sir James Dewar reported to the British Association an investigation that showed there to be three times as many chemists working in German as in British industry and amongst these industrial chemists, four times as many as in Britain were graduates.[52] Yet not everyone saw the German labour force as educationally superior to the British. Siemans considered the German higher technical institutes, the *technische Hochschulen*, to be too practical, putting too little emphasis on underlying principles; he considered the engineering faculties of Cambridge, Manchester and London to be better in this respect.[53] At a lower level, a Greenock shipbuilder told the Royal Commission on Depression in the mid-1880s;

> I give preference to the home workman certainly; I think he produces rather more than the German, especially when working on piecework; he is a more skilful workman to a certain extent and he is a more hardy workman; and I do not think that he is easily discouraged.[54]

All was not necessarily better in Germany, but since von Humboldt's reorganisation of the Prussian educational system in 1809–10 after the defeat by Napoleon at Jena, there had been a centrally-administered, well-articulated system in Prussia that had been much imitated throughout the German states and which, after 1870, became the predominant influence upon German educational administration. Private schools were almost non-existent. All children went through the *Volksschulen*, and those intending to stay beyond the minimum legal leaving age proceeded after the age of ten through what grew to be a complex system of secondary schools with different leaving ages and differing emphases on the classics, science or modern languages – the amount of science taught in the classical *Gymnasium* was greater than in the average British grammar school, and the standard of the *Abitur*, the examination allowing entry to university, was so high that in the 1860s one English professor considered a successful candidate could have passed a Cambridge honours examination.[55]

Work had high status in Germany; the word, *Beruf* – a vocation – had been applied to most occupations, whether surgeons or chimney sweeps, for centuries and was extended to the new occupations in the even more finely divided labour force after industrialisation began in the middle of the century. There was a long tradition of apprenticeship and also of daytime continuation schools after leaving *Volksschule*. From early in the nineteenth century the *Gymnasien* and other secondary schools were seen as providers of educated manpower for the civil service and the professions. Hence, later in the century, when the Prussian junkers showed no aversion to entrepreneurial activity in industry, these schools easily extended their function to becoming sources for industrial and commercial managers. Finally, military service was universal and considered to have educational implications; one important result was that ready obedience replaced the need for a favourable attitude to change in the labour force.

The high status of education and its links with industry also had effects at the university level. From the 1840s the universities were international centres of scientific research. They would not permit practical subjects to enter their curricula, but had no objection to work of a similar level being done in other institutions to which the status of universities was granted. Thus in Germany, from the later part of the nineteenth century, there developed a parallel institution, the *technische Hochschule*, a source at university level of applied scientific education.[56]

In Germany the educational system, well developed at every level except, perhaps, in the provision of part-time evening facilities for operatives who wanted to help themselves, encouraged a good general schooling with a scientific component which was without shame seen as applicable in industry and commerce. A well-educated and disciplined labour force seemed to be the result. How much of the German economic success was due to her educational system?

Causes and effects

We now know that, whereas in 1860–80 the annual percentage rates of industrial growth in the UK was 2.4 and in Germany 2.7, in 1880–1900 the rates were 1.7 and 5.3 respectively.[57] Contemporaries noted that Britain won very many fewer prizes at the Paris Exhibition of 1867 than at the Great Exhibition of 1851 and that, in 1886, the USA and, in 1893, Germany overtook the British annual output of iron and steel.

The rhetoric of the time constantly compared British education unfavourably with that of its main competitors, particularly Germany. But there were important economic effects which the educational system could not have offset even had greater reform occurred during the late-nineteenth century. The older basic industries had to withstand export difficulties exacerbated by tariff barriers and using plant that inevitably was older than that of their overseas competitors. In one particular industry, iron and steel, the case has been made that, given the size of the market and the existing tariffs, once costs became roughly the same in Britain, Germany and the USA, the rate of growth in Britain had to be lower than previously and that this equalisation of conditions, with the consequent effect in Britain, occurred in the final two decades of the century.[58]

Furthermore, a form of industry, coming to be known – even before the 1860s and the growth of scale – as 'the American system of manufacturing', was developed in the United States, based on quantity runs of standardised products with interchangeable parts. Usually, this development was attributed to the high cost of labour and the lack of craft skills in the USA, but more important, and less often noted, were such characteristics of the American social structure as the high level of ambition associated with an open stratification system and the great degree of adaptability that labour seemed to display.[59] This system was really appreciated in Germany by managers oriented towards applied science whose labour force was extremely deferential. In both countries major *educational* reforms could have had little quick effect.

Looking back with hindsight, we now know that there were industries in which, whatever the detrimental effect of the educational system, British productivity was greater than that of their German or US competitors. Examples were the manufacture of shoes and bicycles.[60] However, above all we must remember that in the latter part of the century a massive restructuring of the British economy was occurring. If one compares 1851 with 1901, 13 per cent less of the work force was employed in the primary sector of agriculture, forestry and fisheries; but of the labour that shifted, only 3.4 per cent moved into the secondary or manufacturing sector, the remainder moving into the tertiary sector, though only 1.1 per cent was taken up within domestic service.[61] In 1948, Heaton commented that although the 'laments of iron masters, bankers and investors were grievous, the soap workers were never happier' and, more recently, Wilson (1965) has pointed out that 'the Armstrongs, Whitworths and Brasseys were giving way to (or being joined by) the Levers, the Boots, the Harrods, Whiteleys and Lewises'.[62] The retailing revolution that depended greatly upon 'the American system of manufacturing' was upon Britain. Its educational demands were neither those of the early prophets who had gathered round Prince Albert in 1851, nor those of the visionaries of the later technical education movement. Economic developments were probably once again ahead of educational rhetoric.

Historical timing. The British (and American) political revolutions preceded the German; the German (and American) educational revolutions preceded the British; and, finally, the British industrial revolution preceded the German (and American). Any attempts to explain the rate at which the German economy caught up with the British must consider the stage of development of all other social institutions and not merely of education. Thus, a possibly more educated, but subservient German worker under a more aptly educated manager must be balanced against a possibly less educated, certainly in the upper levels, British work-force that was set in a less rigid system of social stratification. All relevant attitudes and their relationships with the social structure must be examined.

The ethos of stratification. The English, and probably the Scottish, labour force was set in a society basically aristocratic in nature and, despite the growing power of the unions, workers who often had only recently left the land were, if not subservient, at least still deferential to their 'superiors'. They could only, unlike their American cousins, work out their lives in industry or, increasingly as the century drew to a close, in commerce. Even though a narrow meritocratic educational ladder was introduced in the 1880–90s its economic significance was influenced by the nature of the ambitions of the middle classes and by the character of the secondary schools that had high status. The ambition of those in the middle class, if not for themselves at least for their children, was to break their connection with *banausic*[63] affairs and to move into the high status professional, political or pro-consular sphere. If industry in 1900 was not yet badly hampered by the ruling aristocratic and amateur ethos, the longer the relevant attitudes prevailed, particularly when one remembers the nature of contemporary economic change, the more was dysfunction likely.

In all probability the educational system had not greatly checked the development of the economy up to 1900. The labour force in Britain – and those of its competitors – was enmeshed in a total social structure, of which education was but one, albeit an important, factor. Furthermore, any balanced account of the situation must also weigh in any advantages gained from the contemporary educational system. What economic benefits, for example, came to the mother country from its empire whose rulers were at the time probably aptly educated in the public schools? However, in spite of manifest quantitative and some qualitative changes, the British educational system was in 1900 neither appropriate for the older basic industries, as then operating, nor for the new dimensions along which the economy was being diverted.

Conclusion

The links between the educational system and the rest of the social structure are peculiar to the society concerned. Separate analysis of the economy and education, therefore, if used to explain differential levels of economic performance, may lead to over-simplified accounts and optimistic hopes, through quick changes in educational policy, of rapid alleviation of malfunctions, the roots of which lie in complex interrelationships between a wide range of social institutions whose characteristic quality may depend upon the apparent vagaries of historical development. The outstanding differences demonstrated here between the educational systems of Britain and Germany, two societies whose economies were then at rather similar levels of development, show this to be true.

The more detailed evidence given earlier concerning attitudes within the British labour force indicate some of the more crucial of the structural constraints upon the ways in which educational change, mediated by the labour force, might benefit the economy. Three fundamental points can be made:

The amateur tradition. To over-simplify, British management might be ruled by the cult of the amateur but German managers worshipped the expert. Both extremes have their advantages and disadvantages. The expert knows a great deal, but can not see the wood for the trees; the amateur should question much, but often sees no trees and barely discerns the wood. Yet within the specific social structures the Germans seem to have come nearer in educational terms to what was economically appropriate in the balance between pure and applied knowledge, between general and specialised education, and between vocational and non-vocational curricula. But such generalisations are relative to the time, the social structure and even to the level of the labour force within one specific industry,[64] although, because we live as societies, some overall national judgement must ultimately be made if only to direct future policies.

Research to-date on the matters considered here supports the conclusion that, despite the rhetoric of the later part of the nineteenth century, the nature of the educational system probably had not yet a large causative role in contemporary British economic ills, though it did probably play some part in Germany's remarkable leap into the industrial world. However, there is enough evidence to consider very seriously the hypothesis that the contemporary slow rate of educational change was a detrimental factor for Britain's economic development in the twentieth century.

Notes and References

1 MUSGROVE, F. (1961), 'Middle class education and employment in the nineteenth century. A rejoinder' *Economic History Review*, 14 (2), December, pp. 320–9.

2 Quoted in WARD, D. (1967) 'The public schools and industry in Britain after 1870', *Journal of Contemporary History*, 2 (3), July, p. 49.

3 *Iron and Coal Trades Review*, 1 September, 1899, p. 385.

4 HARRISON, J.F.C. (1957) 'The Victorian gospel of success' *Victorian Studies*, 1 (2), December, pp. 155–64.

5 *The Economist*, 1 October, 1864, p. 1225.
6 *Royal Commission on the State of Popular Education* (Newcastle Commission), 1859, II, p. 246.
7 *Iron and Coal Trade Review*, 5 February, 1886, p. 206.
8 See, for example, evidence given to the *Royal Commission on Depression of Trade and Industry*, 1886.
9 LANKASTER, E.R. (1890) *The Advancement of Science*, London, Macmillan, p. 199.
10 *Journal of the Iron and Steel Industries*, 1881, I, p. 161.
11 *Iron and Coal Trade Review*, 28 August, 1891, p. 266 and 27 December, 1895, p. 814; *Journal of the Iron and Steel Institute*, 1896, I, p. 177. The last phrase occurs several times in the journals.
12 *Select Committee on Scientific Instruction*, 1868, Q. 1514.
13 SANDERSON, M. (1972) *The Universities and British Industry, 1850–1970*, London, Routledge and Kegan Paul, pp. 25–6 and 212–3.
14 MUSGRAVE, P.W. (1967) *Technical Change, the Labour Force and Education*, Oxford, Pergamon Press, p. 90.
15 MUSGRAVE, P.W. (1966) 'Constant factors in the demand for technical education, 1860–1960', *British Journal of Education Studies*, XIV (1), May, pp. 173–87.
16 *The Economist*, 25 January, 1868, p. 87.
17 Quoted in ERICKSON, C. (1959) *British Industrialists: Steel and Hosiery, 1850–1950*, London, National Institute of Economic and Social Research, pp. 35–6.
18 Quoted in BURN, D.L. (1940) *The Economic History of Steelmaking, 1867–1939*, London, Cambridge University Press, p. 214.
19 Quoted in ERICKSON, C. (1959) *op. cit.*, p. 43.
20 MAGNUS, P. (1910) *Educational Aims and Efforts*, London, Longman, pp. 109–10.
21 ROSE, M.E. (1977) 'Rochdale man and the Stalybridge riot. The relief and control of the unemployed during the Lancashire cotton famine', in DONAJGRODZKI, A.P. (Ed.) *Social Control in Nineteenth Century Britain*, London, Croom Helm, p. 185.
22 *Royal Commission on Labour*, Final Report, 1894, pp. 54, 112–3, and 146–7.
23 MITCHELL, B.R. and DEAN, E.P. (1962) *Abstract of British Historical Statistics*, Cambridge, Cambridge University Press, pp. 64–5.
24 SAMUEL, R. (1977) 'Workshop of the world: steampower and hand technology in mid-Victorian Britain', *History Workshop*, 3 Spring, p. 13.
25 *Royal Commission on Depression of Trade and Industry* (1886), Qs. 6383 and 5169.
26 MAGNUS, P. (1910) *op.cit.*, p. 111.
27 For this paragraph see McCANN, W.P. (1960) *Trade unionist, co-operative and socialist organisations in relation to popular education, 1870–1902*, (unpublished PhD thesis), University of Manchester.
28 ROBERTS, R. (1971) *The Classic Slum*, Harmondsworth Penguin Books, pp. 28–31.
29 *Op. cit.*, *Royal Commission on Depression of Trade and Industry* (1886), p. 24.
30 *Ibid.*, Qs. 1758–73.
31 *Ibid.*, p. XV.
32 *Hansard*, 3rd series, Vol. 198, Cols. 168–9.
33 *Royal Commission on Children's Employment* (1864), 3rd report, p. 187 and 198.
34 RUSKIN, J. (1888) *Crown of Wild Olives*, London, G. ALAN, p. 28.
35 *Census of Great Britain, 1851*, Education, Reports and Tables, 1854, p. XV.
36 *The Economist*, 15 December, 1866, p. 1457.
37 *Op. cit.*, *Royal Commission on Depression of Trade and Industry* (1886), lxiii.
38 *Royal Commission on Labour Laws* (1894), Q. 513.
39 Quoted in POLLARD, S. (1959) *A History of Labour in Sheffield*, Liverpool University Press, p. 29.
40 DINGLE, A.E. (1977) 'The rise and fall of temperance economics', *Monash Papers on Economic History*, No. 3. See also HARRISON, B. (1971) *Drink and the Victorians*, London, Faber, p. 305.
41 *Royal Commission on Depression of Trade and Industry* (1886), Q. 3351.
42 DINGLE, A.E. (1972) 'Drink and working-class living standards in Britain, 1870–1914', *Economic History Review*, 25 (4), November, pp. 608–22.
43 SADLER, M.E. (1902) 'The unrest in secondary education in Germany and elsewhere', *Special Reports on Educational Subjects*, IX, p. 80; PAULSEN, F. (1908), *German Education Past and Present*, London, T. Fisher Unwin, 1908, p. 193.
44 *Royal Commission on the State of Popular Education in England*, (Newcastle Commission), (1859), I, p. 243.
45 TROPP, A. (1957) *The Schoolteachers*, London, Heinemann.
46 LAYTON, D. (1973) *Science for the People*, London, Allen and Unwin.
47 SADLER, M.E. (1899) 'Problems in Prussian secondary education for boys, with special reference to similar questions in England', *Special Reports on Educational Subjects*, III, p. 108.
48 *Op. cit.*, I, p. 136.
49 *Royal Commission on Technical Instruction* (Samuelson Commission), III, (1884), pp. 323–4.

50 MUSGRAVE, P.W. (1967) *op. cit.*, p. 89.

51 Board of Education, *Annual Report, 1908–9*, 1909, p. 90.

52 CARDWELL, D.S.L. (1957) *The Organisation of Science in England*, London, Heinemann, pp. 157–8.

53 SANDERSON, M. (1972) *op. cit.*, pp. 22–3.

54 *Royal Commission on Depression of Trade and Industry* (1886), Q. 11902; similar evidence was given concerning the chemical industry.

55 *Select Committee on Scientific Instruction* (1868), Q. 2384.

56 For a fuller treatment of the German situation along the lines outlined here see MUSGRAVE, P.W. (1967) *op. cit.*, especially Parts I and II.

57 PATEL, S.J. (1961) 'Rates of industrial growth in the last century, 1860–1958', *Economic Development and Cultural Change*, IX (3), April, pp. 316–30.

58 TEMIN, P. (1966) 'The relative decline of the British steel industry, 1880–1913', in ROSOVSKY, H. (Ed.) *Industrialisation in Two Systems*, New York, Wiley, pp. 140–55.

59 SAWYER, J.E. (1954) 'The social basis of the American system of manufacturing', *Journal of Economic History*, 14 (4), pp. 361–79.

60 SANDERSON, M. (1972) *op. cit.*, pp. 24–5.

61 DEANE, P. and COLE, W.A. (1967) *British Economic Growth, 1688–1959*, (2nd edition), Cambridge, Cambridge University Press, p. 142.

62 WILSON, C. (1965) 'Economy and society in late Victorian Britain', *Economic History Review*, XVIII (1), August, pp. 189 and 192.

63 Significantly this word, Greek in origin, according to the *Shorter Oxford English Dictionary*, was first used in 1876 with the meaning of 'pertaining to mechanics'.

64 For evidence concerning this last point see MUSGRAVE P.W. (1966) 'The educational profile of two British iron and steel companies with some comparisons, national and international', *British Journal of Industrial Relations*, IV (3), July, pp. 201–11.

Population and the Biosocial Background

W.H.G. Armytage

If it were universally known that the birth of children could be prevented, and this was not thought immoral by married persons, would there not be great danger of extreme profligacy among unmarried women, and might we not become like to 'arreois' societies in the Pacific?

Charles Darwin to G.A. Gaskell,
15 November 1878, *More Letters of
Charles Darwin* 1903, ii, p. 50.

The new morality

Darwin's reply to a Bradford-based missioner for the eight-year old Malthusian Society – the first organisation in the world formed to promote family planning as a prescript for poverty – is doubly ironic. First, because it was a sentence of Malthus' which he read forty-five years earlier, to the effect that population when unchecked doubles every twenty-five years, that set him on the road to his theory of natural selection.[1] Second, at the same time, he involuntarily provided us with a classic example of an individual procreational calculus:

Marry
Children – (if it please God) – constant companion, (friend in old age) who will feel interested more, object to be beloved and played with – better than a dog anyhow . . .

Not marry
No children (no second life), no one to care for one in old age . . . have the expense and anxiety of children – perhaps quarrelling . . . less money for books, etc. – if many children, forced to gain one's bread . . . [2]

Such procreational calculi were, in official opinion, so rare that the government had adopted the policy of claustralising into workhouses those whose prolificity was a burden on the rates. A special brand of sick humour was evoked by the whole scheme of governmental interference in the procreational freedom of the poor.

Thomas Carlyle's macabre Malthusian character, Hofrath Hauschreke, (in *Fraser's Magazine* in 1834) was so savage that it 'excited the most unqualified disapprobation' as Hauschreke (House wrecker) being haunted by 'open mouths, open wider and wider' and by a world which would terminate 'by its too dense inhabitants, famished into delirium, universally eating one another'.[3] John Eagle's gruesome fantasy of 'New Scheme for Maintaining the Poor' (in *Blackwood's Magazine*, April 1838) envisaged three quarters of the inmates of a workhouse being put down as 'aged and infirm', bones boiled down into soup for the living inmates, their bones made into spoons and ladles and skins for binding books, cushioning the Poor Law commissioners chairs or used in making shoes for the relieving officers; the skins of the young being sold to pay for the salaries of the Poor Law commissioners as 'the innocency of this source of income would make this office more profitable'.[4] But perhaps the most notorious (because still unknown) was 'Marcus' who called for the gassing of all superfluous children above two in poor families in order to contain the 'pauper herd'. For 'Marcus' did not believe that the workhouses' could prevent the fecklessly fecund from breeding and suggested fixing the number of children.[5]

Was it the exfoliation of this macabre humour at the time which led Darwin to record that he turned to Malthus 'for amusement'?. He certainly transcended Malthus' prescript of six children by having seven who survived him. He also transcended Malthus' concept of 'struggle'. For whereas Malthus used 'struggle' to mean 'a zero-sum competition for a *scarce* resource (subject to the law of diminishing returns)', Darwin used it to mean 'an effort to overcome a difficulty (through relations of dependence, chance, variation, *or* competition)'.[6]

Prudence institutionalised

Two Asian students in England in 1838–40 were astounded at the way in which one Englishman sacrificed his 'private comfort for the good of his country' by fathering fourteen children and forming three banks, one gas light and one railway company, as well as serving as a magistrate.[7] To these Indians such prolificity was to be seen 'in conjunction with the colonial enterprise and maritime enterprize' of England.[8]

This is why an emphatic negative could be given in 1840 by Carlyle to the question: 'will ... twenty millions of working people ... in universal trade-unions [pass] a resolution not to beget any more [children] till the labour market becomes satisfactory?'.[9] Carlyle's negative answer depended on the increase of factory inspection, sanitation and emigration, the last especially. 'Our little Isle', he wrote, 'is grown too narrow for us; but the world is wide enough yet for another six thousand years ... Why should not London long continue the All-Saxon-home, rendezvous of all the "Children of the Harz-Rock" arriving, in select samples, for the Antipodes and elsewhere, by steam and otherwise, to the "season" here'.[10] (That's good pre-vision! London has since become a tourist Mecca!) But his endorsement of emigration underlined the defects of the English socio-industrial system in that he advised 'every honest willing workman who found English too strait, and the "organization of Labour" not sufficiently advanced, might find a bridge built to carry him into new Western Lands, there to "organize" with more elbow room some "labour for himself"'.[11] Else, as he crisply put it, how was 'the alarming problem of the Working Classes . . . to be managed'?[12]

To an increasing number (because numbers were increasing) blind belief in 'Providence' was giving way to the exercise of reasonable foresight to discern hazards to their life chances and insuring against disasters. 'Life tables' or 'tables of mortality' no longer bore the names of particular towns like the Northampton (1780) or the Carlisle (1815) but were national, like those compiled by Seventeen Insurance Offices in 1843 and the Institute of Actuaries in 1869.[13] Only extend life assurance to the working classes, argued the actuary of the Legal and General, and they would acquire the basis of prudence. His insistence (voiced in 1832 before beginning a thirty-two-year stint with the Legal and General) on social mobility through mechanics institutes and provincial universities was most timely, being taken up in Parliament in the following year. It was also in the true spirit of Malthus who also looked to schools to teach prudence.[14] For actuaries of these insurance companies were the 'new men' of an investment society. Thus, Charles Ansell of the Atlas Insurance Company (which bore many a family burden by wise investment) was elected FRS in 1835, two years before the General Register Officer was created by the efforts of his colleagues. He also served the National Provident, the Friends Provident, the Custom Annuity and Benevolent Fund and (what else?) the Clergy Mutual Life Offices. When reproved by the Bishop of London for charging more than the annual salary of most curates he replied 'That may be but actuaries are bishops'.[15] Rightly he was known as 'the father of the profession of actuaries'. This was right in that his profession transformed life chances in this world both for their clients and for industry. Friendly Societies, in the words of an Act of 1819, were designed to encourage people 'to make provision for themselves or their own family out of their own industry'. Big insurance companies aimed higher as their very names signified: The Eagle Star (1807), The Norwich Union (1808), The Sun Life Assurance (1810) and the Scottish Widows (1815). Because Friendly Societies could not afford the actuarial skills, another act of 1829 empowered Justices of the Peace to ensure their 'safety'.

But it was the Prudential (founded in 1848) which was the first to take infant lives on its books. Even more enterprising, the Equity and Law (1844), the Royal Assurance (1845) and the Commercial Union (1862) (four of what have now become the big twelve of such companies controlling in 1978 investment funds of £16,722 million); insured the wage-labourer for old age, dependency, and burials at a penny or twopence a week, thereby superseding a host of petty assessment societies without its actuarial backing.[16] The Prudential was so effective that though the British Government undertook a similar insurance service through the Post Office after 1864, by 1882, when the blind Malthusian economist Henry Fawcett was Postmaster General, he found that in the intervening seventeen years the average number of insurance policies granted annually was under 400. And thirty three years later 'the Pru' was described as:

absolutely the highest shareholder in the Bank of England, as it was in the River Company, the most extensive owner of railway securities as well as of freehold ground rents; the most considerable holder of Indian and Colonial Government Bonds and Stocks; one of the greatest London ground landlords owning more than half of a square mile of the Metropolis, and probably the greatest owner of freehold property in the United Kingdom.[17]

Filtering immigrants

The other insurance was to emigrate, especially if one didn't want to practice Malthusian 'prudence' and have only the children one could afford, for many hoped that through emigration they could build a family. Indeed emigration was often helped by the extended family networks. Writing home from Wisconsin in the 1840s, one such emigrant hoped to place himself 'in circumstances one day or another so that I can see my children smiling about me in contentment and be able to assist their parents in their Declining Years'.[18]

There was much in England to propel them out. Rent, taxes and tithes deprived capital and labour of its just rewards. Leases limited farming operations. Labourers too wished their hire to be more profitable. Craftsmen wanted a fair wage for the long years of apprenticeship. Cobbettian 'forebodings' about the future, and fears that Britain 'was in the throes of a long decline' possessed other emigrants to the United States of America in the first four decades of the nineteenth century. And the push increased so that, whereas in 1843 people were leaving the country at a rate of over a thousand a week, by 1852 the same number was leaving daily.[19]

There was much comment. One who wrote over a thousand leading articles for *The Times* suggested that to dispense with inherited wealth and to compel people to work would release 'hidden springs of energy and genius'.[20] Were those 'hidden springs' in the total annual average of 200,000 persons a year (286,000 between 1846 and 1854 propelled by the Irish famine and Australian gold) provided with free or assisted passage by the Colonial Land and Emigration Commission between 1840 and 1873? Some like J.H. Elliott (1868) thought so. But they were wrong, as only a twentieth (10,000) were provided for. As he saw it, the mother country was left to struggle 'with an ever increasing proportion of lame, lazy and helpless persons' who had to be 'maintained by the labour of a less and less proportion of workers'. He particularly lamented the 'large immigration of Irish' as having both raised the percentage and increased the ratio of what he called 'the ill-conditioned population' and 'an unfair proportion of our criminals'.[21]

Though the net loss by migration oscillated in the nineteenth century from between 182,000 in 1846–50 to 787,000 in 1851–56, it was never less than 373,000 (in 1864–65) and only once (1881–85) rose above 700,000. By 1911–15, it rose to the staggering total of 2,584,000. Describing the net loss of peoples by emigration overseas during the second half of the nineteenth and early part of the twentieth century as 'heavy', Tranter (1973) has estimated it as no less than 8.6 million i.e.

over one third of the actual increase in the population between 1841 and 1939. The bulk of this of course went before 1915 as after it there was a net immigration balance of plus 1,017,000. And since as he says 'a significant and rising proportion' of those leaving the country were professional and skilled men, and men themselves forming sixty per cent of emigrants, increasingly the British Empire, and decreasingly the United States, received the benefit.[22]

'The safety valve of emigration' had, in Bernard Shaw's (1889) view, failed to relieve the pressure of population. Rather, he saw it as having

> forced us to begin the restitution to the people of the sums taken from them for ground landlords, holders of tenant right, and capitalists, by the imposition of an income tax, and by compelling them to establish out of their revenues a national system of education, besides imposing restrictions – as yet only of the forcible-feeble sort – on their terrible power of abusing the wage contract.[23]

'The Irish bull is always pregnant'

The original punster – J.P. Mahaffy – was married in the year in which William Farr (1877) identified a 'strong counter-current to the emigration of the English race' that was flowing into England.[24] With the 'Irish' in the lead (followed by 'Scottish, colonial and foreign settlers'), Dr. Farr admitted that they were literally innumerable because 'fear of removal to Ireland' might well have led some of them 'to have assigned England as the birth place of their children'.[25]

Perhaps one most revealing Census indicator was the increase from one per cent (in the 1780s) to five per cent (in 1850) of Roman Catholics in the population of Great Britain, escalating to 6.5 by 1900:[26] a figure which excited at least two predictive fantasies about the glowing future of that church that Macaulay's New Zealander might have thought plagiaristic.[27]

But no figures of speech could do justice to the terrible fall in the percentage of the population that remained in Ireland to that of the combined population of Britain. For it fell from nearly a half in 1781 to about a tenth in 1911.[28] And central in this fall was the horrific famine of the 1840s with its revelation that the administrator of the British relief projects regarded the famine as a divine punishment for Irish perversity. This should be coupled with a British historian's view of America forty years later as 'a grand land if only every Irishman would kill a negro and be hanged for it'.[29] Well might Sir William Harcourt acknowledge the existence of an Irish nation in the United States, . . . hostile, with plenty of money, absolutely beyond our reach and yet within ten days sail of our shore'.[30]

Even those emigrants who had achieved middle class status 'believed that an independent Ireland would help them be assimilated in the United States'. So many non-Irish Americans supported home rule in the hope that it would ease ethnic and religious tensions in the United States. As one Boston WASP put it on 16 April 1886, 'here our two races – the Irish and Anglo-Saxon – will amalgamate and form the great American race'.[31] But if there was a race between the races, the Irish would seemingly have won as they retained their polyphiloprogenitivity during the early twentieth century: J.F. McDonnell, head of the Wall Street firm of that name, having fourteen children.[32]

Lofty Jews

Race was also becoming a suspect word as the Jewish refugees poured into Saltonstall's New England, as well as Farr's Old England. Later to be aggravated by the propaganda of the British Brothers League, it contributed to the passage of the Aliens Act of 1905.[33] Contemplating the descent of these alien immigrants in the last two decades of the century, the gentle Archdeacon Cunningham (1897) acknowledged that, in the past, England had learned much from immigrants but questioned whether new refugees from the ghettos would bring similar skills. And were they needed? Did not England need the newest machines? Being a Liberal he agreed that to stop them would be retrograde.[34]

The former British Ambassador to the United States who had also been much affected by the *fin de siècle* views of New Englanders, dismissed the editor of the *Dictionary of National Biography* (in which ironically, immigrants do not figure largely) as 'a Jew-boy by the name of Lee (later Levi)', sneering at him as a 'Jew biographer' for not being able to contain his 'enthusiasm for the healthy great achievement of the dramatist [Shakespeare], namely the good investment of his capital'.[35] In that sneer is embodied all that was arreois in 'English' culture at that time, especially in view of denigration of the capitalist and educated class as being those 'least able to be trusted in the great racial questions'.[36] For if French Huguenot emigrants 'lifted England's industrial and technological level and pushed her into the role of industrial leader in the eighteenth and nineteenth centuries',[37] German and Russian Jews kept it there. If Hirsch and Cassell enabled the future King Edward VII to emulate his horses and set a fast pace, their humbler counterparts made life much easier for those in the unpalaced industrial towns north of Windsor.

No graduates in marketing were required to sell the products of nineteenth century Lancashire because, as a Manchester economist of the time observed, Greece and Spain and Germany, 'have come, in a sense into Manchester'.[38] Here foreign merchanting firms rose from 2 (in 1784) to 420 (in 1870). Jews, like Charles Hallé, enabled them to taste the brandy of music instead of the gin of despair, and Chaim Weitzman removed a bottle neck in the mass manufacture of high explosives.[39] Alphabets of 'aliens' from Aaronovitch to Zangwill can be compiled that would include such families as the Behrens, Cassells, Disraeli, Engels, Ferranti, Goldschmidt, Heymanns, Jacobi, Laski, Marks, Neumann, Polanyi, Rothenstein, Schuster, Woolf and Zangwill. They should be reinforced by some simple case histories from one of the by-ways of Jewry: Nottingham. Here one of the first shipping houses was launched in 1835 by Moritz Jacobs, whilst the lace specialists, Simon, May and Co. (founded by Jacob Weinberg from Hamburg) even had some contacts in

Moscow. By the 1880s, Albert Cahn from Cologne founded the furniture firm of Jays and Campbells (now part of Wolfson's Great Universal Stores): his son was knighted and ran a special cricket eleven. As elsewhere these Jews were anxious to improve the cultural facilities in Nottingham. Thomas Carlyle's friend and translator, Alfred Neuberg (who arrived in 1820), presided over the literary department of its Mechanics' Institute, and when that burned down, a pioneer of the curtain trade, Lewis Hayman, capped his introduction of street lighting in 1857 by giving (anonymously too) £14,000 to building its successor, Nottingham University College.[40]

Cephalization versus Civilization

Both the Irish and the Jews provided steam for those who drove new social reforms through the hereditary thickets of British politics. Even Cardinal Manning, perhaps the most English of all the Victorian clergy, confessed in 1882 that he had 'given up working for the people of England to work for the Irish occupation in England'. The Irish delivered the ethnic vote and the Jews, in the persons of Liberals like Rufus Isaacs and Herbert Samuel, provided the leadership.[41] But the Irish had one further disadvantage, in that they were depicted as prognathous and cranially inadequate according to what can literally be called the 'skull-diggery' of that day. These estimations of the cranial (and, as they saw, the mental) capacity of the various races of the globe in rank order found a vent in *Punch* as well as the most learned of all the journals.[42] Exquisite callipers for this purpose were devised, and in this hierarchy of measurement, the English woman found herself aligned (maligned might be a better word) with the backward races. She, like them, was deemed incapable of profitting by such environmental influences as education. This (and exercise) were especially to be shunned if the psalmists precept – 'be fruitful and multiply' was to be fulfilled. Behind this was the belief that brain power severely handicapped ovulation. Clever women tended to be barren. 'Neither the "emancipated" woman at one end of the scale, nor the prostitute at the other, propagates her kind' observed yet another medical practitioner at the close of the century, gratuitously adding 'Society has reason to be thankful in both cases'.[43]

Women's 'surplus' numbers, very real in an age when marriage was above all a circumspect Malthusian operation, led to the devising of schemes to send them abroad to breed. The Colonial Land and Emigration Commission used to send two females to every male assisted by them, but, since this did not do the trick, many other societies – like the London Female Emigration Society (1850), the British Ladies Emigration Society (1859), The Female Middle Class Emigration Society (1861) and the United English Womens Emigration Society (1889), to say nothing of the mysterious activities of Mr. Vere Forster – all sprang from this particular social problem, which no doubt was due to the low opinion of their capacities and their personality.[44]

What can now be seen as the considerable contributions of Byron's only daughter, Augusta,[45] to computing, and of Sara Marks (later Mrs. Ayrton)[46] to electricity, shows that women's intellectual potentiality was consistently and regularly denigrated. In the weight of brain alone they were held to be far inferior to men, and indeed more kin to the negro: a belief held from the 1840s (when Thomas B. Peacock researched on the cerebrum and cerebellum) to 1870 (when John Cleland showed that the temperal and temporo spheroidal lobes of the woman's brain were more 'childlike' than that of the male). The momentum of this research built up such a formidable dossier of feminine physiological disadvantage that medical men considered that it was almost criminally foolish to suppose that women could ever possess the same 'brain power' as men.[47] (see *table 1*)

Cull-ture or anarchy?

James Mill (1824), in his article on 'Colony' in the *Supplement to the Encyclopaedia Brittanica*, held that one alternative to emigration was 'to discard the superstitions of the nursery'. He might have added (but didn't) that many did their best to get rid of the foetus before it reached the nursery.[48] For despite the endorsement of vaginal sponges by Francis Place in the 1820s, and of post-coital douches in the thirties by Dr. Charles Knowlton, so many pregnant English women resorted to abortion, that Disraeli in *Sybil* (1845) described it as 'practised as exclusively and legally in England as it is on the banks of the Ganges'. And this in spite of a considerable tradition of contraceptive practice.[49] Medical men confirmed this. One Manchester doctor estimated the proportion of abortions to births as 1 in 7; another put it at 1 in 3; and yet a third reported that 'ladies were habitually beginning to take exercise' when they were pregnant in order to make themselves abort.[50] Even the great William Acton found it 'grievous that children should be born dependent for support on the caprice or good feelings of the father' ... and that 'the object of unlawful love' was to the mother such 'an intolerable burden and cause of shame' that her natural desire was 'to hide her reproach from the world, and to rid herself of the burden; hence the concealment of birth, baby farming and infanticide'. By 1868, the editor of the *British Medical Journal* was overcome by 'a shudder and a loathing' ... when he 'looked back on the matter of fact details in our late numbers on baby farming or allied trades'. The Journal even had 353 replies to a sham baby-farming advertisement in its own pages.[51]

Though the editor of *The Cornhill Magazine* suspended publication in 1860 of Ruskin's articles which derided 'Colonization'; 'Bringing in of waste lands'; or 'Discouragement of Marriage' as illusory and the Malthusians as implying that the poor were 'of a race essentially different from ours and unredeemable',[52] by 1867 he was publishing the opinion of one of Her Majesty's Inspectors of Schools suggesting that it was 'a little unjust ... to attribute to the Divinity exclusively this polyphiloprogenitiveness, which the British Philistine, and the poorer class of Irish, may certainly claim to share with him'. Was he too wittily suggesting that the true cull was culture? For without 'culture' came 'anarchy'. Culture, in Arnold's definition of it, would provide the knowledge of how to prevent accumulation of children and would underline the lesson that

Table 1

| Races | Brain-weights of the Skulls of MEN | | | | | | | Brain-weights of the Skulls of WOMEN | | | | | | | Mean of Sexes | | Mean of Series | | |
| | Number | Heaviest | | Lightest | | Average | | Number | Heaviest | | Lightest | | Average | | | | | | Mean internal capacity |
	1	2	3	4	5	6	7	8	9	10	11	12	13	14	15	16	17	18	19
i. European Races	299	52.68	1493	43.61	1236	48.25	1367	94	46.02	1304	39.56	1121	42.49	1204	45.73	1296	47.12	1335	92.3
ii. Asiatic Races	124	50.27	1425	41.57	1178	46.00	1304	86	45.95	1302	37.48	1062	42.13	1194	43.94	1245	44.44	1259	87.1
iii. African Races	53	47.37	1342	41.93	1188	45.63	1293	60	43.91	1244	39.59	1122	42.74	1211	43.66	1237	43.89	1244	86
iv. American Races	52	48.16	1365	43.50	1233	46.17	1308	31	45.44	1288	39.13	1109	41.89	1187	44.92	1273	44.64	1265	87.5
v. Australian Races	24	50.86	1441	36.96	1047	42.83	1214	11	42.98	1218	34.77	985	39.22	1111	41.02	1162	41.81	1185	81.9
vi. Oceanic Races	210	49.25	1396	42.90	1216	46.54	1319	95	44.61	1264	41.01	1162	43.00	1219	44.52	1272	45.63	1293	89.4
Numbers and Averages	762	49.76	1410	41.74	1183	45.90	1301	377	44.81	1270	38.59	1094	41.91	1188	43.96	1246	44.58	1263	87.3

Source: Philosophical Transactions of the Royal Society CLV, III, (1868), pp. 525–7.

to bring people into the world when one cannot afford to keep them and oneself decently and not too precariously . . . is by no means an accomplishment of the Divine will or a fulfilment of Nature's simplest laws, but just as wrong, just as contrary to season and the will of God, as for a man to have horses, or carriages, or pictures, when he cannot afford them.[53]

Had Arnold in mind what has been called the 'field of narrowed opportunity'? For this has been held to be partly responsible for the so-called 'Great Depression' in industry and trade.[54]

The British distemper

By 1870 even Ruskin discerned 'hope of the nation's giving some of the attention to conditions affecting the race of man, which it has hitherto bestowed only on those which may better its races of cattle', adding 'ugly and fatal as is every form and agency of licence no licentiousness is so mortal as licentiousness in marriage'. Ruskin envisaged 'permission to marry' as 'the reward held out to youth 'during the entire latter part of the course of their education': a certification that the first portion of their lives had been rightly fulfilled.[55]

With a staggering 36.5 per cent of the population revealed by the 1871 Census as under the age of fifteen, Montague Cookson (1872) (later Crackenthorpe and a QC) boldly followed Ruskin's example and shed the anonymity that had hitherto cloaked writers on contraceptives by publishing advice to parents on the need to plan their families if they wished to cope with the great 'examination' race.[56] The climax of such 'speaking out' was of course the courting of prosecution by a clergyman's former wife and a rationalist republican for republishing a birth control tract. Apart from publicising the case, the prosecution led to the formation of the Malthusian League with the twin objectives of agitating 'for the abolition of all penalties on the public discussion of the population question' and of spreading 'among the people, by all practicable means, a knowledge of the law of population, of its consequences, and of its bearing up on human conduct and morals'.[57]

But all this was of little use to those begotten in the days before contraception was so discussed and they represented what even Thomas Hughes (a father of nine children) was now calling 'the British distemper', which he diagnosed as 'the determination of blood to the head and heart', and prescribed its 'carrying out to the extremeties'.[58] To practice what he preached, he placed one of his sons in Canada and another in Texas, and joined Sir Henry Kimber (who had 'settled' two of his own six sons in South Africa) in establishing a 'colony' for other middle class sons at Rugby, Tennessee. The trade unions, which he had done so much to help, agreed with him [59] and, let it be said, so did Charles Darwin. For when someone asked him whether contraception was the answer the sage replied:

Suppose such checks had been in action during the last two or three centuries, or even for a shorter time in Britain, what a difference it would have made on the world, when we consider America, Australia, New

Zealand and South Africa! No words can exaggerate the importance, in my opinion, of our colonization for the future history of the world.[60]

Were the best withdrawing?

This was in his reply to the Bradford-based Gaskell with which we began. For Gaskell was challenging Darwin's statement, in the *Descent of Man* (1871), that man had 'no right to expect an immunity from the evils consequent on the struggle for existence', arguing instead that man had such a right thanks to 'the conquest of nature and the growth of altruism' and that this right could be enforced' without any deterioration of race and decline of virtue'. Not only did Darwin doubt whether an 'artificial check' to population 'would be advantageous to the world at large at present, however, it may (sic) be in the distant future', [61] but he suggested that Gaskell ponder over an article by Francis Galton ('I forget when published ... in which he proposes certificates of health (etc.) for marriage and that the best should be matched').[62] Unlike Malthus, Francis Galton believed in early marriage, but the early marriage of human beings of superior quality. He wished to encourage 'those who determine to live celibate lives through a reasonable conviction that their issue would be probably less fitted than the generality to play their part as citizens'.

Far from encouraging contraception, Galton considered it merely exaggerated the tendency for the responsible to curb their reproduction and the irresponsible not to. His conversion to early marriage was effected by a Scots obstetrician father of thirteen who had enquired into *Fecundity, Fertility and Sterility* (1866).[63] Moreover, Galton had given a prescription for 'the best form of civilisation in respect to the improvement of the race'. This was contained in his subsequently much maligned *Hereditary Genius* (1869). (If he later regretted using the term 'genius' instead of 'talent',[64] he never regretted his prescription). The prescription called for a society which was not costly and in which:

> incomes were chiefly derived from professional sources, and not much through inheritance; where every lad had a chance of showing his abilities, and, if highly gifted, was enabled to achieve a first-class education and entrance into professional life, by the liberal help of the exhibitions and scholarships which he had gained in his early youth; where marriage was held in as high honour as in ancient Jewish times; where the pride of race was encouraged (of course I do not refer to the nonsensical sentiment of the present day, that goes under that name); where the weak could find a welcome and a refuge in celibate monasteries or sisterhoods; and lastly, where the better sort of emigrants and refugees from other lands were invited and welcomed, and their descendants naturalized.[65]

Nor was he alone in rejecting contraception. Even his great opponent at the British Association for the Advancement of Science and at the Statistical Society, the environmentally-minded Dr. William Farr, (a father of eight) joined him in condemning 'the precocious procreation of feebly built children in India', and refused to accept what he called 'the policy advocated by Malthus, by John Stuart Mill (and) by Dr. Drysdale'.[66] Not so Dr. Farr's medical successors at the General Register Office. One argued that emigration was no cure for over-population because it took away 'most of the vigorous and enterprising of our working men, to the necessary deterioration of the residue left at home'.[67] With this G.A. Gaskell (1890) agreed.[68] Developing the case, he urged the state to endow motherhood, and undertake the rearing of children in order to foster greater responsibility in conception: ideas promoted by the wife of the Foreign Secretary of the Royal Statistical Society who a year later published *The Rapid Multiplication of the Unfit* (1891), and started a journal to convince women of this.[69] Even the non-conformist divine (who once earned Matthew Arnold's disapproval for euphorically exclaiming 'the whole earth breeds and God glories') was now denying that the poor could or would profit by any assistance whatsoever. So Robert Buchanan (1891) added his shrill treble in *The Coming Terror* to the many 'futopias' or Tiresian predictions of disaster for Britain: without colonies, in a socialist Europe,[70] a 'shoddy feudalism'[71] perhaps even a republic.[72] But that the republic should be forecast by a future editor of the *The Cornhill Magazine* (where Arnold originally published his criticism of Buchanan) and later of *The Spectator*, was not so significant,[73] as another proposal that, if the population of the British Isles should be reduced to twenty millions through 'a gradual process of race improvement', it would 'rule the world'. Such 'race improvement' would be effected through Socialism and 'the removal of the disabilities of birth . . .'[74] This was G.S. Carr (1895) who put the 'standing room only' argument of our own day: forecasting that the limit of space for world population would be reached 'far sooner than most people imagine' and continued 'if the rate of increase that prevailed in the USA were to persist among the present population of the globe for 250 years, there would be left but one square yard of standing room for each individual, and a market garden in Jupiter would be wanted'.[75]

Averting an arreois society?

But such socialist sentiments were by no means to the liking of the disciples of Herbert Spencer (the real Social Darwinists) who argued that both private and public philanthropy were misplaced in that they 'set aside the harsh but ultimately salutary action of the great law of Natural Selection without providing an efficient substitute for preventing degeneracy'.[76] Other fears were heightened by the forecast that birth cohorts relatively stable for two decades would, given the continued operation of the socio-economic forces which had brought this about, so reduce the rate of growth of the population that by 1995 it would stand at a maximum of 37,316,007.[77] The forecaster was on the staff of the new London School of Economics, whose founder, Sidney Webb, was worried about the increasing practice of women 'adopting neo-Malthusian devices to prevent the burden of a large family'[78] as well as by what he called 'the breeding of degenerate hordes of a demoralised "residium" unfit for social life'.[79]

These fears intensified when the Boer War broke out. Hence the Webbs' so-called 'Co-efficients'. Hence too, the sub-committee of the Fabian Society concluding that the population was being increasingly recruited from 'our most inferior stocks': 'Irish Roman Catholics and the Polish, Russian and German Jews ... and the thriftless and irresponsible – largely the casual labourers and other denizens of the one room tenements of our great cities the other'. The result (according to Sidney Webb), could 'hardly result in anything but national deterioration; or as an alternative, in this country gradually falling to the Irish or the Jews'.[80] With this, the medical officer for Brighton and the assistant medical officer for the LCC education committee agreed:

> Whether the less fit are now contributing a greater share to the general population than in the past is by no means certain. Very few would venture to assert that the line of intellectual ability or of physical endurance is horizontal and not oblique, or possibly almost perpendicular in relation to social position.[81]

Their painstaking inventory of the fall of the birth rate in English towns was also a stark endorsement of the effectiveness of Gaskell's persuasive tactics. The birth rate in Bradford fell more rapidly between 1881 and 1901 than in any of the other towns they listed (30.63 in 1881 to 21.95 in 1901) except in nearby Huddersfield (30.20 to 19.47). Brighton was third. Realistic people had discovered that the 'human niche'[82] of the British was not as wide as Darwin conceived it to be.

Notes and References

1 The sentence was: 'It may safely be pronounced, therefore, that the population, when unchecked, goes on doubling itself every twenty five years, or increases in geometric ratio', MALTHUS, T.R. (1826) *Essay on the Principle of Population*, 6th edition, p. 6, and Dalton noted: 'until the one sentence of Malthus, no one clearly perceived the great check amongst men ... Even a *few* years plenty, makes population in man increase ... One may say there is a force like a hundred thousand wedges trying (to) force every kind of adapted structure into the gaps in the economy of nature, or rather forming gaps by thrusting out weaker ones', DE BEER, G., ROWLANDS, M.J. and SKRAMOVSKY, B.M. (1971) 'Darwin's notebooks on transmutation of species', Part III, *Bulletin of the British Museum (Natural History) Historical Series*, Vol. 3, 1962–69, pp. 162–3.

2 For a full version of this balance sheet drawn up in 1837–38 see ALLEN, M. (1977) *Darwin and His Flowers*, London, Faber and Faber, p. 121.

3 FROUDE, J.A. (1882) *Thomas Carlyle, a History of the First Forty Years of His Life*, ii, 404; TRAILL, H.D. (Ed.) (1891) *The Works of Thomas Carlyle*, London, Chapman and Hall, Vol. 1, pp. 180–1. T.H. Huxley (Darwin's Watchdog) also found Carlyle's *Sartor Resartus* and *Miscellanies* essential reading, listing those as 'among the few books devoured partly by myself and partly by the might horde of cockroaches' in his cabin during the cruise of the *Rattlesnake* ten years later and confessed that his 'sense of obligation' to them remained 'extremely strong', *Nineteenth Century*, January, 1890, p. 5.

4 Though the article was unsigned it is now known thanks to the Wellesley Index as one of the many contributions of the Red John Eagles (1783–1855) as prolific an author as he was a propagator. (The DNB records him as leaving 'a numerous family').

5 MARCUS (1838) *An Essay on Populousness*, MARCUS (1825) *On the Possibility of Limiting Populousness*.

6 The suggestion, WEBB, S. and B. (1929) *English Local Government*, London, Longmans, pp. 163–4, that the author might have been the Benthamite Lord Brougham is interesting in view of MANIER, E. (1978) *The Young Darwin and his Cultural Circle*, Boston, D. Reedel Publishing Company, p. 82.

7 NOWROJCE, J. and MARWANJEE, H. (1841) *Journal of a Residence of Two Years and a Half in Great Britain*, London, W.H. Allen, p. 490.

8 *Ibid.*, p. 489.

9 TRAILL, H.D. (1891) *op. cit.*, XXIX, pp. 200–1.
10 TRAILL, H.D. (1891) *op. cit.*, X, p. 26.
11 *Ibid.*, p. 266.
12 *Ibid.*, p. 269.
13 EDMONDS, T.R. (1832) *An Enquiry into the Principles of Population, Exhibiting a System of Regulations for the Poor; Designed Immediately to Lessen, and Finally to Remove, the Evils which have hitherto pressed upon the Labouring Classes of Society*, London. E.H. Wilson. EVERSLEY, D.E.C. (1959) *Social Theories of Fertility and the Malthusian Debate*, Oxford, Oxford University Press, p. 43.
14 Cornelius Walford, 'Charles Ansell FRS, FAS, 1794–1881', *DNB*; 'The families of the world', *Statistical Journal*, xli, 433–526, xlii, pp. 79–265, *Insurance Encyclopaedia*, 5 vols., 1871–78. Walford founded the Colonial Assurance Corporation in 1867 and was manager of the New York Assurance Company for Europe in 1820.
15 GOSDEN, P.H.J.H. (1961) *The Friendly Societies in England 1815–1875*, Manchester, Manchester University Press; and (1973) *Self Help, Voluntary Associations in the Nineteenth Century*, London, B.T. Batsford.
16 BARNARD, R.W. (Ed.) (1948) *A Century of Service: The Story of the Prudential, 1848–1948*, London, Prudential Assurance, p. 3.
17 CLAYTON, G. (1971) *British Insurance*, Elek Books, p. 123.
18 ERICKSON, C. (1972) *Invisible Immigrants: The Adaptation of English and Scottish Immigrants in Nineteenth Century America*, London, Weidenfeld and Nicolson, p. 25.
19 *Results of the Census of Great Britain in 1851*, Table XXIII, p. 56.
20 BRODERICK, G.C. (1881) *English Land and English Landlords*, London, Cassell Petter and Galpin, p. 355.
21 ELLIOTT, J.H. (1868) 'The increase of material prospects and of moral agents compared with the state of crime and pauperism', *Statistical Journal*, XXXI, pp. 307–8, 311.
22 For the full figures see TRANTER N.L. (1973) *Population since the Industrial Revolution. The Case of England and Wales*, London, Croom Helm, pp. 53–8.
23 SHAW, B. (Ed.) (1889) in *Fabian Essays in Socialism*, p. 154.
24 FARR, W. (1877) *Thirty Ninth Report of the Registrar General.*
25 FARR, W. (1865) 'Our infant mortality and the alleged inaccuracies of the census', *Statistical Journal*, XXVIII, pp. 134–5.
26 TRANTER, N.L. (1973) *op. cit.*
27 UPWARD, A. (1904) *The Fourth Conquest of England*, London, Tyndale Press; ROLFE, F.W. (1904) *Adrian the Seventh*, London, Chatto and Windus.
28 TRANTER, N.L. (1973) *op. cit.*
29 McCAFFREY, L.J. (1976) *The Irish Diaspora in America*, Bloomington, Indiana University Press, p. 57.
30 *Ibid.*, pp. 101–2.
31 BROWN, T.N. (1966) *Irish-American Nationalism, 1870–1890*, Philadelphia, J.B. Lippincott Company, p. 165. For other ethnic 'manifestoes' see GRIFFIN, W.D. (1973) *The Irish in America 1850–1972*, Ethnic Chronology Series, No. 10, New York, Oceana Publications.
32 BIRMINGHAM, S. (1973) *Real Lace America's Irish Rich*, London, Hamish Hamilton, p. 9.
33 GARTNER, L.P. (1973) *The Jewish Immigrants in England 1871–1914*, 3rd Edition, London, Simon Publications.
34 CUNNINGHAM, W. (1897) *Alien Immigrants to England*, Swan Sonnenschein.
35 GWYNN, S. (Ed.) (1929) *The Letter and Friendships of Cecil Spring Rice: A Record*, London, Constable, ii. pp. 170–1.
36 *Ibid.*, p. 110, p. 121. See also a 'pioneer' of birth control, Montague Crackenthorpe, QC, in WHITE, A. (Ed.) (1892) *The Destitute Alien in Great Britain*, Swan Sonnenschein, p. 57.
37 SCOVILLE, W.C. (1960) *The Persecution of the Huguenots and French Economic Development 1680–1720*, California, The University of California Press.
38 CHAPMAN, S.J. (1904) *The Lancashire Cotton Industry*, Manchester, Manchester University Press, p. 141.
39 FRANGOPULO, N.J. (Ed.) (1964) *Rich Inheritance*, Manchester, Manchester Education Committee, p. 115.
40 From one of whose librarians, Mr. Michael Brook, I obtained the following references: ARONSFELD, C.C. (1954) 'Nottinghams Jewish lace pioneers', *The Guardian Journal* 19, 20 April, 1954; *Jews in Nottingham*, A.J.R. Information, December, 1955, p. 8.
41 For further examples of such prejudice see CURTIS, L.P. (Jr.) (1968) *Anglo-Saxons and Celts*, Bridgeport, Connecticut, The Conference on British Studies, p. 63.
42 BARNARD DAVIS, J. 'Contributions towards determining the weight of the brain in the different races of man', *Proceedings of the Royal Society of London*, xvi, 1867–68, pp. 236–41. *Philosophical Transactions of the Royal Society*, CLVIII, (1868), 505–27; 'On the weight of the brain of the negro', *Anthroplogical Review*, VII, (1869), pp. 190–2. 'No rational man' wrote T.H. Huxley in the year the civil war ended 'cognizant of the *facts*, believes the average negro is equal, still less the superior, of the average white

man . . . it is simply incredible that, when all his disabilities are removed/that/ . . . he will be able to compete successfully with his *bigger-brained* and *smaller-formed* rival, in a contest which is carried on by thoughts and not by bites. The highest places in the hierarchy of civilization will assuredly not be within reach of our dusky cousins'. Huxley, T.H. (1865) *Emanciption – Black and White* quoted in Chase, A. (1980) *The Legacy of Malthus: The Social Costs of the New Scientific Racism* London, University of Illinois Press, p. 635.

43 SUTHERLAND, A. (1900) 'Woman's brain', *Nineteenth Century*, XLVII, p. 805. HUTCHINSON, W. (1895) 'The economics of prostitution', *American Medico-Surgical Bulletin*, V. For a wider canvas see HALLER, J.S. (Jr.) and HALLER, R.M. (1974) *The Physician and Sexuality in Victorian America*, Illinois, University of Illinois Press, pp. 47–87.

44 HAMMERTON, A.J. (1979) *Emigrant Gentlewomen: The Victorian Distressed Gentlewomen and Female Emigration from Britain 1830–1914*, London, Croom Helm.

45 AAL (i.e., Lovelace) translated and edited 'Sketch of the Analytical Engine by Charles Babbage', by L.F. Menabrea for TAYLOR, R. (1843) *Scientific Memoirs*, ii, pp. 666–731, and corresponded with Andrew Crosse, CROSSE, C.A.H. (1857) *Memorials Scientific and Literary of Andrew Crosse the Electrician*.

46 Awarded the Hughes medal of the Royal Society in 1906 for researches on the electric arc and said ripples.

47 BOYD, R. (1870) 'Tables of the weights of the human body and internal organs in the same and insane of both sexes arranged from 2614 post-mortem examinations', *Philosophical Transactions of the Royal Society*, CLX, pp. 117–74; PEACOCK, T.B. (1861) *Tables of the Weights of the Brain and of some other organs of the Human Body*; CLELAND, J. (1870) 'An inquiry into the variations of the human skull', *Philosophical Transactions of the Royal Society*, CLX, pp. 117–74.

48 His son went further. Regarding an uncontrolled birth rate as all that stood between men and ultimate utopia, he did so much to strip the superstitions of the nursery that the wits repeated:

> There are two Mr. M..ls, too, whom those who like reading,
> What vastly unreadable, call very clever;
> And whereas M..l senior makes war on *good* breeding,
> M..l junior makes war on all *breeding* whatever.

49 FRYER, P. (1965) *The Birth Controllers*, London, Secker and Warburg; GREEN, S. (1971) *The Curious History of Contraception*, Ebury Press; McLAREN, A. (1978) *Birth Control in Nineteenth Century England*, London, Croom Helm, p. 52.

50 GREAVES, G. 'Observations on the causes of infanticide, *Transactions of the Manchester Statistical Society*, 1802–3.

51 Quoted in POTT, M., DIGGORY, P. and PEEL, J. (1977) *Abortion*, Cambridge, Cambridge University Press, pp. 156–7.

52 COOK, E.T. and WEDDENBERN, A. (1905) *The Works of John Ruskin*, London, George Allen and Unwin, xvii, pp. 420–2.

53 ARNOLD, M. 'Culture and anarchy' in SUPER, R.H. (Ed.) (1965) *The Complete Prose Books of Matthew Arnold*, Ann Arbor, University of Michigan Press, pp. 214–6.

54 BANKS, J.A. (1954) *Prosperity and Parenthood: A Study of Family Planning Among the Victorian Middle Classes*, London, Routledge and Kegan Paul, p. 129.

55 'Time and tide' in COOK, E.T. and WEDDERHURN, A. (Eds.) (1905) *Works*, xvii, London, George Allen, p. 420.

56 COOKSON, M. (1872) 'The morality of married life', *Fortnightly Review*, XII, p. 400.

57 LEDBETTER, R. (1976) *A History of the Malthusian League 1877–1927*, Columbus, Ohio State University Press, xiii.

58 HUGHES, T. (1975) *Rugby Tennessee*, Macmillan and Co., republished Philadelphia, Porcupine Press.

59 ERIKSON, C. (19) 'The Encouragement of emigration by British trade unions 1850–1900', *Population Studies*, Vol. iii, pp. 248–77. CLEMENTS, R.V. (0000) 'Trade unions and emigration', *Ibid.*, Vol. ix, pp. 167–80.

60 Quoted in CLAPPERTON, J. (1885) *Scientific Meliorism and the Evolution of Happiness*, Kegan Paul, Trench and Co., pp. 94–5.

61 'This note is badly written and expressed' he added in a postscript, 'but I have not the time or strength to rewrite it' quote in CLAPPERTON, J. (1885) *op. cit.*, pp. 339–41. Gaskell's other works include *The Futility of Thrift as a Means to General Well-being*, (1890), and *Social Control of the Birth Rate and Endowment of Mothers* (1890).

62 Partly republished in BAJEMA, C.J. (Ed.) (1976) *Eugenics Then and Now*, Stroudsberg Penn. Dowden, Hutchinson and Ross Inc., pp. 97–101.

63 DUNCAN, J.M. 1826–90, *DNB*.

64 FORREST, D.W. (1974) *Francis Galton: The Life and Work of a Victorian Genius*, Paul Elek, p. 267 suggests that this was 'probably because he found the subject distasteful, but possibly because he did not wish eugenics to be associated with the struggles of the pioneers of birth control'.

65 GALTON, F. (1869) *Hereditary Genius*, London, Macmillan, p. 362.

66 FARR, W. (1877) 'On some doctrines of population', *Statistical Journal*, December, XL, pp. 568–79. LEDBETTER, R. (1976), *op. cit.*, pp. 31–8.

67 OGLE, W. (1905) 'On marriage rates and marriage-ages with special reference to the growth of population', *Statistical Journal*, Vol. LIII, p. 22, 16 May.

68 GASKELL, G.A. (1890) *Social Control of the Birth Rate and Endowment of Mothers*, London, Free Thought Publishing Co., p. 10.

69 Mrs. Victoria Chaplin Woodhull, a women's rights leader, much helped by Cornelius Vandenbielt, came to England in 1877. In December of that year after lecturing in St. James' Hall, John Biddulph Martin proposed to her, but his family objected so strongly that it was six years before the wedding could take place. *Dictionary of American Biography*, Oxford University Press, 1936, XX, pp. 493–4.

70 ANON (H.C.M. WATSON) (1890) *Decline and Fall of the British Empire or the Witches' Cavern*, Trischer.

71 ANON, *The Christ That is To Be*, (1891) London, Chapman, envisaged China becoming a great power and all Europe a Socialist community.

72 ANON (A. MORRIS) (1891) *Looking ahead: a tale of adventure*, Henry. Forecast a state of industrial feudalism.

73 STRACHEY, J. ST. L. (1891) *How England became a republic: a romance of the Constitution*, Arrowsmith.

74 CARR, G.S. (1895) *Social Evolution and the Evolution of Socialism*, London, W. Stewart and Co., p. 100.

75 *Ibid.*, p. 63.

76 PLATT BALL, W. (1890) *Are the Effects of Use and Disuse Inherited?*, London, p. vii.

77 CANNAN, E. (1895) 'The probability of a cessation of the growth of population in England and Wales during the next century', *Economic Journal*, December, V, pp. 505–14.

78 WEBB, S. and B. (1897) *Industrial Deomocracy*, ii, p. 658.

79 WEBB, S. (1896) *The Difficulties of Individualism*, London, Fabian Tract, p. 6.

80 *The Times*, 16 October, 1906, p. 7.

81 SEARLE, G.S. (1976) *Eugenics and Politics in Britain 1900–1914*, London, Nordhoff International Publishing.

82 COLINVAUX, P. (1980) *A Biological Theory of History*, New York, Simon and Schuster.

2
Case Studies

The Coal Industry

Neil K. Buxton

During the nineteenth century, Britain can aptly be described as an economic civilisation based on coal. Technological advance in the previous century, particularly the inter-relationships forged between coal, steam and iron,[1] had paved the way for an upsurge in industrial production which later became known as the Industrial Revolution. To sustain the growth of manufacturing output, continued increases in the supply of coal were necessary, with the result that coalmining itself experienced changes that were hardly less 'revolutionary' than those taking place in other sectors of the economy. Whether or not the improvements effected within the coal industry amounted to a 'technological revolution' is rather a sterile debate. Certainly the period before 1850 witnessed the opening up of new areas of supply, with inland coalfields assuming a national prominence due to the emergence first of a canal network and later of railways.[2] At the same time, increasing use of steam power and iron, above and below ground, profoundly altered ways of winning and moving the coal. More intensive working became possible, in the form of deeper sinkings and the re-opening of previously abandoned collieries.

Equally, technical improvements in the industry allowed improved forms of ventilation, illumination, haulage and winding to be introduced.[3] It is true that by the 1850s, a significant gulf had developed between 'best practice' techniques, found mainly in the Northumberland and Durham coalfield, and those used in other parts of the country. But at least in the former, most of the ground rules had been laid for the solution of the major problems confronting the industry. The rest of the century was to be spent largely in further refining these improvements, in ensuring that the men observed the codes laid down for their safety, and in the attempts of other coalfields to catch up with the relatively advanced technology known and used in the north. Since employment in the industry had increased from about 50,000 in 1800 to over 200,000 in the 1850s, fairly sophisticated industrial management techniques developed to become a model for other industries of follow.[4] All in all, the nature of coalmining and the environment within which it operated changed dramatically during the first half of the nineteenth century.

The successful response of the industry to the steady expansion of demand for coal was reflected in figures of output. Whereas production had increased by a factor of four in the eighteenth century,[5] it rose between 1800 and 1900 by more than 20 times, from 10.1 million tons to 225.2 million tons. Growth was particularly rapid between 1830 and 1860, and continued at only slightly lower a rate during the industry's 'drive to maturity' in the later nineteenth century. Hence the industry achieved a doubling of output in each of the periods 1800–30, 1830–45, 1845–70, and 1870–1900. Advance on this scale enabled the country to consolidate the developments made in manufacturing during the Industrial Revolution and to become in every sense the 'workshop of the world' during the second and third quarters of the century.

Nor was the continued expansion of the British coal industry purely a matter of domestic importance. Indeed from mid-century, the chief success of the industry lay in the exploitation of overseas markets. Between 1855 and 1900, the volume of coal retained for domestic consumption rose by almost three times, from 60 to 167 million tons. On the other hand, coal shipments abroad increased by about 12 times, from 5 to nearly 60 million tons. Perhaps more significant, in 1855 coal shipped abroad (including bunkers) amounted to less than one-tenth of Britain's coal output and to only 3 per cent of the value of total exports. By the first world war, one-third of output was sent overseas and coal accounted for 10 per cent of the value of the country's exports.[6]

Shipments on this scale not only enabled Britain to become by far the largest coal-exporting nation in the world but also made an important contribution to the nation's favourable balance of payments. Unlike textiles, coal did not depend on an imported raw material and the income it earned was almost all pure gain.[7] Moreover, the mineral dominated British shipping. By reason of its weight, it afforded a vital outward freight from this country. At the end of the nineteenth century, more than four-fifths of the weight of British exports consisted of coal. Without it, the great bulk of shipping entering our ports with food and raw materials would have been compelled to leave in ballast.[8]

For the greater part of the Victorian era, therefore, the coal industry experienced a prosperity and rate of expansion that were rarely to be achieved in the present century. Of course, there were wide price fluctuations in domestic markets, and hence in profitability, especially from the 1870s.[9] Within a quarter of a century, the total value of coal output rose from 3 per cent of National Income in 1885 to over 5 per cent in 1890, increased further to almost 7 per cent in 1900 and then fell back again to about 4 per cent in 1905.[10] But, on balance, there is no doubt that these were generally good years for the coal industry: that the Victorian age as a whole witnessed the heyday of British coalmining. Accordingly, the discussion which follows must be considered in proper perspective. On the one hand, it is true that, like other sectors of the economy, the coal industry experienced growing difficulties from the 1870s. These included ageing coalfields and collieries, diminishing returns to effort, districts which remained technologically backward, and problems associated both with the management and labour sides of the industry. On the other hand, it is important to remember that in contrast to the years after 1918, these difficulties were set against a trend of steadily rising output, exports and employment.

In absolute terms, there would seem to have been few problems on the demand side of the industry during the Victorian era. As noted earlier, markets at home and abroad steadily expanded and if the latter developed more rapidly, the fact remains that even by 1900 consumption of coal per head of population was still higher in Britain than in any other country of the world. At just over 4 tons *per capita*, domestic consumption was roughly half as much again as in 1855 and significantly higher than the average of 3.08 tons in the USA, 2.89 tons in Belgium and 1.72 tons in the German Empire.[11] Yet from mid-century difficulties began to develop in the domestic market, mainly due to the declining share of output absorbed by the largest coal-using sectors. This is shown in Table 1.

Table 1: Distribution of Coal Raised in the UK, 1869–1913.
(figures expressed as a percentage of the total)

	1869	*1887*	*1913*
Domestic Consumption:			
Iron and Steel Industry	30	16.5	11
General Manufacturing	26	26	22.5
Mines	7	7	7
Steam Navigation	5	12.5	6
Gas and Electricity	6	6	8
Household etc	17	17	13
Total Domestic	91	85	67.5
Exports	9	15	32.5
Total Consumption	100	100	100

Sources: Report of the Commissioners Appointed to Inquire into the Several Matters Relating to Coal in the United Kingdom, Vol. III, Report of Committee E, c. 435–2, 1871 (Henceforth Royal Commission on Coal, 1871, Committee E); DEANE P. and COLE W.A. (1962), *op. cit.*, pp. 218–9.

In absolute terms, the demand of colliery companies, railways, gas and electricity increased rapidly during the second half of the century with the result that, as Table 1 shows, these sectors maintained or expanded their respective shares of a growing output. On the other hand, principal consumers such as Iron and Steel, General Manufacturing and Households declined in relative importance.[12] Economies in fuel use,[13] the fuel savings achieved by the change from coke to coal on the railways[14] and the gradual emergence of substitutes inevitably affected the proportion of coal output absorbed by both manufacturing and household consumers. However, ample compensation for the relative decline of certain important sections of the home market was found in the expansion of demand abroad.

As industrialisation advanced in several European countries, a steadily rising demand for coal developed from the middle decades of the century. Such was the rate of progress in manufacturing that, although the world's coal supply increased by almost three times between the 1880s and 1913, world demand increased faster still. Industrial demand was supplemented by the requirements of rapidly developing transport facilities and by the creation of gas and electricity undertakings. To some extent, Britain's dominant position in world coal markets was fortuitous. Her geographical position gave the ports of England and Wales easy access to markets in Europe and South America. This advantage was reinforced by the swift decline of freight charges due to improvements in the efficiency of shipping. For instance, outward freight rates per ton from Cardif to major foreign ports such as Bombay, Buenos Aires, Genoa and Port Said fell by anything between one-half and three-quarters between 1863/65–1913.[15]

But the success of Britain's coal-exporters depended on more than geographical accident and declining freight rates. Of major importance was the fact that pit-head prices in this country were generally much lower than those of most of our European competitors. Germany alone could match British prices; other countries were in no position to compete effectively. Prices at the pit-head were determined by a multiplicity of factors including quality of the coal mined, accessibility of seams, extent of royalties payable, cost of labour and the efficiency of operation. Only in the last of these did Britain enjoy a distinct competitive advantage over her European rivals until the years immediately preceding the first world war. In terms of quality and accessibility of coal, this country was no more advantageously placed than Germany, France or Austria. Royalty payments were also greater than in other European countries, although these never amounted to sufficiently high a proportion of selling price to be a serious weakness.[16] In addition, while data on mining labour costs in different countries are far from comprehensive and difficult to compare, annual average wages in the British industry in 1889 were almost certainly far in excess of those paid elsewhere in Europe.[17] By 1913, the length of the working shift was shorter in Britain than elsewhere, yet earnings per shift were almost half as high again as in France or Belgium, and one-fifth higher than in the Ruhr.[18] The fact was that wage costs accounted for a higher proportion of total costs in Britain than in other countries. Between the 1870s and 1910 wage costs per ton in British coal-mining amounted on average to between two-thirds and three-quarters of total costs. In contrast, in 1890, the proportion of average selling-price per ton taken in wages was 54 per cent in Belgium, 50 per cent in France and 33 per cent in Westphalia.[19]

Thus comparitively low pit-head prices in Britain were achieved in spite of, rather than because of, the price of labour. Rather, the success of British coal exporters during the Victorian era can largely be attributed to a much higher level of labour productivity than existed elsewhere. This is a matter which is examined in greater detail below (p. 90) but it may be noted here that throughout the nineteenth century output per head in the British coal industry remained significantly higher than in continental coalmining. It was this above all that allowed British owners to produce coal relatively cheaply and thus dominate foreign markets.

Yet, even in the export-field, not everything was as promising as appeared at first sight. Expansion and prosperity remained the hallmarks of the export-sector until the first world war, but there was growing evidence that Britain's predominant position was being seriously threatened. First, during the last quarter of the nineteenth century, rapid advances in technique and the opening of new sources of supply threatened several traditional British markets. Russia, Japan and certain of the principal British possessions[20] emerged as important producers for the first time. In the United States, coal output rose from 115 million tons in 1885–89, 29 per cent of world output, to 458 million tons in 1909–13, 43 per cent of world output. As a result, while British tonnage over the same period increased in absolute terms from 165 to 270 million tons, her share of world output fell from 41 to 25 per cent.[21]

Second, and perhaps more significant, was that the long-standing trend of steadily rising labour productivity in British coalmining was reversed in the 1880s. Although output per man fluctuated widely over the next 30 years, the underlying trend was markedly downwards. Indeed, over the period 1870–1914 as a whole, Britain alone among the chief continental coal-producers lost ground in terms of output per man-year. Although by the end of the Victorian era, labour productivity was still higher, in absolute terms, than elsewhere in Europe, the gap was steadily narrowing. Thus while the greater part of the nineteenth century must be regarded as a halcyon period for the coalowners, factors on the demand side both at home and abroad, were already at work which, in the long-term, were to have serious consequences for the coal industry. It is important that the effect of these before 1914 should not be exaggerated. More significant for the competitive position of coalmining were growing weaknesses on the supply side and it is to a consideration of these that we turn in the section which follows.

Of greatest concern both to contemporaries and later observers was the marked fall in labour productivity which occurred in British coalmining during the last quarter of the nineteenth century. From a peak of 319 tons above and below ground in 1879–83, output per man fell by 20 per cent to reach 257 tons in 1909–13. *Table 2* shows comparative movements in output per man-year in Britain and her chief overseas rivals between the 1870s and 1913.

Table 2: Output per Man-year of Miners Employed Above and Below Ground 1874/78–1909/13
(Annual Average, Tons)

Period	UK	USA Bituminous	Germany	France	Belgium	Austria/ Hungary
1874/78	270	341[a]	209	154[b]	135	NA
1884/88	319	449	269	196	173	180[c]
1894/98	287	511	262	208	174	176
1904/08	283	617	251	194	162	188
1909/13	257	698	256	195	159	190[d]
Percentage Increase (+) or Decrease (−)						
1874/78–1909/13	−5	+105	+22	+27	+18	+8[e]

Sources: Royal Commission on the Coal Industry, 1925: GIBSON F.A. (1922) op. cit., p. 227.
Notes:
a. Figure for 1874 represents only one-fifth of the industry.
b. Relates to 1876/78 only.
c. Relates to 1885/88 only.
d. Relates to 1908/12 only.
e. Increase measured over the period 1885/88–1908/12.

It should be emphasised at the outset that output per man-year provides only a crude indication of differences in coalmining efficiency since it often conceals wide variations in the accessibility and quality of the seams, the organisation of mining and methods of working. However, more precise measurements are not available and at least relative movements over time in output per man offer some guide to changing relationships in productive efficiency between competing nations. Table 2 shows that in both absolute and relative terms, the bituminous mining area of the USA was far in advance of any country in Europe, a reflection both of relatively easy mining conditions and a more rapid adoption of mechanised equipment. Within Europe, Britain maintained a distinct competitive advantage until just before the first world war. It was this that allowed her to produce coal relatively cheaply and thus dominate foreign markets. In part, Britain's greater efficiency stemmed from the adoption of sound mining practice, particularly a rapid expansion in the use of steam power, compressed air and much improved haulage and winding techniques.

One of the most important advances in mining technology in the second half of the century occurred in methods of conveying the coal from the workings of the mine to the bottom of the shaft. Between 1850 and 1880 the practice of moving moderate amounts of coal by manual or horse power generally gave way to the traction of large amounts of mineral by means of ways fitted with ropes actuated by engines. The introduction of both Main and Tail and Endless Rope systems employing steam power significantly increased the amount of coal that could be shifted from the working faces.[22] However the use of steam boilers underground involved constant risk of fire and explosions, with the result that compressed air began to be extensively used underground from 1865. The new form of power was applied not only to haulage but to pumping and cutting machines in use at the longwall faces.[23]

Despite these advances, the retention of a relatively high level of productivity in Britain came to depend on the exploitation of the best and most easily accessible seams. By the last quarter of the nineteenth century, many of these seams were approaching exhaustion. Reserves had been worked earlier in Britain than in most coalfields abroad, with the result that continued development involved deeper working, the extraction of thinner seams and a longer travelling distance from the face to the shaft. The whole process of mining became steadily more difficult and entailed steadily rising costs. In effect the law of diminishing returns was taking its toll, more so than in the USA, Germany or Belgium where exploitation of the coalfields had come later. Despite such conditions, there was an apparent reluctance to mechanise the processes of production in Britain. By 1913, 51 per cent of total output was won by machine in the bituminous mining districts of the USA, where seams were generally thicker, flatter, closer to the surface and freer from faults than in coalfields elsewhere in the world. In Belgium 10 per cent was mechanically cut, in Britain 8.5 and in Germany (the Ruhr) a mere 2 per cent.[24]

Mechanisation is, of course, only one of the determinants of productivity growth. Collieries which innovated the new technology in the late nineteenth century did not necessarily become 'efficient'; nor were they guaranteed a relatively high level of profits. Emphasis is placed on mechanical cutting and conveying partly because these were, indeed, the main technical advances but also because data on other aspects of colliery development are almost entirely absent. The relatively slow acceptance of machine mining in Britain contributed directly to the steady erosion of her competitive advantage in world coalmining. Indeed, she was the only country of those specified in Table 2 to lose ground in output per man-year over the whole period. A number of factors have traditionally been held responsible for the reluctance of British collieries to innovate mechanical equipment. Prominent among these have been a reluctant and largely uneducated work-force and the apathy, conservatism and lack of technical education of colliery management who failed to keep abreast of, or perhaps improperly understood, the latest techniques known and extensively used in the United States.[25] As a result, the factor-mix employed in the coalfields was inappropriate and could not prevent a rapid deterioration in output per man.

However, it is contended here that criticism of management for neglecting the new technology, and of labour for organising a deliberate restriction of output has been over-done. It is undeniably the case that mechanisation was delayed in the British coalfields from the 1880s but there were often good reasons why this should have been so. Again, while the individual miner may have worked less hard after the 1880s than before, there is no evidence to suggest that this was a planned and concerted attempt to limit output. Since they lie at the heart of so many criticisms which have been made of coalmining practice, the following two sections examine the quality and education of those involved in the industry. Attention will be focused mainly on the second half of the nineteenth century in order to consider the extent to which managerial and labour deficiencies were responsible for reversing the long-term trend of rising productivity. The final section broadens the scope of the argument by investigating other factors which adversely influenced output per man. While not exonerating those responsible for the conduct and operation of the industry, the conclusions reached in this section suggest that there were other important forces at work, leading to a long-term decline in the relative efficiency of the British industry.

Allegations that there was a decline from the 1870s both in the dynamism of management and the work-effort of labour are not, of course, confined to coal-mining. Similar charges have been made about the quality of the factors of production, enterprise and labour, across the range of British industry. There is, indeed, an extensive literature on the weaknesses exhibited by both management and workers in this country relative to their counterparts abroad. These are held to have signi-ficantly affected Britain's ability to compete, in this way contributing to the retarda-tion in the rate of growth of output experienced by most of the country's traditional industries. The complex debate which has subsequently developed on these issues lies beyond the scope of this paper.[26] It is sufficient to note here that, in the context of the coal industry, the growing complexity of technology by the middle of the nineteenth century made it increasingly necessary that those in charge of colliery operations should not only possess adequate general education but also be conversant with the latest technical and safety practices. The 1854 Select Committee of the House of Commons on Accidents in Coal Mines made a fundamental contribution to underground safety by urging that a standard should be maintained by all mines in the country.[27] This should take the form of seven 'General Rules' laying out the basic safety requirements which had to be observed. In addition, each *individual* colliery should be required to enforce its own code of 'Special Rules', devised in collaboration with the Home Office, and appropriate to its particular physical characteristics.

By accepting these recommendations, the Mines Act of 1855 made it imperative that colliery managements throughout the country should, as a minimum, possess the ability to read and write. If the rules were to be properly observed, managers must at least have the capacity to read them. For the men, too, these elementary requirements became increasingly necessary, particularly since the number both of 'General' and 'Special' Rules expanded rapidly during the rest of the century. However, possession of the ability to read and write was far from common, not only among the men but also among large sections of the managerial class. This was thrown into sharp relief by the explosion in 1849 at the Darley Main colliery near Barnsley which cost 75 lives. It was found that the agent, upon whom devolved all responsibility for underground operations between the monthly visits of the viewer,[28] possessed virtually no education or experience. He could neither read nor write and in consequence was inadequately equipped to supervise the running of the pit.[29] That this was far from being an isolated case was evident from the repeated warnings of the first inspector of mines, H.S. Tremenheere.[30] He emphasised that a large proportion of the viewers and agents operating the collieries which he visited were incompetent, largely due to lack of proper education. This he regarded as a 'prominent cause' of the accidents occasioned by inadequate ventilation, roof-falls and defective machinery. For instance, the Northumberland and Durham coalfield consisted by mid-century of about 140 collieries, in each of which there was, on average, three subordinate positions of authority and trust filled by 'men from the ranks'. In aggregate, therefore, about 400 such posts existed upon which depended the smooth and efficient functioning of the coalfield. Yet, Tremenheere found that often such jobs were filled due to favour, or through inadequate knowledge of the candidates, many of whom did not possess even the rudiments of an elementary education.[31]

The most ill-regulated and badly managed collieries were to be found in North and South Wales and in Staffordshire; management in parts of Yorkshire, Derbyshire, Lancashire and Scotland was considered only marginally better; but mines in Northumberland, Durham and Cumberland were operated with some semblance of efficiency.[32] The superiority of collieries in the north was largely due to the experience gained, at a relatively early stage, in mining at considerable depths and in coping with a high incidence of inflammable gas. Out of sheer necessity, knowledge had rapidly been acquired in these collieries about the efficient use of different forms of ventilation, the use of machinery and the need for adequate propping.[33]

In other districts, colliery practice remained for the most part extremely backward. Rather than the wilful neglect of management, the chief failing was simply ignorance of what could be accomplished – indeed, already had been accomplished – by many collieries in the north. This was particularly true of ventilation since most overmen, it was alleged, had 'little or no notion of what firedamp actually is, how it arises, or its properties'.[34] Such ignorance was borne largely out of a lack of education. It was necessary to be able to read about use of the latest techniques and practices in relatively efficient collieries in order to determine their suitablilty for use elsewhere. For an overman not to be able to read or write should be considered 'a perfect disqualification for the post'.[35]

The truth was that by the middle of the century management in the majority of districts relied, in their quest for profits, more heavily on exploiting the workforce than on innovating efficient and safe practices in their mines. As the 1842 Children's Employment Commission[36] had shown, an inadequate concern for the health and safety of those working in the pits, long hours and the exploitation of children were common to all coalfields in the country. Although improvements were gradually introduced from that date in the conduct of colliery operations, evasions of the law and the abuse of both adults and children remained widely in evidence.[37] Particularly difficult to control throughout the Victorian era was the operation of the truck and butty systems. Their survival in the nineteenth century can be attributed directly to an unwillingness to condemn the system of contracting *per se* and a failure on the part of the authorities to enforce their own legislation.

The process, started by the Children's Employment Commission of exerting pressure on the Government to accept a larger measure of responsibility for the conduct of the mines, came to fruition in the third quarter of the century. In 1865, the Miners' Petition was submitted to the House of Commons and referred by it to a Select Committee which reported two years later.[38] Along with several other demands, the Petition called for certain minimum standards of competency in mining management. In arguing that accidents in mines were 'mainly caused by a want of skill in agents, overmen and chief managers of mines and collieries, and from lack of diligence or want of care on the part of the subordinate officers', it urged that all mine officers be required to sit a scientific examination and attain a certificate of competence before a mine was placed in their charge. In the short-term, this plea for some evidence of competency found little sympathy. The Select Committee concluded that owners would be unwilling to have their selection of managers controlled in this way; that leaving selection uncontrolled placed greater legal and moral responsibility on owners to make the correct choice; and that no examination could possibly take the place of the owner's personal knowledge of the character and qualities of those he employed.

But these sentiments were brushed aside in the 1872 Coal Mines Regulation Act. Under the provisions of the Act, colliery managers had in future to be registered as holders of a certificate of competence, granted after a State examination. In addition, the men were given certain rights in areas previously regarded as the prerogative of management. Apart from some minor exceptions, payment by weight of coal raised was made universal and workmen were given the right to hold periodic inspections of the mine in which they worked. The Act was a landmark in the development of the industry. It stablilsed and codified mining law for the next 15 years, subsequent legislation simply revising and refining principles which had already been established. The Mines Act of 1887 extended the system of certification by introducing second-class certificates for under-managers. The process was completed by the Acts of 1903 (see below) and 1911 when the system of management certification was thoroughly revised and regulations laid down for the appointment of other mine officials including firemen (otherwise known as examiners or deputies).[39]

A colliery manager, who had to be at least 25 years of age and hold a first class certificate, was required to give personal supervision daily. On those occasions when he was absent the under-manager, or other person with a first or second class certificate, could be placed temporarily in charge but only for a period of up to four months. In addition, no person could manage more than one mine if the *aggregate* number of persons employed below ground exceeded one thousand, or if all the shafts of the mines did not lie within a circle having a diameter of four miles. Where these conditions did not apply, a manager could supervise several small mines, provided he had the permission of the inspector of mines and that an under-manager was appointed to each separate mine.

At the same time, important changes took place in the provision of further educational facilities. As early as 1838, classes in mining engineering had been started at King's College, London, and in the same year the Durham University School of Mines had been inaugurated. Perhaps most important was the creation in 1852 of the North of England Institute of Mining and Mechanical Engineers, the purpose of which was to promote discussion of, and research into, the prevention of accidents in collieries and other aspects of colliery practice. It soon became a respected and influential body, disseminating information on mining to other districts with the object of raising the standard of colliery management. Along with similar institutes later set up in other districts, it formed the Institution of Mining Engineers in 1889. Two years earlier, the National Association of Colliery Managers had been created to encourage the better education and technical expertise of colliery officials.[40]

From the 1880s, there were also growing opportunities for miners with ambition to register for classes in technical and mining education with a view to acquiring certificates of competence. The Technical Instruction Act in 1890, empowering local authorities to provide technical and manual instruction, was followed a year later by the Local Taxation (Customs and Excise) Act. The latter supplied the county, and county borough councils with various sums of money each year to provide for secondary and technical education.[41] As a result, a number of technical schools were established, providing a variety of courses and lectures in coalmining instruction. In Yorkshire, for instance, efforts were made to bring local classes in mining instruction into closer contact with the Coal Mining Department of the Yorkshire College (later Leeds University) and the University College, Sheffield. Moreover, courses in mining practice were provided by the Barnsley Technical School, established in 1896, and shortly after by similar institutions established at

Batley, Dewsbury, Wakefield, Normanton and Castleford.[42]

The provision of courses in mining education was further stimulated in 1903 with the Amendment made to the Coal Mines Regulation Act (1887).[43] Under the terms of the Amendment, the five years of practical mining experience required of those competing for certificates of manager or under-manager, could under certain conditions, be reduced to three. To qualify for this exemption, candidates had to hold a diploma in scientific and mining training after a course of at least two years in an educational institution approved by the Secretary of State or have taken an appropriate degree in an approved university. However, throughout the Victorian era, an intractable problem remained of ensuring that sufficient working men of ability took advantage of the facilities available. On the one hand, evening classes could provide the necessary instruction once the working day, or shift was over; but on the other, great stamina and ambition were required to attend classes regularly after a hard day's work below ground. This problem was made more acute by the passing of the Eight Hour Day Act which introduced, in some districts, the three – rather than two-shift system.

However, the opportunities for working men to acquire managerial status had certainly improved by the end of the Victorian period. They were further enhanced by the creation of the Workers' Educational Association in the early years of the present century to widen the scope of working-class participation in further education. The achievement of these early efforts must not be exaggerated since many miners lacked the ability, inclination or powers of endurance to benefit from the facilities which were provided. But, at the same time, the requirement that both managers and under-managers must hold certificates of competence had important implications. No longer were favouritism or family preference adequate qualifications for managing a colliery. Managers had to be properly certificated and could not, as in the past, depend for their profits on the blatant manipulation of the workforce. In this industry at least, charges of amateurism and neglect, commonly levied against management in other sectors, were to a large extent inappropriate.

Moreover, throughout the second half of the nineteenth century, management in coalmining was subject to an even higher authority in the shape of the mining inspectorate. The number of inspectors increased over the period from 4 in 1850 to 38 in 1906 and to 82 in the years following the passage of the 1911 Mines Act. Their duties and responsibilities grew more or less in line with the complexity of the regulations, in the form of General and Special Rules, which governed the conduct of the industry. By 1911, there had also been a complete reorganisation of the grades of inspectors and their districts. The inspectorate consisted of one chief inspector, 8 inspectors-in-charge, 11 senior inspectors, 32 junior inspectors, 22 sub-inspectors of mines and 8 sub-inspectors of quarries. Impressive though the increase in grades and responsibilities may have sounded, the fact remained that even by the end of the Victorian period there were still not enough inspectors to carry out adequately the tasks demanded of them. They provided invaluable assistance to colliery management, advising and communicating latest ideas and methods, as well as carrying out the supervision of mine-safety as required by law but severe strains had been placed on the system. The Royal Commission which reported in 1909 pointed out that at least one inspection per mine each year had to be undertaken. In practice visits were more frequent, averaging between 2–3 per mine by the early years of the present century.[44] Even this number fell far short of that regarded as necessary by many sections of the mining community. The men, particularly, had for long wished to see a greater frequency of visits and it was urged that each colliery should be thoroughly inspected once per month.[45] Moreover, inspection was undertaken 'by sample', a particular section of the mine being examined and accepted as representative of the whole. This was clearly unsatisfactory; yet adequate inspection of each mine would have required more time than could possibly have been allocated by the existing number of inspectors.

Although far from ideal the inspection of mines, carried out by conscientious and highly qualified officials, at least provided an extra safeguard for those engaged in winning the coal. Management was permitted neither to become complacent nor to neglect safety standards, a feature which had been all too common in the industry before 1850. It was also argued that a greater frequency of visits would entail an undesirable shifting of responsibility for the conduct and safety of mining operations from mine owners and managers to inspectors. The job of the manager was to manage and he should not be able to rely on the opinions of Government inspectors and use these in mitigation if things went wrong.[46] Indeed, it was argued by one representative of the owners that many collieries in his district were already so carefully managed that they were *in advance* of legislation, taking precautions not provided for in existing statues.[47] How far this observation could genuinely be applied to other coalfields of the country is, to say the least, questionable. But there is no doubt that the greater concern which management was forced to show for mine safety, together with the higher standards of mines inspection, acted to improve working conditions above and below ground. This was reflected in a marked reduction in fatality rates during the latter half of the Victorian period. The death rate from accidents per 1,000 persons employed in the coal mines fell from 4.30 in 1851–55 to 1.33 in 1903–12.[48] In relation to other types of work, coalmining still remained a high-risk occupation[49] but at least the Victorian period witnessed a significant improvement in mortality rates arising from accidents in the industry.

Along with the higher standards demanded of colliery management, went an improvement in the general level of education of the men employed in working the coal and in the educational facilities provided for them. If there was some justification for the charges made around the middle of the century that the mining communities were 'brutish' and 'ignorant', with children ill-educated and unwilling to learn,[50] the responsibility for this lay less with the miners themselves than with the industry in which they worked and the attitudes of an intolerant society. Until that date, the education of the miners and their children was almost wholly dependent upon the paternalism of mineowners. Many employers accepted their responsibilities seriously, genuinely wishing to remedy deficiencies in educational provision in their areas.[51] At the same time of course, they recognised that by supplying such facilities, the prospects of higher productivity in their own mines would be enhanced. As colliery workings, especially ventilation, grew more complicated, miners who could neither read nor write became a source of inefficiency and possible danger.[52] Accidents causing loss of machinery, manpower and delays in production cost money; it was important therefore that the men fully understood how equipment should be used and the general principles governing the safe operation of the colliery. Moreover, the provision of educational facilities and other benefits served as a useful bargaining weapon. By withdrawing, or threatening to withdraw, such benefits the owner could often force the men into a more compliant frame of mind.

However, as the 1842 Children's Employment Commission made clear, benevolent owners were by no means common to all coalfields. Indeed, by that time paternalism was in decline, the inevitable corollary of a steady fall in the number of landed coalowners. Many put the working of their minerals into the hands of professional coal and iron-masters. Others made way for new groups of self-made owners and later for joint-stock companies which could more readily raise necessary capital. In many areas, therefore, miners lost an important safeguard which had provided them with some relief from the harsh conditions under which they worked. It is true that education in one form or another was still available in most districts. Sunday schools constituted an important form of part-time education in the first half of the nineteenth century and Voluntary Societies operated, mainly in the industrial areas, to provide formal instruction for working-class communities. In addition, 'enlightened employers' continued to establish and support works schools for the children of their employees. These, along with the colliery schools established in the north of England and in Wales were generally maintained by making a small levy on the wages of employees. From about the middle of the century most factory and mine owners sought government grants through the Voluntary Societies for the upkeep of the schools which they had promoted, in addition to the charges made on wages. Hence, enlightened benevolence was coupled with compulsory contributions and State support to ensure that as far as possible, elementary education was available to those who wished to take advantage of it.[53]

Although playing an important part in the voluntary elementary schools structure of the nineteenth century, such piecemeal measures were, of course, no substitute for an organised system of formal education. Mining communities, isolated and generally regarded with some disdain by the rest of society, tended to be the most educationally deprived. Facilities were inadequate and there was widespread illiteracy among both adults and children. The problem was exacerbated by the fact that in many districts colliers were little concerned about the provision of education for their children. The latter were regarded as supplementary wage-earners because they could serve as trappers or putters in the mine. Indeed, they commonly worked longer hours than adults since trappers, working the ventilation doors in the underground roads, were required to go down the pit with the first and ascend with the last of the miners.

Since the impetus for reform would not come from the industry itself, the State increasingly intervened to establish conditions governing safety, employment and the right of inspection. The work of the 1842 Mines Act, prohibiting the employment below ground of women and girls, and boys of less than 10 years of age, was carried a stage further by the Mines Inspection Act of 1860. Henceforth, children between 10 and 12 years old working in the mines had to possess a certificate allowing them to miss education on the grounds that they could already read and write. Those without a certificate were obliged to attend school for three hours per night, twice a week. However, the Act was difficult to enforce and was constantly evaded. It was expecting too much of children of that age to work an average 12 hour shift exclusive of journeying time (as in the North of England) and then attend school in the evening for three hours. They were simply too weary and fell asleep over their books.[54]

Failure to observe the provisions of the 1860 Act induced strong reaction in the Miners' Petition presented to the House of Commons later in the decade. The Petition deplored the lack of facilities available for the education of miners' children and demanded that boys be prevented by law from descending the mine until they were at least 12 years old. Further, hours of work should be limited to eight per day for all under the age of 14. The Select Committee which considered the Petition heard from virtually all witnesses on the labour side of the industry that boys working in the pits below the age of 14–15 were almost entirely lacking in education. The age limit for boys working underground should be at least 12 and most considered 14 more appropriate.[55] However, strong objections to the Petition and to any tampering with the 1860 Act were raised by the employers' representatives called before the Committee. In the event, the 1872 Coal Mines Act inclined more to the owners' view. Boys below the age of 12 were not prohibited from going below ground. The working shift of boys below the age of 14 was limited to 10 hours and those who did not possess a certificate of ability to read and write were required to attend school for 20 hours in every fortnight. These measures were largely superceded by the Elementary Education Acts of the 1870s, although not until 1887 were boys below the age of 12 legally prevented from going down the pit.[56] By that time, the provision of formal elementary education had removed the need for specific 'education clauses' in mining legislation. Standards of literacy steadily improved and miners' leaders were able to concentrate on other issues.[57] By the end of the century, the educational standard of the work-force was far removed from that of fifty years earlier. The miners had become an articulate and powerful group within the labour movement, increasingly aware of the influence which they could exert at national level through their new national union, the Miners' Federation of Great Britain (MFGB). Based on outright opposition to the sliding-scale system of determining wages, the MFGB was itself a reflection of how far the miners had travelled from the 'brutish' and 'ignorant' group which, a few decades earlier, had been manipulated with impunity by many employers.

To say that the general education of the working classes, and the standards required of management were improving from the 1870s is not to claim that they were high or that the position could be viewed with complacency. Improvements were gradual rather than dramatic and the provision of technical education compared most unfavourably with that of Germany. There was particular concern that the field from which managers could be appointed was unduly narrow. Eligibility for the posts of manager or under-manager depended on five years' practical experience in mining, or three years if the applicant held an approved degree or diploma. It was felt that this unduly favoured men of 'practical experience' at the expense of those of high ability, and good general education, who might otherwise have been drawn into the industry. Indeed, even if highly educated, entry into the managerial side of coalmining was far from easy for those not already having family connections with the industry.[58]

It is also pertinent to ask why, in a period when for the first time qualifications were demanded of management and the quality of labour had improved, productivity in coalmining should have started to decline. Both sides of the industry have, in varying degrees, been held responsible, and these arguments are examined below, but dominating all other influences on output per man, and of particular relevance in the case of an extractive industry, is the law of diminishing returns. As the best deposits are worked out, deeper and thinner seams require an increase in oncost (non-productive) labour for such tasks as timbering, road maintenance, and shifting the coal underground. Inevitably, the increase in non-productive workers will cause aggregate output per man to fall, unless this relationship is upset by technological development and the greater utilisation of capital above and below ground.

It is argued that, in Britain, in the latter part of the Victorian period, little was done to offset the tendency to diminishing returns. Innovation of the new technology in coalmining was at best modest and traditional methods continued to dominate. But the extent to which this can be blamed on a technically inferior (in relation to the USA and Germany) and ill-informed management is open to question. It is true that even though they were faced with increasingly difficult physical conditions, many colliery managers were less than enthusiastic about underground mechanisation. Given a rising and relatively inelastic demand from 1850, profits were generally high: in consequence, many managers were content to leave well alone. Moreover, it had not been fully established by the end of the Victorian period that the mechanical coal-cutter reduced costs of production in the thick seams as well as thin, and management needed to be fully convinced before risking a heavy capital outlay on equipment and the inevitable reorganisation of underground operations.[59] One district, Scotland, *did* respond to the problem of rapidly diminishing returns by more readily accepting the new face technology. Deteriorating physical conditions compelled the greater use of mechanisation in the district.

But what was appropriate for Scotland was not necessarily appropriate for other coalfields. There were often good reasons for the apparent reluctance to innovate the new forms of mechanical equipment.[60] It was in fact precisely the wide variety of physical conditions in the different coal-producing districts which constituted a major stumbling-block to the greater use of machinery. At one extreme, geological conditions were, for instance, extremely difficult in the long-established Lancashire coalfield. With deeper and thinner seams being worked, the coalfield would appear to have been in a situation similar to that of Scotland, and therefore ready for extensive mechanisation. But steeply inclined seams and a high incidence of faulting meant that much of the new technology, at the level of refinement then existing, was impossible to apply. At the other extreme, in South Wales the major factor inhibiting the adoption of face-cutting equipment was simply the ease with which coal could be won by hand. To this should be added that the coal would hardly stand to be cut since mechanical cutters, when applied to the face, were frequently buried by falls. The extremely rapid innovation of face conveyors before 1914 dispels any notion that management in the district was technically inferior or ignorant of the new methods. Rather than complacency or lack of technical expertise the virtual absence of mechanical face-cutters in South Wales indicated that the requirements of the district were totally different to those existing elsewhere.[61]

The other coalfields of Britain were variously placed between these two extremes. The situation can be contrasted to that in the USA where the uniformity of mining conditions (level floors and relative freedom from faults) greatly facilitated the introduction of mechanical methods of working. In Britain, the lack of such uniformity meant not only that it was difficult to devise machines adaptable to the needs of all but that in some areas the use of mechanical equipment was precluded altogether. In addition, mechanisation in this country was beset with technical difficulties. Breakdowns were frequent and repair and maintenance costly and rarely wholly successful. For certain tasks, neither the appropriate materials nor engineering skills were available. The chain-cutting machine patented in Britain in 1856 had little impact on the domestic industry throughout the nineteenth century but was rapidly innovated in the United States where seams were thicker and the coal softer. Another British invention, the compressed air turbine, used as a source of power, was also quickly adopted in the United States but not in this country. American machine tool practice was far in advance of that in Britain and could provide the degree of accuracy necessary in construction.

Finally, the problem of distributing power underground delayed acceptance of face mechanisation in Britain. By the end of the Victorian era, compressed air was still the most important source of power, although it was of little value in seams of two feet or less. In addition, persistent leakages and the high cost of carrying pipes for the air did not encourage management to accept the new technology readily. Even the introduction of electricity below ground did not resolve problems of transmission and an exhaustive code of rules was quickly adopted, restricting the use of the new source of power in firey mines. For similar reasons, there was little enthusiasm for the face conveyor in Britian. Problems of power transmission and the many failures associated with the earliest conveyors ensured that at the close of the Victorian period, the pattern of underground transport had changed little since the introduction of the Main and Tail and Endless rope systems in mid-century.

Hence, there were often valid reasons for the relatively slow introduction of mechanised methods of production. It was already apparant that in *thin* seams, mechanical cutters could reduce labour costs at the face. But the problem of whether this gain was sufficient to offset the capital charges involved in the introduction of such equipment had not yet been resolved. Failure to innovate the new methods more rapidly meant that there was little to prevent the inexorable law of diminishing returns from taking its toll of the industry. Yet a blanket condemnation of management would be inappropriate and unjust. Several districts persevered with traditional methods due to conservatism or complacency and thus contributed to the decline in output per man at national level from the 1880s. But in others, management had good reason to delay and charges of incompetance or inadequate technical expertise are simply not relevant.

Equally, on the labour side of the industry, there is little evidence to support the contention that planned and organised efforts were deliberately made to restrict output.[62] Nor did the men make any concerted attempt to oppose the introduction of machinery. On the other hand, it is undoubtedly the case that in the generation preceding the first world war, miners were working less hard than formerly. In part, this has been associated with the growing strength and militancy of mining trade unionism from the 1880s. By 1900, some 66 per cent of total employees in mining were union members and by 1913 the proportion had reached 80 per cent.[63] A relationship, albeit tentative, had been established between the output of coal and the incidence of unionism. As the number of members rapidly expanded, so productivity in the industry steadily declined. Hence, total output would have been significantly larger in 1913 had the proportion of miners unionised remained the same as in 1900.[64]

In turn, of course, the development of mining unionism owed a great deal to the rapidly rising demand for coal after the 1880s. As noted earlier, domestic prices of coal delivered at market fluctuated widely but the underlying trend from the floor of 1883–87 was decidedly upwards. The bargaining position of labour strongly improved and so too did the price it was able to command.[65] Against a background of steeply rising money and real wages, there is evidence that miners could and did adjust their efforts in accordance with the prevailing levels of remuneration. Information on the level of mining wages is admittedly sketchy but it has been estimated that between 1888 and 1914, hewers employed on piece-work experienced an increase in money wages of some 86 per cent, firemen 70 per cent, putters 78 per cent and underground labourers 88 per cent. Since there was a relatively modest rise in the cost of living over the period, the real gains cannot have been much below these nominal rises.[66] But as real wages rapidly increased, labour productivity tended to move in the opposite direction.

To some extent, this was because miners made an 'appropriate' adjustment to their work-rate. In South Wales, where hewers were paid by the ton of coal produced, they were able in the short-term to determine their own rate of exertion and hence earnings. When wage rates were low and falling, productivity tended to increase to maintain wage levels. Conversely, when wage rates were rising, correspondingly less effort was required to maintain a given level of earnings.[67] Hewers were able, therefore, to adjust their rate of exertion in the short-term in response to financial pressures. More debateable is whether in the long-term they could have sustained a higher intensity of effort and thus a higher level of output per man. On balance the evidence available for South Wales suggests a positive answer. For instance, the rapid increase in voluntary absenteeism, not only in South Wales but also in other coalfields, gave employers growing cause for concern since it clearly had implications for the level of labour productivity achieved in the pits. Before the Eight Hour Day Act of 1908, absenteeism due to all causes reached as high as 10 per cent, well above the 4.5 per cent normally regarded as 'unaviodable'.[68] In both South Wales and Durham for example, the effect of higher wages in bringing about a fall in labour productivity was exacerbated by a rising rate of voluntary absenteeism.[69]

The growing muscle of the mining unions had further implications for labour productivity. It enabled the men to fight successfully in some districts for a reduction in the number of hours worked, although at national level such a reduction was of little consequence before the passing of the 1908 Eight Hour Day Act. More important was the growing militancy of mining unionism, reflected in the total number of working days lost through disputes. Figures provided by the Labour Department of the Board of Trade, created in 1893, show that between that year and 1900 coalmining accounted for no less than 60 per cent of the total days lost in British industry due to disputes, this falling to 53 per cent between 1901 and 1913.[70] In short, the prosperity of coalmining in the latter part of the Victorian period, together with growing union strength, induced, or encouraged, a reduction of work-effort on the part of miners. Given the industry's preference for utilising labour rather than capital in a period of growth, the miner was less fearful of disciplinary action by his employer, thus inclining him to work less industriously.

But the decline in output per man cannot, of course, be attributed solely to the shortcomings of management and labour. By the late nineteenth century, the unplanned and unco-ordinated nature of past development strongly militated against the sustained growth of labour productivity. Inevitably, the best and most easily accessible seams had been worked first with the result that in several of the older coalfields a larger number of collieries had long since passed their peak years of productive efficiency. As coal beds were depleted, the average product of labour was driven down. As late as 1925, the Royal Commission on the Coal Industry showed that almost one-third of miners in Britain were employed in colleries sunk before 1866.[71] As noted, the wide variety of colliery ages and physical mining conditions made the introduction of machinery, at the level of technological refinement then existing, inappropriate in several districts. Unless there were compelling technical reasons, management preferred to increase inputs of labour and move more men to the face rather than risk innovating expensive capital equipment, the returns to which were uncertain.

Indeed, the very existence of a plentiful supply of labour at a price which the industry could afford reduced the incentive to substitute capital for labour. As output expanded in response to the growth of demand, unskilled workers were sucked into coalmining from other industries such as agriculture and building. As a result, between the 1880s and 1913 the labour force in coal doubled, this reflecting the relatively high level of money wages in the industry and the conditions of less than full employment existing in other sectors of the economy. But the corollary was an inevitable dilution of the skilled labour force in coalmining. Even with unchanged attitudes to work on the part of the individual miner, the persistent heavy addition of inexperienced recruits to the industry's labour force could only have reacted unfavourably on productive efficiency.[72]

Finally, output per man was adversely affected by a fall in the proportion of productive underground workers (hewers) in relation to other workers in the industry. While the relative proportion of underground and surface workers remained unchanged between the 1870s and 1913,[73] a significant change occurred in the *composition* of the underground labour force. The share of non-productive, or oncost, underground workers rapidly expanded at the expense of productive underground workers. For instance, in 1889, 50 per cent of total UK mining employment consisted of hewers, 32 per cent of underground oncost workers, and 18 per cent of surface workers. By 1914, the proportions were respectively 40 per cent, 41 per cent and 19 per cent.[74] The increased share of underground oncost workers had inevitable consequences for output per head. Deeper mines and faces further from the pit-bottom meant more men were constantly needed to act as putters, trammers, and for maintenance and safety work. Although output was rising, it was not growing fast enough from the 1880s to compensate for the increased number of men taken on, particularly the increase in underground oncost men.

Hence a number of factors contributed to the long-term decline in productive efficiency of the coal industry. Inadequate and inappropriate educational facilities played their part but much of the responsibility lay beyond the control of both management and men. The earlier development of the British coalfields and the approaching exhaustion of many of the better and more accessible seams resulted inevitably in a tendency to diminishing returns. The level of mechanisation was not sufficient to halt the downward movement of productivity, in part because of the conservatism and disinterest of owners but also because in several coalfields geological conditions rendered the application of the early technology inappropriate. Moreover, the ready availability of labour deterred management in several districts from looking further ahead. But, as noted above, the huge expansion of employment in the industry involved a heavy long-term cost. In several ways, it contributed to, and accentuated, the decline in output per man-year.

What the industry required, despite the prosperity of the late Victorian period, was a strong measure of reorganisation. A greater emphasis should have been placed on coalfields of more recent origin, with labour and capital concentrated on newer and more productive seams. As the MFGB pointed out in its submission to the 1925 Royal Commission, rather than the personal shortcomings of those who managed the industry the root of the problem lay with the system within which they worked.[75] The time was not yet ripe for the State either to encourage the necessary reorganisation of the industry or to change the environment within which it operated. In the meantime, mineowners and miners had to come to terms with the fact that they were living in an old country and working in coalfields past their prime from which the best pickings had long since been taken.

Notes and References

1 See among others HYDE, C.K. (1974) 'Technological Change in the British Wrought Iron Industry 1750–1815: A Re-Interpretation', *Economic History Review*, second series, Vol. XXVII, pp. 190–206: VON TUNZLEMANN, N. (1970) 'Technological Diffusion during the Industrial Revolution: the Case of the Cornish Pumping Engine', in HARTWELL R.M. (Ed.) *The Industrial Revolution*, pp. 77–98: HILLS, R.L. (1970) *Power in the Industrial Revolut.on*.

2 Transport improvements allowed inland collieries, particularly in the Midlands, Yorkshire and Lancashire, to compete directly for markets with those in Northumberland and Durham. See *House of Commons, Report of the Select Committee on the State of the Coal Trade*, 522, 1836.

3 Mining Association of Great Britain, *Historical Review of Coalmining* (1923); GALLOWAY, R. (1898) *Annals of the Coal Mining and the Coal Trade* (Reprinted 1971), Vol. 1, p. 418ff; House of Lords, *Report from the Select Committee Appointed to Inquire into the Best Means of Preventing the Occurrence of Dangerous Accidents in Coal Mines*, 613, 1849.

4 POLLARD, S. (1965) *The Genesis of Modern Management* p. 79.

5 From about 2.6 million to 10.1 million tons.

6 JEVONS, S. (1915) *The British Coal Trade* (reprinted 1969), Kelley (USA), p. 676.

7 TAYLOR, A.J. (1968) 'The Coal Industry' in ALDCROFT D.H. (Ed.) *The Development of British Industry and Foreign Competition 1875–1914*, London, Allen and Unwin, p. 41.

8 THOMAS, D.A. (1903) 'The Growth and Direction of our Foreign Trade in Coal During the last Half Century', *Journal of the Royal Statistical Society*, Vol. LXVI, p. 454.

9 House of Commons, *Report of the Select Committee on the Causes of the Present Dearness and Scarcity of Coal*, 313, 1873; Mines and Quarries, *General Report with Statistics for 1913 by the Chief Inspector of Mines*, Part III, Cd. 7741, 1914.

10 DEANE, P. and COLE, W.A. (1962) *British Economic Growth 1688–1959*, Cambridge, Cambridge University Press, pp. 329–31.

11 *Statistical Tables Relating to the Production, Consumption and Imports and Exports of Coal in the British Empire and the Principal Foreign Countries in Each Year from 1886–1910*, 284, 1911.

12 For details of trends in the home market, see BUXTON, N.K. (1979) *The Economic Development of the British Coal Industry: from Industrial Revolution to the Present Day*, Batsford, pp. 85–91.

13 Royal Commission of Coal, 1871, Report of Committee E.

14 HAWKE, G.R. (1970) *Railways and Economic Growth in England and Wales, 1840–1870*, Oxford, Oxford University Press, pp. 294–5.

15 JEVONS, *op. cit.*, pp. 692–3.

16 See *Final Report of the Royal Commission Appointed to Inquire into the Subject of Mining Royalties, c. 6980,* 1893.

17 Average money wages amounted to £60 6/- in British coalmining; £47 18/4 in France, £46 13/- in the Saar and £38 16/8 in Belgium. *Royal Commission on Mining Royalties*, 1893.

18 *Royal Commission on the Coal Industry* (1925), Cmnd. 2600, Vol. III, (1926).

19 *Royal Commission of Mining Royalties*, 1893.

20 Including British India, Canada, Australia, New Zealand and South Africa.

21 *House of Commons, Statement showing the Coal Production, Consumption and Number of Persons Employed in the Principal Countries of the World from 1883 to 1893, 317, 1894; Statistical Tables Relating to the Production, Consumption etc of Coal in each Year from 1886 to 1910*, 284, 1911; GIBSON, F.A. (1922) *The Coalmining Industry of the United Kingdom, the Various Coalfields thereof, and the Principal Foreign Countries of the World* pp. 213ff.

22 JEVONS, *op. cit.*, pp. 215–8.

23 For a discussion of the importance of longwall methods of working see evidence of T. Evans, Inspector of Mines, to Committee C on 'Waste in Working' *Royal Commission of Coal 1871, General Minutes and Proceedings of Committee A–E, c. 435–1*, 1871; JEVONS *op. cit.*, pp. 202–6 and 208–9.

24 *Royal Commission on Coal 1925, Minutes of Evidence* (1926); League of Nations *Memorandum of Coal*, Vol. 1, pp. 39–40; International Labour Office, *The World Coal-Mining Industry*, Vol. 1, Economic Conditions (1938) pp. 106–10.

25 Although according to one observer, the quantity and quality of resources rather than differences in capital inputs wholly explain the differential between American and British productivity – See McCLOSKEY, D.N. (1971) 'International Differences in Productivity? Coal and Steel in America and Britain before World War I' in McCLOSKEY, D.N. (Ed.) *Essays on a Mature Economy: Britain after 1840*, London, Methuen, pp. 289–95.

26 For details, see among others ALDCROFT, D.H. (1964) 'The Entrepreneur and the British Economy,

1870–1914', *Economic History Review*, second series, Vol. XVII, pp. 113–30; PAYNE, P.L. (1974) *British Entrepreneurship in the Nineteenth Century*, Macmillan; McCLOSKEY D.N. and SANDBERG, L.G. (1971) 'From Damnation to Redemption: Judgments on the Late Victorian Entrepreneur', *Explorations in Economic History*, Vol. IX, pp. 89–108; ALFORD, B.W.E. (1977) 'Entrepreneurship, Business Performance and Industrial Development', *Business History*, Vol. XIX, pp. 116–33; COLEMAN, D.C. (1973) 'Gentlemen and Players', *Economic History Review*, second series, Vol. XXVI, pp. 92–116.

27 *House of Commons, Fourth Report from the Select Committee on Accidents in Coal Mines*, 325, 1854.

28 Until late in the nineteenth century, colliery managers were known as viewers. In general, they fulfilled a wide variety of roles, including that of manager, engineer and surveyor. Where an undertaking consisted of several pits, there would usually be only one viewer for the whole undertaking, but an overman or agent, for each pit. These undertook the day to day operation of the mine.

29 *House of Lords, Report from the Select Committee of the House of Lords Appointed to Inquire into the Best Means of Preventing the Occurrence of Dangerous Accidents in Coal Mines*, 613, 1849.

30 Tremenheere acted as inspector of mines under the provisions of the 1842 Mines Act from 1843 until 1859. He was, indeed, the only inspector until four additional posts were created under the Mines Act of 1850 (subsequently raised to six in 1852).

31 *Report from the Select Committee of the House of Lords, 1849, Minutes of Evidence.*

32 See *Annual Reports of Inspectors of Coal Mines to HM Secretary of State*, HMSO; evidence of Sir H.T. De la Beche, Director of the Museum of Practical Geology in London, *Report from the Select Committee of the House of Lords, 1849, Minutes of Evidence.*

33 *Report by Matthias Dunn, Inspector of Coal Mines, to HM Secretary of State*, HMSO 1851.

34 Evidence of Sir H.T. De la Beche, *op. cit.*, Firedamp (methane gas) was the miner's chief enemy since it could give rise to instant explosions.

35 *Ibid.*

36 *First Report of the Commissioners for Inquiring into the Conditions of Employment of Children in the Mines*, 380, 1842.

37 LEWIS, B. (1971) *Coal Mining in the Eighteenth and Nineteenth Centuries*, Harlow, Longmans, pp. 59–60; Galloway, *op. cit.*, II, p. 152.

38 *House of Commons, Report from the Select Committee Appointed to Inquire into the Operation of the Acts of Parliament for the Regulation and Inspection of Mines*, 496, 1867.

39 The Act also removed much of the danger commonly associated with the butty system by making the owner, rather than the contractor, legally responsible for providing all necessary materials, such as pit props, and for employing such firemen and other officials as were necessary for the safety of the mine.

40 GRIFFIN, A.R. (1977) *The British Coalmining Industry: Retrospect and Prospect*, Moorland, p. 42.

41 For details of the effects of these measures in Yorkshire, see NEVILLE, R.G. (1976) 'The Yorkshire Miners and Education, 1881–1930', *Journal of Educational Administration and History*, Vol. IX, pp. 30–7.

42 *Ibid.*, p. 32.

43 By 3 Edw. 7, *c.* 7.

44 *Second Report of the Royal Commission on Mines*, Cd. 4820, 1909.

45 JEVONS. *op. cit.*, pp. 436–444.

46 See the evidence of Mr. George Hollingworth and Mr. William Maurice, appearing on behalf of the National Association of Colliery Managers, and Mr. Evan Williams, representing owners in the western district of South Wales. *Minutes of Evidence Taken before the Royal Commission on Mines*, Vol. IV, Cd. 4667, 1909.

47 *Ibid.*, evidence of Evan Williams.

48 *Second Report of the Royal Commission on Mines, 1909; Mines and Quarries, General Report with Statistics for 1913 by the Chief Inspector of Mines*, Part 1, Divisional Statistics, Cd. 7452, 1914.

49 HALDANE, J.S. (1923) 'Health and Safety in British Coal Mines', in *Historical Review of Coal Mining*, Mining Association of Great Britain.

50 *Reports of the Commissioner Appointed to Inquire into the State of the Population in Mining Districts*, 1850 and 1855.

51 DUCKHAM, B.F. (1970) *A History of the Scottish Coal Industry, Vol. 1, 1700–1815*, Newton Abbott, David and Charles, pp. 283ff; *House of Commons, Second Report of the Select Committee on Accidents in Coal Mines, Minutes of Evidence*, 258, 1854. See particularly the evidence of George Elliot, agent of the Marquis of Londonderry.

52 BENSON, J. (1970) 'The Motives of Nineteenth Century Colliery Owners in Promoting Day Schools', *Journal of Educational Administration and History*, Vol. III, p. 16.

53 EVANS, L.W. (1971) *Education in Industrial Wales 1700–1900*, Avalon Books, pp. 169–70.

54 Evidence of Thomas Burt, *Report from the Select Committee Appointed to Inquire into the Operation of the Acts for the Regulation and Inspection of Mines, with Minutes of Evidence*, 431, 1866.

55 See among others the evidence of T. Burt, B. Owen and J. Wilkins, respectively miners from the Northumberland, Staffordshire and Nottinghamshire district. *Report from the Select Committee Appointed to Inquire into the Regulation and Inspection of Mines, Minutes of Evidence*, 431, 1866; also 496, 1867.

56 The limit was subsequently raised to 13 by the Mines (Prohibition of Child Labour Underground) Act, 1900.

57 According to one authority, major literacy improvement did not have to await public (government) initiative. Rather, improvement had steadily been taking place under a mixed private and public school system from the 1830s. WEST, E.G. (1978) 'Literacy and the Industrial Revolution', *Economic History Review*, second series, Vol. XXXI, pp. 378–83.

58 *Royal Commission on the Coal Industry* (1925), p. 190.

59 TAYLOR, A.J. (1961) 'Labour Productivity and Technological Innovation in the British Coal Industry, 1850–1914', *Economic History Review*, second series, Vol. XIV, pp. 60–2.

60 The following paragraphs are drawn largely from BUXTON, N.K. (1979), *The Economic Development of the British Coal Industry: from Industrial Revolution to the Present Day*, Batsford, pp. 112–20.

61 WALTERS, R. (1975) 'Labour Productivity in the South Wales Steam Coal Industry', *Economic History Review*, second series, Vol. XXVIII, pp. 296–7; BUXTON, N.K. (1970) 'Entrepreneurial Efficiency in the British Coal Industry Between the Wars', *Economic History Review*, second series, Vol. XXIII, pp. 483–4.

62 *Royal Commission on the Coal Industry* (1925), pp. 115–6, 120–1.

63 In absolute terms, membership of the MFGB rose from 38,000 in 1888 to about 360,000 by the turn of the century and to almost 900,000 by 1920.

64 PENCAVEL, J.H. (1977) 'The Distribution and Efficiency Effects of Trade Unions in Britain', *British Journal of Industrial Relations*, Vol. XV, pp. 140–5.

65 The extent to which rising real wages generated an increase in union membership or conversely, whether the expansion of membership was responsible for a rise in real wages, lies beyond the scope of this paper. But see POLLARD, S. 'Trade Unions and the Labour Market, 1870–1914' *Yorkshire Bulletin of Economic and Social Research*, Vol. 17, (1965), pp. 109–11; PENCAVEL (1977), *loc. cit.*, pp. 142–3.

66 GRIFFIN, *op. cit.*, p. 79.

67 WALTERS, *loc. cit.*, pp. 288–92.

68 *Royal Commission on the Coal Industry* (1925), p. 183.

69 TAYLOR *loc. cit.*, p. 54.

70 The total number of working days lost through disputes is an aggregate of days lost in building, metal manufacture, engineering and shipbuilding, clothing, transport and mining and quarrying. MITCHELL, B.R. and DEANE, P. *Abstract of British Historical Statistics*, (1971), p. 72.

71 *Royal Commission on the Coal Industry* (1925), Vol. III, p. 175.

72 TAYLOR (1968), *op. cit.*, pp. 50–1.

73 Surface workers commonly accounted for about one-fifth of the total.

74 Calculated from *Mines (Hours of Labour), Return Showing the Average Number of Hours and Days Daily and Weekly Worked by Men and Boys from Bank to Bank in and About Mines in the UK*, 284, 1890: GIBSON, *op. cit.*, pp. 140–3.

75 *Royal Commission on the Coal Industry* (1925), p. 113.

Iron and Steel

J.K. Almond

Introduction

To a considerable extent the Victorian period in Britain is synonymous with the AGE OF IRON, many public and domestic objects being based upon the material. The period also saw the introduction of the allied AGE OF STEEL, the expanding engineering industries of the time being founded upon iron, but becoming more and more dependent on bulk steel; steam engines for winding and draining mines, textile machinery, ships to carry the increasing volume of trade goods, every aspect of the railways, all were enabled to meet the fresh demands made upon them by calling on iron and steel. During the first half of the nineteenth century, it was in Britain that the major proportion of the world's iron was made and improvements in working efficiency were developed. In the decades after 1850 it was also in Britain that there occurred some – but by no means all – of the innovations which enabled steel to take its place as the world's most important engineering material.

As far as iron and steel were concerned, the Victorian period was an exciting time of great activity and expansive development; although, by contrast, it also included occasions when depressed trading conditions brought financial misery, forcing the closure of plants and facing hundreds of employees with destitution. At times of relative prosperity, the achievements of the iron-and-steel industry could be regarded as reflecting the vigour and success of the British Empire. However, by the close of the period the image unfortunately had become somewhat tarnished, for critics could point to the following adverse features of the British industry:

    (i) it had failed to keep pace with world demand;

   (ii) it permitted other countries to sell iron-and-steel items in traditional British markets, including even Britain herself; and

  (iii) it was in a far-from-flourishing condition, whether seen from the viewpoint of management, of capital, or of equipment.

The validity of these criticisms is discussed in the following sections. First, however, it seems desirable to outline the nature of the materials which the industry was producing: the chief commodities were pig iron, wrought iron, and bulk steel.

The industry's materials

Among the significant factors governing iron-and-steel production, the nature and availability of the raw materials are of primary importance. In the earlier part of the nineteenth century Britain was fortunate to possess deposits of both ironstone and coal which were adequate to meet the prevailing demand for pig iron. By smelting the ore with coal (in the form of coke) in a suitable vessel supplied with air – i.e. a blast furnace – crude liquid iron could be drawn off from the bottom portion and run into moulds. If the iron solidified into the shape desired for some particular purpose, the product was called *cast iron*; on the other hand, if the blast-furnace iron was simply cooled into bars for subsequent re-heating and treatment elsewhere, the result was *pig iron*. Cast iron, cheaply produced, was the major material used for the new structures and machinery of the earlier part of Victoria's reign: it possessed decided advantages over available alternatives such as wood and stone. Cast iron's disadvantages, however, were that it could not be hammered, bent, or squeezed to a new shape – e.g. to form the plates for steam boilers – and it was weak when loaded in tension, as numerous failures to engine beams and bridge segments came to testify.

To obtain iron with improved qualities, the pig metal resulting from the primary smelting furnaces could be treated further at high temperature. In the period up to 1870, and indeed for some considerable time afterwards, this was done by 'puddling', maximum British output being achieved in 1882. The result from the puddling furnaces, after squeezing, was *malleable iron*. By further working and manipulation by machinery, the iron could be persuaded to adopt the desired product shape: in this way *wrought-iron* plates for boilers and ships' hulls, rails for railways, and rods for anchor chains and various other engineering purposes could be produced. In contrast with the crude cast iron, wrought iron was strong in tension and it was ductile; it was, however, costly for to make it involved the expenditure of substantial quantities of coal and manpower.

At the beginning of Victoria's reign, *steel* was known as an expensive material, obtainable in small bulk and used to make the cutting edges of knives, swords, scissors and chisels, as well as the springs of clocks and carriages. A large proportion of the country's total steel-making capacity was to be found concentrated in the neighbourhood of Sheffield, where it had been growing strongly from *circa* 1800, using as starting material high-grade iron bars imported from Scandinavia. (In the eighteenth century, a fair proportion of Britain's small production of cementation steel, made from similar iron, had been prepared in several small works near to the Tyne.)[1]

One of the most important achievements of the nineteenth century was the discovery of cheaper ways than puddling for refining pig iron to yield material with equivalent desirable mechanical properties. Such metal was called *steel*, although it differed substantially from the older material known by the name (and 'ingot iron' was perhaps a more-accurate designation for the new material which some preferred). It was from *circa* 1860 that bulk steel started to become available for engineering purposes. By the end of the century, of the British pig iron made, more than one-half was being refined to steel, with a further 12 or 15 per cent being treated by puddling to yield wrought iron; the balance was used for founding objects of cast iron. By this time, too, for special purposes such as armour plate, a certain amount of steel with modified properties was being produced by addition of alloying agents.

Production trends and the changing scale of the industry

Plenty of evidence concerning the declining predominance of the British iron-and-steel industry in world markets can be obtained from curves such as those of *figure 1* (for pig iron) and *figure 2* (for steel), which show the proportion of world output contributed in any particular five-year period. For both pig iron and steel the trends are similar: before *circa* 1870 the British share of world production was close to one-half but as time moved on so the proportion contributed became less. At the end of Victoria's reign, British pig-iron output amounted to rather more than one-fifth of the world total, whereas steel production accounted for a somewhat-smaller fraction. By the 1920s, British output of both commodities had fallen to only one-tenth of world out turn.

In contrast with the British performance, output of pig iron in Germany showed

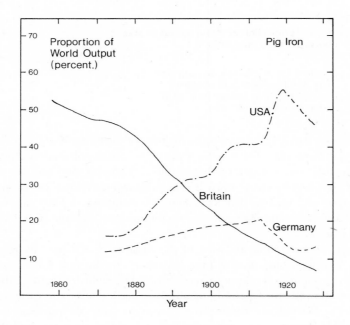

Fig. 1
British proportion of world output of pig iron,
between 1860 and 1930.

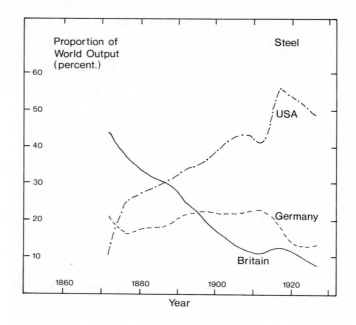

Fig. 2
British proportion of world output of steel,
between 1870 and 1930.

Figures 1 and 2 based on data given by
T.H. Burnham and G.O. Hoskins
Iron and Steel in Britain 1870-1930
Allen & Unwin, (1943) 275

a more buoyant trend, at any rate up to the time of the Great War (1914–18), while the USA was responsible for ever-increasing proportions of world output. British steel production was exceeded by that of the USA around 1887 and was overtaken by that of Germany by about 1895. It is an inescapable fact that the proportion of world output provided by Britain declined throughout the last quarter of the nineteenth century – and the trend was to continue through the twentieth century to the present day.

However, a more-optimistic view of the situation is obtained by plotting the variation of British output with time (*Figure 3*). In the first forty-five years of Victoria's reign, pig-iron output increased by nearly eight-fold; although pig-iron production showed some periods of absolute decline after the early 1880s, the quantity of steel produced continued to rise right up to the post-war depression *circa* 1920. (Moreover, from 1930, the British yield of steel resumed its former upward direction, to exceed 20×10^6 tonnes in some years after 1955, compared with a world output of the order of 500×10^6 tonnes.) Growth in pig-iron production during the Victorian period is summarised in *Table 3*, while in *Table 4* are

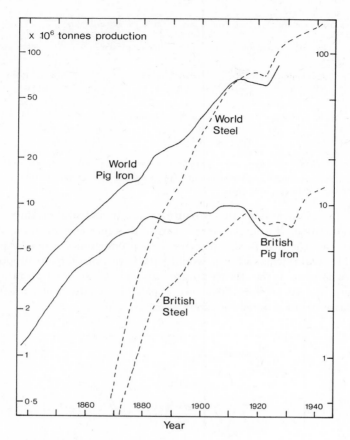

Fig. 3
Iron and steel output trends; Britain and the world.

Table 3: Pig iron production in 1837, 1883, and 1895–99

Country	1837 (30)		1883 (30)		1895–99 (31)	
	tonnes/yr	prop'n of total	tonnes/yr	prop'n of total	tonnes/yr	prop'n of total
Britain	1,140,000	41%	8,650,000	40.5%	8,800,000	26%
USA	300,000	11%	4,700,000	22 %	10,800,000	32%
Others	1,350,000	48%	8,000,000	37.5%	14,100,000	42%
Total	2,790,000		21,350,000		33,700,000	

(for figures relating to 1837 and 1883) BELL, I.L. (1887) and WARD, T.H. (Ed) 'The iron trade and its allied industries', in *A Survey of Fifty Years of Progress*, Vol. 2, London, Smith, Elder and Co., p. 198.
(for 1895–99 figures) BURNHAM, T.H. and HOSKINS, G.O. (1943) *Iron and Steel in Britain 1870–1930*, London, George Allen and Unwin, p. 275.

Table 4: Growth in production of pig iron, wrought iron, and bulk steel outside Britain

Years	Pig-iron production		Wrought-iron prod'n		Steel prod'n	
	(world minus Britain)	prop'n of total	(world minus Britain)	prop'n of total	(world minus Britain)	prop'n of total
1870–74	7.1×10^6 tonnes	52%	4.4×10^6 tonnes	63%	0.56×10^6 tonnes	56%
1880–84	12.0	59%	6.1	70%	3.75	67%
1890–94	18.5	71%	6.7	77%	9.8	75%
1900–04	34.5	80%	3.7	79%	28.2	85%

(derived from Burnham, T.H. and Hoskins, G.O. (1943) *Iron and Steel in Britain in 1870–1930*, London, George Allen and Unwin, pp. 275, 320).

presented figures quantifying the proportions of iron-and-steel products that were made outside Britain during the last 30 years of the nineteenth century.

Clearly, it is true that British iron-and-steel production did not keep up with the growing world demand but it would have been ridiculous to suppose that it might have done so. As the century progressed, a number of other countries became increasingly able to produce their own expanding requirements, together with varying quantities of material for export sales (*see figure 4*).

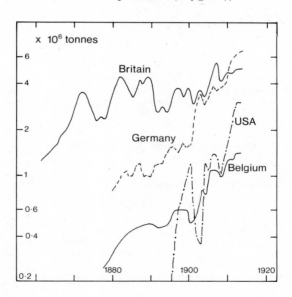

Fig. 4
Levels of national Iron-and-Steel exports, 1875–1913.

Based on T.H. Burnham and G.O. Hoskins:
Iron and Steel in Britain 1870–1930
Allen & Unwin, (1943) 276-77

British performance in world markets

As has been already stated, in the earlier years of the Victorian period, British output of pig iron amounted to nearly one-half of the world total, and it was in Britain that there took place much of the technical development by which blast-furnace performance was improved. This activity was a natural accompaniment to the fact that Britain was the industrial leader of the world and without iron the newly-required machines could not have been constructed. The iron industry met the new demands made on it handsomely and up to *circa* 1870 'anyone with command of coal and iron could count on gaining a fortune'.[2] More than anything else, it was the building of railways which caused the demand for larger quantities of iron; conveniently, this demand did not arise simply within Britain's own confines but it also led to increasing exports to the continent of Europe (including Russia), and to North America (later to South America). Cast iron, puddled iron and then the new bulk steel – all were required for railway-building. In these earlier years, before 1870, the other significant producers of iron included Belgium, France, Germany and the USA. In Belgium a part, at least, of the iron industry had been started with British labour and British business knowledge by William and John Cockerill at Seraing. In the USA, the iron industry was built up largely using workers and engineers from Britain and other parts of Europe.

During the first two-thirds of the nineteenth century the iron-and-steel industry of Britain enjoyed favourable trading conditions, both at home and abroad, and exports exceeded 1×10^6 tonnes *circa* 1850.[3] In the 1860s, there was considerable satisfaction that exports to the continent and to the USA were at high levels, providing scope for further expansion of plant and equipment, and by 1871 exports amounted to 3×10^6 tonnes, mostly associated with the phenomenal growth in world railways. By the early 1880s, exports temporarily reached new heights of more than 4×10^6 tonnes, as the British trade received some further encouragement by way of orders from the USA (*figure 4*). However, these were to be the last from that quarter: in the event they persisted for only a few years – long enough to encourage British producers into thinking they had a revival on hand, only then to dash their hopes. By any standards, the British exportation of iron and steel was on a big scale, and up to the years around 1880 it accounted for three-quarters of world exports. By the early 1890s, this proportion had dropped to between 50 and 60 per cent and after 1901 it fell to less than one-half. This marked change in the relative predominance of British exports in world trade was brought about by the substantial increases that occurred in exports from Germany (from about 1880), and from the USA (after 1895), with those from Belgium contributing to a lesser extent. In spite of the increased competition, however, British exports dropped below 3×10^6 tonnes in only four years in the twenty-year period 1880–1900 while, in the years between 1906 and the onset of World War 1, iron-and-steel goods sent abroad reached new high levels of more than 4.5×10^6 tonnes.

It was the recessions in trade which caused the alarm and led to the disorganization of the industry – in the mid-1870s, in the early-1880s and again after 1889. During this latest falling-off in demand, British exports to the Empire, to South America and to the Far East dropped by one-half, from just over 2×10^6 tonnes (in 1889) to 1×10^6 tonnes (in 1894).[4] Although the recessions were of world-wide effect and were not confined to the iron-and-steel industries, they tended to hit the British industry with particular severity. Various causes were responsible for bringing about the substantial change in the outlook for British trade. First and foremost, the producers in other countries became better able to meet their own home demands for metal; especially was this so in Germany and the USA. Besides this, once these producers had supplied the needs of their home markets, they turned to exporting. The pressures to export varied with the extent of local consumption so that in some periods there came considerable incentive to export in order to keep productive capacity occupied.

From this situation there grew the economic system of 'dumping', under which materials were sold in export markets at prices considerably lower than those for which the same goods were sold in their countries of origin. (The Scottish-American entrepreneur, Andrew Carnegie, writing at the end of the century, pointed out that, to the detriment of the US industry, British traders had been unscrupulous 'dumpers' of iron goods when it was young and defenceless.[5]) During the 1890s and early 1900s, there was formidable evidence that iron-and-steel goods were being 'dumped' by producers in Germany and the USA. Whatever the relationship may have been between the cost of production and the price of selling, these foreign materials competed successfully in markets that had formerly been dominated by the British – i.e. in the imperial markets of India, Canada and Australia, as well as in South America.

What was even more damaging for British morale, foreign iron and steel had little difficulty in gaining entry to this country, for here there were no import restrictions or financial levies to contend with. As a result, steel girders from Belgium were incorporated into British structures, and steel plates from the USA were employed in the building of British ships. Taking into consideration the welfare of all sections of British industry which depended upon iron or steel as their raw materials – e.g. shipbuilding and the various forms of engineering – there were advantages in the importation of such foreign metal: price-wise the iron or steel was likely to be competitive with the home-produced alternatives and quality-wise it might be more reliable. Imports also performed useful functions by keeping down the prices of home-produced materials, and encouraging the industry to meet the needs of its customers.

One group of factors which influenced selling prices was connected with the costs of raw materials (including their transport to the iron-and-steel works), and of transport of the finished items to market. During the years up to 1880, Britain was in a favourable position compared with her possible competitors, for coal was at least as cheap in this country as in any other, and ore suitable for ironmaking, including puddling to malleable or wrought iron, was adequately available. Moreover, the new material, bulk steel, during the first twenty years of its existence – from 1860 to 1880 – required for its manufacture a grade of pig iron which was free from the troublesome element phosphorus; such iron was produced in Cumbria from the high-grade hematitic ore that occurred there, while in other districts –

notably Cleveland and South Wales – suitable hematitic ores were imported from North-Western Spain. At the German ironworks' sites such imported ores were more costly.

After 1880, and the British demonstration of how phosphorus could be success-fully eliminated from the metal during steelmaking, the pattern of raw-material costs changed substantially, as the German producers were able to draw on the iron deposits of Lorraine (which had been obtained from France in 1871) with consequent lowering of their expenses.

Concerning the costs involved in distributing the products to market, British iron-and-steel makers came to believe that railway freights in this country were exorbitant and they pointed to the more-favourable treatment enjoyed by their rivals abroad. As Duncan Burn (1961) noted later, however, against the cheaper rates (per ton mile) which operated elsewhere there should be set the degree of service provided by the railway company.[6] In Britain, more than in other steel-producing countries, the railways were involved in handling small consignments from congested works' sidings, and these goods were conveyed over relatively-short distances. For delivery to export markets, transport by sea was necessary. Here again, during the earlier part of Victoria's reign, Britain was favourably situated in command of much of the world's shipping and with few rivals. But towards the end of the century the situation had changed, with other nations (such as the USA) taking a significant fraction of the ocean trade. Rather than despatching iron-and-steel goods directly from a British port to their overseas destination, there were occasions when it was said to be cheaper to send them first to Antwerp, for transhipment into foreign vessels which charged lower freight rates for carriage to India.[7] All of these features of transport had a bearing on the competitiveness of British iron and steel in world markets.

Adverse trading tariffs

Another factor – and a major one – which affected the British industry adversely in the latter part of the nineteenth century was the existence in many other countries of tariff barriers, while Britain herself had none. These barriers safeguarded and promoted the industries of Britain's competitors, but throughout the second half of the century Britain believed in free trade. This allowed items of iron and steel to be imported without restriction. Such imports came, notably, from Belgium, Germany and (later) the USA at the same time that both of the latter countries operated tariffs which discouraged imports from Britain.

During the earlier part of the nineteenth century, the USA had been a great importer of British goods, which included pigs and castings of crude iron and bars, nails and chains of wrought iron.[8] In 1862 the first steel rails to be laid in the USA were imported from Britain[9] and in the same year one Pittsburgh maker of crucible steel imported 'several hundred English workmen' to ensure success with a big new plant.[10] Only two or three years later, the first American Bessemer steel was made and, during the 1880s, open-hearth steelmaking began to gain ground. By the 1890s, the USA had begun to be an exporter, sending iron-and-steel goods into British markets. US exports of steel and its manufactures, *circa* 1899, were valued at $119,000,000.[11]

In the USA in 1891 the McKinley tariff imposed a duty on imported tinplate in order to foster the growth of an indigenous industry. At that time, most of the USA's capacity consisted of 'dipperies' which tinned imported blackplate. Some of these plants had been built by Welsh manufacturers and were worked with Welsh labour but, as a result of the tariff, Welsh exports of tinplate to the USA fell by 100,000 tonnes a year and the loss of this market had serious effects in the Welsh industry.[12]

In Germany, ironmakers prevailed upon Bismarck in 1879 to re-impose tariffs – that on pig iron being set at around £0.50 a tonne. From that date, the entire German iron-and-steel industry was protected.[13] The principle of unrestricted trade that prevailed in Britain throughout the second half of the nineteenth century was called in question by a minority of those who participated in the Royal Commission on the Depression of Trade in 1886. In the wider industrial sphere, a number of manufacturers naturally believed that they profited from a system of free trade for it meant they could obtain their requirements of steel and iron at lower prices than would otherwise have been the case. Viewed from inside the British iron-and-steel industry, however, the heavy importation of goods from abroad – particularly in the 1890s – was serious and, in certain circumstances, it was calamitous to individual proprietors. Yet even so, among those in the industry, there does not appear to have been any appreciable body of opinion in favour of curbing the flow of damaging imports by the imposition of tariffs. The majority view in favour of free trade held, in spite of the fact that Britain's industrial competitors – Germany and the USA – sheltered behind substantial tariff walls.

Shortly after 1900, Joseph Chamberlain headed a campaign for a return to tariff protection, and as a consequence of this a Tariff Commission was set up to enquire into the main sectors of British industry, including iron and steel. In its report, issued in 1904, the Commission recommended modest import duties to protect the British industry, but nothing came of these proposals until much later.

There is no doubt that, by increasing the prices payable for iron-and-steel commodities imported into this country, import tariffs would have afforded some protection to British producers and helped them to combat their economic problems. At the same time, higher prices for steel would *not* have helped other branches of British industry.

The condition of the industry at the end of the Victorian period

The British policy of free trade led to the iron-and-steel industry having a market of smaller size than would otherwise have been the case. At the same time it ensured that, in order to transact any business, selling prices had to be kept at very low levels. Both of these features had the effect of severely restricting the amounts of money available for renewals and fresh installations of plant and as a result the industry fell behind its overseas competitors in efficiency. This unhealthy state became pronounced in the 1890s at just the time that, in other countries, the corresponding industries were being assisted to develop by their protective import tariffs. By the close of the century, it was not only the machinery of British works which had become in need of renewal but the directors of the works as well. The great advances in the British industry had been made in the 1850s, 1860s and 1870s by men of optimism and vigour: men who invested their money and efforts in euphoric confidence that their investments would be handsomely repaid. The slump in demand for puddled iron in the later 1870s showed this to be misplaced trust, as dozens of small firms were forced out of business.

The changed trading conditions of the 1880s and 1890s demanded from the proprietors of iron-and-steel works qualities different to those that had sufficed in the earlier expansive years: more attention needed to be devoted to market conditions, larger sums of money were involved in prosecuting the business and greater technical ability was required by the increased complexity of the equipment used. At the close of the nineteenth century, there was some evidence that the British iron-and-steel industry was directed by old men, at least some of whom were unable to adapt to meet the changed circumstances and most of whom were frightened to take major decisions in the uncertain and hazardous economic climate that prevailed. This conservative outlook by manufacturers was sometimes reflected in their sales methods which contrasted poorly with the helpful, even though aggressive, technique adopted by foreign competitors – in particular by Americans. The British were in the habit of selling iron and steel to customers and taking no more interest in the matter: the makers were ready to supply the relatively small, individual orders for a multitude of items yet unprepared to go part of the way to meet any special requirement the customer might have. In a highly-competitive situation, such attitudes were not helpful to survival.

The changed industrial conditions that required a modified attitude on the part of proprietors and managers also called for qualities in workmen that differed somewhat from those that had been of prime value in the earlier part of the century. As the volume of materials turned out became greater, there was bound to be a shift in emphasis, even in Britain, with the machine usurping the position of the workman. The ability to keep up to the regular pace set by machines – especially by rolling mills – came to have more value than well-placed muscle, while some tasks needed the changed state of mind that came from a familiarity with machinery. In the USA, the chronic labour shortage provided great stimulus to engineers to introduce a high degree of mechanisation into the operations involved in making iron and steel. In the changed climate, the English habit of absenteeism was not helpful to the maintenance of high production efficiencies and in the last quarter of the nineteenth century there was a considerable degree of labour unrest manifested by frequent strikes.

As a legacy of the relatively-long establishment of the British iron-and-steel industry, much of the plant in existence at the close of the Victorian period tended to be poorly laid out, sometimes adversely situated and unduly fragmented when compared with more-recent works built in other countries. The latter had the advantage of being able to profit from the experience of earlier endeavours. Thus, one of the chief needs of the British industry was rationalisation. To some extent this came about, in the years after 1900, often as the result of sheer economic necessity – e.g. there would occur the merger of several small works into one of more-viable size or the integration of blast-furnace plant with nearby steelworks and rolling mills. It became clear that for greatest economic benefit not only should a plant be 'integrated' on one site, but in addition it required to be favourably situated. The iron-and-steel works needed cheap supplies of good iron ore and coal together with transport facilities whereby its products could be easily placed on the market. The old-established inland sites in Staffordshire, and at the heads of the valleys in South Wales, were at a distinct disadvantage compared with locations close to seaports. (Three-quarters of a century onwards, in the 1970s, the British steel industry was still attempting to come to terms with the economies of situation).

Another of the factors which frustrated the growth of British steel output during the last one-third of the nineteenth century was the conservative attitude taken up by responsible official bodies. Thus, although bulk steel had begun to be available about 1860, it was not until nearly twenty years later, in 1878, that the British Board of Trade sanctioned use of the material for bridges. Within a few years, the world's first major steel bridge was being built to carry the railway across the Firth of Forth, using 54,000 tonnes of open-hearth steel. In the years that followed, bridges were to become one of the main structural applications for steel. In terms of quantities used, shipbuilding was the largest consumer of steel in Britain in the latter years of the nineteenth century. Whilst the construction of naval vessels was controlled by the Admiralty, that of commercial ships was regulated by Lloyd's Register. Lloyd's had first published rules covering the construction of ships of iron in 1855, and in the boom period of the early 1880s shipbuilding was the largest consumer of *iron*, but after 1885 it was *steel* rather than iron which predominated; in each of the years 1889 and 1890, British shipbuilders took 1.2×10^6 tonnes of steel.[14] Although it is true that the Admiralty was prepared to experiment, and had begun to use steel in 1867, both the Admiralty and Lloyd's were cautious in the sanctioning of steel for ship-building purposes. Plates of steel made by the Siemens-Martin (acid open-hearth) method were approved for a wide range of purposes, but use of Bessemer steel was restricted to applications where loading would be relatively light. Basic open-hearth steel was accepted in 1890.

Technical developments

Not only was the scale of the industry greatly increased during the 60 years of Victoria's reign, but the period saw the introduction of considerable technical development. As far as ironmaking was concerned, there occurred a steady incorporation of improvements in order to produce larger quantities of metal at lower unit cost in terms both of manpower involved and of coke needed. Many of these developments took place in Britain. The idea of heating the air that was pumped into the furnace had been patented by the Glasgow gas engineer, Neilson, in 1828: for the following half-century, methods of applying this idea in practice proved fruitful areas for technological development with important economic consequences. Neilson's heated blast was later described as 'a means of developing the national wealth, of equal value with Arkwright's invention of cotton-spinning'.[15] Another major step forward in fuel efficiency, as well as incidentally abating pollution of the surroundings, was derived from the notion of channelling the top gases from the furnaces to good use: this proposal was of French origin but, coupled with the air-blast heating stoves of Whitwell and Cowper, it was from the 1860s applied increasingly to British iron-making situations. During the second half of the century the size of individual blast furnaces increased dramatically.

The technique of refining the crude blast-furnace metal by 'puddling' – re-heating it in small coal-fired furnaces – after 1840 proved not to lend itself to any significant improvements although during the 1870s the process was the subject of extensive experiments which had mechanisation as their aim.

Of very different outcome were the attempts made to obtain *liquid* metal – bulk steel – at the end of the refining process instead of a pasty mixture of metal and slag. In this field, Henry Bessemer's name was, and remains, pre-eminent. Bessemer was a self-made, though literate, businessman/inventor; son of a French immigrant. He stumbled by chance upon his successful, revolutionary new treatment for liquid iron in his London workshop while engaged in the long-standing British occupation of making armaments for sale abroad. Bessemer was crucially aided to practical success by Robert F. Mushet, a metallurgist from the Forest of Dean, and by G.F. Görannsen, a Swedish ironmaster.[16] From 1860, Bessemer's method of making steel spread to all the industrialised countries of the world.

After 1870, however, Bessemer was not alone in being able to offer a way of refining pig iron to metal with good mechanical properties at less cost than by the tedious puddling process. At the Paris Exhibition of 1868 there were shown items of steel made on the 'open hearth' of a reverberatory furnace (of the kind in wide use for puddling) by the brothers Martin at their Sireuil Works. The high temperature which enabled the Martins to achieve liquid metal at the end of the refining operation was obtained by means of the furnace-heating developments of C.W. Siemens and his brother Frederick. A member of a German family and trained in science at Göttingen, C.W. Siemens first came to England in 1843 as the family's representative in selling an electro-plating process[17] but from the 1850s he promoted improved furnaces and the recuperation of heat. Some writers point to Siemens' thorough German training as a definite advantage in enabling him to develop the ideas of heat conservation that had been patented by Stirling, of Scotland, in 1816. However that may be, from 1870, and based on Siemens' work coupled with that of the Martins, the world had available to it a second, alternative method of producing bulk steel.[18] During the 1870s, to make good bulk steel required, as starting material, iron ores low in phosphorus: such ores were only to be found in the minority of known deposits. Ways by which this limitation might be overcome attacted considerable attention from investigators in the later 1870s, in Germany and France as well as in Britain. A solution was produced, in 1879, by two British technologists, Sidney G. Thomas and Percy C. Gilchrist, who developed practical conditions for 'basic' working which were taken up with energy and enthusiasm on the continent where, before the close of the century, they were to lead to Germany's overtaking British steel production. The solution to the phosphorus problem also opened up the way to much wider exploitation of iron deposits in the USA.

The work on the phosphorus problem, unlike the earlier innovations in steel-making, can be clearly linked with the positive value of technological training – indeed, it forms one of the earliest examples of the application of British academic instruction and systematic investigation to the solution of a technological difficulty. At the same time, it is ironic that, by the application of the 'basic process' elsewhere and especially to German plants, the British iron-and-steel industry's economic difficulties in the closing years of the nineteenth century were substantially aggravated. Thomas and Gilchrist had both studied at the Royal School of Mines in London and two other past students of the school, G. J. Snelus and E. Riley, made significant contributions to the successful solution of the problem.

In the rolling and other forms of 'working', which were used to produce the shapes required from puddled iron and ingot steel (plates, rails, angles and girders), there were many minor developments and improvements made in the period 1840–1900, although outstanding innovations were few. Nasmyth's steam-powered hammer was applied to forging from the 1840s, while another notable advance was the introduction of reversible rolling by Ramsbottom of the LNWR Works at Crewe in the mid-1860s. This scheme substantially increased the amount of material that a rolling mill could process, while it decreased the quantity of labour associated with the operation. Outside Britain, there occurred other developments in rolling and working of perhaps equal significance: thus, although British manufacturers did not necessarily lag behind those of other countries, they were not pre-eminent in setting the pace of development.

Not long after bulk steel had been brought within the reach of skilled and energetic makers everywhere, metal with even better properties started to appear from a limited number of sources. The improvements were achieved by adding deliberate amounts of elements, to yield alloy steels. Before 1880, Robert Mushet's 'self-hardening' alloy for cutting tools was an early, and relatively-small-scale example. In the 1880s, in Sheffield, Robert Hadfield introduced the iron – manganese-carbon alloy which was to successfully carry his name. James Riley of Glasgow gave publicity to nickel steels *circa* 1890 for purposes such as ships' armourplate, and in succeeding years both nickel and chrome steels were developed in various countries, including France.[19]

In summary, there was an abundance of technical progress made in the iron-and-steel industries during the Victorian period. While a creditable proportion of this progress stemmed from Britain, the other manufacturing nations – the USA, Germany, Belgium and France – contributed their shares also. Developments in the making of steel, and its subsequent forming to shape, could be considered as international, especially during the last quarter of the nineteenth century.

The place of education in the British iron and steel industry

In the second half of the nineteenth century there crept into the iron and steel industry a marked increase in technology, and with it the need arose for some knowledge of mechanical engineering. The close chemical control that came to be recognised as necessary to maintain the most-efficient production from blast furnaces and from steel-making plant needed knowledge of chemical-laboratory practice for analysis. So there came into being the works' engineer and the works' chemist; the latter, especially, being regarded as an undesirable necessity to be relegated to some obscure corner of the site. As with the 'business' side of the industry, the acknowledged method of entry to any position of authority was by apprenticeship: the apprentice might come straight from school or, alternatively, be a graduate of one of the colleges that offered higher academic instruction. In either case, he would require the financial backing that would enable him to survive during the period of the apprenticeship.

The question of whether British educational facilities were adequate for the industry's needs has been discussed in detail by several writers, and the much-greater provisions available in Germany have afforded a fruitful field for comparison.[20] Limitations of space do not permit any review to be made here. Suffice it to remark that at least one analyst has concluded that in the last years of the Victorian period, despite the meagre opportunities, 'the supply of educational facilities and of trained men matched the demand'.[21] It is possible that better general education would have produced improvements in the efficiency of the industry; on the other hand, there is little indication that the British iron and steel industry either valued or wanted those coming to it with academic technical knowledge.

Facilities for metallurgical instruction

For those who aspired to greater technical knowledge than would result from apprenticeship, formal instruction in metallurgy was offered at the School of Mines in London throughout the second half of the nineteenth century. The professor of metallurgy at the school in the third quarter of the century, Dr. John Percy, MD., produced a textbook in 1864, *The Metallurgy of Iron and Steel*, and was an acknowledged authority, albeit self-made. However, the number of graduates from the School of Mines who played leading administrative parts in the British steel industry was negligible: more important was the influence that past students had, particularly during the last two decades of the century, in the establishment of centres for the teaching of metallurgy in other places. Examples of these Minesmen include: W.H. Greenwood (first professor of engineering and metallurgy at Firth College, Sheffield, 1885–89), Humboldt Sexton (first head of department of metallurgy, Glasgow and West of Scotland Technical College), Thomas Turner (lecturer in metallurgy at Mason College, Birmingham, 1886–94, and first professor of metallurgy in the University of Birmingham, 1902–26), Henry Louis (lecturer in metallurgy and professor of mining at Armstrong College, Newcastle upon Tyne), and A.K. Huntingdon (professor of metallurgy at King's College, London, from 1879 to 1919).

From the 1860s, metallurgy was among the subjects examined and encouraged by the Department of Science and Art, and from 1880 the City and Guilds of London Institute conducted examinations which provided some incentive to local evening classes. However, in general, the steel industry did not give notable support to these endeavours.

Concluding summary and comments

The British iron and steel industry underwent considerable expansion during the sixty years of Victoria's reign, the scale of pig-iron production increasing from a little more than 1×10^6 tonnes a year in 1837 to 8.8×10^6 tonnes in 1895–99. The level of exported material also rose commensurately, from about 180,000 tonnes (in 1837), to more than 3×10^6 tonnes (in the 1890s). Despite this growth, cause for disquiet arose from the fact that, during the same period and beginning on smaller scale, the quantities of iron and steel produced by other countries grew at a much-greater rate. The industry occupied a basic position in the nation's economy but, as with other primary industries, it was entirely dependent upon sales. If difficulties were encountered during the last quarter of the nineteenth century, they were difficulties to a large extent brought about by economic factors and by changed patterns of demand: the British iron and steel industry was a victim of altered circumstances, and it was thwarted by commercial factors, not technological ones.

In order to meet the increasing demands for larger quantities of metal at lower prices and possessing desirable mechanical properties, some notable advances were made in the period 1840–1900. However, in common with many other sectors of the British economy and in spite of the extensive developments that had taken place, at the close of the Victorian period a major proportion of the iron and steel industry remained nepotistic and ignorance-ridden. There were some outstanding exceptions but, in general, the technologist was kept firmly in the background. (Throughout much of British industry this state of affairs was unfortunately to persist into the 1970s, for it is, alas, well-established that the path to responsible industrial positions does not necessarily follow from thorough technological training.)

As a final point, attention may be drawn to certain features which the industry of the 1880s and 1890s exhibited, and which appeared to remain as problems in the British iron and steel industry ninety years later, in the 1970s. These features are: disruptions to orderly production caused by labour unrest; mistakes made and ill-judged decisions and unwise courses of action taken by works' proprietors; the problem of raw materials – particularly the provision of good coke – accompanied by fears of energy shortages; the growing encroachment of foreign-produced goods into the British markets – not only former markets overseas but the British home market as well; and the need (sometimes acted on) to improve efficiency of working by rationalization within the industry. The difficulties that beset the industry towards the end of Victoria's reign did not change with the new century, but nonetheless it seems sad, as well as nationally discreditable, that some disharmonies – symptoms of malaise – have been persisting now for nearly 100 years and still British society has not resolved them for its betterment.

Acknowledgement

The writer is grateful to Dr. S.G. Denner of the British Gas Corporation's Research and Development Division for reading the typescript and for making a number of suggestions for useful improvements; at an early stage, Dr. Denner also drew attention to a comprehensive review published in 1968.[22]

Notes and References

1 BARRACLOUGH, K.C. (1976) Steelmaking before Bessemer: the importance of the north east of England, *Cleveland Industrial Archaeological Society Research Report, No. 1.*

2 SKELTON, H.J. (1927) 'Iron and steel home and export trade', *Iron Coal Tr. Rev., Diamond Jubilee issue*, December, p. 173.

3 CLAPHAM, J.H. (1967) *An Economic History of Modern Britain*, Book 3, Cambridge, Cambridge University Press, (first printed 1932), p. 227.

4 BURN, D. (1961) *The Economic History of Steelmaking 1867–1939*, Cambridge, Cambridge University Press, (first printed 1940), p. 84.

5 CARNEGIE, A. (1901) 'Development of steel manufacture in the United States', in SEDGWICK, A.G. et. al., *The Nineteenth Century a Review of Progress*, New York and London, Putnam, p. 146.

6 BURN, D. (1961) *op. cit.*, p. 167.

7 BURN, D. (1961) *op. cit.*, p. 161.

8 CLAPHAM, J.H. (1926) *An Economic History of Modern Britain*, Book 2, Cambridge University Press (1967), pp. 483–4.

9 *Iron*, Vol. 22, 19 October, 1883, pp. 355–6.

10 CARNEGIE, A. (1901) *op. cit.*, p. 146.

11 CARNEGIE, A. (1901) *op. cit.*, p. 154.

12 CARR, J.C. and TAPLIN, W. (1962) *A History of the British Steel Industry*, Cambridge, Mass., Harvard University Press, pp. 116–8, 185.

13 CARR, J.C. and TAPLIN, W. (1962) *op. cit.*, p. 173.

14 CARR, J.C. and TAPLIN, W. (1962) *op. cit.*, p. 110.

15 KITSON, J. (1890–91) 'British contributions to the metallurgy of iron and steel', *Trans. Amer. Inst. Min. Engrs*, Vol. 19, p. 808, quoting Mushet.

16 BRANDT, D.T. (1956) 'Bessemer steelmaking process, its history, development and future', *Iron Coal Tr. Rev.*, 4 May, pp. 548–9.

17 FAY, C.R. (1950) *Great Britain from Adam Smith to the Present Day*, Longmans, 5th edn., p. 275.

18 TYLECOTE, R.F. (1976) *A History of Metallurgy*, London, The Metals Society, p. 144.

19 *Ibid.*, pp. 147–8, and KITSON, J. (1890–91) *op. cit.*, pp. 832–3.

20 MUSGRAVE, P.W. (1967) *Technical Change the Labour Force and Education A Study of the British and German Iron and Steel Industries 1860–1964*, Oxford, Pergamon Press, pp. 1–127, and CARR, J.C. and TAPLIN, W. (1962) *op. cit.*, pp. 48–9, 151–2.

21 BURN, D. (1961) *op. cit.*, p. 214.

22 PAYNE, P.L. (1968) 'Iron and steel manufactures' in ALDCROFT, D.H. (Ed.) *Development of British Industry and Foreign Competition, 1875–1914*, London, George Allen and Unwin, pp. 71–99.

The Textile Industries

Stanley D. Chapman

In a short essay it is not possible to examine all the branches and locations of the textile industries in detail but perhaps that is hardly necessary. In general, two or three major centres (particularly Lanchashire, Yorkshire and the Midlands) set the style and pace in their respective sectors (cotton, wool, and hosiery), while the lesser or satellite centres – Glasgow, Norwich, Coventry, Macclesfield, Kidderminster, Trowbridge, Dundee, and others – followed at a greater or lesser distance. However, a serious attempt will be made to assess the design, finishing (bleaching, dyeing, printing, etc.), machine building and commercial sectors of the industry, as well as technical education in the more familiar manufacturing processes. It will be seen that the main British strength lay in manufacturing, so that some attention to these neglected aspects of the history of the textile industries may result in a more complete understanding of the nature of the problem facing the Victorian reformers.

The pioneers, 1770–1830

The Industrial Revolution in the textile industries has attracted scholarly attention for many years, so that quite a number of studies of entrepreneurs and firms are available for study. Most of the vanguard firms of the first generation – Arkwright, Strutt, Peel, Robinson, Thackeray, Douglas, Drinkwater, Owen, McConnel and Kennedy in cotton; Gott, Davison and Hawksley in wool and worsted; Marshall in linen – have been the subject of systematic research in recent years. The innovating entrepreneurs in such specialisms as hosiery, lace, textile printing and engineering have also been well written up. But few of these studies approach anything like full-length biography, for the original sources are much too thin for this and one searches them in vain for any substantial amount of information on education and training. A fragment of evidence crops up here and there but it is quite insufficient to provide any easy generalizations.[1]

However, even if these biographical studies were eloquent on the training of their subjects, they would not necessarily solve our problem. If we take only cotton spinning, there were already something like 900 firms in the industry before the end of the eighteenth century and information of any kind is available on less than twenty of the leaders – that is, little more than two per cent.[2] Moreover, those whose careers have found a historic record were mainly the large successful entrepreneurs whose experience was probably not typical of cotton spinners as a group. Economic historians have already made too many generalizations on the basis of small and unrepresentative evidence and we do not want to repeat the error here. Clearly, some other approach to the subject must be made and, in the absence of adequate school or apprenticeship records, this is not easy. However, two alternative possibilities are worth examining. One is to look at the nature of the technology introduced in the Industrial Revolution period to try to identify what levels of education and training were required to master them and keep abreast of constant changes. The other approach is to attempt to identify the sector (or sectors) of society that provided the leadership of the industry and work back from this interpretation of the representative entrepreneur to the typical education received by that class. These two approaches are evidently complementary and it is to be hoped that the findings from each will reinforce the other.

Let us take the technology first, using cotton as our mentor, for the new fibre proved to be easiest to manipulate with machinery and so generally led wool and linen. During the course of the century or so before 1760, the growth of the textile industries allowed and encouraged increasing specialization of function, and hence growth of skills, in the workshops clustered about the clothier's (or fustian manufacturer's) house. This development is already apparent in Defoe's attractive descriptions at the beginning of the century and can be identified in numerous insurance inventories through the century.[3] However, the manufacturing unit was still essentially domestic in the sense that it was centred on the family and, if we may take William Radcliffe's experience as representative, a child brought up in such a household learned every process from the cotton bag (or wool sack) to the conventions of selling on market day. The sequence of specialized processes that composed the industry was the child's and youth's early environment and formative experience and no doubt they were etched on his mind with all the clarity of such early-life pre-occupations. If formal schooling came into the experience it was as an ancillary, rather than central, experience. The economies and improving standards conferred by division of labour were combined with an overall knowledge of the total manufacturing process.[4]

This point may be taken as a pretty obvious one but it has to be re-stated because it represents the real foundation of British manufacturing success in the eighteenth century and, hence, the foundation of British belief about the essential nature of industrial training. It is still too often supposed that British supremacy began with inventors like Arkwright, Crompton, Cartwright, Bell and their successors but these men were building on well-established traditions and their innovations had to be interpreted by lesser men. The point is perhaps best made by an acute Alsatian observer of the success of English printed cottons, writing in 1766: 'All the world knows this people, whose industry and plodding patience in overcoming every kind of difficulty exceeds all imagination. This nation cannot flatter itself with having made many discoveries but it may glory in having perfected all that has been attempted by others, from which comes the saying "to have a perfect thing it must be invented in France and worked out in England" . . . in this, as in all other manufactures, [they have maintained] that superiority which results from their accuracy and patience"'.[5] Two or three decades later, the writer may have revised his opinion about British inventiveness, but there is no reason to suppose that he would have abandoned his view about British artisans and manufacturers reaching their standards by the persistence of a long sequence of minor improvements.

The 'great inventions' of the late eighteenth century are generally chronicled as something apart from these less dramatic developments but as one draws closer to the events they merge into their setting. They were the product of that specialism and search for perfection noticed above, necessitated not only by rising costs but more particularly by the need of better quality yarns and fabrics. They were mechanically simple contrivances that drew on techniques already familiar in the industry or elsewhere. And they themselves continued to be improved by a long sequence of local and generally anonymous advances, continuing the upward trend of both quality and productivity. In other words, the Industrial Revolution in Britain did not inaugurate uneducated empiricism in industry, it simply sustained and confirmed it as the basis of British manufacturing achievement. British faith in empiricism was born of generations of successful practice, both before and during the Industrial Revolution, and the eagerness with which foreign governments and employers tried to recruit British artisans for their factories is sufficient commentary on the achievement of the time-honoured method.[6]

But this is not to say that training-by-doing left nothing to be desired. Even in 1830, the most acute observers might have noticed the limitations of the new technology. Empirical know-how is limited because it characteristically develops along one particular path which is dictated by specific local experience and needs, while other possible paths are ignored or explored by only the occasional individualist. Thus, in hosiery, we find that the path that led from Lee's stocking frame was exhaustively explored over two centuries, while the equally promising warp-knitting was ignored. In cotton spinning, Crompton's mule dictated a path that was minutely explored for three or four generations, while the equally important throstle spinning, which began with Arkwright, was all but abandoned to the Americans. In textile printing, where Lancashire achieved unrivalled expertise following through the possibilities of Bell's roller printing apparatus, neither designing nor colour chemistry were taken very seriously for most of the nineteenth century. The limits of empiricism are already discernable in the Industrial Revolution period.[7]

Before pressing this theme any further, we must turn to the other approach to our subject, the recruitment of entrepreneurs. The subject is not a difficult one to measure but it has been obfuscated by the 'self-help' propagandists of last century, who insisted that all entrepreneurs worth their salt were risen from the lower ranks, and by the innumerate historians of this century, who have tried to generalize on inadequate samples. The only good work which has been published is Charlotte Erickson's *British Entrepreneurs, Steel and Hosiery, 1850–1950* (Cambridge, 1959). This demonstrates that the normal hereditary leadership of the industry lost ground to newcomers during periods of fundamental technical change but, when more normal times returned, sons followed fathers in the traditional way while, even in periods of change, the hereditary leadership was by no means eclipsed. Unfortunately, this work comes rather late for our immediate purposes, and only applies to one branch of the textile industries. However, work now in the pipeline or at the thesis stage points to similar conclusions for cotton and lace. The great number of the 200 or so entrepreneurs who followed in Arkwright's shoes up to 1788 were drawn from the hereditary leadership of the industry, as were most of the Bolton mule spinners in 1830. The Nottingham lace industry had a reputation for 'self-made' men, but most of them were in fact small masters of hosiery workshops before they made the shift over to the new technique. The minority were for the most part tradesmen and shopkeepers who had some earlier acquaintance in trading in the commodity.[8]

The implications of all this for training and education hardly need underlining. Even during periods of technical upheaval, the hereditary forms of training were most largely represented in the industry and the handful of biographies suggest that the new men who were drawn in characteristically trained themselves on the job in the factories, workshops and warehouses of the hereditary elite – Robert Owen at Peter Drinkwater's factory, Charles Hulbert in the printing workshops of Daniel Burton & Sons, Samuel Bamford in the warehouse of Hole, Wilkinson and Gartside, and so on.[9] It is of course possible to find a few cases of individualists who do not easily fit into these categories, notably the better-educated migrant Scots millwrights and engineers (McConnel and Kennedy, Adam and George Murray, Fairbairn, and their connections[10]) but we must not lose sight of the total picture. So far at least as the textile industries were concerned, British supremacy was founded on the fullest exploitation of specialization of function and empirically developed mechanical devices and entrepreneurs were generally unwilling to depart from the path that had led to such brilliant success until they were forced to do so.

The middle period, 1815–75

In the generation after the French Wars, Lancashire industry and social conditions became a major focus of interest both for foreign manufacturers, who liked to tour the industrial areas, and for British moralists and politicians, who produced a whole genre of polemical literature on the new phenomenon. The problem in this period is not, therefore, so much shortage of material as that of obtaining objective commentaries. The earliest and most reliable of the post-war accounts appears to be that of Alexandre Andelle, who was reporting to the French government. In 1818 he wrote:

> At Manchester, spinning has been carried to the highest degree of perfection, partly by the fine construction of the machinery, partly by the particular care given to the preparation and the regularity of work . . . In general, the English are remarkable for the simple and methodical administration

of their business, their managers are almost all trained. The simplest worker, man, woman, or child, can read, write, and count, for which they are indebted to the celebrated Lancastrian school established at Manchester for a long time.

But Andelle, like so many other foreign visitors, examined only the most successful works, so that he obtained an unusually favourable impression of both managers and workmen, and his enthusiasm needs to be qualified by reference to some more critical contemporaries.[11]

The writers of the technical manuals of the period were not, of course, concerned with education and training as such but some of their *obiter dicta* are revealing. Thus Robert Scott, the author of the popular *Practical Cotton Spinner and Manufacturer* (various editions, from 1851), noted in his preface that 'Having been engaged in the different departments of the cotton business for many years, I have found a great deficiency in theoretical knowledge amongst practical persons filling important situations in cotton and other factories'. And the other successful textbook writer of the period, James Montgomery of Glasgow, alluded darkly to something worse than ignorance when he wrote in 1832 that 'considering the amount of capital invested in these establishments [cotton mills] it might be expected that proprietors would be much more scrupulous in the choice of those to whom they confided the charge of them than they frequently are: for it is now become proverbial that interest and influence, not merit, are the only means by which these situations are obtained'.

Mechanics' Institutes were particularly thick on the ground in the textile districts of Lancashire and Yorkshire (in the 1850s and 1860s there were about a hundred of them in East Lancashire and 130 in the West Riding) and an optimist might suppose that they contributed substantially to the elementary technical training of mill hands and overseers. In fact, the main problem here, as elsewhere, was lack of basic literacy and numeracy and, having discovered this deficiency at an early stage of their development, some of the institutes turned their attention to the uphill task of providing remedial classes, characteristically with volunteer teachers. The truth about reports on artisan education was no doubt discerned by Gustave d'Eichthal in 1828:

> People generally assume that English workers are far better educated than they really are. The more intelligent of them are sent up to London in deputations and people imagine that the rest are of the same calibre, which is quite untrue. A Mechanics' Institution has been established at Bolton; good lectures are given and it has a good library of one thousand volumes [but] . . . out of a population of 40,000 souls there are less than a hundred members . . .

Another lucid commentator touring Yorkshire confirmed in 1849 that 'In too many towns, the Mechanics' Institute really means a cheap news room, with an 'occasional trashy concert for the subscribers'.[12]

But what standard of education was required to run a cotton spinning and weaving mill? Another of Robert Scott's books, a pocket manual titled *Guide to the Theory and Practice of Spinning, Manufacturing, etc.* (Burnley, 1843) makes an assessment which seems to be confirmed by the contents of other manuals of the period:

> In treating of machinery, the rules and examples will be laid down in the most simple manner, so that persons possessing only a knowledge of the fundamental rules of arithmetic will be able to comprehend them, and . . . may acquire every necessary qualification that will be requisite (so far as regards calculations) for persons filling the important situations of managers or overlookers . . . [13]

The tabulations that formed the principal contents of such manuals enabled the mill managers and spinning room overlooker (or 'gaffer') to make regular calculations of inputs, outputs, and qualities (or counts) of yarns. For most of the nineteenth century this work constituted the technical component of the management function within a spinning mill for the mule spinners were quasi-independent artisans who regulated their own machines and employed their own assistants, usually two or three women or juveniles. The 'gaffer' answered to the general manager (often a partner or director) and worked in liaison with the engineer (who supervised the steam engine and transmission system), the carder (who controlled all the preparatory processes) and the warehouseman. Each department of the mill was a self-contained entity responsible only to the general manager. This system of delegation and demarcation ensured that few management skills were looked for beyond the insistence on the quality of the product. The *original* skills of the cotton spinning, and also weaving, lay with the machine builders, a small group of specialist firms whose expertise continued to dominate both the national and international market until after the end of the century. If, as Scott and others noted, some managers and overlookers were deficient in education, it was the ability to read and use the four rules of arithmetic that was lacking. This is all the Lancasterian and National Schools provided and these were the institutions that drilled the 'three Rs' into working class boys, the brightest of which might step up from the mule gate to be 'under-gaffer' and perhaps 'gaffer'.[14]

The spinning and weaving processes were mechanical but the finishing processes – bleaching, dyeing and printing – were of course chemical and here a much greater degree of technical expertise was required within the factory. It was here that the most lamentable deficiencies in training became apparent in Lancashire quite early in the nineteenth century. While the value of a good understanding of chemistry was fully recognised in the eighteenth century, little was done to extend knowledge of the subject for another half century or more. According to the biography of John Mercer (1791–1866), a self-taught chemist who was one of the two outstanding innovators in calico printing of the post-war generation:

> When I became connected with calico printing in 1818, the only printing firms in this country who employed a man possessing a knowledge of chemistry were the Thompsons of Clitheroe and the Hargreaves of Accrington . . . The want of chemical knowledge was most obvious

among the managers of smaller works ... An amusing volume might be written about ludicrous mistakes, and equally ridiculous attempts to rectify them ... The majority of managers and colour men in printworks, being practical only, are so jealous of, and offer such decided opposition to, 'the chemical man' as they term him, that the principal is compelled to give way when sometimes he would gladly engage such a person.

This was written in 1853, shortly after Mercer's retirement. Hargreaves, Dugdale and Co. of Broad Oak Print Works, Accrington, employed a French chemist called Steiner, while James Thompson of the Primrose Work, Clitheroe, was a graduate of Glasgow University who had been trained in management with the Peels but whose technical outlook was more strongly influenced by the premier French printer of the late eighteenth century, Oberkampf of Jouy. Mercer became a parner in Forte, Taylor and Bury of Oakenshaw Works, Accrington. All the remaining Lancashire printers – ninety-three of them in 1840 – muddled through on the old 'recipes' and empirical techniques, 'borrowing' or buying French designs and imitating them as well as they could. These numbers provide an all-too-rare objective assessment of the extent of the application of science to industry in the heyday of British industry. If textile printing enjoyed a reasonably prosperous term in Lancashire, it was on the basis of cheap yarns and weaving rather than original colours or design.[15]

Some twenty-five years later, in 1867, it was claimed in evidence to the Taunton Commission that educational attainments of the partners in Lancashire printworks had improved considerably, a 'great many' of the new generation having studied at Owen's College, Manchester, or at London or Glasgow University. Nevertheless, the French retained the leadership in the quality end of textile printing, the sector of the industry calling for originality in design and colour chemistry, while Britain continued to rule in the cheaper mass-produced goods. A similar story came from the hosiery manufacturing districts, where A. J. Mundella reported that Nottingham silk hosiery was sent to Lyons to be dyed because there were no colour chemists in the town, a deficiency attributed to the lack of scientific education in that part of England. A similar complaint was made by a spokesman for the Scots' woollen manufacturers when he appeared before the same Commission.[16]

British machine builders retained their lead through this period, and indeed increased it in some sectors, but this was not primarily due to the standards of education and training; the evidence suggests that their supremacy would have been more marked and more easily won if the artisans, and particularly the foremen, had been better prepared for their exacting work. The experience of Platt Brothers of Oldham, the leading firm of cotton spinning and weaving machine builders, is instructive. The firm began as a small workshop in 1824 and in 1846 employed 873 workers but the dramatic expansion came after that year when the ban on the export of British machinery was lifted. Britain had by far the largest domestic market for textile machinery and colossal export of yarns to Central Europe that was the foundation of a reservoir of demand there. Consequently, Platts were able to indulge in a specialisation of men and machines that enabled them to outpace their continental rivals. Earlier competition from Belgium (the British emigrés, Cockerills of Liége) and Zurich fell away, and Platts grew so rapidly that after twenty years of unrestricted exporting they were employing between five and seven thousand men. However, the second generation leadership were already realising the limits of workmen who, with little education, had learned their skills on the job. John Platt found that their primary schooling was quite inadequate and sent his apprentices to his factory school for two hours a day until they were 14 years old. Skilled men were persuaded to attend classes in draughtsmanship and mechanics at the Oldham Science and Art School and the best were rewarded by being sent abroad to supervise the assembly of export orders. This was also a necessary test, for it had been found that uneducated machine erectors lacked the means to diagnose erection and running faults. Unfortunately, there were very few firms with the resources to remedy the deficiencies of the public educational system and the determination to overcome the apathy of parents. Platts' educational programme was almost unique at the period.[17]

The exporting success of Platt Bros. cannot be said to have been the product of unaided British genius for the marketing side, like that of many other English cotton manufacturers and machine builders, was largely conducted by foreign-born – more particularly German and Greek – commission agents. Platts' greatest success was achieved in Russia where they had an agent called Ludwig Knoop, a German merchant who worked through his former employers, De Jersey and Co. of Manchester. Knoop, who was styled 'the Arkwright of Russia', drew technical expertise from Oldham and finance from London to build an industrial empire of cotton mills on the Lancashire plan.[18]

It was, of course, inevitable that British technology should find its way abroad but the extent to which foreigners controlled the export of textiles and machinery again points to the inadequacy of British education, particularly on the commercial side. The problem was explained by Jacob Behrens, a German Jew who became the foremost merchant in Bradford. In the West Riding, young men:

> leave school early and are taught in their father's mill the father's trade in the same practical manner in which he himself has learned it, and which has enabled him to rise to his present position, when England possessed exceptional advantages over all other countries ... In no other country has practical technical education [on the job] been more perfect than in England, and ... no school can ever give the same practical education as that which is given in the real workshop; but it is evident that in places like Bradford where this branch of education is so thoroughly satisfactory, teaching of a more scientific character would be doubly beneficial.

Whatever the merits of this practical apprenticeship, it could contribute little to the manufacturers' need of markets. Behrens believed that ignorance of foreign languages, laws, customs and geography – even among the 'affluent classes' – was a great bar to their commercial progress and was the reason for 'throwing almost the whole of our continental export trade into the hands of foreigners residing in this town' [Bradford]. He went on to explain that,

The German clerk, who has a good knowledge of three of four languages, who has been taught to understand the working of the [commodity] exchanges in the whole world, the tariffs of different countries, and their commercial laws and usages, will find employment and rise into an important position, or to independence, much sooner than the English clerk who has not received the same educational advantages.

Of course, there were large numbers of British commission agents stationed abroad, some 1,500 of them at mid-century according to a pioneer enquiry but, in the third quarter of the nineteenth century, competition intensified and the inadequacy of British education became painfully apparent. One of the most penetrating comments came from Russia, where British and German merchants met on neutral ground:

The old race of British merchants ... is rapidly dying out, and I greatly fear that the rising generation will not be equally successful. Times have changed. It is no longer possible to amass large fortunes in the old easy-going fashion. Every year the conditions alter and the competition increases. In order to foresee, understand, and take advantage of the changes, one must have far more knowledge of the country than the men of the old school possessed ... Unless some change takes place in this respect, the German merchants, who have generally a much better commercial education and are much better acquainted with their adopted country, will ultimately, I believe, expel their British rivals. Already, it is said, many branches of commerce formerly carried on by Englishmen have passed into their hands.

The inadequacy of British education evidently threatened on more fronts than one but it was to take a more ugly situation before there was an adequate response.[19]

Later Victorian years, 1875–1901

It is clear that, by the last quarter of the nineteenth century, the pressures of foreign competition were making the more perceptive textile manufacturers and merchants increasingly conscious of the need for more technical and commercial education. However, there was still considerable local apathy, and sometimes hostility, to the establishment of schools and colleges. Resistance rose from various causes but particularly from the feeling that the methods that had brought success in the past were the best guarantee for the future; as one Bradford merchant interpreted the popular view in 1884: 'we had better keep to our traditions and go on as we have done before, relying entirely on the skill and energy and industry of our people'. There was also an underlying fear that education would create an intellectual élite which might overturn the hereditary leadership, or migrate to America where they might then drive the home manufacturers out of business. These fears were also expressed in a continuing reluctance to employ educated managers. Thus it was said in 1884 that the managers in Alsatian textile printing factories were all chemists, while in Lancashire there were still very few chemists in such places, even though competition had intensified.[20]

The superiority of French designs on silks, printed cottons and lace produced the first serious attempt to provide technical education in the textile towns. In the eighteenth century, copper plate printing had been perfected first in London and English designs led European taste in the period 1760–85. Lancashire printers first emerged as popularisers of London designs so, when the London industry collapsed in the recession following the French Wars, Lancashire had to look to Lyons or to Paris for their inspiration. As early as 1818, a French designer made a fortune by selling 10,000 sample patterns, of one or two inches square, in Manchester at seven to eight shillings each; half a century later, leading printers were paying £25,000–£30,000 *per annum* for French designs. Similarly, Nottingham machine-made lace was originally a popular imitation of cushion lace, with no local tradition of design. The Jacquard loom – which was adapted to the needs of Manchester, Huddersfield, Coventry, Nottingham, Kidderminster and other textile towns from the late 1830s – was, of course, a French invention so here again there was no indigenous tradition of design.[21] A handful of leading merchants and manufacturers who had travelled extensively in France believed that the foundations of French success lay in their schools of design. In particular, the Lyons School, which was founded about the middle of the eighteenth century expressly for the instruction of draughtsmen engaged in preparing patterns for the local silk industry, was seen to have contributed to French success in cotton printing (for cotton tended to follow the more expensive productions in silk) and in the 'blond net' (silk lace) manufacture. Then, in 1833, the Mulhouse printers, Manchester's closest rivals, established their own school of design. The British government appointed a Royal Commission to investigate the arts and their connection with manufactures and its 1836 report pressed for the foundation of schools of design in industrial centres throughout the country. Manchester School of Design was opened in 1838, Nottingham in 1842, Paisley and Norwich in 1846, and so on, but these schools were by no means uniformly successful. The Manchester one was never accepted by the local manufacturers and the Nottingham School only triumphed over the prejudices of the lace manufacturers when a particularly determined principal was at the helm (1865–80). The Paisley manufacturers did not value their school enough to want to contribute to its upkeep. Only the Halifax School made any real impact on its region, perhaps because of Crossleys' lead in the design-conscious carpet industry.

The establishment of Owens College, Manchester, in 1851, and the appointment of Henry Roscoe as professor of chemistry, created some serious local interest in the chemistry of dyestuffs. Roscoe said that Lancashire manufacturers had previously been compelled to recruit young Germans but in the 1860s Owens College products began to take their place. However, as is well known, this initiative came too late to retain the synthetic dyestuffs industry in Britain, despite the fact that the original break-through (Perkin's synthesis of mauve in 1856) was made in England and that the largest market was here. German success was undoubtedly due to their educational system and, in particular, the numerous universities which were cheap and open and had close connections with industry.[22]

Design and colour chemistry were of course relatively peripheral to the main

British interest in textiles, which was in the machinery of mass-production, and it was not until 1875 that this entered higher education. This time the initiative came from Leeds, supposedly because of the West Riding's recognition of continental achievements at the Paris Exhibition of 1872 but more likely because of growing competition and loss of traditional export markets to Germany. Unfortunately there is no economic history of the West Riding for this period but the basic export record can be read in modern German sources:

	Great Britain	Zollverein
1833	£6.54m.	£5.10m.
1850	£10.05m.	£11.40m.
1864	£23.95m.	£28.60m.

The strongest German exporters were the big firms in the Aachen fine cloth industry and the Chemnitz (Saxony) hosiery manufacture. The West Riding trade launched a public appeal to found a college in 1872 but the scheme looked like failing for want of adequate subscriptions when the City of London Clothworkers' Company stepped into the breach. The Company offered to maintain a Department of Textile Industries, an idea that had not been part of the original scheme. This initiative gave fresh momentum to the project and the new textile-centred college was opened in Leeds in 1874. A Dyeing Department was added in 1880 and an Art Department after that. In 1895, the professor reported that in general 'the students attending the day classes are the sons of manufacturers, managers, and designers, but the evening classes are chiefly attended by artisans'. The class division was fairly typical of the period.[23]

The ignorance of proprieters, manufacturers and foremen in the Nottingham hosiery industry were exposed by A.J. Mundella in his evidence to the Taunton Commission in 1867. Anxious to identify the reason for successful Saxon competition in foreign markets, he had acquired a firm in Chemnitz and sent out an English manager, H.M. Felkin, to assess the situation. Felkin soon concluded that the main difference between Nottingham and Chemnitz was the latter's polytechnic school which trained the superior class of workmen, the NCOs. of the industrial world. A decade later, a University College was launched in Nottingham on the impetus of the endowment of an emigré German merchant but, as Dr. Tolley shows in Part 3, the evening classes in the hosiery and lace manufacture found little support from local industrialists. The main value of Mundella's initiative was that he induced H.M. Felkin to write *Technical Education in a Saxon Town* (1881), a book that generated the publicity necessary for the appointment of the Samuelson Commission on Technical Instruction.[24]

Working through the middle years of the so-called 'Great Depression' (1874–96) in British industry and commerce, the period when German and American competition really began to bite, it is not surprising that the Commissioners' enthusiasm for foreign travel began to rub off on the anxious leadership of northern industrial towns. The period was also one of strident German nationalism and of showy civic pride in Britain and on the continent. Manchester, as befitted the metropolis of manufactures, had to have a technical institution that would put the

Germans in their place and its satellites did not want to be left far behind. It was not until after the benefits of the 1870 Education Act began to be felt that the Mechanics' Institutes could launch more advanced classes. Anticipating this change, the Keighley Mechanics' Institute changed itself into a technical college in 1870 and during the next twenty years Huddersfield, Leeds, Dewsbury, Halifax, Manchester and Bradford followed suit. However, the Mechanics' Institutes were not the only sponsors of elementary technical education in this period. In Lancashire, the initiative was taken up by such diverse foundations as the Bolton Church Institute, Oldham Lyceum, Bury Athenaeum, Salford Working Men's College, and Harris Institute, Preston. The Royal Technical Institute, Salford, was opened in 1896 with departments of dyeing and calico printing, spinning and weaving, but this was to appear as a preface to the conurbation's real prestige performance. The Manchester Municipal School of Technology took seven years to build and equip and was finally opened by the Prime Minister in 1902. According to one of its proud sponsors, the School was 'a serious attempt to place at the service of English industry an institution which shall be adequate to its needs and importance, and comparable in respect of equipment with the great institutions of the continent and the US'. The Department of Bleaching, Dyeing, and Printing was 'claimed as the most completely equipped institution for textile finishing in any country'. Nearly 5,000 students were enrolled for the first session, 1902–03, and from 1905 they were able to read for Manchester University degrees. Manchester's *Dreadnought* was only the flag-ship of a flotilla of smaller ventures; already in 1895 there were said to be 68 centres for teaching spinning and 70 for weaving, all launched within the last twenty years. National and civic pride had, almost overnight it seemed, transformed chronic neglect into something like over-production.[25]

Even so, there were still blind spots. In particular, there was very little serious consideration of the claims of commercial education. At the end of the century, a large part of the exporting from Manchester, Bradford, Nottingham and London was still being conducted by German and Greek emigrés or their descendents and financed by Anglo-German banks (Rothschilds, Schroders, Kleinworts, Brandts, and others) in the City. In 1897, Alderman Swire Smith of Bradford described the problem in much the same terms as Jacob Behrens had done thirty years earlier; frankly stating that 'the merchanting of the yarn here is practically in the hands of the Germans', and that they had held this position for two generations on the basis of superior technical education. German-born clerks were everywhere; in 1887 as many as forty per cent of the clerks in many central London offices were said to be German.[26] At the close of Victoria's reign there was still no degree course in commerce at any of the British universities or university colleges. The problem seems to have been solved more by the German emigrés becoming anglicised than by any very serious attempts to emulate the achievements of German commercial education.

Conclusion

In the 'take-off' period of the industrial revolution the British won world leadership in the development of machinery for the mechanized mass-production of cotton, wool, worsted and linen and, with few exceptions, this leadership was retained through the nineteenth century. This strength was reinforced after 1846 when free trade in textile machinery provided a great stimulus for the Lancashire and York-shire builders. Success was founded on a highly-developed specialization of func-tion (itself produced by a vast international market) and the kind of continuous small improvements that had won the day for British empiricism in the eighteenth century. But, in other branches of the textile industries, continental competition was always a close rival and sometimes conspicuously ahead. The challenge of French design found a response in the schools of design but the educational solution was not very successful so the British clung to their empiricism and bridged their deficiencies by importing better-educated foreigners, especially French designers, German merchants and chemists, and Greek traders. This 'policy' met with a great measure of success in the sense that it helped to retain British leadership, at any rate in cotton, though the dyestuffs industry was lost to the Germans and Swiss. It was only in the 1870s, when the basic manufacturing sectors came under severe pressure, that the textile manufacturers began to think that French, German, and now American competition must be met on equal terms. Even so, in some areas the manufacturers were too poor, ignorant, conservative, or individualist to show much interest in technical education before the 1920s.

Notes and References

1   Bibliographies may be found in CHAPMAN, S.D. (1972) *The Cotton Industry in the Industrial Revolution*, MACMILLAN and HUDSON, P. (1975) *The West Riding Wool Textile Industry: a Catalogue of Business Records*, Edgington. See also RIMMER, W.G. (1960) *Marshalls of Leeds, Flax Spinners*, Cambridge, Cambridge University Press.

2   CHAPMAN, S.D. (1972), *op. cit.*, p. 70.

3   CHAPMAN, S.D. (1974) 'The textile factory before Arkwright', *Business History Review*, XLVIII. WADSWORTH, A.P. and DE LA MANN, J. (1931) *The Cotton Trade and Industrial Lancashire 1600–1780*, Manchester, Manchester University Press.

4   RADCLIFFE, W. (1828) *Origins of Power Loom Weaving*, Stockport, cf. LAWSON, J. (1886) *Progress in Pudsey*, Stanningley, J.W. Birdsall.

5   RYHINER, J. (1865) 'Traite sur la fabrication et le commerce des toiles peintes', in DOLLFUS–AUSSET, D. *Materiaux pour la Coloration des Etoffes*, II, Basle, p. 5.

6   CATLING, H. (1978) 'The development of the spinning mule', *Textile History*, IX, HILLS, R.L. *The Development of Jenny and Roller Spinning* (forthcoming paper).
    For the setting of innovation, see especially RADCLIFFE, W. (1828) and LAWSON, J. (1886).

7   CHAPMAN, S.D. (1974) 'Enterprise and innovation in the British hosiery industry, 1750–1850', *Textile History*, V. CATLING, H. (1978) *op. cit.*, HILLS, R.L. *op. cit.*
    For calico printing see below.

8   HONEYMAN, K. (1977) *Social Mobility in the Industrial Revolution*, (unpublished PhD thesis), Nottingham. CHAPMAN, S.D. *The Arkwright Mills, 1768–88* (forthcoming).

9   BAMFORD, S. (1893) *Early Days* (1848–49) London, Fisher Unwin, pp. 276–8. CHALONER, W.H. (1954) 'Robert Owen, Peter Drinkwater, and the early factory system' *Bull. John Rylands Lib.*, XXXVII. HULBERT, C. (1952) *Memoirs of Seventy Years . . .* , Shrewsbury, the author, p. 165ff.

10 LEE, C.H. (1972) *A Cotton Enterprise – a History of McConnel and Kennedy*, Manchester, Manchester University Press, POLE, W. (Ed.) (1877) *Life of Sir William Fairbairn.*

11 Archives Nationales (Paris), F12/2295 (transcript kindly provided by M.S. Chassagne). The school was opened in 1813 and the two rival National schools in 1812.

12 ASTON, J. (1816) *A Picture of Manchester*, Manchester, E.J. Morten, pp. 143, 145. For some other travellers of the period see HENDERSON, W.O. (1968) *Industrial Britain under the Regency*, London, F. Cass.

13 SCOTT, R. (1843) *op. cit.*, pp. iv, 25. MONTGOMERY, J. (1832) *Carding and Spinning Master's Assistant*, Glasgow, J. Niven, pp. 209–10. RATCLIFFE, B.M. and CHALONER, W.H. (1977) *A French Sociologist in Britain*, Manchester, Manchester University Press, p. 93. REACH, A.B. (1974) *The Yorks. Textile Districts* ASPIN, C. (Ed.) Helmshore, Local History studies, p. 6. HEMMING, J.P. (1977) 'The Mechanics Institutes in the Lancashire and Yorkshire textile district from 1850's *Journ. Educ. Admin. and History*, IX; SMITH, T.A. (1967) *The Effects of National Development on Technical Education in Bury, Oldham and Preston before 1889*, (MA thesis) Liverpool.

14 SCOTT, R. (1843) *op. cit.*, p. 13. CATLING, H. (1970) *The Spinning Mule*, Newton Abbott, David and Charles, pp. 149–54. See also MONTGOMERY, J. (1836) *Theory and Practice of Cotton Spinning*, Glasgow, pp. 248–54.

15 PARNELL, E.A. (1886) *Life and Labours of John Mercer*, London, Longmans, pp. 241–5. TURNBULL, G. (1951) *A History of the Calico Printing Industry of Great Britain*, Altringham, Sherratt, Ch. 5, pp. 423–6.

16 *Select Committee on Scientific Instruction (Taunton Commission)* (1868), XV, evidence of R. Rumney, pp. 299–300, A.J. Mundella, p. 233, R. Gill, p. 386. See also *Select Committee on Schools of Art* (1864), XII, evidence of E. Potter, p. 126.

17 BUTTERWORTH, E. (1856) *Historical Annals of Oldham*, 2nd Edn., Oldham, Hirst, pp. 184–7: *Taunton Commission*, (1868), *op. cit.*, XV, evidence of John Platt, p. 290.

18 SCHULZE–GAEVERNITZ, G. VON (1889) *Volkswritschafthiche Studien aus Russland*, Leipzig, p 86. CHAPMAN, S.D. (1977) 'The International Houses', *Journ. European Econ. History*, V. Platt Bros. registers of machinery exports, Lancashire Records Office.

19 *Reports on Technical Education*, 1867–68, LIV, pp. 28–9. CHAPMAN, S.D. (1977) 'The International Houses', for Palmerston's survey of British Commission agents. MACKENZIE WALLACE, D. (1877) *Russia*, I, p. 277.

20 *Royal Commission on Technical Instruction (Samuelson Commission)*, (1884), XXXI, evidence of H. Mitchell, p. 248, R. Haeffeley, p. 2.

21 Archives Nationales (Paris) F12/2295. *Samuelson Commission*, (1884), *op. cit.,* evidence of J.S. Rawle, pp. 68–70; ROTHSTEIN, N. (1977) 'The introduction of the Jacquard loom to GB' in GERVERS, V. (Ed.) *Studies in Textile History* (Toronto) Royal Ontario Museum. *Select Commission on Schools of Art*, (1864), evidence of E. Potter, p. 132.

22 *Royal Commission on the Arts and their Connexion with Manufactures*, 1836, IX. *Select Commission on Manufactures, Commerce and Shipping*, 1833, VI, pp. 240–4. Taunton Commission, (1868), *op. cit.*, XV, evidence of R. Rumney, p. 300, H.E. Roscoe, p. 279. Samuelson Commission, (1884), *op. cit.*, evidence of J.S. Rawle, pp. 68–70. READER, W.J. (1976) *ICI, A History 1870–1926* Oxford, Oxford University Press, pp. 12–14.

23 TEUTEBERG, H.J. (1975) 'Das deutsche und britische Wollgewerbe um die Mitte des 19 Jh' in WINKEL, H. (Ed.) *Vom Kleingewerbe zur Grossindustrie*, Berlin, pp. 95–6. *The Record of Technical and Secondary Education*, IV, 1895, pp. 471–9. BERESFORD, M.W. and JONES, G.R.J. (Eds.) (1967) *Leeds and its Region*, British Association for the Advancement of Science, pp. 278, 283.

24 Taunton Commission, (1868), *op. cit.*, evidence of A.J. Mundella, pp. 232–5. BECKETT, E.M. (1928) *History of University College*, Nottingham, pp. 48–9. *Calendars* of University College. Nottingham, 1882 onwards. ARMYTAGE, W.H.G. (1951) *A.J. Mundella*, London, Ernest Benn, p. 209.

25 *The Record*, I, 1892, p. 176ff, 429–31; VII 1898, pp. 51, 349; XII, 1903, pp. 466–76; XIV, 1905, p. 347. *Royal Commission on Depression of Trade and Industry*, 1st Report, (1886), evidence of H. Mitchell, p. 131; 3rd report Sir J.C. Lee, p. 14. HEMMING, J.P. (1977) *op. cit.*; SMITH, T.A. (1967) *op. cit.*

26 *The Record*, VI, 1897, pp. 77–9. ANDERSON, G. (1976) *Victorian Clerks*, Manchester, Manchester University Press, pp. 61–5. HOOPER, F. and GRAHAM, J. (1901) *Commercial Education at Home and Abroad*, Manchester, Manchester University Press, especially, pp. 223–4. The authors were concerned with the promotion of their subject in the West Riding.

Engineering

Geoffrey Sims

Introduction

Never before had there been such an abundance of talent in the general field of engineering as that which was to be found in England during the early reign of Queen Victoria. Brunel, Stephenson, Maudslay, Nasmyth, Crompton and Whitworth, to name but a few, were all part of a movement which justifiably earned England the prestigious title of 'the workshop of the world'. The contribution of these men towards the development of technology was immense and at no period in history has so much technological innovation sprung from so few hands in such a short time. The Victorian era saw the development of a major railway network, the first ocean-going iron-clad ship, the movement towards mechanisation on the farms and the beginnings of large-scale steel production. There were, too, the adventurous bridge-building feats of the civil engineers whilst, towards the end of the century, there dawned the age of electricity and the motor car. In the majority of these areas Britain was the world leader and engineering manufacture was a major factor in the economy.[1]

Why was it then that a hundred years later the British did not see themselves in so pre-eminent a state? Had Britain really lost her lead or was she just indulging in the favourite British pastime of self-denigration? Was there already writing on the wall which the Victorians had failed to recognise? These are some of the questions with which this chapter will deal although there are few simple answers and historians generally fail to find a consensus about the relative importance of the many factors which caused Britain's position in the world of engineering to change.

It has been argued by historians that one of the reasons for the decline of the competitiveness of British industry was the fact that it 'lead' all others into the industrial revolution. There is undoubtedly much truth in this for the innovative skill to which we have referred, and which started to be utilised well before the early reign of Queen Victoria, had enabled Britain to produce goods which were available nowhere else in the world. Furthermore, a relative abundance of cheap labour, as well as cheap materials from the Empire, enabled the country to indulge in an almost dilettante way in the luxuries of engineering development without the necessity of paying too much regard to adaptability, profitability and productivity which were to become so crucial later on. The year 1851, – with the Great Exhibition visible through the windows of Paxton's glazed masterpiece, the Crystal Palace – represented a peak of achievement arrived at through a rare combination of talent which had flowered fortuitously in a friendly environment. None of the men who had brought these miracles about had received any formal education in science and technology. * It was a climate in which genius could win the day and where basic business sense, as we would interpret the term today, was perhaps less critical to success than now for if you are the only manufacturer of a product, the monopoly situation tends to make you less self-critical or forward looking than if you have rivals.

In discussing the development of the industry therefore we shall need to consider not only the importance of the undoubted talent for invention but the extent to which Britain succeeded in adapting to changes in social background and technology. This immediately calls into question the development of engineering in other countries and the ways in which Britain responded to foreign competition. How well were British engineers educated, and managers forward looking? Was Britain merely the victim of circumstance or could she have positively chosen a different path. First, however, we must look briefly at the progress of engineering and the change in social and economic background which characterized the nineteenth century. We shall return to many of the issues which appear in this brief survey in more detail later but first it is important to have an overall perspective against which their influence can be evaluated.

Victorian industry and engineering – a synopsis

Table 5 gives some picture of certain key events and inventions in the Victorian period. It is not comprehensive and among the omissions are civil engineering achievements and much that relates to the development of consumer goods. To be seen in perspective, it has to be remembered that before the Victorian period Britain had gained a prodigious lead in steam power through men like Trevithick and Newcomen. Much of the subsequent success of the railway and the shipbuilding industries rested on this factor. The table shows how, throughout the century, other countries were following Britain's lead in railway development though, as is explained in the text, after 1850 Britain reigned unchallenged in shipbuilding. The disturbing features which become all too apparent towards the end of the century are to be seen in both the emergence of original invention abroad (much of it in Germany) and its development in many countries which soon became successful industrial competitors. It is particularly noticeable that many of the foundations of today's industries, particularly the science-based ones, were laid elsewhere

---

*The first chair in engineering in a British University was not to be filled until 1840, in Glasgow, where the unfortunate professor was denied the use of lecture rooms by his colleagues, who disapproved of the development. Only the intervention of the Lord Advocate allowed him properly to take up his duties.

Table 5

	Developments		Fundamental Discoveries and Achievements	
	Home	Abroad	Home	Abroad
1820			Electromagnetic rotation (Faraday)	First 'ironclad' Steamship (America)
1825	Stockton-Darlington Railway First railway tunnel (Liverpool-Manchester Railway)		Portland Cement (Aspdin)	First practical ship's propeller (Ressel)
1830	Stephenson's Rocket 'Wins' Liverpool-Manchester Railway	First Steam Locomotive in America (Baltimore-Ohio)	Electromagnetic Induction (Faraday/Henry)	'Needle' – telegraph (Weber/Gauss)
1835	First London Train First regular steamship communication between Britain and America SS Great Western and Sirius First 'screw' Steamer crosses Atlantic (SS Great Britain)	First European Railway (Brdweis-Linz) First Canadian Railway	Nasmyth Steam Hammer Photographic Negative (Fox Julbot)	Daguerrotype (Daguerre)
1840	Whitworth's 'Standard Thread' Export of machinery legalised	First telegraph message in America sent (Washington-Baltimore) (Morse)		Arc lamps for Street Lighting demonstrated (Paris) Carbon/Zinc battery (Bunsen)
1845	Railway gauge standardised	Zeiss Factory opened (Jena) Colt opens 'Hartford' Armoury		Sewing Machine patent (E. Howe) (America)
1850	Dover-Calais submarine cable laid Colt's London Armoury opened			Reinforced Concrete (Monier) Vacuum Freezing Machine (Carre) Singer Sewing Machine (America)
1855	SS Great Eastern Launched			First 'elevator' for tall buildings (Otis)
1860		First machine-chilled cold store (Sydney)		10 barrell gun (Gatling) (America) Universal milling maching (J. Brown) (America)

Table 5 (continued)

Year	Developments — Home	Developments — Abroad	Fundamental Discoveries and Achievements — Home	Fundamental Discoveries and Achievements — Abroad
1865	Metropolitan Railway opened Transatlantic cable successful			Bone shaker invented (Lallement) (France) Dynamite (Nobel) (Sweden)
1870		Bicycles (Michau) (France) Meat packing factory (P.D. Armour) (America)		Westinghouse brake invented (America) Dynamo (Gramme) (France)
1875	First electric lighting in London First telephone exchange	Electric filament lighting (St. Petersburg Docks) Remington typewriter produced (design of C.L. Scholes) Frozen meat shipped Argentina – France First American Bicycles produced (Pope) Electric railway demonstrated (Siemens) (Berlin)	Electromotive power poineered (Ayrton)	Telephone (Bell) (America) Phonograph (Edison) Reinforced concrete beam (Monier) (Swann) Filament – Lamp (Edison)
1880	Electromotive power	First electric generating station (New York) (Edison) Electrical exhibition – Munich		Petrol Engine (Daimler) (Germany)
1885		Canadian Pacific Railway finished First Railway in China Aeronautical exhibition (Vienna)	First practical Turbo generator (Parsons) Rover 'Safety' bicycle (Stanley)	Single cylinder motor car engine (Benz) Internal Combustion Engine (Daimler) Radio waves produced (Herz) (Germany) Box Camera (Kodak) (America)
1890	First tube railway beneath Thames First power station (Deptford)	Trans Siberian Railway started	Pneumatic tyre (Dunlop)	4-Wheeled car (Benz)
1895		First petrol tractor (America) Paris metro started	Oxygen liquified (Dewar) Wireless telegraph (Marconi) Electron discovered (J.J. Thompson)	Flying machine successful (Langley) Air liquification (Linde) (Germany)
1900	First Motor bus		First transatlantic telegraphy (Marconi)	Zeppelin trial flight (Germany)

although there was no lack of genius in truly fundamental discovery. This aspect of the picture is considered further later in the chapter.

The commencement of the Victorian era marked the beginning of a halycon period in the country's history as a manufacturing nation which persisted until the depression of the 70s and 80s. Even from 1880, however, machinery exports continued to rise at a steadily increasing rate so that by 1913 they were worth three times their value in 1880. This in itself was good but cannot be evaluated properly without making comparison with the success of foreign competitors who rapidly prospered, both in numbers and in strength, from the period of the depression onwards. The period began with an abundance of cheap labour, and, until 1900, wages climbed continuously whilst, as *table 6* indicates, prices both fell and rose.

Table 6

	Prices	Real Wages
1830–1852	Falling slowly	Rising slowly
1852–1870	Rising	Rising considerably in the whole period
1870–1873	Rising fast	Rising fast
1873–1879	Falling fast	Rising fast
1879–1887	Falling	Rising
1887–1892	Rising and falling	Rising
1892–1897	Falling	Rising
1897–1900	Rising	Rising
1900–1914	Falling and rising	Stationary

Source: (After Professor Bowley, see 'Dictionary of Political Economy' Palgrave, (1908) (Ed.) Appendix, p. 801)

Much could be said of the influence of wages and prices during this period but space does not allow a full discussion of this matter here. Suffice it to say that, by the end of the century, labour had become much less cheap, though still plentiful, and that attitudes stemming from the early part of the period, coupled with a persistence of skills which in some cases were now much less relevant, posed one of the more severe threats to the future. Indeed, it was cynically predicted that Britain would soon only have a relative advantage in trades which involved the exploitation of irreplaceable raw materials or which depended on the resources of sweated labour!

Some significant aspects of the background to engineering development during the period are set out in *Table 7*. It must be recognised that the dominant growth area in the first half of the century was the textile industry. Indeed by 1840, textiles accounted for some two thirds of total domestic exports and only after 1850, due to the emergence of new industries, did they become relatively less important.

As *table 7* might be taken to imply, * the need for adaptation of industry generally, in the face of the new situation, became all too apparent but by the turn of the century it seemed to some commentators that the readjustment had been effectively completed and there was great expansion in all of the staple trades, including iron

*For further expansion of the historical background to this period see, for example, KNOWLES, L.C.A. (1966).

Table 7

Period	The background to engineering development 1815–1900
1815–1850 'The most rapid period of development of domestic resources in Britain's economic history'.	·Modern industrial structure was beginning to evolve. Many industries migrated from the south to the coal producing areas, to become steam based. Foreign trade was basically a simple process of 'new countries' producing raw materials and 'old countries' manufacturing them. Britain moved steadily towards a policy of freer trade, which operated in her own interests. By 1850 the volume of exports was three times that at the beginning of the century.
1850–1875 'Growth continues but more slowly'.	Britain's developing metallurgical trades supported much of the world expansion in material equipment – especially through the development of railways and shipping. British foreign investment enabled many countries to purchase machinery and transport equipment. The boom created by the Franco-Prussian war marked the peak of Britain's industrial supremacy. Tariff policies became increasingly liberal until checked by the 'Great Depression' of 1874 when increasing import duties caused damage to some British industries.
1875–1900 'The growth of overseas challenge'.	Newly unified countries in Europe began to produce and export manufactured goods. The advantage of Britain's early start lessened, as newly established industries elsewhere began with more advanced manufacturing processes. Britain's iron and steel industry lost supremacy. The textile industry came under challenge from others. The hardware trades were unable to equal 'scientific' German competition. Other industries also could not match American large-scale production methods. Exports still expanded, but more slowly, and only those relying on cheap labour (including coal) prospered. Optimism was replaced by doubt and uncertainty!

and steel and engineering. This was accompanied by a rapid growth in exports, particularly those of metallurgical products, helped by heavy British investment abroad during the period. New industries like the motor, the cycle, the rubber and the electrical apparatus manufactories were beginning to take an important place in the industrial life of the country. Whatever the state of relative decline, it was unimportant, or so it was argued, in the face of an absolute expansion even if the old supremacy could no longer be claimed. There will, nonetheless, be many who, with hindsight, will need to be convinced that much more could have been achieved had Britain been more willing to observe, and then learn from her new competitors.

The decline – some specific contributory factors

As we have already seen, by 1870 the country's position was beginning to decline, for other forces were at work elsewhere. There was no reason why Britain should maintain a monopoly of genius even if it had for a while enjoyed a monopoly in terms of uniqueness and excellence of product. Indeed, it was rapidly to become apparent that, in order to maintain a competitive position, one had to have not only the bright ideas in the first place but the means to develop and market them competitively. This, in turn, implied that manufacture at minimum cost was a matter of extreme importance and it was not only in Britain that manufacturers bankrupted themselves by cutting prices to a point where ultimate insolvency was the only conclusion.

What then were the crucial factors in Britain's decline and how did they differ from those of her competitors? This is in many ways one of the most difficult questions to answer because there is a considerable lack of detailed documentation of the period, not only as it relates to Britain but also regarding Germany and the United States, which were to become the main rivals. Some of the factors which we shall discuss, although they could be taken as indicators of deficiencies in the British system, were undoubtedly influential in other countries too and therefore it is not only difficult but dangerous to draw conclusions too rapidly. Of the points mentioned below, there seem to be two which can be referred to with reasonable certainty as having a persisting effect and we shall refer to these first.

Educational influences

Whereas in France the origins of technological education date back to the middle of the eighteenth century, and in Germany engineering was prominent as a university-level study early in the reign of Queen Victoria, nothing in England remotely connected with engineering studies appeared either in Oxford or Cambridge until the 1870s. It should be remembered, too, that academic preferment at this period was still mainly to be obtained through non-scientific channels and even the sciences, which were by that time represented in the universities, were far from being favoured subjects. Many an Oxford or Cambridge science professor discontinued his lectures or, if they were obligatory, gave them to empty classes.[2]

The existence of an educated class of engineer was to prove vital to the continuing success of the industry and indeed of industry generally but the country did not have the talent to retain its competitiveness because it lacked suitably prepared people. It was common enough practice for those who had made their wealth in the early days of the engineering industry to send their sons to university but what they read there was hardly calculated to predispose them to the engineering apprenticeship which they would later have to take up with a view to running the works when fathers passed on. There were many cases of firms which perished through the incompetence or disinterestedness of the nepotistic process. One can see, in this period, the seeds of the feeling, still prevalent in Britain today, that engineering is not a first class profession whereas in Germany it has commanded respect for a very long time and therefore has always attracted the best and most able people to it. In late Victorian England, even when more suitable education was starting to become available, it was commonly accepted that engineering was for the artisan whereas any respectable professional man would read the humanities.[3]

Even the artisan, however, was not too well served, for although there were Mechanics Institutes, where evening studies could be carried out in many fields, they flourished for only a short period and eventually many become little more than social clubs. The point is well illustrated[4] by an appeal launched in 1883 in Sheffield (already a thriving centre of steel production and manufacture) to raise money for a technical institution in this wealthy city. In four months only £5,000 had been raised and, by the end of six months, the sum had risen to a mere £10,000 after much effort and additional 'encouragement' had been applied by its sponsors. At this stage, it was reluctantly concluded that the manufacturers of Sheffield did not want technical education and the project was seriously delayed.

Management

A second consideration which seems to be generally acknowledged relates to the lack of application of the principles of 'scientific management'.[5] Towards the end of the century, F.W. Taylor, in the United States, was giving considerable attention to incentive schemes, workshop layout and rudimentary work study techniques which were to pave the way for the mass-production methods so successfully used by America from the turn of the century. Taylor, who was far from being a lone voice in his own country, received only a cool reception in the United Kingdom and, indeed, some of his proposals were dismissed as inhuman – an odd comment to be made in a country where, only some fifty years before, punishments for children whose work did not satisfy their employers ranged from deprivation of pay to beating and confinement to the factory. Although there were certain exceptions (like Nasmyth's great Bridgewater Foundry, where even in 1840 he had utilised a basic but well-thought-out production-line technique) it is clear that there was a far from systematic approach to the organized use of labour. It seems reasonable to suggest that much of this disinterest may have sprung from the 'second generation managers', referred to earlier, who had been brought up within the protected shadow of prosperity which their fathers had produced and who, in many cases, lacked the imagination and education to fit them for the next round of development.

Standardization and mass production

This same lack of appreciation was manifest in many of the mechanical engineering works which exhibited at the same time a strange contrast of commendable dedication and gross negligence. Many were equipped with first class machines which had been allowed to deteriorate through lack of maintenance, and there were many examples of shops where it was impossible to turn cylindrical objects because of worn lathe beds which no-one had ever thought to re-grind. Instead, time-consuming, ill-adapted corrective hand techniques were applied in finishing the product to the required standard rather than remedying the basic fault in the machinery – an attitude which still persists in some works even today.

Along with poor maintenance went a reluctance to standardize and some of this must be related to an unwillingness, if not exactly an inability, to manufacture to precise tolerances. Many of the machines which were produced tended to be one-off manufactures and, as suggested above, they were often produced by manufacturing concerns for their own purposes in the manufacture of some secondary product. Where home buyers sought the help of outside producers to make their tools for them they were frequently extremely particular about certain detailed features that they wanted to see incorporated and, indeed, it was a matter of some pride to the producer that he should be able to manufacture to a one-off specification. This particular syndrome was blatantly apparent in the locomotive industry but it seemed to be true in most other areas of mechanical engineering also. This was hardly conducive to fostering the right atmosphere for a future which was going to depend very much upon mass production and ready replacement of parts.

Nasmyth again was a notable exception[6] and even by 1839 was selling standardized machine tools manufactured in advance of orders. The idea of making engineering products in runs and selling them off the shelf by catalogue was novel indeed! Another exception, which in some respects boded ill for the future, was the sewing machine industry which had been established in Scotland, on American initiative, by Singer. Here, everything was as it should be in terms of organization, precision and ready availability of spares but the initiative was not British and, sadly, its desirable characteristics did not prove to be contagious.

The market and marketing

Britain was certainly not going to be able to sell for ever into the markets of the world on the basis of orders for one-off products, which were not only expensive to produce but where also a rapid spares service could not be guaranteed, however good the quality. Yet it was to a large degree upon the excellence of the manufacture that the country's reputation rested and a highly diversified market was the result. The dependence upon the varied demands of diversified foreign markets may account in some measure for Britain's tardiness in adopting the policies of standardization and specialization which had helped the Americans, in particular, to lower their costs and win markets. This, in turn, caused many factories to remain smaller than those of the continent and America. It was, perhaps, to be expected that the

Americans, with a large home demand for uniform products and with a relatively slender supply of skilled labour, would adopt different methods from the British but this, in itself, could not explain Britain's slow rate of adaptation. Indeed, there were those who even then accused industry of complacency and inertia – yet another criticism with a familiar present day ring.

Towards the end of the century, trends in marketing[7] were changing rapidly. Much of Britain's enterprise in the nineteenth century depended on merchants who bought goods and used their growing experience of the foreign markets to sell them abroad. It was the merchant who carried the risk but, while Britain remained the only manufacturing centre, the risk was not large and the merchant played a vital part in the creation of her great export trade. There was often high competition between manufacturers for a good merchant's trade. This led to price cutting at the expense of the working conditions of employees although, from the point of view of the development of the export trade as a whole, the system worked well enough. Once foreign competition began to grow,the merchants were no longer obliged to buy from British suppliers and they began to purchase their wares abroad as well. They continued to sell very happily using experience which they had accumulated on the basis of selling British goods, thus promoting German and other industries at the expense of the British. So Britain tended to suffer from having been first in the field and foreign competitors were not slow to offer incentives to potential customers to win our markets.

Overseas competition – a contrast in attitudes

Industrial development in England in the nineteenth century owed almost nothing to state aid, whereas in France and Germany the state afforded generous assistance. The fact that the British inventor received neither capital nor encouragement is, perhaps, another symptom of the low regard in which the professional engineer was held. From evidence given to the Royal Commission on the Export of Machinery in 1841[8] it was clear that Prussia was already carefully studying the machinery that was being developed elsewhere. Indeed, not only did they have numerous examples of English and American machines, developed for industrial use, in their possession but they were already designing their own machines, many of which embodied more than one of our own patents. The attitude of the Prussian government stands in sharp contrast to the English *'laissez faire'* approach to both industry and technical education. The constrast between British and continental attitudes is all too apparent in a paper which appeared in 1820 on the state of science in England and France which stated that,

> the Government (of France) is the great protector and prompter of science: and not only urges on but even directs the pursuit of the learned.
> In England the Government does less because the subject does more.

It is only in relatively recent times that signs of change have appeared in the UK, whilst Japan seems to have learned much from Germany and France.

The explanation of these attitudes is to be found in the lack of capital and the destruction of economic life and individual initiative – the inheritance of the feudalism of the governments of Prussia, France and Russia – which meant that *only* the government could lead in the introduction of all major innovations in the late nineteenth century. We had no such problems to contend with. The attitudes of mind suggested in the foregoing have persisted to some extent up to the present time and were quite crucial in fashioning our approach during the Victorian period.

Mechanisation, technological adaptation and change

In many cases we cannot state with any certainty that more sophisticated American methods, alone, produced goods which were strongly competitive in price with those produced in Britain for, as Saul[9] points out in relation to the example of textile machinery, tariff and transport costs could give America a price advantage of up to forty-five per cent in their home market. It is, nonetheless, beyond question that the dearer labour costs in America provided an incentive to mechanise which was not present at that time in the UK. The principal difficulty is to determine just how, when and why the substitution took place for, where mechanisation saved both capital and labour per unit of output, it was not unnaturally the logical approach in both countries. By contrast, where the method saved labour at the expense of capital, there was greater incentive for it to be adopted in America than in the UK.

As we have already argued however, the American manufacturers were always more ready than the English to scrap existing machinery and replace it with new, whilst we continued to repair what we already had and, when necessary, spent much time and labour on hand finishing products.

The barriers to change

Laissez-faire and its consequences

Nationally we have always been reluctant planners and our attitudes to free enterprise today have their roots in the '*laissez-faire*' approach to the development of industry which ruled British attitudes in the nineteenth century.

The impetus given by the rate of new technical discovery made it imperative that all industries must face the need to adapt to new conditions continually or perish. This was a necessary concomitant of '*laissez-faire*' and, while the drive for success still depended upon the profit-seeking entrepreneur, success could only be achieved through flexibility of mind and approach as well as through a high measure of mobility of both capital and labour. No, one, industry, however much it had been dominant in the past, could expect to maintain its position in the face of a radical change of technology without anticipatory planning and, even with good anticipation of technological change, there were still other factors which could supervene to prevent the achievement of success.

Returning to the arguments which stressed the need for flexibility of function and organisation to enable the industry to adapt, particularly towards the end of the century, we can see a situation not dissimilar from that which exists today. In areas with a diversified economic life and small industrial units, changes could be effected with comparative ease. However the advance of industrialisation had often resulted in the creation of large producing units and specialised manufacturing facilities. Such units had high costs and they often perished, causing not only capital loss but substantial social distress. Even today labour is not particularly mobile but at that time movement to geographically distant areas was even harder to achieve.

The attitudes of labour

Britain had for so long enjoyed a plentitude of reasonably cheap labour that it had not been over-concious of the need to mechanise and (as today) overmanning, stemming from attitudes formed in the first half of the century, persisted. Even at this early stage people were arguing not only about whether machinery should be introduced but also about the conditions for its introduction. Fear for threatened jobs frequently led to demands for conditions which made it unprofitable to intro- duce relatively straightforward machine tools and it is of interest that, in the 1890s, machinery was introduced into the shoe industry on terms which maintained production costs at the same level as that of purely manual manufacture. There seemed to be little persuasion that increased productivity might actually generate more jobs in the long run and labour thus imposed a check on the modernization of British industry of a magnitude unknown in the USA.

A spokesman for the English boot and shoe manufacturers said in 1901 (quoted by Habbakuk):[10]

> for years labour has been so cheap and has been content to work under such conditions as to render it a matter of small importance as to the mechanical existence with which it should be furnished ... Men have been cheaper than machines. Today men are getting dear and machines are getting cheap. The whip of cheap labour was applied to the backs of American manufacturers years ago ...

This quotation not only appears to sum up the general situation perfectly but is also interesting for the light that it casts on the management attitudes of the day, although these have to be judged strictly within the context of their own time. Now, although management has had plenty of experience of dear labour, labour attitudes towards more advanced forms of mechanization often still follow the pattern of a hundred or more years ago whilst management, in many cases, remains as un- successful in reassuring its workforces!

The entrepreneur and technical expertise

We have already commented on the reluctance of the workforce to consider new technologies but there is no doubt that, in some quarters at least, there was a lack of what we would now call 'lateral thinking' on the part of entrepreneurs. It was, perhaps, not altogether surprising that Britain had lost some of the drive which goes with the initial stages of industrialization and that, whilst it was in the second and third generations of the 'clogs to clogs' process, the Americans and Germans as late entrants were still fired both by the magnitude of their task and their relative freedom to start with better processes than those which had formed the foundation of Britain's earlier pre-eminence. Perhaps it is true that many of her abilities had ceased to be relevant but it is beyond question that she had entered an age where innovations were going to require a degree of technical expertise beyond the abilities of the ingenious artisan. Among other qualities, a breadth of knowledge and perception were to be required, for much was to stem from the cross-fertilization which occurs when the techniques developed in one industry are applied to another. The problem of 'technology transfer' was arising for the first time and Britain was failing to cope with it.

The entrepreneurs were on the whole 'commerical men' and the type of technologist who was now needed to capitalise upon the rapidly unrolling tapestry of scientific discovery had never been developed. Habbakuk,[11] referring to the later part of the century, observed:

> Scientific knowledge became more important as a source of invention compared with empirical, artisan trial and error, than it had been earlier ...

Narrow technical mastery, upon which previous success had been based, would no longer suffice, however superb the craftsmanship.

We have already discussed the educational differences which better predisposed some of Britain's rivals for the decades to come but there were other social attitudes which influenced us as well as those which conditioned education. Whilst in Britain the professions absorbed most of the best brains,* in America there were few competitors to business success as a source of social prestige. Britain's landowning, traditional ruling class had set its own standards which were reinforced by hereditary privilege, a powerful bureaucracy and were accompanied also by a professional military class. This resulted in a rigidified society where each knew his place. In America there were no such problems and the 'land of opportunity' offered ways of success which were open to all and which, in time, produced a type of dedicated entrepreneur unknown in Europe.

Changing patterns of development and technology utilisation

There were other problems of adaptation to new technologies and the exploitation of electricity illustrates many of them. Although the principle of electromagnetic induction was discovered in Britain in 1831, even the genius of Faraday was not enough to enable Britain to lead in the development of the new industry which the discovery presaged. Even had the technological problems which at that time

---

*It is commonly quoted that Morris (later to become Lord Nuffield) only entered business because his father was unable to afford the lengthy education necessary to fulfil his intention to make him a surgeon.

made efficient distribution of electricity impossible been solved, there was little incentive for development in Britain. Once efficient means of electric lighting had been developed, it was other factors which largely determined from whence the developmental thrust was to come. Britain already had a very efficient, well developed gas industry: America did not.[12] The demand for electricity was largely urban-centred and the urban population of America was growing much more vigorously than that in Britain. High cost American coal made gas dearer than in Britain – clearly America must develop an electricity system. Yet, as is indicated in the right hand column of *table 5*, many of the fundamental discoveries arose in Europe – not to mention the preliminary development work which was later to be capitalized upon by American successors.

This should not be taken to suggest that the process was in any way parasitic for then, as now, (though to a lesser degree) Europe has remained an active centre for the discovery of new scientific principles, whilst their development and utilisation – which often depended upon mechanical ingenuity, vision and the ready availability of markets – remained an outstanding area of American contribution.

The research – development – exploitation chain, so characteristic of the high technology of today, was already taking on an international dimension whilst we remained largely a nation of small, if highly skilled, specialists. It is argued with some force that pioneers of the British electrical industry, Swan, Crompton and Siemens were little behind Edison and Brush technically and that the systems developed by the Americans were rapidly imported, suggesting that entrepreneurial activity was not a major factor. Enough has been argued above, however, to indicate some of the weaknesses and disadvantages which hampered Britain's development and which can still be recognised in many of the frustrations and inhibitions of today.

Finance and Free Trade[13]

The attitudes and implicit policies (or lack of them) which have been the main burden of this section so far cannot be divorced from questions of finance or of trade policy, which were, at this period, mainly attitude manifestations.

Until the end of the nineteenth century the typical manufacturing business was controlled by individuals or partners who themselves owned the capital. The capital was raised by loans from banks or from merchants through whom they dealt but additions to their fixed capital usually came from re-investment of profits. At the same time, the savings of the professional classes tended to be invested in foreign enterprises and government stocks and there was thus a clear division between the sources of foreign investment and the ways in which industry was provided with capital. Clearly, however, overseas investment brought substantial orders from foreign railways, shipping and public utilities which further stimulated Britain's own industries and their profit margins. A further consequence was an increase in the ability to secure raw materials and foodstuffs but the export of capital nonetheless had a two-edged impact. Whilst it offered immediate domestic advantages it also stimulated the creation of new foreign industries threatening the existence of long established British exporters and hastening the need for a redistribution of British productive resources. Thus, whilst the stimulus of competition was welcome, there was at the same time a high business mortality rate and, as is the case today, each recession saw the extinction of innumerable operating units from every industry.

Conclusion

It is of course extremely difficult to single out points of this kind as critical symptoms of future failure. The real difficulty, in the face of a mass of conflicting information in an ill-documented field, is to identify those things which may have been crucial. It was relatively easy for the United States, with little capital investment, to start the twentieth century on the right foot with new techniques and processes and scientific management. Britain had already made her investment on many fronts within the general field of engineering and was reluctant to change while that investment was still earning her a substantial profit. Furthermore, in an atmosphere of labour scarcity such as that in the United States, it became essential to pursue the path of increasing productivity, if only because of high labour costs. At that time, no such stimulus existed within the United Kingdom. Having said all of these things, it is not difficult to understand our lack of aggression in relation to second-phase development of the kind needed to compete with the professional Germans and the late-starting Americans. Britain's early lead had made her complacent. The fact that she was still in profit meant that she needed a lot of convincing to accept new technologies and, hence, there was a conservatism in her approach which is still evident in many industries today. Whether or not influence could have been brought to bear to make matters otherwise must remain a matter for speculation though, in the absence of an informed professional class to promote the adoption of new and more productive techniques, it is unlikely. The accounting methods of the time were also primitive and cost accounting had not yet replaced double entry bookkeeping so that the country was not exactly geared for any reliable quantitative assessment of its competitive position.

Perhaps in the light of the above analysis, the best that Britain could hope for was to learn from her mistakes. It is easy, with hindsight, to identify the mistakes of one's forbears but one must always beware of falling into the trap of making judgements of yesterday based on today's knowledge and standards. We should not, therefore, be passing a judgement on the Victorian era which can, in the field of engineering, be regarded as a great success story. If, however, we had examined the Victorian situation in a critical way and had identified factors which were adverse to Britain's future development as a competitive trading nation, we could have embraced the solutions to which they pointed and shown respect for our predecessors by learning from them. As long ago as 1902, a Trade Union delegation (the Mosley Commission)[14] commented, on its return to Britain from the United States, that the techniques that they had seen·in operation in American industry were ahead of those in Britain. We have long been aware of the commercial success of German industry in terms of the reliability, quality and timeliness of its products.

This has sprung primarily from the quality of the people who entered the respected profession of 'engineer'. Britain dishonours the titanic figures of the nineteenth century by her lack of response to indications of an earlier failure to uphold their tradition.

Notes and References

It is not easy to quote a comprehensive set of references to cover what is at once a large and often in-adequately documented field. The works quoted below, however, convey the flavour of the period and the author has drawn on several of them extensively.

1 ROLT, L.T.C. (1970) *Victorian Engineering*, Harmondsworth, Penguin Books.
2 ASHBY, E. (1966) *Technology and the Academics*, London, Macmillan.
3 KNOWLES, L.C.A. (1966) *The Industrial and Commercial Revolutions in Great Britain during the Nineteenth Century*, London, Routledge, Kegan and Paul, p. 111, et seq.
4 CHAPMAN, A.W. (1955) *The Story of a Modern University – a History of the University of Sheffield*, Oxford, Oxford University Press, p. 37, et seq.
5 LEVINE, A.L. (1967) *Industrial retardation in Britain 1880–1914*, Garden Press Ltd., p. 60, et seq.
6 MUSSON, A.E. (1977) 'James Nasmyth and the early growth of mechanical engineering, in TUCKER, K.A. (Ed.) *Business History*, London, Cass.
7 ALLEN, G.C. (1970) *British Industries and their Organisation*, London, Longmans, p. 11–12.
8 KNOWLES, L.C.A. (1966) *op. cit.*, p. 171, et seq.
9 See for example, SAUL, S.B. (1970) 'The market and the development of the mechanical industries in Britain 1860–64', in SAUL, S.B. (Ed.) *Technological Change: The United States and Britain in the Nineteenth Century*, London, Methuen.
10 HABBAKUK, H.B. (1967) *American and British Technology in the Nineteenth Century*, Cambridge, Cambridge University Press, p. 198.
11 *Ibid*, p. 194.
12 *Ibid*, p. 209 – see also LEVINE, A.L. (1967) *op. cit.*, p. 39.
13 KNOWLES, L.C.A. (1966) *op. cit.*, p. 138, et seq. See also LEVINE, A.L. (1967) *op. cit.*, p. 142.
14 Moseley Industrial Commission to the United States of America 1902. Reports of the Delegates, Manchester 1903.

The Chemical Industry

Keith Trace

The origins of the modern chemical industry lie in nineteenth century Europe, more especially in Britain. Two distinct, albeit partially overlapping, stages of development are distinguishable prior to 1900.[1] The first stage, which may conveniently be termed the chemical phase of the Industrial Revolution, was associated with quantity production of such inorganic products as soda ash, sulphuric acid and sodium sulphate. The second stage, beginning in the third quarter of the century, was characterized by the growth of new sectors based on the synthesis of organic products.

The first stage was directly linked to the growth of the market. Strong demand for soda alkali from the textile, glass and soap industries threatened, by the mid-1820s, to outstrip the production of alkali from natural sources, notably barilla and kelp, thus hastening the introduction of inorganic processes. The most notable of these, discovered by Nicholas Leblanc, entailed the furnacing of sodium sulphate, calcium carbonate (chalk) and coal to produce sodium carbonate (soda alkali). The production of sulphuric acid was closely linked to the alkali trade; sulphuric acid, then produced by the chamber process, being furnaced with common salt to produce saltcake (sodium carbonate) which was a basic raw material in soda alkali production. Sulphuric acid was also used by the metal trades as well as being employed as a 'sour' by textile bleachers. The patenting in 1841, by John Lawes, of a process for producing superphosphate by the treatment of bones with sulphuric acid, and the subsequent building of his Deptford factory, marked the emergence of the artificial fertilizer industry, enormously enhancing the demand for sulphuric acid. Process innovation in inorganic chemical production intensified in the latter years of the century, the classic example being Solvay's ammonia soda process.

The second stage in the development of the modern chemical industry, characterised by the development of a new range of outputs based on the synthesis of organic products, began in the third quarter of the nineteenth century. Dyestuffs, pharmaceuticals, perfumes and photographic chemicals were amongst the main products for which manufacturing techniques were radically altered by scientific advances during this phase. The natural dyes used hitherto in textile production had been mainly derived from plants. By the 1850s, the limited supply of a range of natural dyestuffs threatened to 'apply a brake to the rapid expansion of the textile industry'.[2] The task of synthesizing natural dyes, which proved to be most complex natural compounds, occupied organic chemists for several decades. The base material for synthetic dyestuff production, as well as that for a wide range of pharmaceuticals and photographic chemicals, was eventually shown to be coal tar, a substance produced jointly with coal gas. Indeed, Svennilson (1954) has characterized the new processes as ones whose raw materials consisted of 'by-products from the coke-ovens and gas-works'.[3]

The British chemical industry was pre-eminent during the first phase of the development of the modern chemical industry. France's early lead in the production of alkali by the Leblanc process was eclipsed by the 1830s and, thereafter, European industrialists looked to Britain for technical innovation in the complex of processes which together constituted the alkali trade. The outstanding innovations relating to the Leblanc process included those by Gossage (1836) which captured hydrochloric acid hitherto discharged into the atmosphere as hydrogen chloride; Weldon (1866) and Deacon (1868) enabling the bleaching agent chlorine to be made from the by-product hydrochloric acid; Elliot and Russell's (1853) revolving black ash furnace which cut labour costs; and the Chance-Claus (1887) solution to the problem of recovering sulphur from alkali waste. British innovators also played a major role in the development of the artificial fertilizer industry. The relatively rapid introduction of these and other improvements, the scale of the domestic market and the availability of raw material inputs provided the basis for Britain's mid-nineteenth century leadership of the chemical industry.

Britain's pre-eminence in the chemical industry began to wane in the late 1870s. By World War I, the British chemical industry had slipped to a poor third place in the league table of world production, the volume and value of British output being substantially lower than that of the United States and Germany. Superficially, the chemical industry would appear to be an example of an industry in which Britain's relative standing declined substantially between 1870 and 1914. This impression needs to be modified in two important respects. First, Britain's market position varied widely between different groups of chemical products. Second, the decline noted is as much a reflection of the very rapid growth of sectors of the United States and German chemical industries as it is of poor performance by the home industry, the British chemical industry continuing to expand throughout the period.

The relative importance of the organic sector of the German chemical industry has been the subject of widespread comment, Landes (1969) noting that it accounted for well over half of the industry's work force and capital investment by 1913.[4] Dyestuffs were of major importance and here only Switzerland, through specialization, could offer competition. Germany's strength in the organic area, however, extended well beyond dyes. Synthesis of cellulose, for example, led to the development of a range of products including photographic plates and film, celluloid, artificial fibres (*soie artificielle* and *viscose*) and explosives.

The strength of the United States' chemical industry, which developed rapidly from the 1890s, lay in the manufacture of sulphuric acid, superphosphate, ammonia and alkali. Widespread adoption of the Solvay process in the 1890s and, above all, the development of electrolytic processes after 1900 'promoted the American chemical industry from a local, comparatively unimportant and technically backward branch of manufacturing to a leading position in the chemical industry of the world'.[5] The adoption of these processes led to rapid growth in the output of ammonia soda, caustic and bleaching powder.

British output of a wide range of chemical products continued to expand in the late nineteenth century, although the rate of growth of output tended to slacken over time. The volume of sulphuric acid production, for example, virtually quadrupled between 1869 and 1878. Output grew by a further sixty per cent between 1878 and 1900 though growth during the ensuing decade was minimal. Production of soda ash and of ammonium sulphate doubled between 1884 and 1904, whilst that of soap doubled between 1890 and 1910. Employment in the chemical industry also expanded over the period, the rate of growth of employment speeding up in the 1890s. Whereas the industry employed 1.7 per cent of the labour force in manufacturing industry in 1891, the proportion had grown to 2.6 per cent in 1911.[6] Exports likewise continued to expand; the value of chemical exports tripling between 1880 and 1913 [*table 8*]. Although Britain's share of world trade in chemicals declined over the period, from 29.4 per cent in 1880 to 21.9 per cent in 1913, the chemical industry's share of UK exports rose from 0.6 per cent in 1870 to 4.3 per cent in 1910.[7]

Table 8: *British Exports of Chemicals, 1880–1913*

	1880	*1890*	*1899*	*1913*
By value (£ million)	8.0	11.6	12.6	24.0
As % of world trade in chemicals	29.4	26.3	22.6	21.9

Source: SAUL, S.B. (1965) The Export Economy, 1870–1914, in SAVILLE J. (Ed.) Studies in the British Economy, 1870–1914, Special Number of *Yorkshire Bulletin of Social and Economic Research*, 17 (1), May, p. 13.

The debit side of the balance sheet is more readily apparent when specific product areas are considered. In broad terms, British manufacturers were relatively successful in retaining their market shares of heavy inorganic chemicals, notably in alkali production, but lagged in the development of a range of new product types, especially artificial dyestuffs and electrochemicals. The British chemical industry maintained a strong hold on soda ash production, its share of world production falling from 58 per cent in 1884 to 50 per cent in 1904 [*table 9*]. Here the problem was not so much that of a falling market as of low profitability resulting in part from the failure to switch from the Leblanc to the Solvay process. By contrast, the UK industry's share of world sulphuric acid production fell much more dramatically, from 46 per cent in 1878 to 13 per cent in 1913.

British firms failed to capitalise on an early research lead in the field of synthetic dyes, allowing their German rivals a chance to dominate this important branch of the industry. Here German strength contrasts sharply with British weakness. In 1913, the German chemical industry produced 85 per cent of the 161,000 tons of synthetic dyes produced throughout the world, and Germany accounted for almost 90 per cent of world exports of dyestuffs. In contrast, British firms accounted

Table 9: *Market Shares of Key Chemicals, 1913*

	UK	USA	Germany	World
Sulphuric Acid ('000 tons of 100% acid)	1,082 (13%)	2,250 (27%)	1,686 (20%)	8,300
Superphosphates ('000 tons)	820 (7%)	3,248 (28%)	1,863 (16%)	11,750
Soda Ash[a] ('000 tons of Na_2CO_3)	850 (50%)	120 (7%)	325 (19%)	1,700
Chemical Nitrogen ('000 tons)	90 (12%)	36 (5%)	119 (16%)	767
Synthetic Dyestuffs ('000 tons)	5 (3%)	3 (2%)	137[b](85%)	161

( ) Proportion of world output produced in country X.

a. 1904.

b. Including production of German foreign subsidiaries, estimated at 10,000 tons.

Source: SVENNILSON, I. (1954) *Growth and Stagnation in the European Economy*, Geneva: UN Economic Commission for Europe, pp. 286–91.

for only 3 per cent of world production and 2 per cent of exports in 1913. There remains, however, the credit side of the balance sheet. British entrepreneurs were relatively successful in maintaining or improving their share of the markets for a range of chemical products including soaps, explosives, paints and some types of heavy chemicals. The soap manufacturers appear to have been amongst the most successful of the chemical industry's entrepreneurs. Whilst the rate of growth of soap production was slower in the fourth than in the third quarter of the nineteenth century, manufacturers were able to overcome an essentially static home market by expanding their export trade in the first decade of the new century, thereby consolidating Britain's position as industry leader.[8] Three powerful firms – Lever Brothers, Crosfield's and Gossage – emerged in the late nineteenth century. The soap industry's consolidation continued in the early twentieth century despite a temporary check when, in 1906, a proposed merger of the leading soap manufacturers fell through owing to press and public hostility.[9] The failure of the merger did not prevent Lever Brothers from acquiring several smaller firms in the succeeding years, whilst the acquisition of Crosfield's and Gossage by Brunner Mond moved the industry closer to duopoly.

The most frequently cited case in which it is alleged that the British chemical industry failed to adopt overseas best practice is that of the alkali trade. Despite the fact that British producers maintained a substantial share of world production until World War I, the history of this branch of the chemical industry has been seen as a 'dreary tale of defensive and overcautious entrepreneurs clinging to the obsolete Leblanc system long after the superiority of Solvay soda production was recognised by their continental and American counterparts'.[10] The critical issue here is whether, given the pattern of input prices and the nature of the market, British entrepreneurs were justified in retaining their Leblanc works or, alternatively, whether, by switching to Solvay's process of ammonia soda production, they could have achieved higher profit levels. The alkali trade of the mid-nineteenth century comprised a closely integrated group of operations centred on Leblanc's process for the production of soda alkali. Sulphuric acid, manufactured by the chamber process, was reacted in furnaces with common salt to produce saltcake (sodium sulphate). In turn the saltcake was converted, by reaction with limestone and coal in Leblanc furnaces, to 'black ash' from which was extracted soda. Whilst the by-products of this process – sulphur and hydrochloric acid – were at first wasted, the invention of the Gossage tower allowed the recovery of the by-product hydrochloric acid which was then used in place of salt in the production of chlorine for bleaching powder. Leblanc producers also found markets for their intermediate products. For example, saltcake was sold to the glass industry. According to Haber (1958), the period from 1860 to 1880 was the 'golden age' of the Leblanc soda industry.[11] Between 1852 and 1878, British production of soda ash and soda crystals tripled, output of bleaching powder increasing over sevenfold. Whilst a high proportion of output was sold on the domestic market, export markets, particularly in the United States and France, were expanding rapidly.[12] We should, however, note that from 1872 an increasingly competitive market meant that production economies were passed on to consumers, the result being a fall in the profit margin per ton of refined product.[13]

By the mid-1870s Leblanc producers were experiencing additional competition from the Solvay ammonia soda process. Ernest Solvay, a Belgian, devised in 1863 a method whereby salt could be converted on an industrial basis to soda (sodium carbonate) by means of ammonia.[14] It was, however, to take a further decade to perfect the process; not until about 1872–73 was soda, produced by the Solvay process, cost competitive with Leblanc soda. British production of ammonia soda began after Brunner, Mond and Company (hereafter Brunner Mond) were granted in 1872 a licence to produce soda by the Solvay process on payment of a royalty of eight shillings a ton. Brunner Mond began production in 1874. Few other producers followed Brunner Mond's initiative.[15] By-and-large, British soda producers chose to compete by trimming costs and promoting the by-products of the Leblanc process, in particular by introducing Weldon's process for the recovery of chlorine from the by-product hydrochloric acid. Such Leblanc by-products did not suffer from competition from the ammonia soda process. Despite stern warnings in the mid-1880s that the dilemma of the Leblanc soda manufacturers could only be met if 'the less favourably situated manufacturers reduce the nominal book value of their present works, take advantage of cheap capital, cheap salt, cheap ammonia, and cheap coal, and erect ammonia-soda works on the best and most approved principles',[16] Britain continued to lag in the conversion to ammonia soda. In 1894, over 65 per cent of British soda production still came from Leblanc plants, while no other country produced more than 22 per cent by this process.[17] Yet the experience of the leading British Solvay producer was unequivocal; from the mid 1870s Brunner Mond's annual dividends were consistently above 25 per cent. By comparison, Leblanc production and profits began to slump in the 1880s. A defensive merger of Leblanc producers took place in 1890 with the formation of the

United Alkali Company. Despite the closing of less efficient plants and the opening of one small ammonia soda plant, and despite the concluding by 1894 of a price and output agreement with Brunner Mond, United Alkali's profit record was dismal and dividends low and infrequent. United Alkali appear to have ceased production of Leblanc soda ash around 1902 and abandoned the remaining Leblanc alkali products by 1920. Kershaw's (1907) comment 'threatened industries . . . like ailing people, have sometimes a long life'[18] sums up an era in which British Leblanc producers, notwithstanding dire prophecies of imminent collapse, staved off the consequences of technological change for over thirty years.

Qualitative evidence strongly suggests that British alkali producers could have benefited, in the sense of earning higher profits, by switching to the Solvay process at an earlier date. It has, however, been argued elsewhere[19] that to refer without qualification to a country's failure to conform to world-wide best practice, or failure to modernize plant and adopt new processes, is to confuse modernity and machinery with profitability. We should in particular note that comparisons with techniques of production adopted in other countries may be misleading because of differences in cost conditions. In the case in point, three of the four largest items in the extra cost of Leblanc over Solvay – coal, pyrites and capital – were cheaper in Britain than the continent. Labour alone was more expensive in Britain. Nor is it sufficient to contrast the input costs for soda ash production by the Leblanc and Solvay processes, for in so doing the profitability of the important Leblanc by-products – notably bleach obtained by the Weldon or Deacon process and sulphur by the Chance-Claus process – would be ignored. The consequences of failing to shift to ammonia soda production can only be measured by a benefit-cost calculation designed to measure the private profit foregone by a non-optimal choice of technique.

Given that the problem of switching from one technology to another has a time dimension, the choice of a decision date is a crucial element of the calculation. Lindert and Trace (1971) chose to calculate the net benefit of switching to the ammonia soda process in each of the three different phases of its development. First, the incremental profits that might have accrued to British chemical firms if one of them, instead of Ernest Solvay, had perfected and wholly adopted ammonia soda production in the late 1860s were calculated. Second, the returns from converting to the ammonia soda process between 1872 and 1886, given that Solvay had already taken out his patent and sold a licence to Brunner Mond, were determined. Third, the results of a decision to switch techniques in the late-1880s was appraised. The three alternatives were found to yield widely differing results.

Britain's failure to develop, patent and adopt the ammonia soda technique clearly cost her income during the latter years of the nineteenth century.[20] This income loss included the royalties Brunner Mond paid to Solvay, the royalties that could have been received from foreign producers, and the incremental profits that British firms could have enjoyed if ammonia soda had been free of royalties between 1872 and 1886. We should however note that British entrepreneurs appear to have put at least as much money and effort as any other country into ammonia soda research before 1870. The search for a commercially viable ammonia soda process must be seen as a research gamble that Britain failed to win. The granting of the crucial patents for the ammonia soda process to Solvay was followed by a licence agreement between Solvay and Brunner Mond. Whilst this agreement set the royalty payment to be made by Brunner Mond at eight shillings a ton, it contained a clause to the effect that no other British licence was to be granted for less than £1 a ton. The £1 a ton royalty appears to have been sufficient to make conversion truly unprofitable for the following fourteen years, that is until the expiration of Solvay's key British patents. Only Brunner Mond, with its lower royalty rate, might have profitably expanded and competed more vigorously, especially in the market for soda ash and crystals, during this period.[21]

The third calculation relates to the decision to switch to the ammonia soda process in the late-1880s. The expiration of Solvay's British patents in 1886 coincided with a period that appears, with hindsight, highly favourable to innovation. By the late-1880s, the Solvay process was well known; the costs of acquiring and perfecting the technique were relatively low compared to those that would have been incurred, say, in the early 1870s. It was also clear, by the late-1880s, that the price of ammonia would not rise and choke off the growth of the ammonia soda process. The Leblanc process, equally, had attained its highest stage of development, the range of by-products being completed by the Chance-Claus process of sulphur recovery. Capital markets were receptive to new issues in the late 1880s and merger negotiations underway between Leblanc producers concluded with the formation of the United Alkali Company in 1890. Here was a clear opportunity for Leblanc producers to switch to the ammonia soda process. In the event, the opportunity was missed, the essentially defensive, merged United Alkali Company closed some Leblanc plants but was content with only a small scale investment in ammonia soda production.

Hindsight calculations show that a wholesale conversion to Solvay plant, if ordered in 1888 and fully installed by the beginning of 1890, would by 1897 have brought the newly formed United Alkali Company additional profits. Thereafter, additional profits would have been earned during each of the years prior to World War I. The capitalized 1890 value of the 1890–1914 gains and losses from conversion to the ammonia soda process would have amounted to slightly under £2 million.[22] Should the gains revealed by hindsight have been foreseen in the late-1880s? There do not appear to have been any foreseeable changes in the relative prices of inputs used by the two processes which would have given the Leblanc producers any grounds for optimism. Nor can Leblanc producers have realistically expected higher prices for their by-products, the 1883 price agreement for bleach and caustic soda having broken down between 1887 and 1889. The remaining hope was that a merger, eventually accomplished with the formation of United Alkali in 1890, would be able to peg bleach and caustic prices well above the Solvay-determined soda ash price. Such expectations necessarily rested not only on the assumption that a cartel would be strong enough to stabilize prices but also on the assumption that the cartel had nothing to fear from new technology. Yet, by the late-1880s, chemists were experimenting on an industrial scale with the electrolytic production of alkali and chlorine from sodium or potassium chloride and a visit to the electrolytic plant at Griesheim, near Frankfurt, in 1892, convinced Lünge that the process was economically viable.

The case study of alkali production clearly suggests that British entrepreneurs could have earned somewhat higher profits by switching to the ammonia soda process at an earlier date. Major gains would have accrued had British producers made the breakthrough actually achieved by Solvay. But, given the finding that British entrepreneurs were ploughing at least as much into ammonia soda research as their continental rivals, it would be uncharitable to conclude that their failure was other than the outcome of an unsuccessful research gamble. Gains could however still have been made had Brunner Mond expanded production somewhat more rapidly in the period 1872–1886 and/or had the remaining producers abandoned the Leblanc system in the late-1880s.

Britain's early lead in synthetic dyestuffs was not maintained despite a resource-based comparative advantage, German firms totally dominating world production and exports by the late nineteenth century. Prior to the 1850s, natural dyes obtained from plants were used for textile colours. Fears that the supply of such natural dyestuffs would be outstripped by demand, and also of the instability of supply due to the vagueries of weather, led to a search for substitutes. The natural dyes were, however, complex organic compounds, their chemical structure beyond the analytical ability of organic chemists of the day. Early discoveries of synthetic dyestuffs should therefore be seen as the result of inspired guesswork rather than coherent scientific experimentation. Perkin's discovery of mauveine (1856) is a case in point. Taking as his starting point Hofman's belief that quinine could be synthesised from napthalene, Perkin followed a series of empirical steps which led fortuitously to the investigation of the action of dichromate on aniline sulphate and, thereby, to the discovery of a brilliant purple solution, mauveine. Shortly thereafter, Perkin set up a factory to produce aniline dyes. Further *ad hoc* experimentation led to the discovery of a range of aniline colours including magenta (1856), violet imperial (1860), and Bleu de Lyons (1861).[23] A small scale industry developed in Britain to exploit aniline dyes.

It was, however, the synthesis of alizarin, one of the red-coloured substances occurring naturally in the root of madder (a plant cultivated in France and the Levant), that gave the infant synthetic dyestuffs industry of the late 1860s its greatest boost. Independent work by Perkin in Britain and Gräbe and Liebermann in Germany concluded with the latter announcing that they had successfully synthesized alizarin from anthracene and taken out the prior patent. Perkin was thus forced to seek an alternative production method. After a five month delay he was able to file a patent for a novel process. An exchange of licences between Perkin and the Badisches Anilin Company, holders of Gräbe and Liebermann's rights, followed. By 1873 Perkin and Sons were producing over 400 tons of alizarin annually. Thereafter, the focal point of the development of the synthetic dye-stuffs industry switched from Britain and France to Germany. By the mid-1870s, German production of alizarin was double that of Britain. Moreover, the locus of invention and innovation clearly lay in Germany. The slow growth of the British synthetic dyestuffs industry contrasted markedly with the rapid expansion of the German. The British synthetic dyestuffs industry which, judged by the volume of production, had been larger than the German in the early 1870s, was only one quarter the size of Germany's in the 1880s and one twenty-seventh the size in 1913.[24] When World War I broke out, Britain was importing from Germany 200 tons of alizarin a month, 100 tons of indigo, 1,200 tons of aniline dyes and smaller quantities of other dyestuffs; almost nine tenths of UK consumption being satisfied by imports.[25]

Here was an industry, in which Britain apparently held substantial natural advantages and in which early development had taken place domestically, being captured by foreign producers; an industry moreover whose products found ready sale in the home market. To what set of factors was the loss in competitiveness attributable? That Britain held a substantial advantage regarding raw materials appears beyond dispute. Synthetic dye-stuffs, notably the aniline, napthalene and alizarin colours, were obtained from such products of coal-tar distillation as benzene, toluene, xylene, napthalene and anthracene. Other major raw materials used in the manufacture of synthetic dyestuffs included ammonia, coal, sulphuric acid, salt, lime, pyrites, nitrate of soda and iron. According to Levinstein (1886), these materials were, with the exception of sulphuric acid, obtainable considerably more cheaply in the 1880s in England than in Germany.[26] Coal tar distilates were exported in substantial quantities to Germany, some three quarters of Germany's consumption of benzene-toluene being imported from Britain. The competitiveness of British prices for ammonia, salt and iron was reflected, Levinstein argues, in the scale of exports, whilst pyrites and nitrate of soda were available in Britain at a lower cost than Germany because of cheaper freights. To these advantages, accruing from cheaper raw materials, should be added the advantages of a large scale domestic market; the British market for synthetic dyestuffs being substantially larger than the German.

Whilst natural advantages clearly favoured Britain, and British manufacturers had access to a large domestic market, it has been argued that British manufacturers not only incurred higher costs in certain areas but also that they laboured under nationally-induced disabilities. The more important explanations advanced to account for the poor performance of the synthetic dyestuffs industry appear to be those relating to the availability of cheaper and more skilled labour in Germany, the allegation that British patent legislation was defective, the argument that scientists and technically skilled labour were hard to obtain because of deficiencies in the British educational system, and the allegation that research and development was assigned a lower priority in Britain than Germany.

Whilst labour cost differentials existed between Britain and Germany, at least in the 1880s, they do not appear to have been sufficient to justify their being considered a major part of the explanation for poor performance. Levinstein (1886), for example, conceded that a labour cost differential existed but argued that it amounted to only £0.1 per week, that it could be compensated for by more capital-intensive technology and that in any case the differential was narrowing.[27] The difference in labour skills is considered together with the alleged deficiencies of the British educational system.

Defective patent laws may have given a commercial advantage to foreign producers. Prior to 1883, British patent legislation did not compel the holder of a patent to work his innovation in the UK, nor was the holder compelled to license others to work the patent in lieu. Section 22 of the Patents, Designs and Trade Marks Act of 1883 attempted to remedy this defect, empowering the Board of Trade to order a patentee to grant a licence if on petition it was shown that the patent was not being worked in the UK 'by reason of the default of a patentee to grant licences on reasonable terms'. The 1883 Act failed in its purpose. The Act did not specify a fixed time within which the patentee was compelled to 'work' his patent and the wording of Section 22 was in other respects ambiguous and ill-chosen.[28] In contrast, French and German patent law clearly specified the conditions under which a patent might be revoked. French law specified that a patentee who failed to work his discovery or invention in France within two years of the date of his patent being granted would be deprived of his patent rights. German patent laws provided for the revocation of the patent after three years if the patentee failed to work his invention in Germany to an adequate extent or whenever the grant of a licence to others to use the invention appeared to be demanded in the public interest and the patentee refused to grant a license 'upon adequate compensation and good security'.

The impact of defective patent laws remains to be satisfactorily resolved. Complaints regarding British patent law recur frequently in contemporary chemical industry publications, it being alleged that, whilst German firms which took out British patents invariably failed to work them (with the result that their adoption was effectively blocked), French and German patent laws not only ensured that a British patentee had to work his foreign patent but was obliged to license foreign producers under threat of patent revocation. Levenstein argued that not one of the 600 British patents relating to coal-tar products granted to foreigners between 1891 and 1895 was being worked in 1897.[29] Further, albeit negative, evidence of the importance of patent legislation is provided by the effects of the Patent Law Amendment Act of 1907. Following the passing of the Act, which was believed at the time to have tightened loopholes relating to the working of patents, a 'spate of foreign plants' was established in Britain.[30] With hindsight, the 1907 Act was also flawed, a 1915 investigation reporting that its compulsory working clause was a 'dead letter'.[31]

Allegations that Britain's lack of success in the synthetic dyestuffs industry stemmed, at least in part, from defects of the educational system are difficult to resolve. That synthetic dyestuff production required not only trained chemists but also a core of technically-trained production personnel is evident from contemporary accounts. It is arguable that the British educational system failed to train sufficient highly qualified chemists and also failed to develop technical education courses for factory floor personnel. In an 1886 address to the Society of Chemical Industry,[32] Levinstein argued that Britain trained few chemical engineers. He contrasted British experience with that of Germany, implying that the lack of trained chemical engineers made the efficient translation of new chemical processes from the laboratory pilot plant to full scale production extremely difficult. His argument obviously struck a responsive chord in his audience for the ensuing discussion focussed primarily on alleged defects of the educational system. The British educational system's failure to produce sufficient university trained chemists was criticised on numerous occasions.[33] Whilst the educational system undoubtedly left much to be desired, it is by no means clear that the failure to develop synthetic dyestuffs can be directly attributed to such deficiencies. The early synthetic dyestuffs industry was, at least in part, developed by foreign nationals, Levinstein himself hailing from Germany. If the lack of trained chemists was the critical constraint preventing the industry's expansion, it is hard to explain why – at a time of free movement of labour – higher wages were not offered as an inducement to German chemists and chemical process workers. German chemists were, in fact, employed at Levinstein's Manchester works and Levinstein himself acknowledged that 'if the number of these highly trained [British] chemists is not yet large enough to supply the demand, there is no difficulty in getting first-class chemists from Switzerland and Germany at reasonable salaries'.[34]

The intensity of research and development work in synthetic dyestuffs appears to have been considerably greater in Germany than in Britain during and after the 1870s. In the absence of industry statistics, or a representative sample of business records, there is no direct way of measuring the relative intensity of research, with the result that we are forced to use such imprecise indicators as numbers of patents and authorship of scientific papers. As Richardson (1968) notes,[35] German coal tar producers took out eleven times more patents than their British counterparts in the last fifteen years of the nineteenth century and German chemists contributed substantially more articles than their British counterparts to scientific journals, especially those relating to organic chemistry.[36] Whilst warning against the danger of elevating neglect of Research and Development (R and D) into a single factor explanation of declining competitiveness, Richardson (1968) remains the strongest proponent of the thesis that the relative decline of the British chemical industry is explicable in terms of 'the sin of underestimating the returns from investing in R and D'.[37] The essence of Richardson's argument is that British industrialists were reluctant to undertake substantial R and D expenditure, even when research was likely to pay off, because 'British industrial supremacy had been built by practical men' and because the social environment tended to underestimate the benefits of R and D. The fact that R and D only paid off in the long run masked the consequences of this attitude until after 1900.

On the other hand, McCloskey and Sandberg (1971) have argued that it is by no means clear that higher expenditure on research would have been individually or nationally profitable.[38] Their argument, derived from the neo-classical economist's competitive model, centres on the proposition that it may be more profitable to let others bear the risks of innovation, a stand that gains strength because the probability of initially adopting the 'wrong' technique is high. In McCloskey and Sandberg's words 'there is a good argument for being a "fast second" in research'.[39] The unseen assumption is that the successful innovator would grant, or be forced to grant, licences on terms favourable to the potential entrant. But in a world of defective patent legislation, a world in which German firms apparently chose to supply the British market for synthetic dyestuffs from German factories and were not forced – through flaws in British patent legislation – to license British firms, the case for being a 'fast second' loses much of its attractiveness. Greater research outlays by British firms in the 1870s and 1880s 'could have made the defect in the patent law irrelevant for dyestuffs'.[40]

Britain's share of world sulphuric acid production appears to have peaked at around 46 per cent in the late-1870s, thereafter falling to 24 per cent in 1900 and 13 per cent in 1913. The price competitiveness of domestic producers declined in the 1880s. By 1886 a significant price difference existed in the British and German markets, Levinstein quoting the delivered price of acid of a standard strength as £3 per ton in Frankfurt compared to £3.75 in Manchester. Given the existing over-capacity amongst British sulphuric acid producers, and in the absence of any cartelisation, Levinstein argued that the price differences necessarily stemmed either from differences in production technology or differences in plant organisation.[41] He urged that British manufacturers 'remodel their works or alter their processes', failing which, he suggested that their customers combine to set up their own vitriol works, perhaps along the lines of the Griesheim Chemical Works at Frankfurt which had recently adopted the contact process.

The contact process of sulphuric acid production, based on the research of Marignac and Lünge, was adopted by German firms in the late-1880s and 1890s: by 1914 over 25 per cent of German sulphuric acid was produced by the contact process, while American and British proportions were 14 and 11 per cent respectively. Britain's lag in adopting the contact process was less marked than that in artificial dyestuffs or in the Solvay process and, indeed, appears explicable in terms of factor costs and demand patterns. Calculations of the unit manufacturing cost of sulphuric acid suggest that, given the pattern of input prices facing both British and German producers in 1902, it was only worthwhile adopting the contact process for the production of very high strength acid.[42] For low strength acid the chamber process appears to have retained a competitive advantage, although the contact process was a substantially cheaper method of producing highly concentrated acid (97–98 per cent H_2SO_4). The threshold beyond which it paid to adopt the contact process, under either country's pattern of input prices, lay in the region of 93 per cent H_2SO_4.

Why then, assuming unit production costs have been calculated correctly, did Germany adopt the contact process earlier than Britain? The explanation may lie in differences in the nature of demand in the two markets. Prior to World War I the synthetic dyestuffs industry accounted for a high proportion of the demand for concentrated acid. The difference in size between the synthetic dyestuffs sector in the two nations is sufficient to account for the observed difference in market shares of the contact process. The lag in adopting the contact process may thus be related directly to the British chemical industry's failure to translate an early research lead in synthetic dyestuffs into a competitive market position.

Ironically, British output of concentrated sulphuric acid was insufficient in the early years of World War I to meet the demand of the heavy chemical and explosive industries, most of the acid being produced being of too low strength for use in nitro-explosives. Britain then turned to continental techniques to step up production of highly concentrated sulphuric acid.

The chemical industry does not provide an unequivocal answer to the question 'Where Did We Go Wrong?'. The industry's share of world production and exports of a range of chemical products declined, the severity of decline varying widely between product groups. Overall, the chemical industry fared somewhat better than average in export performance with the result that its share of total exports rose during the period. We should, however, note that a relatively rapid increase in imports led to a substantial fall in the hitherto healthy export surplus in chemicals.

When investigated on a disaggregated product line basis, the branches of the chemical industry exhibit a considerable diversity of experience. The manufacturers of soap, paints and heavy chemicals were amongst the more successful in maintaining market shares. Such success stories were counter-balanced by the British Leblanc producers' blunder in clinging to their outmoded techniques, by German dominance in artificial dyestuffs and, perhaps also, by the failure of sulphuric acid manufacturers to switch to the contact process. There was, too, a range of new product lines which the British chemical industry may have, by default, allowed to develop abroad. German producers not only dominated dyestuffs but were a powerful force in world markets for chemical glassware, drugs and photographic chemicals. Electro-chemicals became the semi-exclusive preogative of the United States chemical industry.

In the absence of detailed benefit-cost studies for areas other than the alkali trade, the researcher must necessarily rely on a combination of qualitative and quantitative evidence to assess the likely profitability of product lines under the cost and market conditions facing British entrepreneurs. There is no reason to suspect that synthetic dyestuff production was unprofitable under British conditions. The explanation for the failure to develop this branch of the industry consequently focusses on several areas of alleged deficiency, amongst which patent legislation and the failure to appreciate the value of research and development in a research oriented area may partially explain Britain's poor performance in organic chemicals. Failure to adopt the contact process of sulphuric acid production appears explicable in terms of the available domestic market.

Notes and References

1 For an alternative chronology, based on types of production process, see HARDIE, D.W.F. and PRATT, J.D. (1966) *A History of the Modern British Chemical Industry*, Oxford, Pergamon Press, pp. 81–2.
2 HARDIE, D.W.F. and PRATT, J.D. (1966) *op. cit.*, p. 65.

3 SVENNILSON, I. (1954) *Growth and Stagnation in the European Economy*, Geneva, UN Economic Commission for Europe, p. 162.

4 LANDES, D.S. (1969) *The Unbound Prometheus*, Cambridge, Cambridge University Press, p. 276.

5 Victor Clark 'History of manufactures in the United States', as quoted by FAULKNER, H.U. (1961) *The Decline of Laissez-Faire*, New York, Holt, Rinehart and Winston, p. 129.

6 DEANE, P. and COLE, W.A. (1967) *British Economic Growth, 1688–1959*, Cambridge, Cambridge University Press, p. 146.

7 Share of world trade in chemicals from SAUL, S.B. (1965) 'The export economy, 1870–1914' in SAVILLE, J. (Ed.) Studies in the British Economy, 1870–1914, *Yorkshire Bulletin of Social and Economic Research*, 17 (1), May, p. 13.

8 RICHARDSON, H.W. (1968) 'Chemicals' in ALDCROFT, D.H. (Ed.) *The Development of British Industry and Foreign Competition, 1875–1914*, London, George Allen and Unwin, pp. 280–1.

9 ASHWORTH, W. (1960) *An Economic History of England, 1870–1939*, London, Methuen, pp. 97–100. See also WILSON, C. (1954) *The History of Unilever* Vol. 1, London, pp. 72–88, 115–27 and 129–39.

10 LINDERT, P. and TRACE, K. (1971) 'Yardsticks for Victorian Entrepreneurs', in McCLOSKEY, D.N. (Ed.) *Essays on a Mature Economy: Britain after 1840*, London, Methuen, p. 249.

11 HABER, L.F. (1958) *The Chemical Industry during the Nineteenth Century*, Oxford, Oxford University Press, pp. 55–9.

12 LANDES, D.S. (1969) *op. cit.*, pp. 270–3.

13 LINDERT, P. and TRACE, K. (1971) *op. cit.*, p. 275.

14 The ammonia chemical process, involving reaction between carbonic acid (carbon dioxide) and a concentrated solution of common salt saturated with ammonia, was discovered in 1811 by the French physicist and engineer, A.J. Fresnell. Numerous attempts were thereafter made, in Britain and the continent, to translate this chemical discovery to a production basis, including Muspratt's attempt to operate an ammonia soda process in 1840–42. HARDIE, D.W.F. and PRATT, J.D. (1966) *op. cit.*, pp. 83–4. See also LANDES, D. (1969) *op. cit.*, pp. 271–2.

15 The handful of other producers that established in the mid-1870s small scale ammonia soda works on the Cheshire salt fields, were ultimately taken over and shut down by Brunner, Mond and Company.

16 LEVINSTEIN, I. (1886) 'Observations and suggestions on the present position of the British Chemical Industries, with special reference to coal tar derivatives', *Journal of the Society of Chemical Industry*, 29 June, p. 356.

17 'Report on Chemical Instruction in Germany and the Growth and Present Conditions of the German Chemical Industry' by Dr. Frederick Rose. His Majesty's Consul at Stuttgart, *House of Commons Sessional Papers*, 1901, LXXX, No. 561, p. 192, (46).

18 KERSHAW, J.B.C. (1907) 'The present position and future prospects of the electrolytic alkali and bleach industry', *Transactions of the Faraday Society*, III, p. 45.

19 The paragraphs that follow draw heavily on LINDERT, P. and TRACE, K. (1971) *op. cit.* Note however that it is not possible in this essay to comment in depth on the methodological issues raised by such an approach. The reader is referred to the Lindert and Trace study as well as to McCLOSKEY, D.C. and SANDBERG, L.G. (1971) 'From damnation to redemption: judgements on the late Victorian entrepeneur, *Explorations in Economic History*, IX.

20 The statistical basis for this statement, and for ensuing statements deriving from the benefit-cost analysis, may be found in LINDERT, P. and TRACE, K. (1971) *op. cit.*, pp. 253–64.

21 But note that the range of possible error in the estimates is too great to exclude the possibility that Brunner Mond would have been little better off by expanding production.

22 LINDERT, P. and TRACE, K. (1971) *op. cit.*, pp. 280–1.

23 HARDIE, D.W.F. and PRATT, J.D. (1966) *op. cit.*, pp. 64–7.

24 SVENNILSON, I. (1954) *op. cit.*, p. 290. See also RICHARDSON, H.W. (1968) *op. cit.*, p. 287.

25 HARDIE, D.W.F. and PRATT, J.D. (1966) *op. cit.*, p. 71.

26 LEVINSTEIN, I. (1886), *op. cit.*, pp. 352–4.

27 *Ibid*, p. 353.

28 The referee appointed by the Board of Trade to adjudicate in the 1889 case brought by Levinstein against Meister, Lucius and Brüning, Mr. R.W. Wallace, QC, is reported as saying 'whatever the intention of the people who framed this section (section 22) was, they have not stated it in the clear and definite language in which an Act of Parliament ought to be drawn'. LEVINSTEIN, I. (1898) Section 22 of the Patents Act, 1883, and its bearing on British Industry, *Journal of the Society of Chemical Industry*, 30 April, p. 320.

29 LEVINSTEIN, I. (1898) *op. cit.*, p. 320.

30 RICHARDSON, H.W. (1968) *op. cit.*, p. 300.

31 *Ibid*, p. 300.

32 LEVINSTEIN, I. (1898) *op. cit.*, p. 353.

33 See, for example, 'Report on Chemical Instruction in Germany and the Growth and Present Conditions of the German Chemical Industry' by Dr. Frederick Rose, His Majesty's Consul at Stuttgart, *House of Commons Sessional Papers*, 1901, LXXX, No. 561.

34 LEVINSTEIN, I. (1898) *op. cit.*, p. 319.

35 RICHARDSON, H.W. (1968) *op. cit.*, p. 302.

36 In 1872, the British *Journal of the Chemical Society* published 151 British abstracts against 809 German. Ten years later the margin had widened: 232 British abstracts appearing compared to 1,442 German. In the organic area the German dominance was overwhelming: 574 German abstracts appearing in 1882 compared to 59 from the United Kingdom. RICHARDSON, H.W. (1968) *op. cit.*, p. 303.

37 *Ibid*, p. 306.

38 McCLOSKEY, D.N. and SANDBERG, L.G. (1971) *op. cit.*, pp. 106–7.

39 *Ibid*, p. 106. See also KINDLEBERGER, C.P. (1975) German's overtaking of England, 1806–1914, Part II, *Weltwirtschaftliches Archiv*, III (1), pp. 495–6.

40 LINDERT, P. and TRACE, K. (1971) *op. cit.*

41 LEVINSTEIN, I. (1886) *op. cit.*, p. 365. Levinstein noted that labour cost differentials were only of secondary importance. Material costs tended to favour British producers.

42 *Unit costs in £ per ton of pure H_2SO_4, 1902:*

	At German input prices	At British input prices
Regular 'chamber' acid (60%–80% H_2SO_4)		
Contact process	1.233 to 1.461	1.088 to 1.193
Lead chamber process	1.138	0.931
Concentrated acid (97%–98% H_2SO_4)		
Contact process	1.25 to 1.43	1.01 to 1.16
Chamber process plus Heraeus condensing stills	1.572	1.317

Source: LINDERT, P. and TRACE, K. (1971) *op. cit.*, p. 265.

3
Education and Government

Technical Education 1850–1914

Michael Le Guillou

> Royal Commissions, House of Commons inquiries, and great demonstrations of public opinion were tardy in effect. The employer stood aloof.[1]

This brief extract from the 1927 report of the Association of Teachers in Technical Institutes adequately summarises the main argument contained in this essay. Between the run-up to the Great Exhibition of 1851 and the outbreak of the World War I, a great deal took place within the field of technical education itself but whether it had much effect upon the performance of industry in the United Kingdom is another matter. Numerous contemporary accounts would support a further point made by the Association that 'Technical Education was born of the fear of continental competition'. Again, however, there is little evidence to support the view that the growth in the provision of technical education had any impact on industry:

> Manufacturers were suspicious or indifferent. They feared their trade secrets would become known, or they saw no immediate benefits, or they had no faith that schools or colleges could be of service to productive industry.[2]

If the point is worth making at all without the quantitative evidence to support it one way or another, it was not so much that the changes in the educational system were so slow as to check the economic system but that industry itself failed to take advantage of the changes.[3] To stay with the 1927 report for one further point: 'Within a relatively brief period the world ... passed from a non-scientific to a scientific age.'[4] Educational reformers, in fact, became obsessed with the need to expand the provision of 'science classes', if industry and commerce were to meet 'the competition of scientifically trained rivals'.[5] Unfortunately, when an expansion of 'science classes' did take place, especially in the so-called 'organised science schools' dating from 1872, 'there was too much emphasis on the purely academic teaching of chemistry and physics'.[6] Contrast the condemnation of United Kingdom practices – 'the rigid rules and the theoretical curriculum, together with the system of payment by results, led to stale and unimaginative teaching'[7] – with the report of the 1864 French Commission on German technical education:

In this respect Germany appears to us to have made, as regards the diffusion of the sciences, and particularly their application to the requirements of public works, arts and industry, far more rapid progress than England ... The chemical classes have at their disposal extensive and well organised laboratories, in which students are allowed to perform manipulations and thus join practice to theory. Numerous collections of instruments, models, minerals and technology, and also libraries supplied with all the new publications, complete the means of instruction.[8]

The Theoretical nature of the Science and Art Department's examinations in metallurgy, for example, would have been of little relevance to ironmasters struggling with the difficulties of applying the new *inventions* that were taking place in their industry – the Bessemer, the open hearth and the basic processes. The word *inventions* is used advisedly because the men associated with the discoveries were, for the most part, inventors – not scientists. Significantly, too, the inventions occurred in the United Kingdom – despite the lack of scientific and technical education![9] Prior to 1851 – assuming that it would take at least a generation of technical education to percolate through and have effect – the lack of any such education had led to the United Kingdom having the 'least trained' artisans and the 'worst educated' middle class in Europe.[10]

The workshop of the world obtained little, if any, help from its schools, or even from its ancient and wealthy universities, and only prospered in spite of this great handicap.[11]

Significantly, though, in 1851 it appeared that the United Kingdom was under no severe economic pressure to improve the quality of the working force. The demands placed upon the average artisan were physical ones; with few exceptions he was poorly paid and belonged to a labour force that was as much characterized by its high rate of turnover as anything else. Any technical knowledge that was needed was gained by doing the job. However, even in this very unsatisfactory and far from promising situation, a small number of workmen had sought 'to better themselves' through improving their technical education. As a prerequisite to this untypical trend, the individual member of the artisan class would almost certainly have attended one of the following types of schools – a day-school of the National Society, a Lancasterian school, a Charity school, a ragged school, a 'Free grammar school', a 'Dame' school or even a Sunday school. Attendance at any one such school would have provided the individual with only a very rudimentary child education – basic instruction in the three R's, intensive religious learning and perhaps a little vocational training – which was aimed primarily at making the person aware of his 'place' or 'status' in society. Without in some way being able to undergo a self-taught programme, it would be doubtful if the individual could have taken advantage of any technical education. Equally, by 1851, attendance at any one of the many Mechanics' Institutes would have been 'difficult' for any member of the artisan class who felt ill at ease with members of the clerical and middle classes.

The original aim of George Birkbeck had clearly been to offer classes on the scientific principles underlying their trades to workmen and artisans but, although the Mechanics' Institute idea caught on and grew to the point where, in 1851, there were over 600 separate institutes in England and Wales (with a membership of well over 500,000), the nature of the movement had changed in the process. In most cases, institutes had been taken over by the clerical and middle classes, and science instruction had declined;[12] in areas where iron and steel production occupied a foremost position, for example, no chemistry classes were to be found. Perhaps there is a parallel to be drawn with the fate of the Workers' Educational Association (WEA) in the 1960's and 1970's, although it has to be stressed that both movements could never attract a widespread 'working class' support and, at their best, they would appeal to a working class elite. Indeed, this is true of the way skilled men – 'the aristocracy of mid-Victorian labour' – took advantage of the system of examinations started by the Union of Mechanics' Institutes in the late 1830's and 40's. Criticisms that the Mechanics' Institutes had pitched their classes at too high a level or that their book stocks 'were in pretty poor shape'[13] may give the wrong impression. The same kind of criticism is often levelled at the adult education class of today, and yet, for those people who voluntarily participate in them, they have a great deal to offer. Too often, it is assumed that the only education deserving of the name is that which is provided formally in an educational establishment – the work place and the 'self-help' principle of Victorian England have to be taken into account. The Mechanics' Institutes can perhaps best be seen as acting in a supportive capacity to those people capable and determined enough to improve their technical knowledge. Because so many contemporaries chose to do so, it is of interest to repeat the point that compared with the situation in Germany the technical education of the average English workman suffered largely because of the absence of any elementary education:

> In Germany there was compulsory education for at least six years ... In Britain schools were sparse, attendance was intermittent, and the curriculum was uncertain.[14]

In a very hostile environment, the one thing that, perhaps, would have made voluntary participation in education attractive for the working class would have been if it had meant some tangible monetary reward. Not only did a child at school mean a lost opportunity for earning but there was no obvious connection between education and increased opportunities. The average employer's (master of men) only interest in elementary education was indeed that it would make for an obedient and passive work force.[15]

If we may be permitted to excuse members of the working class from being so poorly educated that to participate in any kind of technical education was virtually impossible, was the situation any better for the middle and upper classes in 1851? At first sight, it would appear not for, as one contemporary put it, 'the English people do not believe in the value of technical education'.[16] Very few of the endowed public schools and grammar schools at this time included a science subject in the curriculum, choosing instead to concentrate upon subjects relevant to the preparation of young gentlemen. Rugby was a notable exception but even then too much should not be made of the fact that physics was added to the subjects taught in 1837. At a higher level of education, neither Oxford nor Cambridge had much to offer in the way of modern and scientific subjects; it was too early for the Honours Schools in Mathematics and Science (begun in Oxford in 1850), or the Cambridge Natural Science Tripos (1851) to have had any effect. Elsewhere, progress was equally slow, although classes in engineering were held in Durham (in 1830's) and a chair of Engineering was founded at University College, London, in 1841.

When J. Scott Russell wrote in 1869 that the English did not believe in the value of technical education, he added:

> Still less do they believe in the value of a national system of universal education. And still less in the duty of the Government, the Legislature . . . to undertake the education of a whole people.[17]

Nevertheless, it was the state, either directly through the schools of design administered by the Board of Trade[18] or the various establishments belonging to the armed forces (Scott Russell himself praised the Royal College of Naval Architecture and J.F.D. Donnelly was perhaps only one of a number of army engineer officers from the Royal Engineers and Royal Artillery influential in technical education), that was putting some resources into such education even before 1851. Lyon Playfair, for example, had been at the School of Mines since 1845 when, in 1850, he was appointed one of the Commissioners to plan and organise the Great Exhibition. Playfair's career up to that time was by no means typical of the day (it was exceptional) but it does show that if the individual was both able and willing, it was possible for somebody in the United Kingdom to achieve a very good scientific education and then rise to a position of influence within the state system. Born in 1818, Lyon Playfair spent some of his formative years on the continent studying under Liebig, the foremost German chemist of his day. At various stages in his career he enjoyed the confidence of both politicians (including Sir Robert Peel and Prince Albert) and leading industrialists (notably Sir Bernhard Samuelson); with regard to the latter Playfair attempted to interest them in education by proving, for example, that they could save money if their workforce could appreciate the causes of waste in the production processes. It was, indeed, a slow development, but more important at this stage in the furtherance of ideas relating to science and technology were the many learned societies. Nationally, the Royal Institute (1800) had considerable influence in spreading knowledge of mechanical inventions and improvements, as, in fact, did both the Society of Arts (1754) and the British Association for the Advancement of Science (1831). Significantly, somebody like J. Scott Russell was a Fellow or Member of a number of societies and institutions including, in Russell's case, membership of the Institute of Civil Engineers, of Mechanical Engineers and of Naval Architects. Finally, it was always possible – both before and after 1851 – for industry to buy its *science* from abroad, if and when it saw the need.[19]

The Great Exhibition of 1851 was seen by at least one contemporary as 'a great school (in which) the civilised nations of Europe had their first lesson in technical education'.[20] According to Russell, 'the genius of Paxton would alone have sufficed to rescue the skill and the manufacturing industry of England from humiliation'. What upset the calm and satisfaction of those who visited the Great Exhibition was the beauty and grace of design of continental glass and pottery exhibits:

> It is curious, but instructive, to notice that the Exhibition of 1851 had disgusted the whole nation with its blue earthenware plates, cups and saucers, borrowed from the 2000 years' tradition of China, and with its huge lumps of glass, called decanters and glasses, cut or moulded into hideous distortions of form.

Four years later, it was the turn of Napoleon III to emulate Queen Victoria with the Paris Exhibition of 1855. In that short space of time, the English had improved the design of their glass and pots but the French and Germans had made even bigger strides in heavy industry; unfortunately, the mass of those English visitors to Paris failed to learn from the second lesson:

> What we saw in 1855 was instructive to the clear-sighted and the thoughtful, but it was not humiliating to the mass of English visitors, and it did not alarm the English manufacturers. Therefore, unhappily, they did not take warning in time.

The third lesson was the British Exhibition of 1862 when, if it did nothing else, it showed that the British should give up the idea of having exhibitions because they only served to advertise to the world 'the more rapid progress of rival nations'. The Paris Exhibition of 1867 provided the final lesson:

> By that Exhibition, we were rudely awakened and thoroughly alarmed. We then learnt, not that we were equalled, but that we were beaten – not on some points, but by some nation or other on nearly all those points on which we had prided ourselves.[21]

Russell was in no doubt as to the cause:

> I have said enough to let him understand how the Exhibition of Paris startled a thinking Englishman, and ended by convincing him that England had been asleep, and that a whole generation of wakeful, skilled workmen had been trained in other countries during the interval between 1851 and 1867. Fifteen years is the time necessary to train a generation of skilled men.[22]

It is, indeed, the case that the 1867 Exhibition led to a flurry of activity amongst those people interested in technical education but, before moving to a consideration of what occurred after 1867, what (if anything) had taken place in the United Kingdom whilst the continent was supposedly training 'a whole generation of wakeful, skilled workmen'? The main agency of technical education after 1851 was the Department of Science and Art set up by the Aberdeen Government in 1853.[23] Lyon Playfair was Secretary for Science until 1858, when Sir Henry Cole took it over, in addition to his responsibility for Art. The grand sum of £898 had been spent on science classes between 1853 and 59, but not to criticize Playfair unduly, the Department had reorganised and renamed the School of Mines[24] whilst Playfair himself had spent a good deal of time 'in lecturing in England on technical education and in visiting science and technical colleges on the continent'.[25] Cole, in particular, was initially opposed to the idea that the state should take a 'dominant part in Secondary Education'; instead, he favoured a system whereby the Department would financially support institutions which had been set up as a result of a local patron or charitable trust.[26] The new system for providing science classes, introduced in 1859' aimed directly at the 'industrial classes of this country', hoped 'to stimulate the public to do the work of scientific instruction for itself as much as possible, the State aid being simply auxiliary'.[27] Similarly, the Department's help to cities which wished to start schools of science put the burden upon the cities themselves to found institutions; Bristol and Birmingham were the first to make use of this rather limited support. For various reasons, not least a combination of the theoretical nature of the syllabuses and the rote-like teaching methods adopted by the teachers who got additional payments on the results of examinations (£3 for a first-class pass, £2 for a second and £1 for a third), it was not long before most employers had become highly suspicious of anyone who had not gained some practical experience in industry in addition to passing the examinations of the Science and Art Department. The reorganised School of Mines also failed to make any impact on industry; even after 1862, when the institution was again reorganized to make the courses more strictly vocational, it was generally accepted that its graduates were not fitted for industry without further training.

At the centre of the activity occasioned by the poor showing of British industry at the international exhibitions was the work of the Parliamentary Select Committee on Scientific Instruction, under the Chairmanship of Bernhard Samuelson, MP. Samuelson was one of the very few industrialists to take a significant part in the campaign for scientific and technical education. Before looking at the home scene, he had been sent abroad by the government (one version says that Samuelson offered his services and the Education Commissioners took up his offer) to see whether or not the chief cause of the continent's better showing at the 1867 Exhibition was due to a superior system of education. Samuelson visited France, Belgium and Germany, taking in as many 'manufacturing establishments ... which stand in direct rivalry to our own':

> He found everywhere in these establishments men of all ranks better edu
> cated than our own; working men less illiterate – foremen and mangers well
> educated, and masters accomplished, well-informed, technical men. He
> traced out the pupils of technical schools to their practical and successful
> results, as the superintendents of large works ... [28]

Samuelson was not prepared 'to estimate precisely what has been the influence of continental education on continental manufacturers', but he contrasted the well-educated continental worker with the 'imperfectly taught British manufacturing artisan' and the 'illiterate agricultural labourers'. Samuelson's leadership of the Select Committee in 1868 was extremely energetic and a considerable amount of evidence was obtained from various sources, including industrialists. The need for more education was clearly linked to the growing threat of foreign competition and some of the views expressed showed that attitudes were slowly changing – even over the question of state aid. In Sheffield, the local Chamber of Commerce seemed to favour the creation of an institution which could teach foremen chemistry and metallurgy; in the Black Country, a Smethwick glass and chemical manufacturer had overcome his dislike of state aid and accepted capitation grants from the Science and Art Department; in Keighley, money from the same source was used to create a system of technical education that was soon to be greatly admired by both Professor T.H. Huxley and the Duke of Devonshire.[29] But the overall message from Samuelson was one that was to be heard over and over again: Britain suffered from the inadequacy of primary and secondary education and the shortage of science teachers. The Select Committee recommended a sound system of secondary education, a new scheme of primary education and improved facilities for teaching science.

The Education Act of 1870 whilst not necessarily stemming from the efforts of those who were championing the cause of scientific and technical education, nevertheless, went some way towards meeting their wishes. Unfortunately, words rather than deeds became the order of the day with regard to scientific and technical education itself and for the next five years a Royal Commission on Scientific Instruction and the Advancement of Science sat under the chairmanship of the Duke of Devonshire. Then, in 1881, Samuelson was asked to head a Royal Commission on Technical Instruction and more voluminous reports were forthcoming. Whilst the former came to the conclusion that there was a dangerous lack of scientists and technologists in Britain, Samuelson's group of like-minded, committed men[30] called for the need to improve primary and secondary education as the pre-requisite to a sound system of scientific and technical instruction. Samuelson's findings were all the more valuable because they came from a group of level-headed men who were realists and who saw not only what was required but what was possible in the circumstances. Essentially, the need for state aid was recognised but, at the same time, it was no good providing science subject classes which were not practically-orientated in their content; consequently, school boards and local authorities would have to seek the cooperation of industrialists. The question of teacher supply was recognised as being crucial but, apart from saying that science in teacher training colleges should be increased and made more efficient, there were few suggestions with regard to how practical men with industrial experience might be attracted into the profession. In effect, this was to prove to be a significant factor in the failure of the education system to serve the needs of industry whilst at the same time contributing to the air of mutual suspicion with which industry and education came to view each other. Swire Smith and Henry Roscoe were also sensible enough to realise that the findings of the Commission would not necessarily lead to legislation and action and what was required was the permanent presence of a pressure group which could promote legislation on technical education and continue to stimulate interest by providing a steady supply of informed literature. The National Association for the Promotion of Technical Education was set up in 1887 and remained a fairly active and influential body down to the early years of the twentieth century.

The Association issued a report within two years of being founded and stressed once again the shortcomings of teacher training: 'the great majority of teachers . . . receive but little, if any, adequate scientific instruction'.[31] Improvements within the provision of state education after 1870 made it increasingly feasible for individuals to reach a level of basic education from which it was possible to progress in scientific and technical instruction. Similarly, money was being made available by the state for just such education. The creation of the new County Councils in 1888 led to the Technical Instruction Act of 1889, by which local authorities were given powers to raise a penny rate in support of technical instruction. Not all authorities took advantage of this legislation but by the end of the 1890's a considerable sum of money was being raised. The Science and Art Department kept a fairly tight rein on the curriculum content of such courses and it also provided grants for buildings and capital equipment. Perhaps even more important (and certainly more popular with all except those who over-imbibed) was the Local Taxation (Customs and Excise) Act, by which certain sums out of customs and excise duties were allocated to local authorities either to relieve the rates or to subsidise technical instruction. Gradually, this 'whisky money' rose to over £860,000 (eight times greater than the sum raised by rates). However, as a result of the legislation of the 1870s and 1880s, there were, in effect, two different bodies supplying education at a local level. School boards, created by the 1870 Act primarily for the purpose of providing elementary education but slowly moving into the fields of secondary and technical education, acted under the authority of the Education Department. The 1889 Act had itself led to the creation of technical instruction committees or technical education boards and, under the guidance of the Science and Art Department, these tended to regard themselves as the providers of both secondary and technical education. A number of towns and cities came to benefit from very influential technical instruction committees, including Birmingham, Sheffield, Leeds, Huddersfield, Liverpool and London. The Mechanics' Institutes in these towns had used the 1889 Act to acquire central funds for the enhancement of local provision and very often the same people took an active interest in the provision of education at all levels. Significantly, those towns which made the most headway with basic scientific and technical instruction also took the lead in the provision of university education – Sheffield (Firth College), Birmingham (Mason Science College), Leeds (Yorkshire College of Science) and Liverpool (University College). London, too, saw considerable development at all levels although, in 1892, a report on Technical Education by A.H. Smith had argued that London was 'not only very far behind Germany and France . . . but also far behind our chief provincial towns'. Once again, particular attention was given to the shortage of trained teachers and the fact that industry viewed with suspicion those teachers who were without practical experience. In April 1893, the Technical Education Board of the London County Council met for the first time under the chairmanship of Sidney Webb, and with William Garnett as secretary. It is probably an exaggeration to say that a revolution took place in the provision of technical and scientific education in London but over the next nine or ten years the efforts of Webb and Garnett were considerable. Support and encouragement were given to Regent Street Polytechnic (opened in 1882 by Hogg) and to the Polytechnic at New Cross (founded and maintained by the Goldsmiths' Company and now, of course, Goldsmiths' College). In addition to the London Polytechnic (Northern, Borough and Northampton were also represented on the London Polytechnic Council), Webb's committee was able to provide financial support for a number of smaller institutions including the Working Men's College (which ran trade classes), Wandsworth Technical Institute and the Brixton School of Building. Webb's skill at persuasion in bringing about a 'fully comprehensive' system of scientific and technical education (he boasted that his polytechnic did more work of a university level than the new provincial universities 'with all their dignity of charters and chancellors, diplomas and degrees', whilst the trade courses provided a 'unique kind of instruction for the intelligent workmen') was seen best in the way that he brought together all the interested parties – the Charity Commissioners, the City Companies, the LCC, the City and Guilds Institute and the individual institutions. The 1902 Education Act, whilst not primarily concerned with scientific and technical education, nevertheless, had a considerable influence upon developments in those spheres down to the outbreak of war in 1914. The legislation of 1899 and 1902, indeed, had both positive and negative effects upon the development of scientific and technical education. A Royal Commission on Secondary Education (the Bryce Commission 1894–95) had published its findings in 1895[32] and had referred to the fact that secondary education at all levels was uncoordinated and illogical. As a result of such findings, the Government decided to reform the central agencies and in 1899 the Education Department, the Science and Art Department and the education sections of the Charity Commissioners were merged into a new Board of Education. Almost immediately, the Duke of Devonshire, as President of the Board, had set up a committee to look into the Coordination of Technological Education. School boards were abolished in 1902, together with the technical instruction committees, and all forms of national education placed in the hands of county councils and county borough councils constituted as Local Education Authorities. So far, so good; the rationalization of resources which had been advocated both by the Technical Instruction Commission of 1881–84 and the Bryce Commission had been brought about. Surprising, perhaps, in view of the presence of men like Sir Swire Smith and Michael Sadler, no answers were found to the question of how to make practical scientific and technical education socially acceptable, or for that matter, recognised as absolutely necessary both by the state and industry. On the one hand, the state had appeared to refuse to accept responsibility for practical instruction – workshop practice – whilst, on the other, resources provided for scientific and technical education remained largely concerned with part-time education provided for the lower wage-earners. The post-1902 expansion of secondary education, especially the provision of grammar schools, concentrated upon supplying people for respectable white-collar jobs – not 'jobs in industry'.[33]

Faced with the difficulties of filling the many gaps in respect of the secondary schools in their areas, LEA's found it almost impossible to spend the sums of money that were required to sustain a momentum in the part-time system of 'further education'. Organizational consolidation there undoubtedly was – continuation schools, technical and commercial schools at both branch and central levels – but, sadly, even in those areas which were able to build and staff well-equipped premises, there was a shortage of students arising out of an inadequate student support system and the socio-economic non-acceptability of technical education. Very few of those students who enrolled for 'basic' scientific and technical education actually moved on to more advanced courses, one reason being the need to devote time (dare we mention it?) 'to the recovery of work which should already have been done at school'. Many of the premises, too, that housed 'evening classes' had been designed (and were used in the daytime) for children; perhaps the closest modern-day analogy we can find is the system of non-vocational adult education which continues in many areas with the use of school buildings (many of which house primary school children during the day) for adult classes in the evenings. Curriculum matters provided another disappointing aspect; a rigid examination system left little room for innovation and the emphasis was very much upon teaching methods that left nothing to chance. However, it was probably in this area that most improvement took place within the system itself up to the outbreak of World War I. The system operated by the Board of Education of 'Science and Art' examinations had meant that students took individual subjects, which might or might not be related, to add up to what in today's terms would be a further education *course*; after 1902, and very much as a result of the efforts of the Union of Lancashire and Cheshire Institutes, a system of 'grouped' subjects was offered. The Board of Education officially adopted this innovation in 1910 and by 1914 most LEA's had fallen into line. Also, the Board of Education fostered the growth of regional examining boards, and the ULCI and the EMEU took over responsibility for drafting syllabuses and setting and marking examinations.[34] One difficulty, which is not present today with the system of day- and block-release operating, was the fact that most 'evening class' students arrived at 'school' after a very long working day. Even in 1921, the total number of day students amounted to only 22,000. In effect, therefore, the combined efforts spread over more than half a century had resulted in the creation of a system of technical education based upon part-time study that involved only a very small percentage of the population.[35] Theoretical scientific instruction, rather than practical and technical studies, formed the basis of much of what was provided, and this led to industry being less than supportive to the efforts of the state. Inadequate financial support to students ensured that no large-scale developments could take place and the low esteem that society held for technical education was seen in the very poor salaries and working conditions offered to teachers. No real attempt had been made to create an educational system that allowed for progression to take place from one stage to another. Junior technical schools, which dealt solely with local industries, were in no way linked to senior technical schools; both groups had little contact with other forms of secondary education. Even the Technical Inspectorate of the Board of Education was said to function in isolation and not to be in touch with colleagues from main-stream education.

Notes and References

1 'Report on an Inquiry into the Relationships of Technical Education to other forms of Education and to industry and commerce', The Association of Teachers in Technical Institutions, November, 1927, p. 8.

2 *Ibid.*

3 MUSGRAVE, P.W. (1967) *Technical Change, the Labour Force and Education*, Oxford, Pergamon, p. 1.

4 ATTI (1927) *op. cit.*, p. 7.

5 SMITH, S. (1916) *The Real German Rivalry*, T. Fisher Unwin, p. 16.

6 ARGLES, M. (1964) *South Kensington to Robbins*, London, Longmans, p. 21.

7 *Ibid.*

8 Quoted by SMITH, S. (1916) *op. cit.*, p. 17.

9 Numerous writers contend that the apparent sloth with which these inventions were put into practice can be attributed to the poor state of education in the United Kingdom. P.W. Musgrave, for example, has written: 'The steel industry provided three good examples of sudden particular change. Between 1856 and 1878 the introduction of the Bessemer, the open hearth and the basic processes revolutionised technique. Such inventions often change the structure of the labour force and not only new skills, but a different proportion of old skills may be needed. This process puts direct demands on technical education and perhaps on training within industry. It also puts indirect demands on the basic education upon which further education is built. However, education plays a perhaps more vital role in the acceptance of sudden technical change. Scientific knowledge is the basis upon which the application and development of such innovation rests. Ready acceptance must, therefore, depend upon the spread of the relevant scientific facts and upon a favourable attitude to science and change. Lack of scientific knowledge or hostile attitudes can check the transmission of an invention; both these faults can be due to malfunctions within the educational system', (p. 2). At first sight much of what Musgrave says is correct – especially of the iron and steel industry in the second half of the nineteenth century – but industrial development is never simply a question 'of malfunctions within the educational system'. The application of the basic process to the making of steel in the Cleveland District provided a good example. Whilst it is indeed true that Cleveland firms encountered technical difficulties when they tried to make basic steel from local ores – not to mention marketing difficulties – it is also the case that it became cheaper to go on making Bessemer steel by the acid process with high quality ores imported from Spain and (later) Sweden. The availability of river-side sites, rather than failings in the educational system, determined which steel-making process would flourish on Tees-side. See LE CUILLOU, M. (1979) *A History of the River Tees*, Cleveland County Libraries, pp. 81–5.

10 SMELLIE, K.B. (1951) *A Hundred Years of English Government*, London, Duckworth, quoted by ARGLES, M. (1964) *op. cit.*, p. 5.

11 SMITH, S. (1916) *op. cit.*, p. 16.

12 'In the large towns of Yorkshire science students were as hard to find as needles in a bunch of hay. In 1866, Leeds had one class at the Mechanics' Institute with 33 students; in Huddersfield, there was one with 26; but in Sheffield, Bradford, Hull, Halifax and so throughout the towns of England – there were no science classes', *Ibid*, p. 15.

13 ARGLES, M. (1964) *op. cit.*, p. 7.

14 MUSGRAVE, P.W. (1967) *op. cit.*, p. 44.

15 ENGELS, F. *The Working Class in England in 1844*, p. 238, et seq.

16 RUSSELL, J.S. (1869) *Systematic Technical Education for the English People*, p. 79.

17 *Ibid*, pp. 78–80.

18 These had been established after W. Ewart, a Liverpool MP, had in 1835 proposed a select committee of Parliament 'to inquire into the best means of extending a knowledge of the Arts and of the principles of design among the people (especially the manufacturing population) of this country'.

19 MUSGRAVE, P.W. (1967) *op. cit.*, pp. 51–2, like so many others who have studied and written upon this subject, appears to condemn this practice – he quotes the Manchester man who exclaimed when told that a junior partner of the main Mulhouse calico printer was qualified at a German polytechnic, 'Oh! We can buy our chemistry', and comments that he thus portrays 'the common belief that managerial ignorance of science could be offset by the employment of a chemist'. Inevitably, perhaps, Musgrave goes on to quote the example of Lowthian Bell who 'from the first maintained a chemical laboratory'. If only he had looked beyond the spoken and written word – by Bell himself – to see just how disastrous an influence Bell had on the Cleveland Iron and Steel Industry because of his much publicised knowledge of chemistry. Bell opposed the basic process (both before and after the successful trials of Gilchrist and Thomas), the introduction of Swedish ores to the United Kingdom and the use of the continental-style cooking ovens – all on the strength of his knowledge of chemistry!

20 RUSSELL, J.S. (1869) *op. cit.*, p. 87.

21 *Ibid*, p. 86.

22 *Ibid*, p. 90.

23 Until 1857, the Department remained under the Board of Trade but in that year it became part of the new Education Department. In effect, it remained separate from the Education Department, which promoted primary education, and took on the responsibility for encouraging secondary and technical education.

24 In 1853 it became the 'Metropolitan School of Science applied to Mining and the Arts'; the 'Royal College of Science' was not used until 1890.

25 ARGLES, M. (1964) *op. cit.*, p. 20.

26 One result, perhaps, of the series of exhibitions was that by 1867 Cole had swung over to the belief that all questions of finance to do with public education should be in the hands of a Minister of Education.

27 Department of Science and Art, 6th Report, 1859, quoted by ARGLES, M. (1964) *op. cit.*, p. 21.

28 RUSSELL, J.S. (1869) *op. cit.*, p. 99.

29 SMITH, S. (1916) *op. cit.*, p. 19.

30 As well as Samuelson and Swire Smith, the Commissioners included Professor Henry Roscoe, a Liverpool scientist who had trained at Heidelberg under Bunsen, and who had been responsible for setting up a strong School of Chemistry at Owens College, Manchester; John Slagg, a textiles industrialist and MP; Philip Magnus, of the City and Guilds Institute; and William Woodall, industrialist of Staffordshire.

31 *Technical Education in England and Wales*, 1889, p. 63.

32 Significantly, perhaps, out of 61 County Councils giving evidence to the Bryce Commission, 19 included representatives of local industries (if not already councillors, industrialists had been co-opted on to councils), *The Royal Commission on Secondary Education* (1895), (*Bryce Commission*), Vol. i, pp. 35–6, and 420–1.

33 ARGLES, M. (1964) draws attention to the fact that H.G. Wells' books provide an amusing commentary on the social and cultural values of lower-middle-class Edwardian England and that it 'was rare for an Artie Kipps to become a mechanic', p. 59.

34 The third important regional body – the Northern Counties Technical Examinations Council – was not founded until 1921, but LEAs in Yorkshire had also taken a lead in introducing grouped courses.

35 The Thompson Commission had reported to Lloyd George, in 1918, that only 7 per cent of the male population was getting any sort of trade instruction in 1914.

The Universities

Gordon Roderick and Michael Stephens

Throughout the nineteenth century Oxford and Cambridge were a favourite target for the numerous critics of the scientific scene in England. The ancient universities were a perpetual thorn in the flesh of those who viewed with concern the rise of the German universities and technical high schools. To such critics, Oxford and Cambridge, with their adherence to traditional studies, were an insidious influence, a stumbling block to progress; the abandonment of outmoded educational ideas and a greater emphasis on science was demanded.

These criticisms were heard before a number of Royal Commissions during the period 1850 to 1870 and resulted in important changes being implemented by the latter date. But it was after 1870 that Oxford and Cambridge, in response to the challenge from an increasingly industrial and commercial society, began to integrate new thinking about the functions of a university and to pay more attention to the need for scientific studies. This was particularly so between 1900 and 1914 and it was during this period, too, that the civic universities became recognizably the institutions we know today.

It was to Scotland that England looked for the production of the 'professional' scientist. Scotland in the eighteenth century had developed a distinctive educational system of its own; at the age of fifteen students entered university for four years of a general education which included philosophy, classics and science. After this general education students undertook a specialist training. England relied heavily on the products of the Scottish universities in the fields of medicine, science and engineering throughout the nineteenth century.

In England the major innovation in higher education in the eighteenth century came from the Dissenting Academies. The revival of the 1559 Uniformity Act in 1662 and the allied legislation known as the Clarendon Code (1662–65), with the demand that clergymen and university tutors should conform to the liturgy of the Church of England, led to the exclusion of those other than Anglicans from teaching posts at the Oxford and Cambridge colleges. The response of the Dissenters was to set up their own Academies. Created primarily to provide higher education for those entering the Ministry, their curricula also included natural and experimental philosophy, mechanics and hydrostatics, geography, astronomy, French and German, as well as navigation and commercial subjects. Oxford and Cambridge, deprived of many of their most able and vigorous dons fell into decline; the curriculum was narrow, standard of tuition low and posts were limited to the clergy. Towards the end of the first decade of the nineteenth century, the Edinburgh Review launched a sustained campaign of criticism. In 1810, it published a scathing attack on the concept of scholar as upheld at the ancient universities:

> A learned man! a scholar! A man of erudition! Upon who are these epithets bestowed? . . . Are they given to men who know the properties of bodies and their action upon each other. No! This is not learning. The epithet of scholar is reserved for him who writes on the Aeolic reduplication . . . His object is not to reason, to imagine, to invent but to conjugate, decline and derive . . . Would he ever dream that such men as Lavoisier were equal in dignity of understanding to, or of the same utility as Bentley and Heyne.[1]

At Oxford the subjects of the BA degree course were ancient history, Latin, Greek, poetry, philosophy, logic and mathematics. There was no chemistry taught at Oxford and, while Cambridge included chemistry in its curriculum, neither Oxford nor Cambridge had laboratories. However, scientific lectures were being given at Cambridge as early as the 1800s by Professor Vince who illustrated his lectures in mechanics with practical demonstrations using apparatus which quickly became obsolete. In the 1820s, Professor Airy, Lucasian Professor of Mathematics, delivered a course of lectures on pneumatics, optics and mechanics. Later Professor Farish, Jacksonian Professor of Experimental Philosophy, concentrated on the teaching of machinery, a practice that his successor, Professor Willis, continued and extended by lecturing on the nature of weaving, steam engine models and machines. George Liveing, Professor of Chemistry at Cambridge, in giving evidence to the Devonshire Commissioners, later claimed that 'the results (in physical science) are very small compared with the noise which has been made about them'.[2] The essential point about these early attempts at scientific instruction was that they were spasmodic, as witnesses to the Devonshire Commission pointed out; they led nowhere, each innovation collapsing as soon as the innovator moved on.

The credit for pioneering the physical sciences and technologies at university level belongs to University College, London, and King's College, London. University College, London was intended for those members of the middle class unable to enter Oxford and Cambridge and was also to provide opportunities for the study of subjects not available at the older universities. Opened in 1826, it was modelled on the University of Berlin. From the outset full scope was given to the sciences and engineering. Two years later, King's College was established. This also adopted a progressive attitude to science and engineering (a distinctive feature of the college). Up to 1850 it was customary for those wishing to pursue a systematic course of advanced study in chemistry to seek it in Germany at Giessen or Heidelburg or Marburg. Leading public figures came to the conclusion that a national college of chemistry was an urgent requirement and, in 1845, the Davy College of Practical Chemistry was founded under a Council whose President was HRH Prince Albert. It was to be devoted mainly to pure science but in order 'to meet the exigencies of this country, and to adopt the latest improvements in the Continental schools an appendage will be provided, devoted to the Economic Arts, where inquiries relating to Pharmacy, Agriculture and the other Arts may be pursued'. As a result of the personal intervention of the Prince Consort, Dr. August Wilhelm von Hofmann was appointed to the post of Professor of Chemistry, being granted two years' leave of absence by Bonn University. Under Hofmann's inspiration teaching and research flourished, the college attracting students of diverse backgrounds.

> Almost all classes of society have been represented in the laboratory – gentlemen following chemistry as a profession, or as an object of scientific taste, chemists and druggists, medical students and medical men, agriculturists, manufacturers in almost all branches of the chemical arts, copper smelters, dyers, painters, varnish makers, soap boilers, brewers and sugar makers have been working side by side.[3]

Although initially not lacking in guaranteed support, the college was, nevertheless, in financial difficulties by 1847 for subscriptions had fallen off considerably. Much of the debt was cleared by twenty three members of the Council contributing £50 a-piece, but developments were seriously affected and financial sacrifices were necessary from all, including Hofmann:

> Dr. Hofmann voluntarily gave up in succession – first a portion of his salary, then his share of the students' fees and lastly his house; yet during this trying period he never in the slightest degree relaxed his efforts to establish the reputation of the college. He not only gave up the money which was his due, but, out of his extreme devotion to the educational objects of the college, abandoned for some years what to a German savant is of still greater importance, his original research investigation.[4]

Meanwhile the Government had founded the Museum of Economic Geology in 1839. Here students received instruction in mineralogy, analytical chemistry and meteorology. Following a Report by a Committee of the House of Lords which expressed concern at the lack of facilities for mining education, the Museum of Economic Geology became in 1851 the 'School of Mines and of Science Applied to the Arts'. Instruction was designed to enable the student 'to enter with advantage upon the actual process of mining or of the Arts which he may be called upon to conduct.[5] So in the quarter of a century between 1826 and 1851 four Colleges had been established in London which between them provided a wide range of scientific and technological studies.

What made higher education, and in particular scientific and technical instruction at university level, widely available across the country generally was the emergence of the 'civic' colleges during the last quarter of the century. Manchester led the way with the creation of Owens College in 1851. Owens, a wealthy merchant of the City, left £100,000 in trust for the express purpose of founding a college open to all, irrespective of creed. Owens College continued the trend, begun by King's College and University College, of providing studies relevant to the commercial and industrial needs of the country. The growing awareness of these needs led to six new colleges being founded between 1871 and 1881, all of which were later to acquire university status.

Oxford and Cambridge after 1850

Although professional studies such as law, medicine and theology were of importance at Oxford and Cambridge in the early nineteenth century, they merely formed the super-structure, the foundation for which was a 'liberal' education firmly based on the classics. Only a minority of students pursued a professional course, the majority being content to confine their studies to classics. A significant innovation at Cambridge during the early nineteenth century was the emphasis given to mathematical studies. However, these studies were not intended to lead to the production of professional mathematicians or to the training of such personnel as would apply this mathematical knowledge within another profession. For instance, between 1800 and 1850 no fewer than 43 men who subsequently became Bishops were successful in the Cambridge Mathematical Tripos.[6] The real significance of this development of mathematical studies was that the concept of 'liberal studies' had now been redefined so as to include mathematics. The philosophical foundations for such a view were to appear in Whewell's *On the Principles of English University Education* which was published in 1837, a theme taken up by Newman in *On the Scope and Nature of University Education* published in 1852. According to Whewell, the virtue of mathematical study was not that it led to increased knowledge or that it was useful as an instrument for other purposes but, rather, that it lay in its power to provide 'intellectual discipline'. The study of mathematics, he said, 'induces solid and certain reasoning' and he argued that 'some insight into the progressive sciences (i.e. mathematics) is an essential part of a liberal education . . . the man of mathematical genius who . . . is led to become familiar with the best Greek and Latin classics becomes thus a man of liberal education'.[7]

In the view of these advocates mathematics became as essential a part of liberal education as was classics. In arguing thus Whewell and Newman would have had the support of such theorists as Huxley and Spencer. On the other hand Whewell's statement that 'the state of Germany . . . has of late years been unfavourable to the intellectual welfare of its students' would have brought strong dissent from Huxley, for he was an advocate of the German model of higher education with its emphasis on professorial teaching and its acceptance of science and technology. This was at the heart of the controversy which focussed on Oxford and Cambridge during the middle decades of the nineteenth century. Huxley challenged the views of Newman and Mill; he called for theoretical studies of technologies such as engineering, agriculture and industrial chemistry to be included within university studies:

> There can surely be little question', said Huxley, 'that instruction in the branches of science which lie at the foundation of these arts ought to be obtainable by means of a duly organized Faculty of Science in every

university. The establishment of such a Faculty would have the additional advantage of providing in some measure for one of the greatest wants of our time and country, I mean the proper support and encouragement of original research.[8]

Support for the importance of research came also from within the ancient universities. The Reverend Mark Pattison, Rector of Lincoln College, Oxford, in his seminal work *Suggestions on Academical Organisation* wrote:

there remains but one possible pattern on which a University can be constructed . . . This is sometimes called the German type . . . the Professor of a modern university ought to regard himself primarily as *learner*, and a *teacher* only secondarily.[9]

This was diametrically opposed to Newman's view which was that the universities should not be concerned with research but only with teaching and education. Huxley's advocacy of technological studies, too, was far removed from Newman's narrow view but it was Huxley's ideas that were to prevail. His desire for technological studies such as engineering, industrial chemistry and agriculture was to find realization in most universities including Oxford and Cambridge by 1914.

Whatever the respective merits of 'liberal' education and of 'scientific' education, there was a growing dissatisfaction with the ancient universities. Many felt that there was an almost total neglect of science; facilities for scientific study were very inadequate and scholarships and fellowships in science were few. The student intake was largely from the public schools and certainly too exclusively from one sector of society. A further adverse factor was that lecturers had to take Holy Orders. But above all, the most universally condemned feature was the dominant influence of the colleges. Royal Commissions on the universities reporting in the early 1850s recommended the abolition of the halls and colleges over the universities, the appointment of professors and lecturers so as to break the hold that tutors then had on instruction and that colleges should contribute out of their revenue towards university developments. Reforms were quickly implemented during the 1850s and 1860s but great disquiet persisted over the state of scientific education at the universities.

The Commission, appointed in 1868 under the chairmanship of the Duke of Devonshire to inquire into scientific instruction throughout the country, examined the work of the universities very carefully. The Commissioners wrote to the heads of the colleges in order to ascertain what sums had been spent on science. Several colleges refused to reply and of those which did reply many had spent no money on science. In the award of fellowships, classics and mathematics still dominated; of a total of 449 at all the colleges, no fewer than 212 (46 per cent) were in mathematics; seven only were in science.

A number of witnesses who appeared before the Commissioners were highly critical of the state of science and technology at the universities. J.C. Adams, Lowndean Professor of Astronomy at Cambridge considered that 'science had largely been neglected hitherto'. At Oxford, N.S. Maskalyne, Professor of Mineralogy, confessed he had only three students and that 'mineralogy is hardly pursued at all at Oxford and geology is only very imperfectly pursued'.[10] G.M. Humphreys, Professor of Anatomy at Cambridge, thought that the Natural Science Tripos, despite being in existence for twenty years, had not flourished as it might have done; the average number of candidates – mainly medical students – was twelve. Of significance was the fact that the standard was not high for 'the route through the Natural Science Tripos was an uncertain avenue to a fellowship'[11] The Rev. James Challis, Plumian Professor of Astronomy and Expermental Philosophy wondered whether 'we perhaps have not made the advance (in physics) that we might do, considering what has been done outside the University'.[12]

Several witnesses to the Devonshire Commission emphasized the research function of the universities but at the same time expressed great dissatisfaction as to the neglect of research at Oxford and Cambridge. Clifton thought Oxford did very little in that direction as:

> the professors' time is so taken up with teaching now that it is impossible for them to do anything more than teach, and in fact not to do that as thoroughly as they would wish ... One main duty of a university is to promote research and another is to supply the country with the very best teachers ... the number of teachers now employed is so small that one of these aims must be neglected.[13]

Sir Benjamin Brodie, Professor of Chemistry at Oxford, also told the Commissioners that in the sciences the university had to supply elementary teaching, a situation which, according to the Master of Sidney Sussex College, also prevailed at Cambridge. The teaching was at an elementary level because those entering for science were not the best material and they had been inadequately instructed in the schools. Teaching loads were high because there were so few appointments in science, and consequently research was neglected. The Devonshire Commissioners provided lists of science lecturers at Oxford, Cambridge and Berlin and they concluded that 'it is impossible not to be impressed with the evidence which the list affords of the abundance and variety of the scientific teaching given in Berlin by professors of great eminence.'[14] Thus the plurality of professorial appointments in any one subject was a key factor in the promotion of research. The Devonshire Commissioners illustrated it by quoting from the evidence of Sir Henry Roscoe, Professor of Chemistry at Owens College, Manchester, and J.G. Greenwood, Principal of the College, who in 1868 had been on a conducted tour of the German universities. They claimed that:

> The number of teachers is considerably larger than in the English universities and colleges ... Provision is thus made for the effective instruction of students and for the zealous prosecution of original research ... the number of skilled assistants attached to each professorship, is greater than we have in England. In Bonn and Berlin, one assistant (often professors) is appointed to every 12–13 students ... whereas I have only two assistants to 60 students in my laboratory. One great expense in working a laboratory

is the cost of the apparatus and chemicals used by the students, and this is especially paid for in German universities by the state . . . In England the greater part of this charge falls on the professors.[15]

Roscoe pointed out that at Berlin University there were four professors of chemistry and seven professors of physics – a situation not untypical of German universities and technical high schools in general. Until late in the nineteenth century it was customary in England to have only one professor in each subject. Greenwood and Roscoe urged on the Commissioners the 'importance of the principle that the existence of a plurality of teachers is an indispensible prerequisite both for breadth and depth of instruction' and pointed out that where there were several teachers in one discipline 'the teachers are also induced by the opportunity of lecturing on special subjects, to engage in profounder investigations'.[16]

Witnesses to the Devonshire Commission agreed that the funds provided by the universities were 'lamentably deficient' and professors complained bitterly that they had to provide their own apparatus and pay demonstrators out of their own pockets. Yet at Cambridge the annual income of the colleges was estimated to be £180,000, whereas the income of the University from endowments was a mere £2,000. A similar situation existed at Oxford. Despite the Royal Commissions, the Universities' development lay largely in the hands of the colleges and the final verdict of the Devonshire Commissioners was that scientific teaching was 'inadequate in amount' at the ancient universities.

Statistical data bears out the evidence presented by the witnesses to the Royal Commissions as to the position of science at mid-century. The Class Lists issued by the Public Examiners at Oxford show that there were 101 successful candidates in classics and 28 in mathematics. At Cambridge 38 had passed the Classical Tripos and no fewer than 131 the Mathematical Tripos but, by this time, success in the Cambridge Mathematical Tripos had become one of the highest honours attainable and to be Senior Wrangler represented the apex of achievement, a distinction eagerly sought after by clerics among others.

At Oxford there were fifty professors of whom ten were in science (excluding mathematics). This certainly gives the impression that science was not neglected but taken on its own it is highly misleading for while there were professors in geology and mineralogy the earlier evidence of the Professor of Geology to the Devonshire Commission points out that the number of students was few. Further, to put it into perspective, there were two chairs in Arabic and one each in Chinese and Sanskrit but there was only one in the growing field of biological sciences. It is very likely that the science professors were entirely engaged in teaching medical students. At Cambridge the total number of professors was far fewer – twenty-three, of whom four were in science (in chemistry, physics, botany and mineralogy). Outwardly it would appear that Oxford with its ten science chairs was in a far stronger position than Cambridge with its four chairs. This is negated, it would seem, by the testimony of witnesses to the Devonshire Commission who invariably pointed to the greater prominence of the sciences at Cambridge. Such judgements, however, may have been coloured by the eminence of Cambridge mathematics.

It is difficult, therefore, to arrive at an objective assessment of the relative strengths of science at the Universities in 1850.

Whatever this may have been in 1850 by 1900 a radical shift had come about in their respective positions. This is illustrated in *table 10*. At Cambridge out of a total teaching staff of 70 there were now 18 (26 per cent) in the sciences. Comparable figures at Oxford were 15 out of 84 (18 per cent). Technology at Cambridge was represented by the chair of mechanical sciences and the recently founded one in agriculture. At Oxford there had been no appointments in technology additional to that in rural economy which had existed in 1850. In mathematics and physics, if not also in chemistry, Cambridge was now clearly ahead. This impression is further strengthened by a survey of student numbers. At Cambridge the successes in Part I of the various Triposes were now: Natural Sciences (136); Classics (126); Mathematics (82); History (49); Law (46); Languages (25); Mechanical Sciences (18); Theology (13); Moral Sciences (9). Thus, while classics still held a dominant position, it had by now been surpassed by natural sciences, while theology had been totally eclipsed. At Oxford, on the other hand, the position was very different. In the Class Lists issued by the Public Examiners classics led the field with 154

Table 10: Staff at Oxford and Cambridge

OXFORD

	1850				1900			
	Professors	Others	Total	Percentage of total	Professors	Others	Total	Percentage of total
Theology	5	—	5	10	7	1	8	10
Classics	5	—	5	10	4	2	6	7
Law	4	—	4	8	5	1	6	7
Arts	19	—	19	36	22	17	39	46
Medicine	6	—	6	11	6	4	9	11
Science	13	—	13	25	11	4	15	18
Technology	1	—	1	—	1	—	1	1
	53	—	53	100	55	29	84	100

CAMBRIDGE

	1850				1900			
	Professors	Others	Total	Percentage of total	Professors	Others	Total	Percentage of total
Theology	6	—	6	19	6	—	6	9
Classics	3	—	3	10	5	—	5	7
Law	3	—	3	10	4	1	5	7
Arts	9	—	9	30	14	7	21	30
Medicine	3	—	3	10	9	4	13	19
Science	7	—	7	21	12	6	18	26
Technology	0	—	—	—	2	—	—	2
	31	—	31	100	52	18	70	100

successes, closely followed by history with 148. Natural sciences came next with 37 but were nearly equalled by theology with 31 and there were only 26 successes in mathematics.

The data strongly suggest that Cambridge was by now the leader in science and it could certainly take a pride in its facilities. Between 1863 and 1900 museums of zoology, of botany and of mineralogy had been built and in addition to the Cavendish Laboratories of Physics, opened in 1871, had been added new chemical laboratories in 1887 and engineering laboratories in 1894.

The civic colleges and universities

Between 1871 and 1881 six new colleges were founded: the Armstrong College of Physical Science, Newcastle (1871); the Yorkshire College of science, Leeds (1874); the Firth College, Sheffield (1874); the Mason College of Science, Birmingham (1880); University College, Nottingham (1881) and University College, Liverpool (1881).[17]

University College, Liverpool, came into existence following a Public Meeting convened by the Mayor at the Town Hall on 28th May, 1878, when a resolution was passed to the effect that it was:

> desirable to provide such instruction in all the branches of a liberal educa-
> tion as would enable residents in the town and neighbourhood to qualify
> for degrees in arts, science and other subjects, at any of the universities
> granting degrees to non-resident [and also] to give such technical instruc-
> tion as would be of immediate service in professional and commercial
> life.[18]

The idea of 'practical utility', in the sense of providing instruction leading to university degrees particularly in the sciences and in technology, stands out in this resolution. Furthermore, it is clear from the titles given to three of the colleges above that the fostering of scientific studies was their principal aim. That science was to be of dominant importance in the work of the College at Liverpool was further stressed by Principal G.H. Rendall in his Inaugural Address:

> This is indeed in intellectual progress the age that science may justly call
> her own ... for the present age and for life's daily needs, science bids fair
> to occupy the larger place; it is invading every department of life; and it is
> in purveying and disseminating this side of knowledge that the College
> will probably find its most special work.[19]

This statement can also be taken to represent the philosophy underlying the formation of the other colleges.

Although a wide variety of technological disciplines were established by the colleges in response to local needs, the credit for pioneering physical sciences, and engineering in particular, belongs to University College, London, (1826) and King's

College, London, (1828). University College had the distinction of being the first college in England to appoint a professor of civil engineering (in 1840).[20] Engineering was a distinctive feature of the teaching at King's College too, soon after its foundation and later it established the first chair of electrical engineering in 1890. The most significant contribution of Owens College lay in the field of chemical studies, for under Sir Henry Roscoe a respectable school of chemical research was established. In 1874, Carl Schorlemmer, a German-trained PhD, who had earlier been attracted to the College by Roscoe as a lecturer, was appointed Professor of Organic Chemistry. This was the first chair of organic chemistry in an English university and the lateness of the appointment is indicative of the neglect of this subject by the universities.

Turning to the newer civic colleges, Newcastle specialised in mining, metallurgy and naval architecture, whilst the college at Leeds also made a valuable contribution to local industries by establishing a wide range of relevant courses in textiles, dyeing and leather processing. A special feature of the work of Firth College, Sheffield and Mason College, Birmingham was the study of coalmining and of metallurgy. A remarkable innovation at Birmingham was the establishment of a Department of Brewing in 1899 following a donation of £28,000 by local brewers. Another innovation was at Liverpool when the Borough Engineer, the Manager of the Yorkshire and Lancashire Railway and the Engineer-in-Chief of the Mersey Docks and Harbour Board were all made Associate Professors in Municipal Engineering, Municipal Electrical Engineering, Railway Engineering and Docks and Harbour Construction respectively.

Despite the fact that the civic colleges owed their origins to common purposes, a principal one of which was the promotion of science and technology to meet the needs of local industries, in practice the studies offered by them differed at many points. These differences cannot be explained entirely as being the reflection of local conditions, and a determining factor may have been the means by which new enterprises were financed. All the colleges were acutely short of funds and thus, whilst college councils may have wished to put in hand particular developments, the possibilities open to them in practice were often dependent on their benefactors. Thus at Leeds, the Clothworkers Company of London donated £15,000 for a Textile Department and £2,500 for a Dyeing Department. At Sheffield Sir Thorpe Mappin, a local cutler, gave £2,000 for the funding of a Technical Department and the Drapers' Company of London gave £4,000 for a similar department at Nottingham. The latter College benefited, too, from the local coal owners' guarantee of £300 for a Mining Department, whilst at Birmingham local brewers gave £28,000 for the development of studies in the science of brewing.

One of the colleges to receive considerable local support was University College, Liverpool. Its original laboratories were built at a cost of £20,000 out of donations from several leading citizens. In 1886 Sir Andrew Walker, a local brewer, gave £32,000 for engineering laboratories and later in 1909 J.W. Hughes and H. Harrison donated £41,000 for additional engineering laboratories. Meanwhile, in 1905, Dr. Edmund Musgratt, a local alkali manufacturer had given £17,000 for physical chemistry laboratories. In the period 1887 to 1914, donations for sites and buildings in science and technology exceeded half a million pounds; by comparison the amount the University received from government sources during the same period was a modest £170,000.

It was not only buildings and laboratories which depended on the generosity of local groups and individuals, but also the creation of chairs. These were sometimes the outcomes of the fancies of wealthy individuals. At Liverpool the policy was that the creation of a chair required a specific endowment, usually to the value of £10,000. The financing of chairs from general college funds was not attempted prior to 1907, presumably because of the precariousness of the general financial position, and when such a policy was implemented the three unendowed chairs lapsed after twelve months. Between 1889 and 1893 endowments were provided for chairs in botany, physiology, pathology and anatomy but there was no endowment for geology until 1916. Sir John Brunner, influenced no doubt by his industrial experiences, endowed a Chair of Physical Chemistry – the first in England. A year earlier, William Johnston, a local shipowner, had endowed the Chair of Biochemistry but no one came forward to offer an endorsement for organic chemistry.

At each of the civic colleges, the first chair in engineering was either in civil or mechanical engineering. Electrical engineering was a later development which usually began as a lectureship in electrotechnics, this later being converted into a chair; King's College (1890) Yorkshire College (1899) Newcastle (1907) and Sheffield (1917). In chemical studies what was remarkable was the neglect of organic chemistry and the late recognition of physical chemistry as a subject in its own right. As late as 1900 there was only one full professor of organic chemistry (Owens College). Liverpool, Leeds and Sheffield had lectureships in the subject and the chemistry of dyeing was included at Owens and at Yorkshire College. In practical chemistry, apart from the chair at Liverpool, there was only one other appointment, that being a special lecturer in the subject at Sheffield.

Although wealthy industrialists, manufacturers and merchants were prepared to endow chairs, sometimes perhaps for reasons of prestige, the appointment of lecturers and demonstrators was financed out of general college funds. Such funds were rarely in a healthy state (the accumulated debt at Liverpool in 1907 was £11,000[21]) consequently junior posts were thinly spread. At Liverpool in 1895 the ratio of junior to professorial posts was 1.6 : 1; many departments consisting only of a professor and one assistant. The ratio for all science and technology post in the civic colleges in 1894 was 1.7 : 1.[22] It followed that teaching duties tended to be heavy, with the result that research was neglected.

Another factor which all the civic colleges had in common was the slow rate of growth in the number of candidates taking degree courses; it was not until the 1890s that substantial numbers of degree successes were recorded. Being a student all too often involved a substantial degree of financial hardship as scholarships were few. Many students were effectively barred from full-time study or could only embark on a limited period of study. Such difficulties were recognised by college authorities who provided a number of alternative courses at different levels. The colleges also established a variety of shorter courses leading to the award of diplomas, certificates and college associateships which met the needs of local industries. There were diplomas in mining, engineering and naval architecture at Newcastle, diplomas in mining at Sheffield and Birmingham, a diploma in brewing at Birmingham and certificates of proficiency in dyeing, textile industries and leather industries at Leeds.

In addition to the provision of day classes, each college arranged an extensive programme of evening classes in a wide range of subjects. During the first session at Liverpool in 1881 the Registrar was able to announce that over 500 students attended the College classes but fewer than a hundred had registered for the day classes. The evening classes, which were open to both sexes for a charge of six shillings per session, continued to flourish throughout the period 1881–1914. In 1889 the subjects of the evening classes included mathematics, physics and chemistry, electrotechnics, technological chemistry, oceanography and geology. The physics course spread over twenty weeks was entitled 'Scientific principles of the electric telegraph' and there were also twenty weeks of elementary practical physics and twenty weeks of electrotechnics. In engineering there were classes in vibration and balancing of machinery, applied mechanics and theory of machine design. Special features of the evening programme at Liverpool were the classes in mechanical drawing and engineering at the Walker Engineering Laboratories; classes by Professor Hele-Shaw were attended by large numbers of artisans (often 200 or more) for a charge of one penny per evening. Liverpool was, however, far from unique in emphasising evening instruction and similar programmes of evening classes may be found in the Calendars of most other civic universities.

The government played little part in the origins and development of the provincial civic universities; financial support was not forthcoming until 1889 when the first Treasury Grant in aid was awarded. Government aid in England was concentrated instead on the two London institutions – the Royal School of Mines and the Royal College of Science[23] – despite the pleas of industrialists to the effect that it was not in London that centres of science and technology should be placed but in areas such as Newcastle and Sheffield, in close proximity to the major centres of industry. In 1907 these two colleges were amalgamated with the City and Guilds Technical College, founded jointly by the London Livery Companies and the Corporation of the City of London in 1884, to form the new Imperial College of Science and Technology, a cooperative venture which involved the Government, the London County Council and the City and Guilds. It paid off handsomely, for it quickly became the leading centre of science and technology and by the outbreak of war it had a staff of nearly forty professors. Its impact can best be seen in the field of engineering for the number of candidates successful in the London Honours BSc in engineering rose from a mere five in 1903 to sixty in 1910, the College contributing 50 per cent of the successes.[24]

Considerable numbers of students succeeded each year in obtaining diplomas awarded by the three colleges after rigorous three or four-year courses in which students specialized in one subject. Because of the length and rigour of the courses and because of the illustrious staff attracted to the colleges – Sir Norman Lockyer (physics), John Percy (metallurgy), Thomas Huxley (biology), Sir Lyon Playfair and Sir Edward Frankland (chemistry), and Sir Warington Smyth and Sir Clement

Le Neve Foster (mining) – the authors feel justified in including these diploma students among those listed as honours graduates in *tables 11* and *12*.

It has been demonstrated that graduate scientists and technologists represented but a small fraction of all those who received some measure of university training. The graduates were the elite, or the fortunate, or perhaps merely the 'fittest', for many students entered full-time courses at the universities after years of evening study at technical colleges and universities only to abandon their studies at a later stage. By no means all students entered degree courses, for other courses had a wide appeal; among those on degree courses the numbers graduating were only a small proportion of those who began the course.

Table 11: Graduate Manpower 1870–1910 (figures represent numbers graduating in the stated years)

	1870	1880	1890	1900	1910
SCIENCE					
B.Sc. Honours Mathematics[a]	1	1	8	22	44
B.Sc. Honours Physics[a]	0	7	16	25	39
B.Sc. Honours Chemistry[a]	3	1	26	48	126
B.Sc. Honours Geology[a]	3	3	9	9	14
B.Sc. General Degree[b]	6	26	77	200	577
Total Science	13	38	136	304	800
TECHNOLOGY					
B.Sc. Honours Engineering[c]	0	0	11	46	183
B.Sc. Honours Mining[d]	3	6	13	14	31
B.Sc. Honours Metallurgy[d]	3	11	3	3	10
B.Sc. Technology (Honours)	0	0	0	0	12
B.Sc. Engineering	0	0	0	0	137
B.Sc. Mining	0	0	0	0	6
B.Sc. Metallurgy	0	0	0	0	3
B.Sc. Technology	0	0	0	0	9
Non-Degree Technology Awards	0	0	3	11	40
Total Technology	6	17	30	74	431
Total Science and Technology	19	55	166	378	1,231

a. Includes Associates of the Royal College of Science.
b. Includes Associates (of Science) of the Armstrong College, Newcastle.
c. Includes Associates of City and Guilds Central Technical College.
d. Includes Associates of the Royal School of Mines.

Source: Calendars of:
i. *Universities:*
   London, Durham, Manchester, Liverpool, Leeds, Sheffield, Birmingham, Bristol.
ii. *Colleges:*
   Imperial College of Science and Technology; Owens College; Yorkshire College; Armstrong College of Science; Mason College, Birmingham; University College, Sheffield; University College, Liverpool; University College, Nottingham.
Note: If Oxford and Cambridge are included the additions to the figures in the final total for science and technology are: 1870 (150); 1880 (148); 1890 (177); 1900 (160) and 1910 (189). The lack of variation in these figures reflects the dominance of mathematics at Cambridge. Mathematics graduates at Oxford and Cambridge accounted for 90 per cent of all English university science graduates in 1870 and 80 per cent in 1890.

Table 12: Cumulative Totals of Graduate Scientists (1870–1910) (figures represent numbers graduating in or before the stated years)

	1870	1880	1890	1900	1910
SCIENCE					
B.Sc. Honours Mathematics[a]	17	33	85	213	443
B.Sc. Honours Physics[a]	0	16	87	286	640
B.Sc. Honours Chemistry[a]	24	49	179	675	2,430
B.Sc. Honours Geology[a]	30	76	113	189	271
B.Sc. General Degree[b]	6	172	614	2,577	7,126
Total Science	77	346	1,078	3,940	10,910
TECHNOLOGY					
B.Sc. Honour Engineering[c]	0	0	60	440	1,553
B.Sc. Honours Mining[d]	28	91	151	312	558
B.Sc. Honours Metallurgy[d]	22	75	140	202	291
B.Sc. Technology (Honours)	0	0	0	0	47
B.Sc. Engineering	0	0	0	0	570
B.Sc. Mining	0	0	0	0	26
B.Sc. Metallurgy	0	0	0	0	30
B.Sc. Technology	0	0	0	0	56
Non-Degree Technology Awards	0	0	18	90	289
Total Technology	50	166	369	1,044	3,420
Total Science and Technology	127	512	1,447	4,984	14,330

a. Includes Associates of the Royal College of Science.
b. Includes Associates (of Science) of the Armstrong College, Newcastle.
c. Includes Association of the City and Guilds Central Technical College.
d. Includes Associates of the Royal School of Mines.

Source: Calendars of:
i. *Universities:*
London, Durham, Manchester, Liverpool, Leeds, Sheffield, Birmingham, Bristol.
ii. *Colleges:*
Imperial College of Science and Technology; Owens College; Yorkshire College; Armstrong College of Science, Mason College, Birmingham; University College, Sheffield; University College, Liverpool; University College, Nottingham.

Scientific manpower and the English civic universities

During the greater part of the nineteenth century there were few openings in industry for scientists and opportunities for research, both at university and in industry, were rare. For many, the opening up of the Dominions and South American countries offered more attractive prospects than were available in England and this accounted for the high 'brain-drain' of trained manpower. To some extent this was offset by an influx of trained scientists from the continental countries, particularly Germany. With the establishment of the new civic colleges, the growth of technical colleges and the gradual change in the attitude of the schools to science, opportunities in teaching and lecturing became increasingly available. The attitude of industry changed also for, while earlier there had been no very great demand for scientists, there was a greater readiness at the end of the century to undertake organized research and this attitude coincided with the production of new nuclei of trained scientists. One result of the availability of English-trained man-power was that progressive firms such as Crosfields of Warrington, who had earlier employed German-trained scientists, were now able to replace these with men trained in the English universities.

During the second half of the nineteenth century, the leading technological centre in England, and the institution most likely to produce the managerial technologist and scientific research worker, was the Royal College of Science and Royal School of Mines. From a survey of the careers of 850 former students,[25] it is possible to draw certain conclusions. Of these 850 students, whose careers spanned a period of forty years, only 170 (20 per cent) had entered industry at some stage in their careers. It is not unreasonable to assume that no other institution contributed as many. Of those who spent some time in industry, the majority entered mining and brewing and frequently they held positions not in management or research but in the inspectorate. Some 32 per cent went abroad, either immediately after qualifying or at later stages in their careers and 28 per cent entered the teaching profession. Some indications of research publications are given and from these it would seem that no more than seventy-five (9 per cent) engaged in research.

Another source of information regarding careers of graduates is Professor Schuster's account of *The Physical Laboratories of the University of Manchester* which was published in 1906.[26] Arthur Schuster was educated at Frankfurt Gymnasium and later studied for a PhD degree under Kirchhoff at Heidelberg University. He was appointed Professor of Applied Mathematics at Owen College in 1881, and his account contains a record of the careers of those who studied at the physical laboratories during the period 1881 to 1906. The increasing opportunities for physicists – following the founding of the civic universities, the development of technical education and the integration of science into the secondary school curriculum – is demonstrated by the fact that, of 115 individuals listed, no fewer than thirty-three obtained some appointment on the staff of a university department, eighteen became lecturers in technical colleges and twenty-one took up school teaching. Fewer than twenty entered industrial firms and of these several went to Mather and Platt or British Thompson Houston as heads of various divisions.

The membership of the Institute of Chemistry in 1901 totalled 683 Fellows. The Proceedings of that year contain a survey of this membership but unfortunately no information is given in the case of 340 of them. Of the remaining 343, it is again clear that the majority were engaged in academic rather than industrial spheres. No fewer than 66 had the degrees of PhD which indicates the strong connections between training in chemistry and the German universities; thirty-three were on university staffs and twenty-three in technical colleges. Fifty went abroad and eighty-four were employed in laboratories of various description. These included the laboratory of Somerset House and public laboratories such as the railways and Borough Council laboratories.

Perhaps the most comprehensive source of information is E. Fiddes, Registrar of Manchester University, in his Register of Graduates of the Victoria University of Manchester (See *table 13*). His survey included all graduates of the closing years of the nineteenth and early years of the twentieth century and reveals that the rate of emigration was slowing down; opportunities in industry for chemists and engineers were improving. But it was still true that the major proportion of graduates, either through choice or force of circumstances, entered the teaching profession.

Table 13: Occupation of Graduates of the Victoria University

	(a) Secondary Schools per cent	(b) University Technical Coll. Training Coll. per cent	per cent	Emigrated per cent	Other per cent
B.Sc. Finals	31	13	11	7	38
B.Sc. Honours Mathematics	36	40	0	2	22
B.Sc. Honours Physics	41	31	9	3	16
B.Sc. Honours Chemistry	21	29	28	12	10
B.Eng.	0	22	32	20	26

Source: FIDDES, E. Chapters in the History of Owens College and of Manchester University, 1851–1914, University of Manchester Publications, number 254, Historical Series, number 174, Manchester, 1937.

In conclusion it would appear that the numbers of fully-trained scientists and technologists in England fell far short of what was desirable in the last quarter of the nineteenth century. In 1910, the number of university students of science and technology was about 3,000 whereas the corresponding figure in Germany was 25,000.[27] On the one hand there was a considerable wastage of latent talents and on the other too many partially or inadequately trained scientists.

One of the main objectives behind the creation of the civic universities was the training of the cadres of scientists and technologists the country needed. The blame for not tackling this problem earlier may be attributed to industry for not creating a demand for scientists; to the ancient universities, for paying too little attention to the physical sciences; and to successive governments, for their failure to establish an efficient unified educational system. It is certainly true that the intake of scientists into industry was not very great, but it may well have been that many firms had every wish to employ scientists but were unable to find enough men of the highest calibre. It seems, therefore, that while industry should not be entirely exonerated, the major portion of blame should fall on the government which left the civic universities to struggle on as best they could, facing immense difficulties in their attempt to achieve their objectives. More government money at an earlier stage, improved primary and secondary systems of education and a national system of scholarships, along the lines of the Whitworth Scholarships, could have eased their task. Neither the Devonshire nor Samuelson[28] Commissions produced a cogent analysis of England's long term needs for scientific manpower.

Notes and References

1 SMITH, S. (1810) *Edinburgh Review*, Vol. XV, pp. 46–7.
2 *Royal Commission on Scientific Instruction and Advancement of Science*, (The Devonshire Commission), (1872) Vol. 1, p. 282.
3 CHAMBERS, T.G. (1896) *Royal College of Chemistry, Royal School of Mines and Royal College of Science*, Hazell, Watson and Viney, p. 31.
4 DE LA RUE, W. (1864) *Farewell Banquet to Dr. Hofmann*, 28 April, cited in CHAMBERS, T.G. (1896) *op. cit.*
5 *First Prospectus of the Government School of Mines* (1852).
6 CARDWELL, D.S.L. (1957) *The Organisation of Science in England*, London, Heinemann, p. 42.
7 WHEWELL, W. (1837) *On the Principles of English University Education*, p. 43.
8 *Science and Education*, Essays, Vol. III, Macmillan and Co., 1893, p. 223.
9 PATTISON, M. (1868) *Suggestions on Academical Organisation*, Edmonson and Douglas.
10 (*Devonshire Commission*) (1872), Vol. I, p. 32.
11 *Ibid*, Vol. I, p. 285.
12 *Ibid*, Vol. I, p. 278.
13 *Ibid*, Vol. I, p. 187.
14 *Ibid*, Vol. III, p. xxv.
15 *Ibid*, Vol. I. First, supplementary and second reports with minutes of evidence, p. 499.
16 *Ibid*, Vol. III, p. xxvl.
17 ARMYTAGE, W.H.G. (1955) *The Civic Universities*, London, Ernest Benn.
18 *University College and the University of Liverpool 1882–1907, A Brief Record of Work and Progress* (Liverpool: University Press, 1907), 4–5, Harold Cohen Library, University of Liverpool.
19 Inaugural Address delivered at the opening of University College, Liverpool, 14 January, 1882, by Principal G.H. Rendall, Harold Cohen Library.
20 BELLOT, H. (1929) *A History of University College, London, 1826–1926*, London, University of London Press.
21 MUIR, R. (1901) *The Need for a University of Liverpool*, p. 65, Harold Cohen Library.
22 *Education Department (1894): Reports from University Colleges Participating in the Grant of £15,000 made by Parliament for University Colleges in Great Britain* (HMSO).
23 In 1889 government aid to these colleges was £14,000, a sum almost equal to the total aid (£15,000) shared between all the civic colleges.
24 *University of London Calendar*, 1910.
25 CHAMBERS, T.G. (1896) *Register of Associates and Old Students of the Royal College of Chemistry, the Royal School of Mines and the Royal College of Science*, Hazell, Watson and Viney.
26 SCHUSTER, A. (1906) *The Physical Laboratories of the University of Manchester*, Manchester, Manchester University Press.
27 KUKULE, R. and TRÜBNER, K. (1910) *Minerva, Jahrbuch der Gelehrten Welt* (Verlag Karl J. Trübner). Also, Board of Education: Reports from Universities and University Colleges participating in the Parliamentary Grant.
28 *Royal Commission on Scientific Instruction and the Advancement of Science Reports*, (*Devonshire Commission*), 1872–75; *Royal Commission on Technical Instruction*, (*Samuelson Commission*), First and Second Reports, 1882–1884.

Technical Education and
the University College of Nottingham

Brian Tolley

During the last thirty years of the nineteenth century, several universities and university colleges were established in provincial centres throughout England. Their foundation was to a great extent a response to a demand for more advanced scientific and technical education which was seen as one means of improving industrial and manufacturing performance at a time when foreign competition seemed to threaten many parts of the economy. Nottingham University College was unique amongst these institutions in that it was almost wholly a municipal project, the Corporation of Nottingham assuming responsibility for its maintenance in the absence of a substantial endowment from private benefactors. The use of municipal resources was justified on the grounds that the College would provide facilities advantageous to Nottingham itself and to the surrounding region and that the instruction offered, particularly in science and technology, would be of great benefit to the East Midlands. This essay demonstrates just how difficult it was to put across this idea to industrialists and manufacturers and to show how the lack of success in integrating the work of the College with three basic economic activities in the region made the survival of the institution even more dependent upon municipal support, with all that this entailed for the longer term development of the University.

The origins of University College, Nottingham, can be traced to 1873 when enthusiasts for University Extension persuaded groups with similar interests in Leicester and Derby to co-operate in forming a lecture circuit for which the newly appointed Cambridge Syndicate agreed to provide staff.[1] An anonymous donation of £10,000 towards the cost of accommodating these classes in some permanent Nottingham centre encouraged the Town Council to erect a building which would serve this purpose as well as providing space for a library and museum. By the time the building was ready for occupation in 1881, the modest centre for extension lectures had become known as the University College.[2] Apart from £400 interest derived each year from the investment of the original donation, the College had no endowment income and in order to meet the cost of running College, library and museum, the Town Council was compelled to commit further resources to the enterprise. It was able to do this because it had considerable revenue at its disposal from profitable municipal gas and water undertakings and the Bridge Estate, property which had accrued to the Corporation since the fifteenth century and whose value had appreciated so much that the income was far in excess of that needed to maintain a bridge across the River Trent. It also made use of a district rate levied under the Free Libraries Act of 1855. Money from these sources was channelled into a joint University College, Free Library, and Museum Account from which the normal expenditure of the College, averaging about £6,400 per annum during the first ten years of its existence, was met. Until substantial benefactors could be found, any expansion of work beyond the original concept of University Extension to include the teaching of a comprehensive range of arts and science subjects had to be paid for by increasing the precept upon the Corporation. A principal objective in the minds of the instigators of the University College scheme was to provide facilities for technical education which would be advantageous to local industry. If seen to be successful, then the much needed financial support from non-municipal sources might be forthcoming. It was with this intention that the first efforts to develop the teaching of technology at the College were directed towards the hosiery and lace industries.

Nottingham was the centre of the East Midlands machine – made hosiery industry. Although technical and commercial considerations had delayed the application of steam power to the knitting machine, factory production had replaced all but a relatively small number of hand frames by 1880 and the full development of semi-automatic machines, such as the patent frame of William Cotton introduced in 1864, had increased the number of unskilled workers, particularly women, employed in the industry. There was strong competition amongst manufacturers to hold their share of home and overseas markets.[3] The lace trade was an offshoot of the hosiery industry. By 1850, the lace-making machines of Heathcoat and Leavers and the application of the Jacquard principle to the Leavers machines had given the industry a secure base in the Nottingham area. Its growth was sustained by a buoyant domestic market and by sales abroad.[4] Lace-making shared, with hosiery, the characteristic of small competitive manufacturing units but, unlike hosiery, the complicated nature of the machines involved and the high cost of the raw materials used, ensured that production remained in the hands of skilled male operators whose trade union, the Lacemakers' Society, was determined to use the apprenticeship system to control entry to the craft.[5] Both the hosiery and lace trades were supported by ancillary activities like dyeing, bleaching and finishing and by an expanding machine making industry.

The attitude of leading figures in the two trades towards technical education was largely determined by their nature and peculiar organisation. In both cases, but for different reasons, the means already existed to enable the production workers to learn their job. In hosiery this was due to the introduction of the semi-automatic frame which in effect reduced the role of the worker to that of machine minder and such skill that was needed could be acquired by observation of other workers and minimal on the spot instruction. In the lace trade the survival of craft apprenticeship gave the skilled twist-hands all the practical training they needed to do their work. The fact that both industries were run by merchants rather than manufacturers also contributed to indifference. Even after the development of a factory system, the key men were entrepreneurs who organised the buying of raw materials, distributed work amongst several contracting production firms and then marketed the finished goods. They were not generally interested in the production processes or the technology involved.

During the 1860s there had been some support for A. J. Mundella's campaign to promote technical education. Significantly Mundella's Nottingham business interests included machine building as well as hosiery and his concern stemmed from his knowledge of the role which technical education appeared to play in the emergence of a strong German hosiery industry.[6] The Nottingham Chamber of Commerce supported his view that the machine building side of the industry and the dyeing and bleaching processes might gain from the development of technical instruction, provided this was based upon an improvement in elementary education. The Chamber's Memorial to the Committee of Council was one of many submissions which preceded the setting up of the Select Committee under Bernard Samuelson to examine science education but, by that time, Mundella, whose political career was in the ascendency, had moved on to other things, and the Chamber's enthusiasm waned.[7]

Interest in technical education was kept alive by the supporters of the Nottingham Mechanics' Institute which became the venue for science classes held in connection with the Department of Science and Art. These began in 1862 and the number of subjects studied grew to fifteen by 1880. They included chemistry, mathematics, machine construction and drawing and, in the absence of alternatives, were the only means of offering systematic instruction in subjects which seemed to be relevant to the needs of the staple trades.[8] Drawing upon the talents of local men who were prepared to teach and endeavouring through prize schemes to attract students, the Mechanics' Institute persisted in its attempt to provide technical instruction. Measured in terms of examination successes and Whitworth scholarships, the venture was a success but prizewinners who departed for the Royal School of Mines were hardly likely to have an impact upon the hosiery and lace trades. The poor basic education of the artisan students was such that most found it difficult to sustain even the elementary stages of the South Kensington courses which made the transfer of these classes to the University College in 1881 seem to be a costly waste of effort.[9]

Undaunted by this attitude Congregational Minister Rev. J.B. Paton, who had been involved in the educational work of the Mechanics' Institute and whose keen advocacy of University Extension had led to his co-option to the University College Committee of the Town Council, pressed for the technical side of the work of the College to be developed.[10] Paton had travelled widely in Europe and was aware of the importance attached to technical education in countries like Saxony whose hosiery industry, as Mundella had indicated, was becoming competitive with that of Nottingham. His contacts with H.M. Felkin who represented Mundella's

Nottingham Manufacturing Co. in Chemnitz, convinced him of the contribution which technical education might make to the continued prosperity of the Nottingham hosiery trade. Felkin was persuaded to write about the beneficial effects of technical education in Saxony but, though the publication of this work by the City and Guilds of London Institute helped to reinforce the growing national consensus that foreign competition might be contained by an improvement in the overall standard of English education, it had little effect at local level.[11] For Paton, complacency in the face of continental developments was alarming and it was therefore necessary to move in advance of local industrial opinion. The setting up of a technical department at University College, in which instruction directly related to the staple trades would be given, thus became a priority, a view shared by James Stuart, the doyen of University Extension and one who advocated, even in 1879, the appointment of a Principal at University College who 'understands technical education'.[12]

The task of establishing such a department fell to William Garnett, fellow extension lecturer and friend of Stuart, who was appointed to the College in April 1882.[13] His low regard for the South Kensington classes led him to separate these from the new Department of Mechanical Engineering within which students of hosiery and lace manufacturing would be taught. While he hired a workshop for the Department, Paton negotiated a grant of £200 from the Drapers' Company to start the project and a further £1,500 grant over five years for its maintenance. The F.C. Cooper Trust agreed to provide £800 over the same period and with an impromptu gift of £800 from lace merchant and Town Councillor J.H. Jacoby, some £2,400 was still needed to meet the estimated cost of the operation.[14] An extensive publicity campaign and appeal to the hosiery and lace trades for money was then arranged through the Chamber of Commerce. The appeal produced a largely negative response. Four lace merchants and one hosiery firm gave £325 and the remaining donations, many of which came from individuals outside the two trades, amounted to less than £130.[15] Garnett resigned shortly afterwards. A second appeal in 1884 was equally unproductive and J. Ryan, who had succeeded Garnett as Professor of Mechanics and Engineering, was forced to reconsider the programme of work which had been devised for the Department. Although a small lace class began in an old warehouse in 1884 and a start was made with hosiery the following year, Ryan's frustration led to his resignation and it was left to J.R. Westmoreland, a former Mechanics' Institute Instructor, to try to keep the venture alive.

There were several reasons why this attempt to obtain financial support from the hosiery and lace trades for technical education was doomed to failure. In the first instance it was difficult to foresee what type of student should be accommodated by the courses offered. For example, the apprenticeship system took care of the young man who wished to become a lace-maker, therefore, any attempt to substitute a technical school workshop for the factory and to offer this as a way into the industry or as a means of promotion within the industry would incur the hostility of a powerful trade union and, at the same time, appear presumptuous to many of the lace merchants themselves. The students who did attend the lace classes were, therefore, not always destined for the industry and Ryan despaired of the clergymen who came for recreational purposes.[16] To attract the attention of young school leavers to the College technical department was difficult under these circumstances and, although few disputed the advantages to be gained by improving the general educational background of would-be recruits to the staple trades, no one was prepared to pay for the setting up of a Junior Trade School on the lines of the Chemnitz model as an adjunct to the College.[17] For reasons already explained it was impossible to attract the sons of the hosiery and lace manufacturers to the classes. If they received any vocational training it would be commercial rather than technical. The second problem also arose from the need to avoid encroaching upon the traditional methods of training skilled personnel. The old notion that principles rather than practice should be taught was seen in an extreme form in the syllabi of the hosiery and lace classes. Lectures on the sources of raw materials, the history of the industries, their geographical distribution and the various types of machines in general usage, rendered the courses innocuous but did not endear them to hard pressed manufacturers already critical of municipal extravagance in setting up the College.[18] In the same way the inability of the technical department to acquire anything other than out of date machinery for demonstration purposes made nonsense of any pretensions the College might make to be keeping abreast of the latest technical developments in the trades.[19] The lack of a suitable text-book relating to the basic manufacturing processes was also bemoaned by the Hosiery Trade Review.[20]

The third problem was intractable at this stage and indeed for many years to come. There was a misconception that the instruction offered by the University College had to be seen to be immediately relevant to the hosiery and lace trades. The result was the provision of courses labelled hosiery and lace manufacturing which, because of the constraints outlined above, were palpably useless to the industries involved. There were no precedents to suggest what more could be done to relate the University College to industry and the fate of the School of Art, which had to be rescued from backruptcy by the Corporation in 1888, was a clear indicator that even an institution acknowledged to produce the best designers then entering the lace trade could not count upon support from the industry it served. In both hosiery and lace manufacturing technological innovations had come from within the industries, usually as a result of an empirical approach to solving production problems. There was no reason to believe that this would change in the future and if a rapport was to be established between the College and the hosiery and lace trades it would be because the College was able to help in the resolution of problems which could not be solved by the industries themselves. Research into the composition of raw materials used in making hosiery and lace and into the dyes and mordants employed in the ancillary processes was one activity too costly for the individual small firm to undertake and too complex for those who lacked the scientific expertise of the College staff. This service to industry could not, however, be introduced overnight, even if its value was recognised by all concerned. The appeal to the staple trades of Nottingham was therefore both misconceived and premature.[21] Hosiery and lace classes survived into the 1890s but the new Technical School in which they were held derived no income from the two trades.

It was built as a result of the continued generosity of the Drapers' Company and the readiness of the Town Council to allocate the newly acquired Beer Money to the project.

The extensive development of the Nottinghamshire and Derbyshire coalfield after 1850 owed much to the establishment of a major railway network which linked centres of production like Mansfield, Worksop and Chesterfield and the new collieries of the Erewash and Leen Valleys to the London market and east coast ports. A second factor in this development was the relative ease with which good quality steam coal could be extracted from the concealed coalfield which lay east of the Nottingham-Chesterfield axis and where favourable geological conditions enabled the deepest mines to be worked profitably even at a time when coal prices were depressed as a result of the general economic malaise.[22] Although some of the older, smaller collieries ceased to operate, the larger companies ploughed back into the industry profits made in more prosperous years and the greater efficiency of their new mines was largely responsible for increasing the output of coal from the Nottinghamshire field from 4.4 million tons in 1880 to 8.6 million tons in 1900. Similarly in Derbyshire coal output increased from 7.9 million tons in 1880 to 15.2 million tons in 1900. During these years the labour force employed in mining increased from 13,892 to 26,982 in Nottinghamshire and from 27,256 to 46,788 in Derbyshire.[23] Workers from the small towns and rural areas of Nottinghamshire, Derbyshire, Lincolnshire and Leicestershire were attracted to coalmining by higher wages, security of employment and company housing. The East Midland coalfield was late in adopting mechanised coal-cutting and such technological changes that were introduced were in areas such as haulage, winding and ventilation.[24] Consequently coal extraction remained labour intensive. Ex-framework knitters and agricultural labourers soon adjusted to life underground once the former had accepted the regular hours of pit work and the latter had learned how to use a pick and shovel in a confined space. There was always a pool of skilled colliers who could be relied upon to train the recruits to the industry in the basic aspects of the job and, rather than pressing for more schooling, there was a conviction that the sooner a young worker entered the pit, the better he would be as a miner.

At the level of management, the greater size and complexity of collieries increased the responsibilities of the mining engineer. In the East Midlands, as elsewhere, these men were usually self-taught and their standing gauged by the number of pupils who paid for the privilege of attending their office and being admitted to the practice of the collieries with which they were concerned. The anxiety of these men to protect their interests by preserving the tutelage system was one reason why so few graduates of the Royal School of Mines were employed in the industry.[25] Changes did occur, however, as a result of the Coal Mines Regulation Act of 1872 which, in the interests of the safe operation of the mines, specified that every colliery where more than thirty underground workers were employed should be under the control and supervision of a certified manager. Certification was awarded on the basis of an examination which included questions on all aspects of coal extraction, ventilation and general safety as well as tests of basic literacy and numeracy, and was administered by a district committee made up of coalowners, engineers, the Inspectorate and representatives of the miners. Continued pressure to improve safety led to the demand that the proficiency of underviewers should also be examined and this was achieved in 1887 when the Second Class Certificate was introduced for this purpose.[26] This safety legislation prompted efforts to devise some means of educating prospective managers outside the tutelage system to the point where they might successfully take the certificate examinations. The Department of Science and Art courses seemed more suited to metalliferous mining than the coal industry and therefore alternatives had to be found.[27] One response was the creation of private venture academies like the Stapleford Mining School, Nottinghamshire, or the Universal Mining School, Derby, the latter being promoted by T.A. Southern who was himself a member of the Mines Inspectorate.[28] A more significant development, however, was the attempt to associate the University College, Nottingham, with education for the mining industry.

Here there was a precedent. The Newcastle College of Physical Science, at which the first chair of mining was established in 1880, was already serving the needs of the Northumberland-Durham coalfield.[29] The problem was how to gain the support of the coalowners of Nottinghamshire and Derbyshire for casting the Nottingham College in a similar role. The intermediary was the Chesterfield and Derbyshire Institute of Engineers, a body upon which the most influential coalowners and mining engineers of the East Midlands were represented and which had been established in 1871 to promote the interests of the industry by disseminating scientific and technical information amongst the membership. A sine qua non of its declared objective of advancing the science of mining was an improvement in the education of all those involved in the industry and therefore an appeal to this body was essential.

In fact, shortly after its foundation, the Institute had resurrected a scheme for a central mining college which H.S. Tremenheere and Chesterfield coalowner Charles Binns had put forward as early as 1858. It had been rejected then because its estimated cost of £60,000 seemed totally unrealistic. However in 1872 a more positive reception was given to the notion of a School of Mines for the East Midlands put forward by G.H. Wright and R.F. Martin of the Babbington Collieries, Nottinghamshire. The School would award its own degree at the end of a four year course, a substantial part of which would be spent down the mines. This advanced course for engineers would be complemented by a scheme to train schoolmasters in aspects of mining so that they could impart knowledge thus acquired to the boys in the elementary schools in the mining districts.[30]

It was this scheme which James Stuart welcomed at a time when the Cambridge Syndicate was assessing the likely support it might receive for putting University Extension on a more permanent basis. Always pragmatic, Stuart suggested that such a School of Mines would gain in prestige if associated with the University of Cambridge. Instead of recruiting its teachers locally, a source of weakness in the South Kensington system, Stuart outlined a plan to use peripatetic professors who would not only teach at the School but who would also conduct classes at centres in other parts of the mining region. The total cost would be less than half the original scheme.[31] To launch the project Stuart himself agreed to lecture on geology and chemistry at Chesterfield but, preoccupation with the depression of coal prices in the late 1870s tempered the enthusiasm of the coalowners for such a grand design.[32] The Chesterfield Institute thereupon fell back upon a less expensive undertaking to build a George Stephenson Memorial Hall in Chesterfield, described by the Derbyshire Times as a 'sub-university complete with laboratory and lecture room'.[33] It was at this point that William Garnett, aided by Stuart, attempted to forge a link between the Institute and University College, Nottingham. The failure of the hosiery and lace trades to support the projected technical department at University College added urgency to the appeal to the mining industry for financial help but a programme of evening lectures on subjects such as coal gases, combustion, colliery explosions and steam power, introduced at Nottingham during the winter of 1882–83, failed to arouse the interest of the industry.[34] Perhaps the most important factor here was the ephemeral nature of this programme. An initiative, which did not meet with the full approval of the University College Committee who were anxious to limit expenditure until there was evidence of outside support, was stifled almost immediately. Garnett's departure to become Principal of the Newcastle College of Physical Science in 1884 was due largely to this impasse.[35]

It was Stuart who kept alive the idea that University College should court the favour of the mining industry. In anticipation of the mining legislation of 1887, Stuart persuaded the College Committee to allow Professors Clowes and Heaton to negotiate with the Chesterfield Institute the latter's support for a scheme of mining instruction which embodied the original Wright and Martin proposals but with the school of Mines being located at University College rather than Chesterfield. The professors would, in the manner of extension lecturers, also take classes on the coalfield in towns like Chesterfield, Alfreton, Mansfield and Eastwood, and they would be assisted by a mining engineer, G.E. Coke, who would be responsible for practical work including surveying. All that was asked of the Institute was the modest sum of £150 to launch the scheme. The fact that yet again there was no response from the industry can be explained by a consideration of three factors.[36]

In the first instance, the Chesterfield Institute was at that moment seeking to amalgamate with the Midland Institute of Mining, Civil and Mechanical Engineers, a body comprising a large contingent of South Yorkshire coalowners. The objective was the creation of a prestigious society which would embrace the whole of the Midlands and South Yorkshire and the likelihood of a chair of mining being established at Firth College, Sheffield, with which the Midland Institute already had connections, was one of the advantages which the Derbyshire coalowners especially valued.[37] In fact, Firth College was experiencing great difficulty in promoting its own mining courses at that time but the prospect of associating with South Yorkshire seemed to preclude a link with Nottingham which, unlike Sheffield, was not at the centre of a coal-based industrial complex.

In the second instance, the Nottingham scheme was opposed by the Chief Inspector of Mines in the Midland region, A.H. Stokes, whose commitment to the development at Sheffield was absolute. For Stokes, the role which Nottingham might play in mining education would be dependent upon the willingness of the University College Committee to set up full extension facilities so that its staff, supported by an elaborate postal tuition scheme, would cover not only the Nottinghamshire and Derbyshire coalfield, but also Leicestershire and Northamptonshire. The instruction would be at a low level, geared to the certification examinations, and there would be no differentiation between the status of the University College and the coalfield centres. Clowes and Heaton could not accept such a proposition which would inhibit the development of advanced instruction at Nottingham and there was little possibility that the Nottingham Town Council would release staff to operate such an elaborate extension system.[38]

Although the East Midlands coalfield was prosperous enough to support mining instruction at both Sheffield and Nottingham, the coalowners had to be persuaded that investment in such instruction was necessary. What was needed was a prophet to preach to the colliery owners that their costs would be reduced if they supported technical education. This was the third factor which reduced the chance of getting the backing of the coal industry for a School of Mines at Nottingham. Existing facilities for sharing knowledge acquired by individual engineers and coalowners were considered adequate. The mining institutes, especially after federation in 1889, were able, through their regular conferences and published transactions, to make known the results of experiments and investigations into current mining problems. Also, the prospect of acting as a validating body for their own diploma, equivalent to that of the civil engineers, was already being discussed at a time when only Durham University was in a position to award a degree in mining, an award which still had to find acceptance in the industry.[39] Furthermore, the 1887 Act which introduced the Second Class Certificate stipulated that each candidate should have had five years experience in the mines before taking the examination and disregarded any educational qualifications which might be possessed. This reinforced the tendency for candidates to be articled students of the established engineers and reduced the number of good people from outside the industry seeking to qualify. The remuneration of mine managers was, in any case, not so good that the job attracted able outsiders.[40] Under these circumstances, the teaching envisaged by Clowes and Heaton at Nottingham was hardly likely to change the views of the coalowners that the existing arrangements for research and the training of mining engineers were acceptable and there was no justification for further expenditure upon advanced education. The trial course of Saturday classes, which University College offered in spite of Stokes' opposition during the winter of 1888–89, terminated abruptly. When mining classes began again at Nottingham in 1894 they were part of a Nottinghamshire County Council scheme of technical education. County Council students were taught by a Director of Mining Education who was appointed by the Council, and the grant of £40 per annum to support these classes was very small compared with expenditure on mining education in other parts of the county. The attempt to draw financial support for the University College from the coal industry had, for the time being, been abandoned.

The third economic activity with which University College sought to establish links was that of agriculture. The initiative was prompted by the convergence of government policy to create regional centres of excellence for agricultural education with the programme of technical instruction devised by the Nottinghamshire County Council to meet the needs of its farming and landowning interests. Government concern stemmed from the depression which affected British agriculture during the late 1870s and 1880s. The severity of this depression varied from region to region depending upon the type of agriculture practised. Thus, although wheat growing areas suffered as a result of a succession of bad harvests and the importation of cheap grain from East Europe and North America, areas like the East Midlands, where the emphasis was upon pastoral and mixed farming, remained prosperous. The domestic market was large enough to sustain prices which were higher than those of the refrigerated and often inferior products that were imported.[41] Nevertheless, comparisons with the good years which had preceded the depression led to the inevitable enquiry as to its cause and the search for palliatives. Better agricultural education was one of these and the responsibilities of the Board of Agriculture created in 1889 included determining the best means of developing educational facilities which would benefit the farming community. The Board's policy of giving financial support to major institutions which served clearly defined regions was quickly established. By 1891 University College, Bangor, and the Yorkshire College of Science were both in receipt of substantial grants which enabled them to develop a number of teaching activities. These included the provision of courses for schoolmasters, so that they might instruct their pupils in basic science applied to agriculture; popular lectures given in the rural districts on a range of topics of interest to the farmer; dairy schools which toured the region and promoted better understanding of modern dairying practice; and the cultivation of selected crops under controlled conditions so that ways of improving growth could be demonstrated. Both Bangor and the Yorkshire College were then able to approach local landowners and neighbouring county councils – which were after 1890, in possession of the Residue Grant – for further financial support and the Board of Agriculture's approval appeared to guarantee the security of any investment they might be disposed to make. While the number of centres receiving grants increased during 1892 to include the Durham College of Science, the University College, Aberystwyth, Glasgow Technical College and the University of Cambridge, the Board of Agriculture made it quite clear that the county councils must take on more responsibility for agricultural education and should associate their work with the new regional institutions.[42]

The decision of the Nottinghamshire County Council to allocate a substantial proportion of the Residue Grant to agricultural education was taken after an enquiry conducted in 1890 revealed that, out of 121 parish authorities consulted, 71 believed that technical instruction applied to agriculture should be given priority. A comprehensive scheme of education was devised, concentrating upon dairying and pastoral farming, in which it was envisaged that the University College, Nottingham, would occupy a key position.[43] At the centre of a well-defined farming region there was every possibility that the institution would receive financial support from the Board of Agriculture. The University College Committee was for this reason anxious to participate and a concordat with the Nottinghamshire County Council led to the setting up of a Department of Agriculture at the College in 1892.[44] The head of this Department was M. J. R. Dunstan, an Oxford Delegacy extension lecturer, appointed by the County Council to organise its programme of agricultural education. Dunstan, who remained the employee of the County Council, was to build up the staff of the Department in subjects such as veterinary science and agricultural practice. Each assistant was appointed to work part-time in the University College alongside the professors in whose departments matters cognate to agriculture would also be taught. The remainder of their time would be spent working outside the College at different centres in the county area.

At county level, Dunstan's efforts to promote agricultural education were successful. Pioneer lectures were used to popularise more systematic study of various agricultural subjects such as poultry-keeping, horticulture, fruit-growing and veterinary practice. These were gradually replaced by district agricultural schools established in selected villages where courses of two years duration were offered to boys and young men seeking to improve their basic knowledge. At several places in the county experimental units were formed for research into the use of manures, improvement of pasture and the growing of root crops, the results of the experiments being printed and distributed by the travelling library service which Dunstan had also initiated. A peripatetic dairy school was used to demonstrate new techniques at agricultural shows, but the most significant development was the setting up of the Midland Dairy Institute at Kingston upon Soar, some twelve miles south of Nottingham, as a joint venture with the Derbyshire, Leicestershire and Lindsey County Councils in 1895.[45] Here students, most of whom were scholarship holders from the contributing counties, came to study advanced dairying methods on a well-equipped 160 acre farm leased from Lord Belper. Whilst this side of the Nottinghamshire scheme expanded, however, the in-college courses at Nottingham made little progress. There was a dearth of students for the two year diploma course launched in 1892 for 'intending farmers, bailiffs, land-agents and colonists' despite Dunstan's efforts to publicise the practical nature of the work done, including instruction in cost-reducing farm management.[46] It was difficult to overcome the prejudice of the farming community and two years full-time study at University College was a commitment which few young men already farming could undertake even if they possessed the necessary educational background. To overcome the obstacle, Dunstan introduced short bridging courses but this did not remove the constraint upon recruitment imposed by the choice of urban Nottingham as the venue. Saturday classes for schoolmasters were begun with more success in 1893 but these were terminated two years later by the Nottinghamshire Technical Instruction Committee, indignant that only four of the 134 teachers who had attended the classes were working in the county's elementary schools.[47] The shortage of students was not in itself sufficient to destroy the viability of the Department of Agriculture, a fact acknowledged by the Board which, in assessing the level of grants to be made to an institution, considered the extra-mural teaching done by college staff and the provision of research and advisory services.[48] This was the basis of the grant of £200 made by the Board of Agriculture to University College in 1893, a grant which was raised to £450 in 1895 and to £600 in 1896. To this grant was added income from fees and a grant from the Nottinghamshire County Council to pay for Dunstan's assistants in the Department and the services of other members of the University College staff when called upon. This combined income was not enough, however, to avoid a regular annual deficit in the finances of the Department, and even before the Midland Dairy Institute was established, the University College Committee was apprehensive about costs as the demands made upon staff and resources increased.[49] It was assumed, by the Joint Agricultural Committee set up by the County Councils contributing to the Kingston Institute, that the Department of Agriculture would continue to provide advanced instruction in the agricultural sciences at Nottingham as well as extension teaching in the region as a whole. To this end grants were made to the Department by Derbyshire, Leicestershire and Lindsey as well as Nottinghamshire but these were regarded as inadequate by the University College Committee, anxious to extract the maximum contributions from the County Councils which would aid the total development of the College while they seemed to be availing themselves of its status as a university centre to draw into the region substantial sums of government money to support other educational ventures.[50]

To a great extent the attitude of the University College Committee was determined by the precarious financial position of the College in the absence of an endowment. Thus, despite assurances from the Joint Agricultural Committee that it would indemnify the College against any deficit incurred by the Department of Agriculture, more positive guarantees were demanded that in the expansion of work being contemplated by Dunstan the longer term financial interests of the University College would not be neglected. The financial problem was exacerbated by the administrative difficulties which also arose because the College was a municipal institution. The University College Committee had no freedom to act independently of its parent body. It could not, for example, take up the tenancy of the farm at Kingston – a move proposed by Dunstan which might have held together the College and the Institute – because it lacked the Corporation's approval for such action.[51] It was also difficult for the University College Committee itself to accept the independence of action which Dunstan possessed, first in his capacity as organiser of agricultural education for Nottinghamshire and subsequently the Joint Agricultural Committee and then as Director of the Midland Dairy Institute. Friction between the University College Committee and Dunstan, who had carefully nurtured the support of influential county councillors including Lord Belper, was a major factor contributing to the latter's determination to elevate the status of the Midland Dairy Institute to that of regional centre, usurping the position held by University College.[52]

In fact, Dunstan had begun negotiations with the Board of Agriculture as early as 1895 for a separate grant for the Kingston scheme.[53] The Board viewed with favour the specialist dairy institutes being set up at Reading and Ipswich and there was every indication that it would adopt the same attitude towards the Midland Dairy Institute. Indeed, by 1897 – acknowledging the success of the Institute in establishing a variety of well-attended intensive dairy courses, in embarking upon an adventurous series of experiments and research, and in making good use of the capital and maintenance of the supporting county councils to erect laboratories, workshops and residential accommodation – the Board divided its grant of £700 between the University College and the Midland Dairy Institute, the latter receiving £300.[54] From this point onwards, the University College ceased to be the key institution as the Institute, guided by Dunstan, assumed increasing importance, not only as a specialist dairy school but also as the co-ordinating centre for agricultural education throughout the East Midlands. When, in December 1899, Dunstan declared his intentions of looking to Cambridge or the Yorkshire College of Science to provide all advanced courses in agriculture which would lead to diplomas and other awards for students from the contributory counties, it was clear that there was little point in continuing to maintain a Department of Agriculture at Nottingham.[55] It was closed in 1900 and the Board of Agriculture grant transferred to Kingston. What had begun as a promising enterprise with relatively secure finances as a result of the partnership with a county council and the patronage of the Board of Agriculture thus came to an abrupt end. The University College remained dependent upon the Corporation of Nottingham for its existence and it had still to prove that it could make a real contribution to the economic development of the East Midlands.

Notes and References

1 PATON, J.L. (1913) *J.B. Paton A Biography*, London, Hodder and Stoughton, pp. 156–64; WELCH, E. (1973) *The Peripatetic University, Cambridge Local Lectures 1873–1973*, Cambridge, Cambridge University Press, p. 71.

2 The gift was made by W.H. Heymann, wealthy lace manufacturer and supporter of the Mechanics Institute movement. Nottingham Chamber of Commerce Annual General Meeting 29 January, 1892. The term 'University College' was used to 'signify that the College is in connection with the Universities' according to the Town Clerk, S.G. Johnson, *Transactions of the National Association for the Promotion of Social Science* 1878, Papers relating to University Extension and Technical Education, p. 368.

3 WELLS, F.A. (1935) *The British Hosiery Trade: Its History and Organisation*, London, David and Charles, pp. 144–6, 184 and 188, 191.

4 CHURCH, R.A. (1966) *Economic and Social Change in a Midland Town: Victorian Nottingham, 1815–1900*, London, Cass, pp. 285–7.

5 CUTHBERT, N.H. (1960) *The Lace Makers Society*, Amalgamated Society of Operative Lace Makers and Auxiliary Workers, Nottingham, pp. 3, 185–6.

6 ARMYTAGE, W.H.G. (1951) *A.J. Mundella 1825–1897*, London, Ernest Benn, pp. 20–3; FELKIN, W. (1867) *A History of the Machine Wrought Hosiery and Lace Manufactures*, Cambridge, Kelley, pp. 502–3.

7 *Nottingham Chamber of Commerce, Minute Book 1863–74*, 4 September, 27 November, 1867, 3 January, 1868.

8 Nottingham Mechanics Institute, Annual Report 1869, p. 5; GREEN, J.A.H. (1887) *The Nottingham Mechanics' Institute*, Nottingham, Appendix B.

9 *Royal Commission on Technical Education*, Second Report (1884), Vol. III, Digest of Evidence, No. 36.

10 PATON, J.L. (1913) *op. cit.*, pp. 157–64. The University College Committee was a committee of the Town Council. In its original form it was made up of 13 members of the Town Council, 5 members from outside the Council but who were nominated by it, and not more than 4 representatives of the subscribers to the Extension Lecture Fund.

11 PATON, J.L. (1913) *op. cit.*, p. 182.

12 *University College Minute Book*, 28 November, 1879, 1069: (1877–81).

13 *Ibid*, 29 June, 1882.

14 F.C. Cooper, hosiery manufacturer, had left his estate in the hands of trustees who were to use the money to promote 'technical education in arts and sciences among the working classes of Nottingham', University Calendar 1882–83.

15 Nottingham Corporation Accounts, The Technical School (1883–88).
16 *Nottingham Daily Guardian*, 30 March, 1883. The manufacturers' point of view was summarised by lace merchant C.G. Hill. For Ryan's comments upon pupils see Technicus 1883. Collection of newspaper cuttings concerning University College, Nottingham.
17 *University College Minute Book* 1071, (1886–90), 17 December, 1886.
18 For details of syllabi see *University College Calendar 1884–85*, pp. 58–61; consultation with Garnett at Newcastle eventually led to the hosiery and lace classes being linked to the examinations of the City and Guilds of London Institute. See *University College Minute Book* 1071, (1886–90), 12 September, 1887.
19 *University College Minute Book* 1070, (1882–86), 8 December, 1885.
20 *The Hosiery Trade Review: Knitters Circular and Monthly Record* (1894), August.
21 *The Journal of the Textile Institute*, Vol. XXII, 1931, pp. 65–6. ABBOTT, A. *Technical Education for the Textile Industry*. Abbott as Chief Inspector of Technical Schools, Board of Education, was reflecting on the reason for the lack of progress in technical education in the hosiery and lace industries.
22 GRIFFIN, A.R. (1971) *Mining in the East Midlands*, London, Cass, pp. 97–9, 105–8; EDWARDS, K.C. (Ed.) (1966) *Nottingham and its Region*, Nottingham, British Association for the Advancement of Science, p. 239; WILLIAMS, J.E. (1962) *The Derbyshire Miners*, London, Allen and Unwin, pp. 175–9.
23 GIBSON, F.A. (1922) A Compilation of Statistics of the Coal Mining Industry of the United Kingdom, Cardiff, *Western Mail*, pp. 23–4.
24 *Reports of the Inspectors of Mines*, 1906, pp. 1907, XIII, (Cd. 3449–vii), p. 8. A.H. Stokes, Chief Inspector of Mines for the Midland District, expressed the opinion in 1906 that 'the economy in the use of such (coal cutting) machines is at present small and offers little inducement to resort to a radical change in the operation of coal cutting'. See also TAYLOR, A.J. (1961) Labour productivity and technological innovation in the British coal industry 1850–1914' *Economic History Review*, second series, XIV, p. 58.
25 *Reports of the Royal Commission on Scientific Instruction and the Advancement of Science (1872–75)*, Vol. I. First Supplementary and Second Reports with Minutes of Evidence and Appendices, pp. 1872, (XXV), Qs. 2333–5.
26 MORRAL, D. (1926) *A Historical Review of Coal Mining*, London, pp. 315–6.
27 *Transactions of the Institute of Mining Engineers*, Vol. II, 1890–91, p. 98. T.A. Southern, There was also a view that the S. Kensington syllabi and examinations were too hard for the young men who might be presenting themselves for the Certification examinations. See *Transaction of the Institute of Mining Engineers*, Vol. XLIV, 1912–13, F.W. Hardwick, Professor of Mining, Firth College, Sheffield (1892–1912).
28 *The Derby Universal School of Mining Prospectus*, 4th Edition, 1889, Derby Public Library.
29 WHITING, C.E. (1932) *The University of Durham, 1832–1912*, London, Sheldon Press, pp. 187–9.
30 *Transactions of the Chesterfield and Derbyshire Institute of Engineers*, Vol. I, 1871–72, p. 151.
31 *Ibid*, pp. 166–7. Stuart was present at the meeting of the Institute when Wright and Martin presented their paper.
32 Accidents in Mines. The Preliminary Report of H.M. Commissioners with Minutes of Evidence, 1881 (Cd. 3036) Qs. 1573–8, Thomas Evans, Inspector of Mines for the Midland Counties.
33 *The Derbyshire Times*, 19 July, 1879.
34 *University College Calendar*, 1882–83.
35 *University College Minute Book* 1070, (1882–86), 4 December, 1883.
36 F. Clowes was Professor of Chemistry and Metallurgy (1881–97); W.H. Heaton was Professor of Physics and Mathematics (1884–1919). For details of Stuart's role see: *Transactions of the Chesterfield and Midland Counties Institute of Engineers*, Vol. XVI, 1887–88, pp. 57–62, and 147.
37 *Transactions of the Midland Institute of Mining, Civil and Mechanical Engineers*, Vol. IX, 1884, pp. 253–6.
38 *Transactions of the Chesterfield and Midland Counties Institute of Engineers*, Vol. XVI, 1887–88, pp. 57–62, 102–5.
39 *Transactions of the Midland Institute of Mining, Civil and Mechanical Engineers*, Vol. XI, 1887, pp. 119–21. The prospect of a Diploma to raise the status of the mining engineer was raised during the discussion of federation.
40 Although in 1903 academic training in certain colleges became accepted as an alternative to two of the five years practical experience underground, the Samuel Commission (1925) considered that the existence of these regulations narrowed the field from which managers could be appointed and thus diminished the number of men of high ability and good general education who were likely to be drawn into the industry. *Report of the Royal Commission on the Coal Industry*, (1925) with Minute of Evidence and Appendices, Vol. I, Chapter XV.
41 FLETCHER, T.W. (1961) The Great Depression of English Agriculture (1873–96), *Economic History Review*, second series, XIII, p. 243.
42 *Final Report of the Royal Commission on the Agricultural Depression* (1897), Appendix A, VII (a), 481–4.

43 Nottinghamshire County Council, *First Annual Report of the Technical Instruction Committee, 1890–91.*

44 *University College Minute Book* 1072, (1890–97), 1 April, 1892.

45 This account is based upon the *Annual Reports of the Nottinghamshire County Council Technical Instruction Committee,* 1890–96, and the *Annual Reports of the Board of Agriculture* for the same period.

46 For details of the syllabus and publicity see the *University College Calendars,* 1892–93 and 1894–95. The average number of students starting the in-College course each year was 4.

47 Nottinghamshire County Council, *Fifth Annual Report of the Technical Instruction Committee,* 1894–95.

48 *Annual Report of the Board of Agriculture,* 1897–98. 1889, (Cd. 9061), LXXVII, p. 327, (vii).

49 *University College Minute Book* 1072, (1890–97), 18 July, 1893 and 19 May, 1896.

50 The Department of Agriculture received £1,013 from the Joint Agricultural Committee in 1896–97. This figure had risen to £1,601 for the year 1899–1900.

51 *University College Minute Book* 1072, (1890–97), 16 October, 1894.

52 Several attempts were made to restrict Dunstan's independence, culminating in accusations that he was over-drawing money from the grant made to the Department by the Board of Agriculture. A special sub-committee of the University College Committee reproached Dunstan for acting without authorisation. *University College Minute Book,* 1073, (1897–1904), 16 March and 27 April, 1897.

53 *Midland Dairy Institute Minute Book I,* 7 June, 1895.

54 *Annual Report of the Board of Agriculture,* 1898–99. 1899, (Cd. 9431), LXXVII, p. 493.

55 *Midland Dairy Institute Minute Book I,* 11 December, 1899.

The Role of Government

Gordon Roderick and Michael Stephens

Hobsbawm (1968) has argued that a positive role of active intervention in support of industry can be ascribed to British government throughout the late eighteenth century because of the policy of wars and colonization, the results of which provided much needed markets for emerging industries.[1] Unfortunately, no such claim can be justified nor even advanced with respect to many other areas affecting industrial progress: higher education; the support of science and technology; promotion of research – government support and intervention was often too little and too late. This is surprising in view of the body of eminent men that advocated such support throughout the second half of the century. This group comprised industrialists such as Lowthian Bell, Parliamentarians such as Lyon Playfair, engineers such as Joseph Whitworth and scientists such as Huxley – a powerful lobby of individuals embracing a comprehensive range of expertise and interests. There were also establishment figures such as Lord Salisbury and Lord Derby who were emphatically in favour of state interference to aid science.

In scientific and technical education, the major instrument of government policy was the Science and Art Department which was set up following a letter by Edward Cardwell of the Board of Trade, on 16 March, 1853, to the Treasury suggesting the formation of a Department of Science to be allied to the already existing Department of Practical Art. The new Department was to control the Government School of Mines, the Royal College of Chemistry, and the Government Geological Department. As we shall see later, much of the financial support provided via the Department was channelled into promoting museums, collections and geological surveys. The two major government-sponsored institutions at that time were the School of Mines and Science Applied to the Arts and the Royal College of Chemistry. The former arose out of the Museum of Economic Geology erected in Jermyn Street in 1837. This was based on the ideas of Sir Henry De La Beche, Director General of the Geological Survey, whose main concern was to apply chemistry to agriculture. It was not in his mind that it should become a School of Mines hence it was not supplied with a laboratory originally and it was not contemplated, at the time, to teach mining or metallurgy. Thus the School of Mines 'was grafted on and not very cleverly at that upon a different plan'.[2] The Royal College of Chemistry had been established initially as a self-financing institution and was only taken over by the Government when it ran into financial difficulties – the Government paying £3,000 for the plant.

Another forty years were to elapse before further government money was forthcoming, again partly as the result of the initiative of a single individual. In 1890 the Government passed legislation reducing the number of public houses. To compensate the publicans an additional duty was placed on wines and spirits, but many members opposed spending the money on publicans and Arthur Acland suggested spending it on education. As a result, Goschen's Local Taxation Act of 1890 placed £750,000 at the disposal of the local authorities for technical education. In the following year, the Technical Instruction Act empowered local authorities to raise a penny rate in support of technical education. Local authorities, however, were loathe to impose rates for this purpose and by 1900 Acland's 'whisky money' totalled £863,847 whilst money spent from rates amounted to only £106,209.

At no time in the nineteenth century could any government have been unaware of the feelings among leading individuals about the national shortcomings in scientific and technical education. One of the earliest critics was Charles Babbage, the Cambridge mathematician. Babbage invented the principle of the automatic computer and was instrumental in founding the British Association for the Advancement of Science and other scientific societies. His book *Reflections on the Decline of Science* which appeared in 1831 referred to a state of affairs which had existed for over half a century. Its publication was inspired by administrative malpractices in the Royal Society, ruled at that time by a coterie of dilettantes. His book helped to air the grievances of those who were concerned at the absence of scientific institutions and the neglect of scientific instruction in higher institutions of learning. His contention was that, in England, the pursuit of science did not constitute a distinct profession; trained for the law, the Church and medicine, English scientists – with few exceptions – were largely amateurs devoting the greater part of their time to their chosen professions. In enumerating official scientific posts Babbage drew attention to the kinds of activities which merited government support. These included the Royal Astronomer, Conductor of the Nautical Almanac, and officers of the Natural History Museum, all of which were poorly paid in comparison with commensurate posts in other areas of life.

Babbage's criticisms, perhaps not unexpectedly, fell on deaf ears for Britain clearly was the leading industrial nation, her success seemingly owing little to education and scientific pursuits. The pinnacle of her power was reached at the Crystal Palace Exhibition opened by Queen Victoria on 1st May 1851. The spirit engendered by the Exhibition, in particular by Britain's success in the award of medals, was 'buoyant, optimistic and arrogant'.[3] The background to this national wave of optimism and euphoria was a growing material prosperity and 'a level of industrial production and foreign trade which set England far ahead of all other countries'.[4] Against the background of this euphoria one prominent figure dared to speak out. He was Lyon Playfair (later first Baron Playfair) who at that time held a post at the Government School of Mines. He later entered Parliament becoming Postmaster General and Vice-President of the Council of Education thus becoming one of the first scientific men of affairs. In the past, he pointed out, the ready availability of cheap natural resources had been in Britain's favour but in the future the development of transport and communication systems would tend to cancel out differences in natural resources; the race would, therefore, go to the nation which commanded the greatest scientific skill. Playfair's Inaugural Lecture on the opening of the Government School of Mines was a prophetic warning. In it he declared, 'as surely as darkness follows the setting of the Sun, so surely will England recede as a manufacturing nation, unless her industrial population become much more conversant with science than they now are'.

Playfair later toured the continent at the request of HRH. Prince Albert in order to study technical education at first hand. On his return he complained that in England there was 'an overweening respect for practice and a contempt for science. In this country we have eminent "practical men" and eminent "scientific men" but they are not united and generally walk in paths wholly distinct'.[5] Thus did Playfair put his finger on the weakness of England's position; in spite of the impressive performances of her industries in winning medals, England was one of the few major competing countries without an organised system of technical education. Until that time, England had a clear start in the industrial field, but Playfair sounded the alarm bells of foreign competition.

Following Playfair's outspokenness many individuals and offical bodies were to voice concern, during the next few decades, at the poor state of scientific organisation in the country. Prominent among the recommendations were proposals for a minister of science, a government board of science and for state endowed laboratories in the physical sciences. In 1855, at the British Association Meeting at Glasgow, the Parliamentary Committee presented its report 'on whether any means could be adopted by the government or parliament that would improve the position of science in the county'. Sir Philip Egerton suggested, and the Committee agreed, that it was desirable to establish a government Board of Science to control the distribution of endowments and funds. The Committee thought that there was a widespread feeling throughout the country of the importance of science but:

> owing to the system which prevails in this country, of each successive government striving to outvie its predecessors in popularity by the reduction of public burdens, there is a temptation sometimes to withhold grants which may swell the total outlay of departments in which reductions are contemplated.[6]

Two years later, in 1857, a proposal to establish a Council of Science was brought before the Government of the Royal Society upon a report from the Government Grant Committee of the Royal Society. This proposal stated:

> We have arrived at the conclusion that much has to be done which will require continuous efforts on the part of the administration unless we are content to fall behind other nations in the encouragement which we give to pure science and as a consequence incur the danger of losing our pre-

eminence in regard to its applications ... These considerations have impressed upon us the conviction that the creation of a Special Ministry dealing with science and with education is a necessity of the public service.[7]

If there was any encouragement the government needed in order to support science it could be found in abundance in the report of the Devonshire Commissioners. Indeed, the Commissioners themselves concluded:

It must be admitted at the present day scientific investigation is carried on abroad to an extent and with a completeness of organisation to which this country can offer no parallel. The work done in this country by private individuals although of great value, is small when compared with that which is needed in the interests of science ... and learned societies do not consider it any part of their corporate functions to undertake or conduct research ... the progress of scientific research must in a great degree depend upon the aid of governments.[18]

The general conclusion following a survey of scientific work in the various departments of government was:

There is a general concurrence of opinion, that, even in the interests of the Departments themselves, more ought to be done by the Government in the way of investigation, particularly in respect of those sciences the practical application of which has been developed within recent years.[9]

Within the pages of the 8th Report high ranking officials were found to make statements damaging to the Government. Thus Captain Douglas Galton of the Office of Her Majesty's Works and Public Buildings stated that, 'Our statesmen do not appreciate properly the value of scientific advice or scientific inquiry'.[10] Mr. Anderson, Superintendent of Machinery at Woolwich, and responsible for the expenditure of the sum of three million pounds pointed out that there were no means at the disposal of state servants to enable them to investigate questions on which large expenditure depends – 'we are groping in the dark in almost everything at present'.[11] Mr. E. J. Reed, M.P., former Chief Controller of the Navy, stated his opinion as:

I think there are many branches of science remaining undeveloped at present, the development of which would be of great advantage to the country. I base that opinion partly upon the experience which I acquired at the Admiralty, in which I continually found that great and important questions were undeveloped for the want of organisation and the means of developing them.[12]

Sir William Thomson (later Lord Kelvin), although an establishment figure, also expressed his concern:

the Government is insufficiently advised and hence great mistakes are sometimes made – a single body would be better than a number of small committees for advising the Government.[13]

Warren de La Rue of the School of Mines advocated a Minister of Science, an Advisory Board for Science and state laboratories for physics and chemistry costing £50,000–£60,000.

One witness to the Devonshire Commissioners who argued the case for state support for science was Colonel Alexander Strange. Educated at Harrow, he entered the Indian Army, returning to this country in 1861. He had marked scientific ability contributing many papers to the British Association and to the Royal Society, being an elected Fellow of the Society. In 1868 he presented a paper to the British Association at Norwich in which he persuasively argued that only the state could adequately support the advance of science and called for a chain of state-sponsored research institutes, a National Science Council and a Minister of Science. He developed his ideas further in papers to the British Association entitled *On Government Action in Science* (1871) and to the Society of Arts on *The Relation of the State to Science* (1872). In evidence, as witness to the Devonshire Commission he stated:

> The State or Government, acting as trustees of the people, should provide for the cultivation of those departments of science which, by reason of costliness, either in time or money, or of remoteness of probable profit, are beyond the reach of private individuals, in order that the community may not suffer from the effect of insufficiency of isolated effort.[14]

His reply to a request 'to enumerate the machinery that exists at present for securing these objects' illustrates the bias towards the natural and the earth sciences and the lack of overall co-ordination. His list included observatories, the Ordance Survey under the Office of Works, the Exchequer Standards Office under the Board of Trade, the British Museum, the Meteorological Office, the Royal Botanic Gardens under the Board of Works and the Geological Survey under the Privy Council.

Like several other witnesses Strange pressed the case for a Minister of Science responsible to Parliament:

> At present votes for science are to be found scattered through the estimates of various departments, they are in the Civil Estimates, Military Estimates, and Navy Estimates. Some years ago when I took up this subject I endeavoured to get at the aggregate amount of money voted annually for science, and I found it quite impossible to do so without personal inquiry. The estimates do not furnish the information, therefore, I think there should be an estimate for science just as there is an estimate for the army and navy.[15]

Strange countered the objections to a Council of Science based on the grounds of expense with the following words:

> If any idea of the importance of science to the state and of the greatly impoverished condition of science in England is correct, then a matter of £20,000 or even £100,000 a year is a mere bagatelle, compared with the enormous interest involved. Therefore, I utterly refuse to consider the

matter of expense. I look upon it that money spent in this way is money invested; it is not money sunk at all'.[16]

These were hardly the kinds of views to endear him to any of the governments of late Victorian England for the reluctance to spend increasing sums of money on science was a major obstacle to a greater measure of government support. The Treasury reflected the policy of governments, all of whom – Liberals most of all – disliked public expenditure in principle. To Gladstone, Chancellor of the Exchequer or Prime Minister for many years, and his colleagues economy and lower taxation came first. As Professor Gowing points out in her Royal Society Lecture of 1976, the Prince Consort had said in 1859 that 'only the long purse of the nation could deal with the needs of science'. But, said Professor Gowing,

> The purse did not open wide for another thirty years and then only because the government was caught between the claims of publicans and teetotallers. Until then governments would not accept that scientific and technical education must be paid for largely by the state. Britain was much richer than its competitors until nearly the end of the nineteenth century yet more parsimonious than any except France. In 1870, government expenditure was a much lower percentage of Gross National Product than in 1850, and in 1890 lower still. But collective expenditure was unpopular and scientific and technical education had little appeal.[17]

Government attitudes to expenditure on scientific education were reflected in the answers of Henry Cole (Secretary of the Science and Art Department) when, as a witness to the Devonshire Commission, he was subjected to a grilling by Thomas Huxley and James Kay-Shuttleworth. When finally challenged by the Duke himself Cole agreed that he would like to confine government aid entirely to the granting of scholarships, to assistance towards buildings and to providing in certain cases apparatus or conveniences of that kind'.[18] Captain Donnelly, who was also Secretary of the Department, in giving evidence to the Commissioners stated:

> The payment of fees by the pupils can be looked upon as the only solid and efficient basis on which a self-supporting system can be established and supported ... as the payments from the state must be expected to diminish and as aid on account of those persons who did nothing for themselves cannot be justified ... committees of schools and classes should be set up to impose as high a scale of fees as they consider can be raised.[19]

In 1868 a Sub-committee of Owens College, Manchester, obtained an audience with Disraeli as Prime Minister. The Prime Minister assured them of the great importance be attached to the subject they had laid before him. It had his fullest sympathy and would command the greatest consideration from his colleagues when he brought its claims before them but

> if Her Majesty's Government in the exigencies of the State should be unable to comply with your request, I am quite certain that the public

spirit and the generosity of Lancashire will not allow the interests of the College to suffer.[20]

No better luck was experienced by the same deputation when the Disraeli Government was replaced by the Gladstone Government.

The belief in individualism and the dislike of state interference and of centralised administration were widespread. There was a real fear, too, that state support would lead inevitably to state control. One member of the deputation to Gladstone was glad the Government had refused them a grant; there was plenty of money to be had in Manchester. Let them look for that and be independent of government help and interference. There were many who advocated the virtues of self-help and were often 'anti-state' at a time when the need for state and municipal intervention was becoming increasingly evident. Whilst there were those arguing for greater state support for education, and in particular for science and technology, there were others who were bitterly opposed to state interference. This conflict bedevilled the debate about scientific and technical education and its relation with industry and often hindered positive action.

Herbert Spencer was one of the most outspoken critics of state interference. He regarded the state as an enemy of man's evolutionary progress, his views being embodied in *State Education Self-Defeating* (1851) and *Man Versus the State* (1884). Robert Lowe, the instigator of 'payment-by-results', expressed the establishment view in the words 'I hold it as our duty not to spend public money to do that which people can do for themselves'. This became a cardinal principle underlying the allocation of government money to universities and all other educational bodies. The dislike of state interference was finally dispelled and overcome only by the fear of losing prosperity; the increasing intensity of foreign competition acted as a great spur to state action. In the meantime, it was left to merchants, manufacturers, industrialists and the livery companies of London to offer support for educational institutions and to take initiatives – a notable example being Joseph Whitworth's endowment of thirty scholarships at £100 a year for three years and the endowment of 60 exhibitions at £25 a year – the first national scheme of scholarships of any kind. At the same time he wrote (4 May, 1868) to Henry Cole suggesting the creation of a faculty of engineering with government-endowed chairs, but no response was forthcoming to this suggestion. To a certain extent government tardiness in supporting education may be excused for there was money already available but lying idle. The Taunton Commission, for instance, exposed mismanagement of funds relating to endowed schools amounting to over half a million pounds and Ralph Lingen, Permanent Secretary to the Treasury, wrote to the Royal Commission on Oxford and Cambridge:

> I cannot see what is the obligation of government while a Royal Commission is sitting on two universities with more than £700,000 a year to dispose of.[21]

But no such excuse can be advanced with regard to original research.

The overwhelming case for support of scientific research was cogently argued by George Gore, Principal of the Institute of Scientific Research, Birmingham. As a witness to the Devonshire Commission he described himself as a researcher in physics and chemistry. His radical views appeared in a book entitled *The Scientific Basis of National Progress*. He began this work with the statement:

> There is uneasiness at present respecting our ability to maintain our position in the race of progress and as our future success is based largely on science, it is desirable to call attention to the great public importance of new scientific knowledge and the means of promoting its development. By the neglect of scientific investigation, we are sacrificing our welfare as a nation. Present knowledge only enables us to maintain our present state. National progress is the result of new ideas, and the chief source of new ideas is original research.[22]

Scientific research was the key to the future according to Gore:

> New knowledge is new power is a maxim which scientific discovery has impressed upon us . . . The time is near when this nation will be compelled by the injurious consequences arising from its neglect of scientific research to acquire a knowledge of the relations of science to national existence and welfare, and to adopt more-means of encouraging discovery . . . England will be. compelled, by the necessities of human progress and the advance of foreign intellect, to determine and recognise the proper value of scientific research as a basis of progress. National superiority can only be maintained by being first in the race, and not by buying inventions of other nations.[23]

In the field of research, government support was largely confined to an annual grant of £1,000 a year to the Royal Society for distribution by the Society. In the period 1849–1914 this assisted some 400 scientists with grants totalling £180,000.

> The Grant was the first, and until 1890, major continuous source of direct government finance earmarked solely for the support of original scientific investigation – it probably was too small to do more than indicate or describe trends in original research.[24]

This grant was the subject of scathing criticism by Colonel Strange to the Devonshire Commissioners:

> I can only say that I think it is a downright absurdity to suppose that in a nation like England £1,000 distributed annually can produce any material effect upon science. There is literally in our government nobody to go to with the hope of making it clear and intelligible to him that this Grant is insufficient.[25]

Apparently, Lord Palmerston, the Prime Minister, was responsible for making this £1,000 as a personal offer. He would have been prepared to offer £10,000 had the Royal Society asked for it. Strange was critical of Sir Edward Sabine, President of the Royal Society, for not having been more demanding.

The absurdity of the grant in terms of improving Britain's economic efficiency is illustrated by the way in which the money was spent in 1850. The appropriation of the grant was: £350 for publication of observations made at Armagh Observatory; £150 for publication of volume I of the Catalogue of Ecliptic stars; £100 for investigations on inflamination; and £100 for drawing of parts of the skeleton of the Megatherium.

In terms of government support, astronomy and the biological and geological sciences fared much better than did physical sciences and engineering. As we have seen, much of the financial support provided by the Department of Science and Art was channelled into promoting museums, collections and geological surveys. Of one Departmental annual expenditure of £318,125, £39,780 went on South Kensington Museum, £10,071 on the Edinburgh Museum of Science and Art and £10,794 on the Dublin Science and Art Museum. Only £147,574 (40 per cent) actually went on schools of science and art. Professor Gowing states that 'money was poured without stint into the Victoria and Albert Museum'[26] and in the 1870s 'the single most expensive science was astronomy'.[27] This bias towards activities which could be pursued by cultured amateurs may be partly explained by the composition of British governments in this period. Between 1868 and the turn of the century, English Cabinets were headed by Gladstone, Disraeli, Lord Salisbury and Lord Roseberry. The influential and critical post of Chancellor was held meanwhile by Robert Lowe, Sir Stafford Northcote, Gladstone, Sir Michael Hicks Beach, Sir William Vernon Harcourt, and Lord Randolph Churchill. Whig or Tory, Conservative or Liberal, the political complexion of the government of the day made little difference. These were men of similar background steeped in the same traditions and deeply influenced by the ethos of the public schools and Oxbridge. The four Royal Commissions of the 1860s were headed by the Duke of Newcastle, the Earl of Clarendon, Baron Taunton and the Duke of Devonshire. Whatever 'progressive elements' were included as Commission members the chances were always weighted in favour of a non-radical report. This is exemplified in the Report of the Clarendon Commission, which, whilst critical of the public schools, nevertheless concluded that:

> among the services which they have rendered is undoubtedly to be reckoned the maintenance of classical literature as the staple of English education, a service which far outweighs the error of having clung to these studies exclusively.[28]

That the Commissioners should be so imbued with the value of classics is not surprising for they themselves were the successful products of the system. In addition to the Earl of Clarendon (privately educated), the Commissioners included the Eleventh Earl of Devon (Westminister and Christ Church, Oxford), the Fourth Baron Lyttleton (Eton and Trinity College, Cambridge), the Hon. Edward Turner Boyd Twistleton (Balliol) and Sir Henry Stafford Northcote, First Earl of Iddesleigh (Eton and Balliol). They contrast strongly with the 'apostles' of science and reform; Lyon Playfair (St. Andrews and Giessen), Thomas Huxley (Charing Cross Hospital) and Sir James Bryce (Glasgow High School). Government attitudes to science were reflected in industrial management.

In Germany, scientists took their place in the management structure of industry; the expert was thus at the centre of the decision-making process in industrial firms. Such was not the case in Britain where scientists and technologists were largely confined to playing a subordinate role as advisers. Professor Allen in his pamphlet *The British Disease* contends that the attitude towards the 'expert' in Britain was a critical factor. The exclusion of the professional scientist and technologist from the essential decision-making processes meant that the last word was with the amateur. 'This may well provide the clue to many failures in British projects that made a promising start'.[29] Professor Allen sees the 'cult of the amateur' and the misuse of the professional expert as being a fundamental fault not only in the industrial world but in the entire structure of society, especially in the system of government. It is the contention of his paper that the decline of Britain had its roots in the failure of the governing class, as well as the industrialists themselves, 'to realise as early as their competitors, that the age of the professional in industrial management had dawned and, in particular, to grasp that the future lay with men equipped by systematic training to promote technological innovation'.

Allen very firmly assigns the blame for Britain's decline to:

> what we now call the 'establishment': political leaders, the Civil Service and those who sat on the boards of the chief industrial companies. They themselves were of course the victims of anachronistic institutions – the English class system and the educational arrangements associated with it.[30]

His final judgement is that Britain's industrial progress was gravely hindered by the strong prejudice in government, and many branches of industry itself, against the expert, a prejudice rooted in social and educational tradition, a prejudice which carried into a technological age the prejudices and attitudes of mind inherited from a pre-scientific time'.[31]

Notes and References

1 HOBSBAWM, E.J. (1968) *Industry and Empire*, Pelican Economic History of Britain, Vol. 3, Harmondsworth, Penguin Books, p. 13.
2 DE LA BECHE, H. *Royal Commission on Scientific Instruction and the Advancement of Science*, 1st report, cp. 30.
3 THOMSON, D. (1950) *England in the Nineteenth Century*, Pelican History of England, Vol. 8, Harmondsworth, Penguin Book, p. 101.
4 *Ibid*, p. 101.
5 Industrial Education on the Continent – Introductory Lecture at the Government School of Mines, session 1852–53 (London 1853). Quoted in CARDWELL, D.S.L. (1972) *The Organization of Science in England*, London, Heinemann, p. 88.
6 Quoted in CARDWELL, D.S.L. (1972) *op. cit.*, p. 78.
7 *Royal Commission on Scientific Instruction and the Advancement of Science (Devonshire Commission)* (1872), 8th report, p. 45.
8 *Ibid*, p. 24.
9 *Ibid*, p. 2.
10 *Ibid*, p. 3.
11 *Ibid*, p. 4.
12 *Ibid*, p. 4.

13 *Ibid*, p. 3.
14 *Devonshire Commission* (1872), First Report, Vol. II, p. 75.
15 *Ibid*, p. 127.
16 *Devonshire Commission* (1872), Vol. II, p. 129.
17 GOWING, M. (1976) *Science, Technology and Education*. The Wilkins Lecture. Reprinted from Notes and Records of the Royal Society of London, Vol. 32, No. 1, July, 1977.
18 *Devonshire Commission* (1872), Eighth Report, p. 17.
19 *Devonshire Commission* (1872), First Report, Vol. 1, p. 400.
20 THOMPSON, J. (1886) *The Owens College*, J.E. Cornish, p. 145.
21 T1 (7522B) 6048/1876, Minute R. Lingen and W.H. Smith, 12 April, 1876. Report of the Commissioners appointed to inquire into the property and income of the Universities of Oxford and Cambridge and of the colleges and halls therein (1973).
22 GORE, G. (1882) *The Scientific Basis of National Progress*, Williams and Norgate, p. 1.
23 *Ibid*, p. 7.
24 MACLEOD, R.M. (1972) 'Resources of Science in Victorian England: The Endowment of Science Movement, 1868–1900', extract from MATHIAS, P. (Ed.) *Science and Society, 1600–1900*, p. 324.
25 *Devonshire Commission* (1872), First Report, Vol. II, p. 75.
26 GOWING, M. (1976) *op. cit.*, p. 73.
27 MACLEOD, R.M. (1972) *op. cit.*, p. 356.
28 *The Clarendon Commission* (1864) Vol. I, p. 56.
29 ALLEN, G.C. (1976) *The British Disease*, London, Institute of Economic Affairs, p. 49.
30 *Ibid*, p. 49.
31 ALLEN, G.C. (1976) *op. cit.*, p. 49.

Conclusions

Gordon Roderick and Michael Stephens

The great debate

The Great Debate, begun in the nineteenth century, continues to rage over what has been described as the 'English disease'; an apparent failure of British industry to keep pace with its competitors leading to a profound dissatisfaction with economic performance. In the 1960s the late Lord Snow was pointing out:

> There is something wrong with us. For 1938 let us take the national product as 100. In the United States it has gone up to 225, West Germany to 228 and in the OEEC countries to 160 but in Britain to only 150. For 1950 take the base 100. West Germany has jumped to 225, France to 170, Italy 202, OEEC countries to 164 but Britain only to 129.[1]

In this debate, Lords Snow and Bowden have filled the roles formerly occupied by Baron Playfair and Thomas Huxley in the nineteenth century as spokesmen for science and technology, the state of which is always cited as one of the many contributory factors leading to the presumed British failure.

In his speech to the Labour Party Conference at Scarborough in 1963 Mr. Harold Wilson (as he then was) said

> Our failure to develop science and technology is leading to a mass sell-out to foreign concerns . . . Britain, once the workshop of the world, is becoming the dumping ground for the products of overseas industries that are just that bit quicker in getting off the mark than we are.

Two years later, Sir Leon Bagrit in his Reith Lectures, commented

> It is essential for our future national prosperity in Britain that we should modernize this country by spreading an understanding of the most advanced forms of technology as rapidly as we can and throughout the whole of our society. We must somehow induce industrial concerns to adopt these new techniques quickly and intelligently, and we must make sure that our universities, our technical colleges and our schools are mobilized to produce the people with the background, the training and the

inclination which is necessary to bring this about. We must also see to it that the correct political decisions are taken to make it easier, not more difficult to realise these aims.

Earlier, in 1956, a Government White Paper had declared:

The aims are to strengthen the economy, to improve the standards of living of our people and discharge effectively our manifold responsibilities overseas. Success in each case will turn largely on our ability to secure a steady increase in industrial output, in productive investment, in export of goods and services of the highest quality at competitive prices.[2]

A century ago leading spokesmen were saying very much the same things. George Gore, an industrial chemist who had set up his own private Institute for Scientific Research in Birmingham, was writing in a radical work entitled *The Scientific Basis of National Progress*:

England will be compelled, by the necessities of human progress and the advance of foreign intellect, to determine and recognise the proper value of scientific research as a basis of progress. National superiority can only be maintained by being first in the race and not by buying inventions of other nations.[3]

In an address on technical education at Manchester in 1887 Huxley was declaring:

Let me call your attention to the fact that the terrible battle of competition between the different nations of the world is no transitory phenomenon, and does not depend upon this or that fluctuation of the market, or upon any condition that is likely to pass away . . . We are at present in the swim of one of those vast moments in which, with a population far in excess of that which we can feed, we are saved from a catastrophe, through the impossibility of feeding them, solely by our possession of a fair share of the markets of the world. And in order that that fair share may be retained, it is absolutely necessary that we should be able to produce commodities which we can exchange with food-growing people, and which they will take, rather than those of our rivals, on the grounds of their greater cheapness or their greater excellence . . . Our sole chance of succeeding in a competition, which must constantly become more and more severe, is that our people shall not only have the knowledge and the skill which are required, but that they shall have the will and the energy and the honesty, without which neither knowledge nor skill can be of any permanent avail.[4]

It is now generally accepted that there was a slowing down in the rate of economic growth in the United Kingdom after 1870, the High Noon of the summer of 1851 turned into chill evening as the century progressed. The euphoria surrounding the Great Exhibition rapidly evaporated as British productivity lagged behind that of her competitors; the loss of Britain's industrial lead which had once seemed impregnable created the great enigma of 'What went wrong'?

Contemporary observers and historians have assiduously sought the answer to this riddle. And yet there may have been no riddle to solve – perhaps nothing had gone wrong, for Britain's industrial supremacy may not have been the outcome of controllable human factors if 'The whole complex of circumstances that produced British pre-eminence before 1873 was fortuitous'.[5] Britain's pre-eminence may have been accidental, the outcome of a perhaps never-to-be-repeated conjuction of a set of favourable factors – geographic, commercial, economic and technological – conspiring together. It was, in other words, an historical event created by the fortune of circumstances rather than the result of planned policy or of human design.

The Industrial Revolution

Historians have found great difficulty in achieving agreement on the exact causes of the Industrial Revolution. Equally, there is little agreement on why it 'took-off' in Britain or the exact timing of the 'take-off'. All that is certain is that by 1851 (the mid-point of the period when, it is claimed, Britain 'was the workshop of the world)[6] she led in the supply of manufactured goods, machinery and textiles. Although she continued to prosper thereafter a retardation set in in the rate of her industrial productivity.

Why did the Revolution occur at the particular time that it did? And why in England? There is no single answer to either of these questions. Many factors have been put forward by historians to characterize what is described as the Industrial Revolution.[7] But it remains obscure as an event. In summarizing the conflicting views advanced to explain the origins of the Industrial Revolution Michael Flinn (1972) concludes:

> It is clear that the precise origins of the Industrial Revolution remain something of a mystery. This is hardly surprising as the origins themselves have been little studied compared with the copious descriptions produced by historians, each generation of whom have reflected the particular point of view of their ages. For the present generation of scholars the Industrial Revolution represents a more complex event than hitherto.[8]

Hobsbawm (1974) has argued the case for a second industrial revolution:

> The transformation of industry since the end of the Industrial Revolution has become continuous, but every now and then the cumulative results of these changes become so obvious that observers are tempted to talk about a Second Industrial Revolution. The last decades of the nineteenth century were such a time.[9]

Landes (1966) also writes:

> The speed of advance and its consequences towards the end of the nineteenth century were far-reaching, and formed part of a much wider

process of change, which included electricity, the internal combustion engine, and assembly-line production, in short a cluster of innovations that earned the name of the Second Industrial Revolution.[10]

The distinctive feature of the second revolution, in marked contrast to the first, was its close connection with pure and applied science. Britain 'won' the first Industrial Revolution decisively, but it can be argued that she 'lost' the second. The key to this may be found in the fact that 'the output of technological progress was a function of the input of scientifically qualified manpower, equipment and money into systematic research projects'.[11]

High noon to industrial decline

At the time of the Great Exhibition in 1851, which Rolt in *Victorian Engineering* has dubbed 'High Noon in Hyde Park', Britain's main competitor was France. By the final quarter of the century the bogy nation had become Germany. Britain faced severe competition from her for markets, particularly in Mesopotamia, Brazil, Chile and Uruguay. As market after market fell into German hands: 'there were times, particularly towards 1900, when foreign competition seemed to be a brooding menace rather than a bracing challenge and the familiar label "made in Germany" was used as the grimmest of forebodings'.[12]

Where did firms fall down? Leaving aside for the moment the question of whether or not firms were *producing* goods as cheaply or as effeciently as they might have done, it is clear from Aldcroft that they certainly were not *selling* goods as efficiently as they ought to have done. Germany and America tackled the problem by building up extensive sales organisations and abandoned the traditional merchant system of indirect selling through agents. The latter practice 'interposed barriers of communication between producer and consumer'. British firms lost export business through a lack of sales drive. In any case, the 'merchant system was geared to selling traditional goods in traditional markets and less suited to selling new and sophisticated products in expanding markets' (Aldcroft). Some firms can be excluded from this criticism but, in cases where a firm met with exporting success, it was often dependent on foreign skills for as Chapman points out, 'The exporting success of Platt Bros. cannot be said to have been the product of unaided British genius for the marketing side, like that of many other English cotton manufacturers and machine builders, was largely conducted by foreign born, more particularly German and Greek, commission agents. The extent to which foreigners controlled the export of textiles and machinery points to the inadequacy of British education, particularly on the commercial side'.

Economic historians, perhaps not surprisingly, are divided over the central question of whether the performance of the economy was satisfactory or not. Aldcroft earlier concludes that the Victorian economy could and should have grown faster and, in his view, there was certainly room for some structural change which would have helped to achieve a better result. He suggests that an improvement in the economy could have been achieved by less concentration on staple industries with low rates of productivity growth and a switch to faster growing sectors; together with a diversion of resources from foreign investment to home investment. Although these often brought profits 'most foreign investments yielded less than the average domestic return' (Aldcroft) and in any case 'the export of capital stimulated the creation of new foreign industries threatening the existence of long-established British exporters' (Sims). In support of his argument Aldcroft cites Kennedy's (1976) suggestion[13] that, had Britain made a commitment of resources to telecommunications, electricity, electrical engineering and car manufacturing similar to that made in the United States, her implied increase in growth would have been sufficient to lift British per capita incomes to 55 per cent above the level actually recorded in 1913.

Aldcroft divides individual industries into four categories according to their performance. The list of those in which there was 'something wrong' includes iron and steel, coal, textiles, engineering, boots and shoes, chemicals, shipbuilding, watchmaking, railways, electrical engineering and automobiles. 'There remained', he claims, 'large sectors of industry which were technically backward compared with American and German practice' and in this respect he cites the electrical engineering industry and chemicals. Aldcroft points out that it is wrong to generalize about industry generally and says 'McCloskey, Sandberg, Harley and others have argued that it is *misleading to generalize* on an economy-wide basis given the wide diversity of performance between industries and between different branches of the same industry'.

Management and the theory of entrepreneurial failure

The belief that Britain's industrial decline was partly, if not mainly, attributatable to bad management was espoused by contemporary observers and has been advanced by numerous critics down to the present day. In particular, during the 1940s and 1950s economic historians argued that the keystone of Britain's industrial decline was the performance of the Victorian entrepreneur. Aldcroft points out 'the origins of the businessman's "bad press" date from the latter part of the nineteenth century' when the rate of growth of total output and industrial production decelerated. The case against Victorian management was built up of many strands: they had failed to adopt new techniques of production, had neglected research, had invested too little in laboratories and technical personnel, had lost markets through the inefficient use of salesmen and had continued for too long to invest in the traditional industries at the expense of newly emerging industries. The case against the entrepreneurs originally seemed damming but a greater degree of sympathy is now extended to their problems. McCloskey (1971), the chief protagonist of those who now exonerate the entrepreneur, states: 'It is fair to say that the late Victorian entrepreneur who started his career in damnation, is well on the way to redemption'.[14] In reply Payne (1974) writes:

So it may prove though the evidence is not completely convincing.

Doubts are entertained by some economic historians ... The sheer in-conclusiveness of the discussion is challenging, so many questions are as yet unanswered ... [15] To continue to accept that British industry stagnated in relative terms but at the same time to reject the hypothesis of entre-preneurial failure faces us with a 'new series of problems'.[16]

Lindert and Trace (1971) confess, as a result of their study of the chemical industry, that the 'calibre of entrepreneurship has yet to be quantified satisfactorily'[17] and Payne (1974) concludes:

> there is still much to be discovered about the nineteenth century entre-preneur and his influence on British economic performance ... The sheer inconclusiveness of the discussion is challenging, so many questions are as yet unanswered, so much new material – in the form of business archives – is becoming available for research. It may well be that explorations in this most difficult territory will never result in completely satisfying conclusions.[18]

Payne raises two interesting objections to the theory of entrepreneurial failure. First, it is commonly assumed that entrepreneurs in the early stages of the Industrial Revolution possessed drive, initiative and enthusiasm. But such may not have been the case for 'the eulogistic aura enveloping the pioneers has been somewhat obscuring because earlier assessments have reflected a biased sample. The majority of records concern firms that were sufficiently successful to have a long life. Many who succeeded in the early years may not have fared so well in later decades'. British errors and hesitations, he argues, were always present; they simply became more obvious in the period between 1870 and 1914. The second is that it may even be misleading to speak at all of 'the British entrepreneur'. According to Payne 'no such person exists' as managers came from varied socio-economic backgrounds, operated within different institutional frameworks and were concerned with the attainment of different objectives. Payne's judgement as to the loss of British pre-eminence in international trade – which he emphazises is in itself an endlessly debatable proposition – shifts the argument from a possible decline in entrepreneurial activity to 'a surfeit of individual entrepreneurs, a multitude of aggressively independent firms each pursuing its own self-interest when any increase in the rate of economic growth demanded more co-operation'.[19]

Aldcroft points out there may well have been technical lags but it does not necessarily follow that entrepreneurs were inefficient or that they behaved irration-ally for 'it is possible to explain their behaviour as a rational response to costs, markets and other conditions peculiar to Britain'. Nevertheless, there were examples of technical lag of productivity, stagnation and of deficient enterprise. Despite the new 'revisionist views' Aldcroft concludes that 'the British economy did not realise its full potential in late Victorian Britain partly due to mismanagement'.

The quality of management seems to have been particularly deficient in the coal industry where 'the growing complexity of technology by the mid-nineteenth century made it increasingly necessary that those in charge of colliery operations should not only possess adequate general education but also be conversant with the latest technical and safety practices . . . but the ability to read and write was not common among the men nor among large sections of the management class' (Buxton). Mechanization was delayed, often due to sound reasons. Nevertheless, whilst some districts were advanced in their use of mechanical technology others were backward. 'Colliery managers failed to keep abreast of, or perhaps improperly understood the latest techniques known and used extensively in the USA'. Colliery practice remained for the most part extremely backward but, 'rather than wilful neglect on the part of management the chief failing was simply ignorance of what could be accomplished, indeed, already had been accomplished by many collieries in the north' (Buxton). Due to Britain's early start, the best seams were played out rather earlier than were those of her competitors, a natural consequence being that productivity was bound to fall unless technological developments were pursued in order to offset this. Unfortunately, it seems that traditional methods continued to dominate. 'The extent to which this is blamed on a technically inferior and ill-informed management is open to question' (Buxton). From 1850 onwards profits generally speaking were high and many managers were 'less than enthusiastic about underground mechanization', being content to 'leave well alone'. Increase of productivity was pursued through inputs of labour due to its cheapness. Hence, the plentiful supply of cheap labour was a factor which contributed to holding back technological development in the coal industry. Cheap labour had a bearing in the engineering industries too. American manufacturers, because of the high cost of labour, were more ready than we were to scrap existing machinery in order to avoid heavy maintenance costs and replace it with new and updated equipment.

Another charge against British management was that it employed relatively few scientists and technologists and there were shortages, too, of educated foremen, supervisers and technicians. Furthermore, industrialists failed to utilize the work-force effectively for scientific management of the labour force was almost unknown in Britain prior to 1914. Although workers themselves were resistant, and sometimes openly hostile to new technologies and attempts to boost output by rationalizing production methods and by the introduction of incentive payments, management itself did little to assuage workers' fears on these matters, a key factor being the wide gulf between management and labour.

It was the attitude to change and innovation that Arthur Shadwell (1888), highlighted as deleterious to industrial advance. Poor relationships between men and management bedevilled English industry as they did not on the continent. In many industries he found that the manufacturers 'fully recognise the necessity of keeping abreast of the times', whereas the workmen on the other hand 'dislike and resent change, and even ridiculed foreign competition'. He took a serious view of the 'deep and abiding' suspicion between employers and employed:

> the habit of distrust is both a sign and a source of weakness in industrial matters . . . the standing objection of workmen to innovations and improvements is rooted in it, and the very large proportion of the dispute between capital and labour can be traced to nothing but mutual distrust.[20]

Of course, the quality of management, particularly in terms of education and qualifications, throughout most of British industry was open to question. Industry had a low esteem and did not necessarily attract the more able. The oft repeated charge that management had practical experience but was deficient in theoretical knowledge seems to have been true at least of the coal industry where 'eligibility for the posts of manager or under manager depended on five years practical experience in mining. It was felt that this unduly favoured men of 'practical experience' at the expense of those of high ability and good general education, who might otherwise have been drawn into the industry. Indeed, even if highly educated, entry into the management side of coalmining was far from easy for those not already having family connections with the industry' (Buxton).

The iron and steel industry, too, according to Almond, did not welcome the academically trained scientist and technologist. The traditional method of entry was through apprenticeship, an apprentice in fact requiring financial backing in order to fund the heavy premiums. To climb the ladder from apprentice to managing director or owner was unusual, for, as Charlotte Erickson (1959) in her study of business leaders found, the iron and steel industry was governed to a very large extent by dynastic heirs or investors. Family men were predominant. Erickson discovered that steel-making was carried out under the leadership of men who, according to their fathers' occupations, were upper middle class. This class maintained its hold on the vast majority of the top positions in the industry with few fluctuations until World War I. As fortunes were culled from the industry, more and more sons went to public schools and to Oxford and Cambridge; marriage with daughters of landed and professional classes were continued and titles were added to their names. The implication is that Britain was ceasing to produce, in the steel industry, a class of leader who found sufficient scope for his ambition in his industrial achievements. Erickson concluded that:

> the normal hereditary leadership of the industry lost ground to newcomers during periods of fundamental technical change, but when more normal times returned, sons followed fathers in the traditional way, while even in periods of change the hereditary leadership was by no means eclipsed.[21]

Chapman points to similar conclusions for the cotton and lace industries; most of the 200 or so entrepreneurs who followed in Arkwright's shoes up to 1788 were drawn from the hereditary leadership of the industry. The new men trained themselves on the job in the factories, workshops and warehouses of the hereditary elite. Postan, in his survey of the industrial managers in Europe, argued that industrial leaders of the type classed as 'parochial' or 'traditional' had established themselves as the predominant type in most of the older industries.[22] A similar charge had been made by Sir Swire Smith (1888) a woollen manufacturer and member of the Royal Commission on Technical Instruction. In his Inaugural Address at Dundee Technical Institute in October 1888 he claimed:

> The wealthy manufacturer sends his son to a classical school to learn Latin and Greek as a preparation for cloth manufacturing, calico printing,

engineering or coalmining ... After his scholastic career he enters his father's factory absolutely untrained[23]

Among Sir Swire Smith's acquaintances there may have been some to whom this applied. Such a charge, however, cannot be levelled at Merseyside industrialists, among whom an awareness of their own educational shortcomings seemed most acute.[24] A notable example is James Muspratt, 'father' of the heavy chemical industry. After meeting and befriending Justig von Liebig (the originator of the first university research laboratories), Muspratt sent his four sons, none of whom went to a public school, to study under Liebig at Giessen. All four returned to Merseyside, three entering their father's firm and making distinctive contributions to its success. Josias Gamble of St. Helens sent his son David to University College, London, to study science and engineering. He returned to his father's firm, eventually becoming its manager and the outstanding manufacturing chemist of St. Helens. Sir John Brunner of Brunner Mond at Northwich sent both his sons to Cambridge to study science. Like the Muspratt family, later generations of the Pilkington glass firm at St. Helens also carried on in the family firm. Richard Pilkington, brother of the firm's founder, was a trained engineer and his son William Windle served an apprenticeship in the firm. George Pilkington, who was trained as a chemist at the Royal College of Chemistry in London also returned to join the firm as its chemist. Elsewhere, firms like Cadburys, Bibbys and W.H. Allen sent their sons to the university for a scientific education.

Industry and training

The final quarter of the century witnessed rapid change as a multitude of innovations succeeded one another. Industrial processes now were more dependent on science and called for a different requirement:

> The major technical advances of the second half of the nineteenth century were essentially scientific; that is to say they required at the very least some knowledge of recent developments in pure science for original inventions, a far more consistent process of scientific experiment and testing for their development and an increasingly close and continuous link between industrialists, technologists, professional scientists and scientific institutions.[25]

In the textile industries Chapman points out that spinning and weaving were mechanical processes whereas bleaching, dyeing and printing were chemical ones requiring greater expertise. Here the most lamentable deficiencies in training became apparent quite early in the nineteenth century.

Tolley's essay demonstrates how difficult it was to put across the benefits of science and technology to industrialists and manufacturers in the Nottingham region. The technical education provided was meant to be of advantage to the local industries of lace and hosiery, agriculture and mining. But support was not forthcoming in sufficient measure and, as a result, the University College of Nottingham became a municipal project with the Corporation assuming responsibility in the absence of endowments from industry. At Sheffield, where Firth College was founded with narrow industrial purposes, 'industrial support was curiously lacking' and 'what is clear is that in 1884 Sheffield industry did not want a technical school sufficiently to pay for it'.[26] Nottingham and Sheffield, however, cannot be taken as typical. At Leeds, for instance, businessmen alarmed by the evidence of foreign competition at the Paris Exhibition of 1867 helped to found the Yorkshire College of Science in 1874.[27] In Birmingham, Josiah Mason founded his College of Science in 1880 as he was 'deeply convinced from his long and varied experience in different branches of manufacture of the necessity and benefit of systematic scientific instruction especially adapted to the practical, mechanical and industrial pursuits of the Midland district'.[28] Later, Sir James Chance, head of the Birmingham glass firm, gave £50,000 to the College for engineering developments. The same pattern was found in many other cities. At Manchester, financial support for Owens College was not forthcoming in the early days but this was because the College tried to adopt the liberal arts education of the ancient universities. Under the influence of Roscoe it was demonstrated that the College was relevant to industry and gifts from industry for industrial purposes began to flow in. At Liverpool, a wealthy city, support came in abundance from the merchants and from the chemical industry. All the 'civic' colleges, however, experienced great financial difficulties from having to rely on endowments and subscriptions. Even at Liverpool, one of the best endowed Colleges, it was found necessary to set up a special Sustentation Fund to see the College through its problems – a process described by Ramsey Muir, a young history lecturer, as a precarious and undignified way of funding a university.

Many enlightened industrial leaders were mindful of their own educational shortcomings and were anxious to ensure that their own sons benefited from such an education. During the first half of the nineteenth century in particular, industrial leaders were patrons of the Mechanics' Institutes and later they gave support to the 'science and art' classes movement. Enlightened firms took an interest in the further education of their employees, both within and outside the firm. Chapman points out that John Platt found the primary schooling of his workmen inadequate and consequently sent his apprentices to his factory school for two hours a day until they were fourteen years of age. Skilled men in the firm were persuaded to attend classes in draughtmanship and mechanics at Oldham Science and Art School, the best were rewarded by being sent abroad to supervize the assembly of export orders. At Crosfields, the Warrington soap firm, most managerial appointments were made from among men who had been brought up in the firm. The firm provided regular lectures and a library of technical books and journals. After entry from school and appropriate training in the laboratories and works departments many continued their education, with the Directors' strong approval, in the evening classes of the technical colleges – attendance being encouraged by payment of the fees and bonuses for passing the examinations.[29]

At Bootle, the firm of Johnsons at one time sent all their boys to the technical school for instruction in chemistry and other subjects but found that for the majority of cases 'it was a pure waste of time owing to the lack of general education of the apprentices'.[30] The firm consequently decided to hold special classes at the works itself, the instruction being provided by the head chemist. Attendance was voluntary but nearly all the boys and men went through the course. Furthermore, boys who wished to attend continuation schools were let off work and had their fees paid. But as Chapman rightly points out 'few firms had the resources to remedy the deficiencies of the public educational system'.

Manufacturers and industrialists sought to overcome their own educational deficiencies and to keep abreast of increasing specialized knowledge through the formation of technical and professional associations. In 1882 the Society of Chemical Industry was established; the membership included alkali manufacturers, chemical engineers, analytical chemists and assayers and university staff. In such bodies were forged the essential links between teachers and academics on the one hand and manufacturers and industrial chemists on the other. Such developments as these were not, of course, confined to chemistry. Each developing field was 'professionalizing' itself in the same manner; as evidenced by the formation of the Institution of Mechanical Engineers (1847), the Institution of Gas Engineers (1863), the Iron and Steels Institute (1869), the Institute of Mining Engineers (1889), and the Institute of Mining and Metallurgy (1892).

The early generation of managerial leaders could not be blamed for their almost total lack of formal instruction in pure and applied science for, until 1850 or so, such facilities did not exist apart from those at the two London colleges. Many industrialists did what they could to ensure that their own sons did not lack scientific instruction and sought to create facilities with sparse aid from the government. There is little doubt that many had positive and progressive attitudes towards the importance of science, technical training and research.

Education

Turning to education generally, it is clear that a transformation had occurred in the English education system by the end of the century but, in all sectors, England was the last of the major industrial countries to effect reforms. West points out that people were more literate at the end of the first Industrial Revolution than at the beginning. There was an upward trend in literacy rates and from 1800 onwards there was an 'educational explosion' in all the major towns.

> Despite the widespread belief to the contrary, education expanded significantly during the periods examined, and at least on *a priori* reasoning there is a fair assumption that it significantly assisted economic growth throughout . . . There was an educational revolution as well as an industrial revolution and both were interrelated.[31]

A major advance was effected with the introduction of board schools following Forster's Act of 1870. School buildings rapidly increased in number, the numbers on school rolls and numbers in attendance multiplied. A remaining obstacle was the imposition of school fees. Mathew Arnold in his report of 1852 pointed out that in an inspection of 112 schools 'half of the total costs had been collected from the scholars themselves[32] and concluded 'that these rates of payment must generally exclude the children of the very poor'.[33] In the 1880s 'school fees were still providing substantial amounts towards costs'.[34] They were not finally abolished until 1891.

No field of education was so badly unco-ordinated as that of secondary education; its origins are to be found in private initiatives and benevolence but progress was stultified in consequence of the state's reluctance to interfere and allocate adequate resources. Looking back at secondary education in the nineteenth century, the Board of Education reflected in its Report for 1908–09:

> That the state has any concern with secondary education is a comparatively modern idea in England ... the term 'secondary' has been left in the air, and this is a sort of symbol of the way in which secondary education itself was for long neglected after a national system of elementary education had been established on the one hand, and on the other university education.[35]

An awareness of a dependence between primary education and technical education on the one hand and industrial productivity on the other came into being long before any such connection with secondary education was envisaged. Secondary education was not seen to be significant for economic prosperity until very late in the century. Michael Sadler (1904), Professor of History and Administration of Education at the Victoria University, when asked by the Liverpool Education Committee to review secondary education found such an attitude widespread in the City.

> The educational problem in Liverpool is the education of commercial England in epitome. Here within the limits of a single city, are all the difficulties and opportunities which present themselves in the great problem of national education as it bears upon the welfare and efficiency of a commercial state ... All that is most significant in the commercial greatness of Britain is represented here[36]

The citizens of Liverpool argued thus to him:

> Out of the estimated ships' tonnage of the world, one half is British, and more than one quarter of that belongs to Liverpool. Why should not things go on as they are? Is not the prosperity of Liverpool due to her geographical position? ... Her port, not her education, it might be argued is the cause of her wealth. Is there likely to be any real advantage in having a higher level of education among the clerks who at present go into business at 15? Why do more than is already done for the upkeep of the secondary schools?[37]

Sadler found widespread indifference to secondary education in England compared to vigour abroad. Britain had enjoyed a long start in industry and commerce leading to the belief that 'it could make shift'. The momentum of past success carried the country along.

As late as 1904 Sadler was able to conclude that:

In no country in the world . . . are the issues involved in any real reform
of secondary education so tangled or so obscure as they are in England,
and we can feel no surprise that we are almost the last of the great nations
seriously to take in hand the problem of educational reform on a national
scale. And yet the urgency of our need is proportional to the complexity
of the problem which we have to solve[38]

Secondary schools in England consisted of those recognized by the Clarendon
Commission in 1864 as the nine leading public schools (Eton, Harrow, Winchester,
Westminster, Merchant Taylors, Charterhouse, St. Paul's, Rugby and Shrewsbury)
together with the ancient endowed grammar schools (often established for children
of the poorer classes) and the new private and proprietary boarding schools which
sprang up with the coming of the railways in the 1840s (many founded as the
result of the dissatisfaction of the middle class parent with the existing schools).
Unfortunately, in the second half of the nineteenth century, the traditional grammar
schools and many of the new secondary schools were unduly influenced by the
classically-oriented public schools. 'The new schools imitated the public schools
in large part because of the demand of the upwardly mobile to establish their children
in the new class' (Musgrave). Later, following the Education Act of 1902, 'the
new type of secondary school which came into being due to the influence of Sir
Robert Morant, the senior civil servant at the Board of Education, became Arnoldian
in spirit and curriculum and not connected with the world of industry and commerce'. As for technical education, this had a low esteem in society and was intended
primarily for the industrial artisans. The middle classes were virtually excluded from
the necessity to receive a technical education.

In higher education universities played little part in producing trained manpower
until the final quarter of the century. The ancient universities were concerned with
the concept of creating 'cultivated human beings', and when the civic colleges
came into being they were hampered in their attempts to promote science and
technical studies by lack of finance, the low esteem of science in the schools and
the poor quality of entrants. The deficiencies in the ranks of manpower requirements
could fortunately be overcome by bringing over trained scientists, technologists
and salesmen from the continent. There has been no attempt to quantify this continental 'brain-drain' into Britain but it was clearly quite considerable. Industrialists
favourable to the employment of trained scientists were probably doubtful of the
quality of English trained men as compared to the Germans. Mond was one such
and was not converted to employing graduates from Owens College until late in
the century. Unfortunately some industrialists and managers continued to harbour
suspicions of the theoretical man preferring instead men who had come up through
the industry from the shop floor. When Lady Chorley's father joined Mather and
Platt in the 1880s the engineering industry had little use for bright young men from
the universities. Most firms preferred: 'lads who had been through the works and
had practical knowledge rather than theoretical knowledge'[39] These attitudes were
still to be found even prior to the World War I: 'There still exists among the
generality of employers a strong preference for the man trained from an early age

in the works and a prejudice against the so-called "college-trained" man'.[40] The prejudice was not confined to industry:

> Britain's industrial progress was gravely hindered by the strong prejudice, in government, and in many branches of industry itself, against the expert, a prejudice rooted in social and educational tradition, a prejudice which carried over into a technological age the practices and attitudes inherited from a pre-scientific age.[41]

Government

It was not, of course, the accepted function of government to iterfere or intervene in education and even less so in the affairs of industry. The century was dominated by the philosophy of *laissez-faire*. which stemmed initially from a belief in the efficacy of a free market economy and whilst some continued to restrict the use of the term to economic questions others extended the concept to embrace the whole field of government action:

> The nineteenth century was viewed as an age dominated, at least until its final quarter, by the principle of *laissez-faire*, expressed in terms both of economic ideas and of social policy[42]

The less government action there was the better the economists liked it. But there were seen to be clear advantages in there being some direction of educational policy. Classical economists:

> saw the education of the masses as the means through which the growth of population could be controlled; as a guarantor of social order; as an instrument of national economic development; and, not least, as an indispensable agent in the promotion of political democracy. To achieve these diverse ends the economists were prepared to accept large-scale intervention by the state[43]

Once Parliament made its first modest educational grant in 1833 the principle of interference was established. Elementary education continued thereafter to be the sector of education which experienced major government interference. It was the Great Exhibition which directed attention to the need for schools of art and design and schools of science. After England's poor showing at the Paris Exhibition of 1867, technical education became firmly established as a field of priority, along with primary education, in the government's mind. In secondary education, despite its chaotic state, the problem was not so much lack of finance as the distribution of funds and a process of rationalization. Between 1860 and the end of the century, no fewer than four commissions were required before some semblance of order was introduced in the form of the 1902 Education Act. Prior to that, the major interference by government had been the setting up of the Endowed Schools Commission in 1869.

Major advances throughout the greater part of the century had been due to initiatives taken by private individuals; this was no less true of universities than of any other sector. It was not until the civic colleges had been well established on the basis of local funding that the government took a hand, in 1889, and even then it was limited to a meagre grant of £15,000.

As to industry, the government stood aside: 'Industrial development in England owed almost nothing to state aid whereas in France and Germany the state afforded generous assistance' (Sims). Nowhere was the connection between State aid, higher education and industry more clearly seen than in the case of the German chemical industry and during the latter part of the century the German chemical industry, the universities and technical high schools were the objects of frequent visits by deputations and observers from England. The visitors were invariably impressed by all they saw. Around the turn of the century, Dr. Frederick Rose (1901), H.M. Consul at Stuttgart, attempted to relate the German investment in higher education with the progress of the chemical industry, or, in his words, attempted 'to show to what extent the German chemical industries have benefited by the sums expended by the German states on chemical instruction'. The field of chemical research and investigation, he said, was so dominated by Germany that 'a knowledge of German is essential – the best manuals are in German and two-thirds of the world's annual output of chemical research work comes from Germany'.

By 1897 German production of chemicals amounted to £50 million, yet there was no complacency. In the view of the Society for the Protection of Chemical Industries, 'It [was] absolutely indispensible for the further progress of chemical industries that the necessary sums for thorough reorganisation of chemical in-dustries be forthcoming'[45] Between 1820 and 1899, state aid to universities in Prussia multiplied tenfold; in 1897, the total income of Prussian universities amounted to £563,584 of which the state gave £412,683. In the 1880s the total capital cost of technical high schools in Germany amounted to some £3 million with a further annual running cost of £250,000. The investment of such vast sums, a considerable proportion of which went on chemical instruction, was, in Rose's (1901) view justified:

> Sums expended on chemical instruction have been amply repaid . . . it is universally recognised that the efforts made hitherto must be increased and more carefully and judiciously applied if the German chemical industries are to maintain and strengthen their position in the future'[46]

Final conclusions

On balance it would seem that the performance of the economy during the period 1870–1914 cannot be regarded as entirely satisfactory; there was 'considerable scope for improvement in performance through structural change, resource alloca-tion, technical progress and better management of resources.' (Aldcroft) But not all industries could be condemned on this score; several performed well and in those which did not there were factors, other than management failure or lack of technical innovations, which accounted for a decline in productivity. Again, within a single industry a blanket condemnation of management would hardly be justified – in some regions of the country management was efficient whereas in others conservatism or complacency delayed the introduction of new techniques.

In part exoneration it can be argued that Britain's early start meant that investment had already been made in plant and processes, and it was natural that whilst that investment was still producing profits there was a reluctance to change; managements needed a lot of convincing before being prepared to adopt new technologies. 'Entrepreneurs were generally unwilling to depart from the path that had led to such brilliant success until they were forced to do so' (Chapman). Of course, 'it is easy with hindsight to identify the mistakes of one's forebears but we must always be aware of falling into the trap of making judgements of yesterday based on today's knowledge and standards' (Sims). Nonetheless, there was plenty of visible and demonstrable evidence, both from the United States and the continent, of the existence of new technologies and especially of the superior education and training existing in those countries. Sims, for example, cites the Trade Union delegation of 1902 (the Mosley Commission) to the United States which on its return stated that the techniques they had seen in operation in American industry were ahead of those in Britain.

Many manufacturers and industrialists made extensive visits to the United States and the continent and brought back a mounting volume of evidence. Arthur Shadwell (1906) carried out an exhaustive study of continental industry and education and analysed the effect of many factors. He found that English industry operated under severe handicaps of antiquated equipment and obsolescent plant. His conclusion was that other nations 'have not only caught up with us from behind but have surpassed us'.[47] Others, including Sir Swire Smith and Sir Philip Magnus who were both members of the Samuelson Commission on Technical Education, generally present the British worker in a favourable light and he is largely exonerated, his deficiencies, such as they were, being attributed to the English system of training and education which was heavily censured on several grounds. To Philip Magnus (1888) the advance of German trade was 'due solely to the superior fitness of the Germans, due unquestionably to the more systematic training they received for mercantile pursuits' whereas England, in the matter of education, was particularly deficient.[48] The Samuelson Commissioners on their visit to Germany found that:

> in nearly every instance we were able to trace the success of German firms to the scientific and artistic training of heads of departments, designers and skilled workers, and not seldom to the superior commercial knowledge and linguistic attainments of employers themselves. The commissioners were satisfied that this and nothing else explained the growing success of Germany.[49]

In his report to the London County Council in 1914, J.C. Smail, Organiser of Trade Schools for Boys, following a visit to France and Germany, defined technical education in those countries in terms of three levels – lower, middle and higher. Germany in particular:

> possessed a national organisation with definite national objectives. No such clear lines of demarcation existed in Britain where there was overlapping between the three levels, often the same institution attempting to attain all three objectives within its programme.[50]

Earlier, in 1897, a deputation from the Technical Instruction Committee of the University of Manchester had visited Austria and Germany. It was likewise impressed by the zeal and thoroughness with which the governments of those countries supplied the resources for technical training. The delegation was particularly interested in textile schools with a view to incorporating one in the new Municipal Technical School then being built at Manchester. At Crefeld they visited the Textile School built by the Prussian Government. They concluded that, 'It is plain that the better education of the dyer is a matter of far more vital moment in Manchester than it can possibly be in Crefeld; and yet the means of securing it here on an adequate and effective scale can scarcely be said to exist'[51]

Smail (1914) summed up the different approaches of Germany and England: 'Germany', he said, 'has come to believe that workshop training alone is insufficient to make a sound industrial training; it must be reinforced by adequate education specialized in trades'. There was a difference of ideals – Germany was aiming to benefit the nation by training all its workers through carefully designed specialized courses, whereas in contrast 'Britain is organized so that individuals may secure what they think best for their own advancement'.[52] Smail's views on technical education found support in the Report of a Canadian Royal Commission on Industrial Training and Technical Education which had also been studying technical education on the continent that same year. Its main conclusion was that:

> In France, Germany, Switzerland and the United States, the power and influence of technical education of the highest types appeared to be greater than in the United Kingdom or Canada. In England the opinion most frequently heard was to the effect that hereafter the industries must somehow secure the services of more men of the highest scientific attainments with thorough technical training, or her manufacturers and merchants will not be able to hold their own against foreign competition[53]

It was the same at school level. The City of Manchester deputation concluded:

> It is by no means a difficult matter [it said] to trace to the influence of the schools and the system of education generally, the improvement which has marked the manufacturing progress of Germany . . . It is high time the effort was made in this country to give our youth the educational advantages which are enjoyed by their rivals abroad[54]

The Samuelson Commission (1884), too, stated that, 'Secondary education of a superior and systematic kind is placed within the reach of the children of parents of limited means, to an extent of which we can form no conception in this country'[55]

Universities formed only part of the German system of higher education which also encompassed technical high schools and academies of technology specialising in particular fields. The technical high schools were created between 1840 and 1890 by converting, at considerable expense, the state small trade or technical schools established earlier in the century. There was nothing comparable to the technical high schools in England and any assessment of them must be set against the relative neglect of higher technical instruction in English universities and the difficulties encountered in establishing technical studies within the English universities. By 1900 there were over 13,000 students attending these schools which had highly qualified staff.[56]

The motive underlying this vast expenditure was simple. The technical high schools, according to the Samuelson Commissioners, were to impart 'a scientific training with its practical applications so that by this means a body of men might be educated in such a way as to make it possible for continental states to compete with the workshop-trained engineers of England'.[57]

In 1868, Henry Roscoe, Professor of Chemistry at Owens College, and J.G. Greenwood, the College Principal, toured the German universities and technical high schools. They presented some of their findings as witnesses to the Devonshire Commission. Their conclusions were:

> That the acknowledged success of the German university system and of the polytechnics, is ultimately bound up with the strict preliminary training of the old Gymnasia and other secondary schools; and in like manner in England the permanent and widespread usefulness of institutions for the higher education will mainly depend upon a corresponding amount of efficiency in secondary schools.[58]

> The results of a systematic government effort is seen in the case of the German universities, in which, for comparatively small amounts of national expenditure, great results are obtained, whilst I fear that with us (for want of a system) the opposite condition of things more nearly holds good.[59]

What part did education really play in Britain's relative decline? Musgrave considers that in all probability the educational system had not greatly checked the development of the economy up to 1900 but by that time 'was neither appropriate for the older basic industries nor for the new dimensions along which the economy was being diverted'.

Sims has drawn attention to the necessity to produce a new breed of men. Britain was entering 'an age where innovations were going to require a degree of technical expertise beyond the abilities of the ingenious artisan. Among other qualities, a breadth of knowledge and perception were to be required for much was to stem from the cross-fertilisation which occurs when the techniques developed in one industry are applied to another. The problem of "technology transfer" was arising for the first time and Britain was failing to cope with it. The entrepreneurs were on the whole "commercial" men and Britain had never developed the type of technologist now needed'.

Germany, according to Musgrave, 'seems to have come nearer in educational terms to what was economically appropriate'. He concludes that 'the nature of the educational system probably had not a large causative role in contemporary British economic ills, though it did probably play some part in Germany's remarkable leap into the industrial world. There is enough evidence to consider very seriously the hypothesis that the contemporary slow rate of educational change was a detrimental factor for Britain's economic development in the twentieth century'.

Notes and References

1 SNOW, C.P. (1963) 'Education and sacrifice' *New Statesman*, 17 May.

2 *Technical Education*, (Cmnd. 9703), (1956).

3 GORE, G. (1882) *The Scientific Basis of National Progress*, Williams and Norgate, p.7.

4 HUXLEY, T.H. (1902) *Science and Education, Collected Essays*, Vol. 3, London, pp. 446–7.

5 PAYNE, P.L. (1974) 'British entrepeneurship in the nineteenth century', *Studies in Economic History*, London, Macmillan, p. 58.

6 CHAMBERS, J.D. (1968) in *The Workshop of the World*; *British Economic History 1820–80*, Oxford Paperbacks University Series, p. 1, defines this as the period between the financial crisis of 1825 and the Great Depression of 1873.

7 See ASHTON, T.S. (1948) *The Industrial Revolution 1760–1830*, Oxford, Oxford University Press; FLINN, M.W. (1972) *Origins of the Industrial Revolution*, London, Longman; HOBSBAWM, E.J. (1968) *op. cit.*; DEANE, P. (1973) 'The Industrial Revolution in Britain' in CIPOLLA, C.M. (Ed.) *The Emergence of Industrial Societies*, The Fontana Economic History of Europe, Vol. 1.

8 FLINN, M.W. (1972) *op. cit.*, p. 93.

9 HOBSBAWM, E.J. (1968) *op. cit.*, p. 172, Industrial Revolution.

10 LANDES, D.S. (1966) 'Technological change and development in Western Europe, 1750–1914' in HABBAKUK, H.J. and POSTAN, M.M. (Eds.) (1966) *The Cambridge Economic History of Europe*, Vol. 6, Cambridge, Cambridge University Press, p. 462.

11 HOBSBAWM, E.J. (1968) *op. cit.*, p. 173.

12 ASHWORTH, W. (1960) *Economic History of England, 1870–1939*, London, Methuen, p. 37.

13 KENNEDY, W.P. (1976) 'Institutional response to economic growth: capital markets in Britain in 1914' in HANNAH, L. (Ed.) *Management, Strategy and Business Development*, Macmillan, p. 183, note 97.

14 McCLOSKEY, D.N. and SANDBERG, G. (1971) 'From damnation to redemption. Judgements on the late Victorian entrepreneur', *Explorations in Economic History* 9, No. 1, p. 108.

15 PAYNE, P.L. (1974) British entrepreneurship in the nineteenth century, *Studies in Economic History*, London, Macmillan, p. 7.

16 *Ibid*, p. 12.

17 McCLOSKEY, D.N. (1971) *op. cit.*, p. 240.

18 PAYNE, P.L. (1974) *op. cit.*, p. 12.

19 *Ibid*, p. 12.

20 SHADWELL, A. (1888) *Industrial Efficiency, a Comparative Study of Industrial Life in England, Germany and America*, Kegan Paul and French, pp. 73, 148 and 8.

21 ERICKSON, C. (1959) *op. cit.*

22 POSTAN, M.M. (1967) *An Economic History of Western Europe*, London, Methuen, p. 281.

23 SMITH, S. Inaugural address at Dundee Technical Institute, October 1888, p. 20, quoted in *The Real German Rivalry, Yesterday, Today and Tomorrow*, T. Fisher Unwin, 1918.

24 RODERICK, G.W. (1971) *Scientific and Technical Education in Liverpool and its relation to industry on Merseyside* (unpublished MA Thesis, University of Liverpool).

25 HOBSBAWM, E.J. (1968) *op. cit.*, p. 173.

26 CHAPMAN, A.W. (1955) *The Story of a Modern University: the History of the University of Sheffield*, Oxford, Oxford University Press, p. 39.

27 SANDERSON, M. (1972) *The Universities and British Industry, 1850–1970*, London, Routledge and Kegan Paul, p. 66.

28 Deed of Foundation of Josiah Mason's Science College, 12 December, 1870.
29 MASSON, A.E. (1965) *Enterprise in Soap and Chemicals, Joseph Crosfield and Sons Ltd., 1815–1965*, Manchester, Manchester University Press, p. 146.
30 SADLER, M.E. (1904) 'Report on Secondary Education in Liverpool' to City of Liverpool Education Committee, p. 181.
31 WEST, E.G. (1975) *Education and the Industrial Revolution*, Batsford, p. 256.
32 SUTHERLAND, G. (1973) *Mathew Arnold on Education*, Harmondsworth, Penguin Books, p. 19.
33 *Ibid*, p. 20.
34 WEST, E.G. (1975) *op. cit.*, p. 240,
35 *Board of Education Report*, 1908–9, p. 31.
36 SADLER, M.E. (1904) *op. cit.*, p. 8.
37 *Ibid*, p. 12.
38 *Ibid*, p. 9.
39 ERICKSON, C. (1959) *op. cit.*, p. 35.
40 *Board of Education Report*, 1909.
41 ALLEN, G.C. (1976) *The British Disease*, London, Institute of Economic Affairs, p. 50.
42 TAYLOR, A.J. (1972) 'Laissez-faire and state intervention in nineteenth century Britain' *Studies in Economic and Social History*, London, Macmillan, p. 13.
43 *Ibid*, p. 46.
44 ROSE, F. (1901) *Chemical Instruction in Germany and the Growth and Present Condition of the German Chemical Industries*, Diplomatic and Consular Reports, Cmnd. 430–16.
45 *Ibid*, p. 24.
46 *Ibid*, p. 75.
47 SHADWELL, A. (1906) *op. cit.*, p. 446.
48 MAGNUS, P. (1888) *Industrial Education*, London, Kegan Paul and French, p. 80.
49 SMITH, S. (1918) *op. cit.*, p. 25.
50 *Trade and Technical Education in Germany and France*, Report by J.C. Smail, London County Council, (1914).
51 The City of Manchester Technical Instruction Committee, *Report of the Deputation appointed to visit technical schools, institutions and museums in Germany and Austria* (1897), p. 5.
52 SMAIL, J.C. (1914) *op. cit.*, p. 11.
53 *Ibid*, p. 7.
54 City of Manchester Technical Instruction Committee (1897), *op. cit.*, p. 18.
55 *Samuelson Commission*, 2nd Report, Vol. I, (1884), p. 23.
56 ROSE, F. (1901) *op. cit.*, p. 25, Diplomatic and Consular Reports, Miscellaneous Series, No. 561, Foreign Office.
57 *Samuelson Commission*, 2nd Report, Vol. I, (1884), p. 192.
58 *Royal Commission on Scientific Instruction and the Advancement of Science* (1872), First Report, Vol. I, First, supplementary and 2nd reports with minutes of evidence and appendices, p. 508.
59 *Ibid*, p. 513.

Notes on Contributors

Derek H. Aldcroft   Professor of Economic History and Head of Department of Economic and Social History, University of Leicester. Author of numerous publications including: *The European Economy, From Versailles to Wall Street, The East Midlands Economy.*

J.K. Almond   Senior Lecturer in Metallurgy, Teesside Polytechnic. Co-author of *Cleveland Iron and Steel, Background and Nineteenth Century History,* and of *Industrial Archaeology in Cleveland – a Guide.*

W.H.G. Armytage   Professor of Education, University of Sheffield. D. Litt, (National University of Ulster and Hull University) Author of numerous publications including: *Civic Universities, Four Hundred Years of English Education, Social History of Engineering.*

Neil K. Buxton   Professor of Economics, Heriot-Watt University. Author of *The Economic Development of the British Coal Industry.* Co-author of *British Industry Between the Wars.*

Stanley D. Chapman   Reader in Textile History, University of Nottingham. Author of *Cotton in the Industrial Revolution.*

Michael Le Guillou   Former Head of Department of Humanities, Teesside Polytechnic. Author of *History of the River Tees.*

P.W. Musgrave   Professor and Dean of the Faculty of Education, Montash University, Australia. Author of *Technical Change, the Labour Force Education: a Study of the British and German Steel Industries, 1860–1964.*

Gordon W. Roderick   Professor of Adult Education and Director of the Division of Continuing Education, University of Sheffield. Co-author of *Education and Industry in the Nineteenth Century* and of *Scientific and Technical Education in the Nineteenth Century.*

Geoffrey Sims, O.B.E.   Formerly Professor and Head of Department of Electronics, University of Southampton. From 1974 Vice Chancellor of the University of Sheffield. Hon. DSc University of Southampton. Member of numerous Government committees. Editor: *Modern Electrical Studies*, Chapman and Hall.

Michael D. Stephens   Robert Peers Professor of Education and Director of the Department of Adult Education, University of Nottingham. Chairman of the National Association for Recurrent Education. Co-author of *Education and Industry in the Nineteenth Century* and of *Scientific and Technical Education in the Nineteenth Century*.

Brian H. Tolley   Lecturer in History, School of Education, University of Nottingham. Publications in the field of local studies, general economic history and the history of education.

Keith Trace   Senior Lecturer in Economic History, Faculty of Economics and Politics, Montash University, Australia. Numerous publications in the field of business and entrepreneurial history including the history and economics of the shipping industry.

Index

Abbott, A. 216
Acland, A. 220
Acton, W. 74
Adams, J.C. 189
Airy, Sir G.B. 186
Albert, Prince Consort 176, 186, 187, 221, 224
Aldcroft, D.H. 29, 30, 104, 123, 168, 234, 235, 236, 245
Alford, B.W.E. 29, 105
Allen, G.C. 154, 228, 229, 249
Allen, M. 79
Almond, J.K. 238
Altick, R.D. 34, 46
Andelle, A. 128, 129
Anderson, C.A. (see Bowman and Anderson)
Anderson, G. 138
Ansell, C. 69
Argles, M. 183, 184
Arkwright, Sir R. 119, 126, 127, 128, 238
Armstrong, Sir W. 26
Armytage, W.H.G. 138, 201, 215
Arnold, M. 6, 11, 74, 76, 78, 81, 242
Aronsfeld, C.C. 80
Ashby, E. 154
Ashton, T.S. 249
Ashworth, W. 168, 249
Aspin, C. 138
Aston, J. 138
Association of Teachers in Technical
    Institutions (ATTI) 173, 183

Babbage, C. 220
Bagrit, Sir L. 231
Bajema, C.J. 81
Bamford, S. 128, 137
Banks, J.A. 81
Barnard, R.W. 80
Barnard Davis, J. 80
Barraclough, K.C. 123
Beckett, E.M. 138
Behrens, J. 132, 136
Bell, T. 126, 127
Bell, L. 219
Bellot, H. 201
Benson, J. 105
Bentley, R. 186
Beresford, M.W. and Jones, G.R.J. 138

Bessemer, Sir H. 119
Binns, C. 209
Birkbeck, G. 174
Birmingham, S. 80
Bismarck, O. Von 116
Board of Education 8, 11, 58, 59, 181, 182, 242
Bowden, Lord 231
Bowman, M.J. and Anderson, C.A. 33, 34, 37, 38, 45, 46
Boyd, R. 81
Brandt, D.J. 123
Brisco, N.A. 31
Britain
    inventiveness of 3, 145, 152, 174
    power of 3
British Association for the Advancement of
    Science 59, 176, 220, 221
British Exhibition (1862) 177
Broderick, G.C. 80
Brodie, Sir B. 190
Brown, T.N. 80
Brunel, I.K. 139
Brunner, Sir J. 195, 239
Brush, C.F. 152
Bryce Commission (1894–5) 184
Bryce, Sir J. 227
Buchanan, R. 78
bureaucrats, conservatism of 118
Burn, D.L. 64, 115, 123
Burnham, T.H. and Hoskins, G.O. 123
Butterworth, E. 138
Buxton, N.K. 104, 106, 237, 238
Byres, T.J. 30

Cahn, A. 73
Cannan, E. 82
Cardwell, D.S.L. 11, 65, 228
Cardwell, E. 219
Carlyle, T. 73, 108
Carnegie, A. 114, 123
Carr, G.S. 78, 82
Carr, J.C. and Taplin, W. 123
Cartwright, E. 126
Catling, H. 137, 138
Challis, Rev. J. 190
Chaloner, W.H. 137 (see also Ratcliffe and Chaloner)

Chamberlain, J. 116
Chambers, J.D. 11, 249
Chambers, T.G. 201
Chance, Sir J. 240
Chance-Claus process 156, 160–161
Chandler, A.D. 30
Chapman, A.W. 154, 249
Chapman, S.D. 137, 138, 234, 238, 239, 240, 241, 246
Chapman, S.J. 80
chemical industry 3–4, 18, 24, 155–167, 235, 236, 239, 240, 245
   by-products 159–161
   capital investment 161
   demand 166–167
   diversity of performance 167
   effects of patent laws 163–167
   inorganic 155–157, 162–164
   labour costs 160, 163, 165–166
   labour force 157
   organic 156, 165
   products 155–159
   profitability 159–160
   provision of further education 241
   raw materials 156, 159, 160, 162, 163
   and technology 155, 161, 163, 166
Church, R.A. 29, 30, 215
Churchill, Lord Randolph 227
City and Guilds Institute 181, 206
City and Guilds Technical College 196
civic colleges (*see universities, civic*)
Clapham, J.H. 123
Clapperton, J. 81
Clarendon Code (1662–5) 184
Clarendon Commission (1864) 8, 9, 227, 243
Clayton, G. 80
Cleland, J. 74, 81
Clements, R.V. 81
Clifton,   190
Clowes, Prof. 210, 211
coal industry 4, 19–20, 85–103, 235–237
   absenteeism 101–102
   child labour 98
   development of 85–86, 208
   labour costs 88, 100–103
   labour structure 103
   problems in 86–90, 99–103, 238
   profitability 208
   provision of further education 94–96, 209–211
   safety in 85, 90, 92–97, 208–209
   and technology 85, 90–94, 99–103
   and transport 85–88, 208
Coal Mines Regulation Act (1872) 93, 94, 98, 208
   Amendment (1887) 95
Cockerill, J. and Cockerill W. 113
Coke, G.E. 211
Cole, Sir H. 177, 178, 224, 225
Cole, W.A. (*see Deane and Cole*)
Coleman, D.C. 105

Cook, E.T. and Weddebern, A. 81
Cookson, M. 76, 81
Cotton, W. 204
Cowper, E.A. 119
Crompton, S. 126, 127, 139, 152
Crosse, C.A.H. 81
Cunningham, W. 72, 80
curriculum
   content 57–58
   control 180
   and economic growth 63
   relevance 187, 193–195, 206–207, 213, 240, 243
   in universities 59, 185–188, 206–207, 213, 240
Curtis, L.P. 80
Cuthbert, N.H. 215

Darwin, C. 67, 68, 76, 77
Davies, P.N. 29
Davy College of Practical Chemistry 186, 187
Deacon, H. 156
Deacon process 160
Deane, P. 248 (*see also Mitchell and Deane*)
Deane, P. and Cole, W.A. 46, 65, 104, 168
De Beer, G., Rowlands, M.J. and Skramovsky, B.M. 79
Defoe, D. 126
De La Beche, Sir H. 219, 228
De La Mann, J. (*see Wadsworth and De La Mann*)
De La Rue, W. 201
Department of Education 11
Department of Science and Art 10, 11, 122, 177–180, 219, 227, 248
Derby, E. Fourteenth Earl of 219
Devonshire, Eighth Duke of 179, 226
Devonshire Commission (1870–1875) 8, 9, 11, 12, 58, 179, 181, 186, 189–191, 200, 222–224, 226–227, 248
Dewar, Sir J. 59
Diggory, P. (*see Pott et al*)
Dingle, A.E. 64
direct selling 22–23
Disraeli, B. (Lord Beaconsfield) 74, 224, 225, 227
division of labour 126, 131, 137
Dollfus-Ausset, D. 137
Donajgradzki, A.P. 64
Donnelly, J.C.D. 176
Donnelly, Capt. 224
Drysdale Dr. G.R. 78
Duckham, B.F. 105
Duncan, J.M. 81
Dunstan, M.J.R. 213, 214, 215

Eagle, J. 68
Edelatein, M. 17, 29
Edison, T.A. 152
Edmonds, T.R. 80
economic growth 16, 17 (*see also education, and economic growth & literacy, and economic growth*)

British 5, 13, 61 (*see also productivity, British*)
foreign 61 (*see also productivity, foreign*)
and immigration 70–73, 77, 119
misplaced British complacency 28
and population 76–79
economic structure 14, 61
need for change 15–18, 21, 28
education (*see also innovation, in education*)
adult 182
agricultural 212–215
British deficiencies 6–11, 24–25, 34, 132–133, 146, 163–165, 173, 175, 178–180, 224, 234, 241–243, 246–247, 249
church control of 7
commercial 132–133, 136, 153, 207, 234
compulsory 8, 42, 44, 45, 55, 98, 176
costs 39–40, 42, 44, 55, 97
and economic growth 6, 56–57, 61–63, 203, 220, 241–249
employer attitudes 24–26, 52–54, 57, 59, 97, 121–122, 134–137, 146, 165, 173, 175–176, 178–179, 207, 243–244
funding 225, 242, 244
further 181, 182 (*see also textile industry, provision of further education & iron and steel industry, provision of further education & coal industry, provision of further education*)
in Germany 6–10, 24–25, 57, 59–63, 99, 119, 121, 134–136, 145, 175, 185, 188, 205–206, 245–249
improvements in 34, 241
and industrial co-operation 179, 182, 209, 241
isolation between levels 182
on the job 174–175, 241, 243
'liberal' and 'vocational' 188–189, 193
parental attitudes 39–40, 42, 175
part-time 7, 54, 59–60, 95, 97–98, 135, 181–182, 195–196, 210
predominance of classics 9, 59, 146, 188, 191–192, 227, 243
resistance to 7, 39–40, 55, 133, 208, 210–211, 243
and science/technology 9–11, 25, 51, 58, 173–174, 177–182, 198–199, 205, 220, 224–225
secondary 8, 50, 57–58, 178–181, 242–244, 247
and social class 10–11, 33–34, 40, 42, 50–55, 58, 62, 136, 174–175, 228, 243
state provision 7–8, 10, 35, 40, 42–44, 52, 180
technical 7, 10–11, 14, 18, 24–25, 52, 54, 58–60, 94–95, 99, 120–122, 125, 129–130, 132–137, 140, 145–146, 151, 164, 173–182, 199, 203–215, 220–221, 224–225, 239–247
in USA 25
workers attitudes to 49, 54, 63, 97, 174 (*see also unions, attitudes to education*)
Education Acts
(1870) 43, 44, 50, 52, 53, 55, 56, 59, 98, 136, 179, 180, 241
(1889) 58, 180
(1902) 8, 58, 181, 243, 244
Edwards, K.C. 216
Egerton, Sir P. 221
d'Eichthal, G. 129
Eight Hour Day Act (1908) 95, 102
electrical industry 4
Elliot, J.H. 70, 80
Elliot, and Russell, 156
emigration 68–72, 78, 200
alternatives to 74
'pull' factors 198
'push' factors 70
employers, conservatism of 103
Engels, F. 183
engineering 18, 139–154, 150, 235
capital investment 152–153
inefficiences in 147
labour costs 139, 141, 149–150, 153
labour structure 146
social status of 146, 148–149, 154
products 139–140
raw materials 139, 141, 152
standardization on 147
table of main historical events 141–142
and technology 139, 149, 151–153
entrepreneurs
biographies of 125–126, 128, 238
conservatism of 137, 151, 153, 158, 161, 165
failure of 6, 13–15, 18–21, 146, 158, 162, 235–236
influences on 17
innovativeness of 125–127, 140, 160
lack of education 137, 174
lack of scientific awareness 18, 132, 135, 151, 241, 248–249
'parochialism' of 132–133
poor salesmanship of 21–24, 132–133, 234–235
quality of 6, 13, 15, 126–129
rationality of 19–20, 28, 236
recruitment of 127–130, 146, 238–239
success of 158
training of 125, 127–129, 132
Erickson, C. 64, 80, 81, 127, 238, 249, 250
Evans, L.W. 105
Eversley, D.E.C. 80
examinations 59–60, 76, 93, 122, 174–175, 178, 182, 205, 209, 211, 240
exports 4–5, 14, 18, 21–24, 61, 86–88, 113–114, 116, 131–132, 135–136, 141, 144, 148, 152–153, 157–159, 162–163, 167, 234

family planning 76–77
Faraday, M. 151
Farish, Prof. 186
Farr, W. 71, 72, 77, 78, 80, 82
Faulkner, H.U. 168
Fawcett, H. 69
Felkin, H.M. 135, 205, 206
Fiddes, E. 199, 200

Fletcher, T.W. 217
Flinn, M. 233, 249
Floud, R.C. 29
foreign competition (*see markets, foreign
    competition in*)
foremen
    conservatism of 52–53
    training of 52
Forrest, D.W. 81
Forster, W.E. 56
Frangopulo, N.J. 80
Frankland, Sir E. 196
Free Libraries Act (1855) 204
free trade 3, 115–116, 137
French Commission (1864) 173
Froude, J.A. 79
Fryer, P. 81

Galloway, R. 104
Galton, D. 222
Galton, F. 77, 82
Gamble, J. 239
Gardwell, D.S.L. 201
Garnett, W. 180, 206, 210
Gartner, L.P. 80
Gaskell, G.A. 71, 77, 78, 79, 82
Gay, J.E. 11
Geertz, C. 46
Gervers, V. 138
Gibson, F.A. 104, 106, 216
Gilchrist, P.C. 120
Gladstone, W.E. 224, 225, 227
Görannsen, G.F. 119
Gore, G. 226, 229, 231, 249
Gosden, P.H.J.H. 80
Gossage,   156
Gourvish, T.R. 30
Gowing, M. 10, 11, 12, 224, 227, 229
Gräbe, and Liebermann, 162
Graham, J. (*see Hooper and Graham*)
Greaves, G. 81
Great Exhibition (1851) 3, 7, 61, 141, 173, 176,
    177, 220, 231, 234, 244
Green, J.A.H. 215
Green, S. 81
Greenwood, J.G. 190, 191, 248
Greenwood, W.H. 121
Griffin, A.R. 105, 106, 216
Griffin, W.D. 80
Gwynn, S. 80

Habbakuk, H.B. 151, 158
Habbakuk, H. and Postan, M.M. 249
Haber, L.F. 159, 168
Hadfield, R. 120
Haldane, J.S. 105
Hallé, C. 72
Haller, J.S. and Haller, R.M. 81
Hammerton, A.J. 81
Hammond, J.L. and Hammond, B. 33, 38, 46

Hannah, L. 29, 249
Harcourt, Sir W. 71
Hardie, D.W.F. and Pratt, J.D. 167, 168
Harley, C.K. 15, 16, 19, 30, 235
Harrison, A.E. 29, 30
Harrison, B. 64
Harrison, H. 193
Harrison, J.F.C. 63
Hartwell, R.M. 104
Hawke, G.R. 104
Hayman, L. 73
Heaton,   210, 211
Hele-Shaw, Prof. 196
Hemming, J.P. 138
Henderson, W.O. 138
Heyne,   186
Hicks Beach, Sir M. 227
hidden curriculum 57
Hills, R.L. 104, 137
Hobsbawm, E.J. 11, 26, 31, 41, 47, 219, 228,
    233, 249
Hoffmann, R.S.J. 30
Hofman, A.W. 162
Hogg, Q. 180
Honeyman, K. 137
Hooper, F. and Graham, J. 138
Hoskins, G.O. (*see Burnham and Hoskins*)
Hudson, P. (*see Macmillan and Hudson*)
Hughes, J.W. 194
Hughes, T. 76, 81
von Humboldt, K.W. 60
Humphreys, G.M. 190
Hunt, J.S. 46
Huntingdon, A.K. 122
Hutchinson, W. 81
Huxley, T.H. 58, 179, 188, 189, 196, 219, 224,
    227, 231, 232, 249
Hyde, C.K. 104

imports 114–116, 163, 167, 212
indirect selling 22–24, 132, 148, 234
industrial relations 27, 53–54, 56, 102, 117, 122,
    237
Industrial Revolution 6, 14, 17, 33–39, 45, 85–
    86, 125–127, 136, 139, 155, 233–234, 236, 241
industry (*see also science, and industry*)
    empiricism in 127–128, 131, 137
    in France 148, 156, 177–178
    in Germany 52, 59, 61–62, 148, 151, 153,
        156–157, 162, 167, 177–178, 205, 228, 245–
        246
    and social class 49–50, 58, 151
    social status of 49–50, 60, 62, 151, 238
    in USA 61–62, 147–149, 151–153, 156–157,
        167, 246
innovation 228, 234, 239
    in British industry 127, 139, 156, 207
    costs of 165
    lack of in British industry 6, 14–20, 23–24,
        26, 28, 53, 134, 148–149, 157–160, 166,

207, 235, 237, 246
  in education 7, 9, 35, 173, 182
    worker attitudes to 150
insurance 69–70
investment 16, 19
  failure of 17
  foreign 2, 15, 17
  lack of 14
  rates of return 17, 233, 244
iron and steel industry 18, 19, 24, 26, 61, 107–
  123, 141, 144, 235, 238
  absenteeism in 117
  capital investment 116–117
  demand 107, 112–114, 117–118, 122
  labour costs 108, 118
  products 107–109, 113, 118
  provision of further education 121–122, 175
  rationalization in 118, 122
  raw materials 108–109, 114–115, 118–119
  and technology 113–114, 118–122
  and transport 114–115, 118
Irving, R. 30
Isaacs, R. 73

Jacobs, 72
Jacoby, J.H. 206
Jenkins, P. 28, 31
Jevons, S. 104
Johnston, W. 195
Jones, G.R.J. (*see Beresford and Jones*)

Kay, J.P. 36
Kay-Shuttleworth, J. 224
Kellogg, W.K. 22
Kennedy, W. 16, 17, 21, 29, 30, 235, 249
Kershaw, J.B.C. 160, 168
Kimber, Sir H. 76
Kindleberger, C.P. 23, 30, 170
Kitson, Sir J. 52, 123
Knoop, L. 132
knowledge
  dissemination of 211
  specialized 241
Knowles, L.C.A. 141, 154
Knowlton, C. 74
Krupp, A. 52
Kukule, R. and Trubner, K. 201

labour (*see manpower*)
Lancastrian School (Manchester) 129
Landes, D.S. 6, 29, 31, 156, 168, 233, 249
Lankaster, E.R. 64
Laqueur, T.W. 35, 36, 37, 46
Lavoisier, A.-L. 186
Lawes, J. 155
Lawson, J. 137
Layton, D. 64
Leblanc, N. 155
Leblanc process 18, 156–162, 167
Le Cuillou, M. 183

Ledbetter, R. 81, 82
Lee T.J. 25, 31
Lee, C.H. 137
Lee, W. 127
Le Neve Foster, Sir C. 196, 197
Le Play, P.G. 56
Levine, A.L. 29, 154
Levinstein, I. 163, 164, 165, 166, 167, 168, 169
Lewis, B. 105
Lewis, W.A. 22, 23, 24, 29, 30, 31
Liebermann, (*see Gräbe and Liebermann*)
von Liebig, J. 176, 239
Lindert, P.H. 236
Lindert, P.H. and Trace, K. 18, 30, 160, 168, 169
Lingen, R. 225
literacy 33–46
  changes in 34
  deterioration in 33, 35–37, 41, 45–46
  and economic growth 37–38, 40, 45
  improvement in 35–38, 40–41, 44–46, 55
  in Lancashire 34–38, 41
  and occupation 37, 50, 55
  rates 33, 37–38, 55, 247
  regional variations in 34, 37
  and schooling 36, 39–46, 50
  sex variations in 38
  and social change 36
Liveing, G. 186
local education authorities (LEAs) 8, 25, 38,
  179–182, 220
  Liverpool 242
  London 179–181
Local Taxation Act (1890) 94, 180, 220
Lockyer, Sir N. 196
London School of Economics 78
Louis, H. 121
Lowe, M. 7
Lowe, R. 6, 56, 225, 227
Lubbock, Sir J. 9
Lünge, (*see Marignac and Lünge*)

machine tool industry 3, 18, 23, 100, 131, 135,
  137, 147, 150
McCaffrey, L.J. 80
McCann, W.P. 64
McCloskey, D.N. 11, 14, 19, 20, 29, 30, 104,
  168, 235, 249
McCloskey, D.N. and Sandberg, G. 105, 165,
  168, 169, 249
McDonnell, J.F. 72
McKendrick, N. 29
Mackenzie Wallace, D. 138
McLaren, A. 81
McLean, I.W. 30
McLeod, R.M. 229
Macmillan, and Hudson, P. 137
Magnus, Sir P. 54, 64, 246, 250
Mahaffy, J.P. 71
Malthus, Rev, T.R. 67, 68, 69, 77, 78
Malthusian League 76

management techniques 27, 85, 147, 149, 150, 153
 Taylor's 'scientific management' 27, 52, 146
managers
 attitudes of 49
 background of 236
 conservatism of 51, 91, 99, 101, 103, 117, 246
 failure of 5, 26–28, 92–93, 122, 147, 235–236, 246
 lack of education 92–93, 103, 130, 146, 237–238
 lack of scientific awareness 18, 91, 93, 122, 129–131, 133, 135, 241
 quality of 45, 140
 poor salesmanship of 117
 recruitment of 238, 240
 recruitment of foreigners 50
 training 52, 59, 62, 92–95, 99, 121–122, 129–130, 208–209, 211, 238–240
Manier, E. 79
Mann, H. 40, 41, 47, 56
Manning, H.E. 73
manpower
 attitudes to management 27, 53–54
 conservatism of 55, 150, 239
 costs of 19, 20, 237
 de-skilling 204–205
 exploitation of 34, 93, 174
 lack of education 10, 14, 33–34, 91–92, 96–98, 103, 129, 132, 146, 151, 174–178, 205, 240–241
 lack of sales training 23
 lack of technical education 24–26
 poor use of 26–27
 recruitment of foreigners 243
 shortage of 200, 237
 skilled 3, 53, 57, 60, 102, 127, 163, 164, 175, 177, 204
 scientific/technical 198–200, 211, 234, 237
 socialization of 56–58, 61, 69
 supply 3, 14–16, 19
 training of 243
 unskilled 54–55, 57, 102–103, 204
manufactures 3–4, 21
 cars 4
 quality of 21
 need for direct selling 22
Mappin, Sir T. 193
Marcus,   79
Marignac, and Lünge, 166
markets
 British advantage in 3–4, 88, 113, 115, 131–132, 137, 139–141, 145, 156, 163, 233
 British failure in 5, 15, 145–146, 231, 236
 foreign competition 4–5, 13, 18, 21–23, 88–89, 107, 113–117, 122, 132–135, 137, 141, 145–148, 153, 157–159, 162–163, 166, 173, 179, 205–206, 225, 231–232, 234, 247
Marks, S. 73
Martin, R.F. 209, 210

Marwanjee, H. (*see Nowrojce and Marwanjee*)
Maskalyne, N.S. 189
Mason, J. 240
Masson, A.E. 249
Masters and Servants Act (1867) 56
Mathias, P. and Postan, M.M. 30
Maudsley, H. 139
Mechanics' Institutes 10, 25, 59, 69, 73, 129, 136, 146, 174–175, 180, 205–206, 240
Menelaus, 56
Mercer, J. 130, 131
Mill, J.S. 50, 51, 59, 74, 78, 188
Mines Acts (*see also Coal Mines Regulation Act*)
 (1842) 97
 (1855) 92
 (1860) Inspection of Mines 98
 (1887) 94, 210, 211
 (1911) 95
Mitchell, B.R. 46, 47
Mitchell, B.R. and Deane, P. 64, 106
Mond, L. 243
Montgomery, J. 129, 138
Moore, Prof. 10
Morant, R. 243
Morral, D. 216
Morris, A. 82
Mosley Commission (1902) 153, 246
Muir, R. 201, 240
Mundella, A.J. 131, 135, 205
Musgratt, E. 194
Musgrave, P.W. 64, 65, 123, 183, 243, 248, 249
Musgrove, F. 63
Mushet, R.F. 119, 120
Muspratt, J. 239
Musson, A.E. 14, 29, 154

Napoleon (Bonaparte) 60
Napolon III 177
Nasmyth, J. 120, 139, 146, 147
National Association for the Promotion of Technical Education 179–180
Neilson, J.B. 119
Neuberg, A. 73
Neuberg, B.E. 46
Neville, R.G. 105
Newcastle Commission (1859) 7, 40–42, 57, 227
Newcomen, T. 140
Newman, J.H. 188, 189
Novaks, D.E. 30
Nowrojce, J. and Marwanjee, H. 79

Ogle, W. 82
Overy, R.J. 29
Owen, R. 128
Owens, J. 187
Owens College 9, 131, 134, 187, 190, 194, 195, 199, 224, 240, 243, 248

Palmerston, Third Viscount 226

Paris Exhibitions
  (1855) 177
  (1867) 61, 119, 177, 178, 240, 244
  (1872) 135
Parnell, E.A. 138
Patel, S.J. 65
Patent Law Amendment Act (1907)
Paton, J.B. 205, 206
Paton, J.L. 215
Pattison M. 189, 201
Paxton, J. 176
Payne, P.L. 30, 105, 123, 235, 236, 249
Peacock, T.B. 74, 81
Peel, J. (*see Pott et al*)
Peel, Sir R. 176
Peel, R. 125
Pencavel, J.H. 30, 106
Percy, J. 59, 121, 196
Perkin, Sir W.H. 162
Pilkington, G. 239
Pilkington, R. 239
Pilkington, W.W. 239
Place, F. 74
Platt, J. 240
Platt Ball, W. 82
Playfair, Sir L. 6, 51, 176, 177, 178, 196, 220,
  221, 227, 231
Pole, W. 137
Pollard, S. 64, 104, 106
polytechnics
  in Germany 248
  Goldsmiths College 181
  London 181
  Regent Street 180
population (*see social change, population*)
Postan, M.M. 249 (*see also Habbakuk and Postan
  & Mathias and Postan*)
Pott, M., Diggory, P. and Peel, J. 81
Pratt, E.A. 27, 31
Pratt, J.D. (*see Hardie and Pratt*)
productivity
  British 3–6, 13–14, 19–20, 61, 89–90, 109–
    113, 120, 122, 127, 140, 150, 156–157, 159,
    162–163, 167, 232
  in chemical industry 159, 162, 167
  in coal industry 86–91, 97, 99, 101–103, 237
  and education 242
  foreign 3–4, 14, 19, 61, 89–90, 109–112, 120,
    122, 156–157, 162–163, 232
  in iron and steel industry 108–113, 117, 122
  possibilities for improvement 16, 26–27
  variations between industries 15, 235, 245–
    246
professionalization 241
profit 15, 19
public schools 227, 238–239, 243

Radcliffe, W. 126, 137
railways 3, 18, 208, 243
Ramsbottom,   120

Ratcliffe, B.M. 29, 30,
Ratcliffe, B.M. and Chaloner, W.H. 138
Reach, A.B. 138
Reader, W.J. 138
Redford, A. 36, 37, 46
redundancy 27
Reed, E.J. 222
Rendall, G.H. 193
research (*see also universities, and research*)
  and economic growth 226–227, 232
  employer attitudes to 24
  funding 225–227, 234
  in Germany 60, 245
  lack of 9–10, 51, 163, 165–167, 235
resources
  British advantage in 6, 108, 221
  foreign advantage in 19, 20
  natural 3, 86
  problems 19
  re-allocation of 14–17, 21, 28
  scarcity 68
  use of 14–15, 26
Rhyiner, J. 137
Richardson, H.W. 165, 168, 169
Riley, E. 120
Riley, J. 120
Rimmer, W.G. 137
Roberts, R. 64
Roberts Austen, W.C. 123
Robertson, A.J. 19, 30
Robertson, P.L. 24, 31
Robson, D. 46
Roderick, G.W. 249
Roderick, G.W. and Stephens, M. 31
Rolleston, Prof. 11
Rolfe, F.W. 80
Rolt, R.T.C. 154, 234
Roscoe, Sir H. 134, 179, 190, 191, 194, 240, 248
Rose, F. 250
Roseberry, Fifth Earl of 227
Rosovsky, H. 65
Ross, F. 245
Ross, M.E. 64
Rothstein, N. 138
Rowlands, M.J. (*see De Beer et al*)
Royal College of Chemistry 219, 239
Royal College of Science 196, 199
Royal Commissions
  (1836) on the arts and manufactures 134
  (1841) on the export of machinery 148
  (1842) on children's employment
  (1881) on technical instruction 179, 238
  (1886) on the depression of trade and industry
    54, 55, 56, 60, 116
  (1894) on labour 53
  (1925) on the coal industry 102, 103
Royal Institute 176
Royal School of Mines 120, 121, 187, 196, 199,
  205, 208, 219
Royal Society 10, 220, 221, 223, 224, 226

Ruskin, J. 55, 64, 74, 76
Russell, J.S. 176, 177, 183, 184
Russell,   (*see Elliot and Russell*)
Ryan, J. 206

Sabine, Sir E. 226
Sadler, M.E. 7, 11, 64, 181, 242, 249
Salisbury, Third Marquess of 219, 227
Samuel, H. 73
Samuel, R. 64
Samuelson, Sir B. 176, 178, 179
Samuelson Commission (   ) 135, 200, 205,
    246–248
Sandberg, L.G. 19, 20, 29, 30, 235 (*see also
    McCloskey and Sandberg*)
Sanderson, M. 25, 31, 35, 36, 37, 40, 41, 42, 46,
    47, 64, 65, 249
Saul, S.B. 29, 30, 149, 154, 168
Saville, J. 168
Sawyer, J.E. 65
Schloss, D.F. 31
Schofield, R.S. 37, 38, 39, 40, 41, 42, 43, 44, 46,
    47
Schorlemmer, C. 194
Schulze-Gaevernitz, G. 138
Schuster, A. 199, 201
science/technology (*see also education and
    science*)
    and economic growth 226, 231–232, 234
    employer attitudes to 239
    funding 221–225, 240
    in Germany 228
    in industry 24–25, 51–52, 130–131, 133
    and productivity 239
    social status of 18, 24–25, 51, 121, 145, 165,
        175–176, 181–182, 198, 221–223, 227–228,
        241, 243–244
Scott, R. 129, 130, 138
Scoville, W.C. 80
Searle, G.S. 82
Sedgwick, A.G. 123
Sexton, H. 121
Shadwell, A. 237, 246, 249, 240
Shaw, G.B. 71, 80
Siemens, C.W. and Siemens, F. 119
Siemens, Sir W. 52, 59, 152
Silk, A.J. and Stern, L.W. 38
Sims, G. 235, 245, 246, 248
Skelton, H.J. 123
Skramovsky, B.M. (*see De Beer et al*)
Smail, J.C. 246, 247, 250
Smellie, K.B. 183
Smiles, S. 50, 52
Smith, A.H. 180
Smith, Sir S. 136, 179, 181, 183, 184, 201, 238,
    239, 246, 249, 250
Smyth, Sir W. 196
Snelus, G.J. 120
Snow, C.P. 231, 249
social change

attitudes to 50, 51, 53
economic 49, 62, 140
educational 63
immigration 36–37
industrial 35–36, 38, 41, 45, 60, 128, 140,
    149–150, 173
political 73
population 36, 38–39, 67–69, 71, 73–74, 76–
    79, 152
technological 160
social stratification 61, 62
Solvay, E. 155, 159, 160, 161, 162
Solvay process 18, 155–157, 159–162, 166
Southern, T.A. and Spencer, H. 78, 188, 225
state intervention 6, 8, 23, 67, 93, 97, 103, 148–
    149, 176, 178–179, 219–227, 242, 244–245
steam power 85, 90, 140, 204
Stephens, M. (*see Roderick and Stephens*)
Stephenson, G. 139
Stern, L.W. (*see Silk and Stern*)
Stone, L. 46
Stokes, A.H. 211
Strachey, J. 82
Strange, A. 223, 226
strikes 56
Stuart, J. 206, 209, 210
Super, R.H. 81
Sutherland, A. 81
Sutherland, G. 249
Sutton, G.B. 30
Svennilson, I. 156, 168
Swan, Sir J. 152

Taplin, W. (*see Carr and Taplin*)
tariff barriers 4, 61, 114, 116, 117, 149
Tariff Commission (1904) 116
Taunton Commission 8, 50, 51, 135, 137, 225,
    227
Taylor, A.J. 47, 104, 106, 250
Taylor, F.W. 27, 146
Taylor, R. 81
teachers
    knowledge of industry 209
    training 180, 212, 213
Teuteberg, H.J. 138
Technical Instruction Act (   ) 58, 94, 180,
    220
Technical Instruction Commission (1881–1884)
    181
technicians
    employers' attitudes to 131
    recruitment of foreigners 50, 131, 134, 176
    shortage of 163–165, 179
'technology transfer' 248
Temin, P. 30, 65
Tennyson, A. Lord 50
textile industry 3, 4, 18, 19, 20, 23, 125–137,
    141, 155, 156, 235, 238, 239
    design in 134, 207
    as family enterprise 126

labour structure 204
organizational structure 130, 205
provision of further education in 132, 134–137, 205
raw materials 204
recruitment of foreigners 132–134, 136–137
and technology 126–128, 131–132, 135
Thomas, D.A. 104
Thomas, S.G. 120
Thompson, D. 11
Thompson, Sir J.J. 9
Thompson, J. 229
Thompson, J. 131
Thompson Commission (1918) 184
Thomson, D. 278
Thomson, Sir W. 222
Tolley, B. 239
Trace, K. 236 (*see also Lindert and Trace*)
trade unions (*see unions*)
Traill, H.D. 79, 80
Tranter, N.L. 70, 80
Trebilcock, R.C. 29
Tremenheere, H.S. 92, 209
Trevithick, R. 140
Trollope, A. 50
Tropp, A. 64
Trubner, K. (*see Kukule and Trubner*)
Tucker, K.A. 154
Turnbull, G. 138
Turner, T. 121
Twistleton, Hon. E.T.B. 227
Tylecote, R.F. 123
Tyszynski, H. 30

unemployment 3, 16, 27, 53–56
Uniformity Act
  (1559) 185
  (1662) 185
unions 53–54, 62, 68, 76, 98, 101–102, 206
  attitudes to education 54–55
  restrictive practices 27
universities 51, 57, 59, 60, 69, 136, 174, 181, 243, 245
  Aberystwyth (University College) 212
  Bangor (University College) 212
  Birmingham 180, 193–194, 196, 240
  Cambridge 9, 145, 176, 185–186, 188–193, 209, 212, 215, 225, 238, 239
  civic 10, 185, 187, 193–198, 203–205, 240, 243, 245
  conservatism of 185
  criticism of 186, 189, 191, 212
  Durham 94, 176, 211
  funding 194–196, 200, 203–204, 206–208, 210–215, 225, 240, 243, 245
  in Germany 186–188, 190, 199, 248
  Glasgow 131, 140
  Imperial College of Science and Technology 196
  lack of resources 207

Leeds, 94, 180, 193–196
links with industry 204
Liverpool 10, 180, 193–196, 240
London 25, 131
London (Kings College) 9, 94, 186–187, 193–194, 241
London (University College) 9, 176, 186–187, 193–194, 239, 241
Manchester 136, 199, 240, 247 (*see also Owens College, Manchester*)
non-degree courses 195–197
Newcastle 193–196
Nottingham 73, 193–194, 203–215, 240
Oxford 9, 145, 176, 185–186, 188–192, 225, 238
  and religion 185, 189
  research 189–191, 195, 198–199, 207, 213
  and science/technology 185–197, 199–200, 203
  Scottish 185
  Sheffield 94, 180, 193–196, 210, 240
Upward, A. 80
Urwick, L. 31

Vernon Harcourt, Sir W. 227
Vince, Prof. 186
Von Hofman, A.W. 187
Von Schule-Gaevernitz, G. 31
Von Tunzleman, N. 102

Wadsworth, A.P. and De La Mann, J. 137
Walker, Sir A. 194
Walters, R. 30, 106
Ward, D. 63
Watson, H.C.M. 82
Webb, R.K. 46
Webb, S. 78, 79, 82, 180, 181
Webb, S. and Webb, B. 79, 82
Weddenburn, A. (*see Cook and Weddenburn*)
Weinberg, J. 72
Weitzman, C. 72
Welch, E. 215
Weldon,   156, 159
Weldon process 160
Wells, F.A. 215
West, E.G. 31, 46, 47, 241, 249
Westmoreland, J.R. 206
Whewell, W. 188
White, A. 80
Whiting, C.E. 216
Whitwell,   119
Whitworth, J. 139, 219, 225
Williams, J.E. 216
Willis, Prof. 186
Wilson, C. 29, 65, 168
Wilson, Sir H. 231
women
  and abortion 74, 78
  attitudes to 73–74
  and emigration 72

employment of 204
intelligence of 73–74
workers (*see manpower*)

Workers' Educational Association (WEA) 95,
175
Wright, G.H. 209, 210